# The Limits of Liberalism

# The Limits of Liberalism

## Josephus Daniels, Henry Stimson, Bernard Baruch, Donald Richberg, Felix Frankfurter and the Development of the Modern American Political Economy

Larry G. Gerber

New York University Press
New York *and* London
1983

Library of Congress Cataloging in Publication Data

Gerber, Larry G., 1947–
    The limits of liberalism.

    Bibliography: p.
    Includes index.
    1. Liberalism—United States—20th century.
2. United States—Economic policy.   I. Title.
JA84.U5G37 1983        320.5'13'0973        82-24756
ISBN 0-8147-2985-1

Clothbound editions of New York University Press books are
Smyth-sewn and printed on permanent and acid-free paper.

# Contents

320.5
Y313l

# Acknowledgments

DURING the long and often tortuous process of researching and writing this book, a number of people have provided me with a great deal of assistance. Early in my years in graduate school, Martin Sherwin introduced me to the fascinating career of Bernard Baruch, the first of the five men I eventually chose to include in this study. Charles Sellers directed my work on this project when it was still in the dissertation stage and gave me important encouragement to maintain a connection between my interests as a scholar and my commitments as a citizen. Michael Rogin was also instrumental in helping me to clarify my conception of liberalism. While I was at Berkeley, his intellectual enthusiasm was a constant source of inspiration. Moreover, his critical reading of the dissertation version of this work was extremely helpful. Stephen Maizlish also was kind enough to read the entire work in its early form. I would also like to thank Leonard Dinnerstein for reading a later version of the manuscript.

My sister, Mary Gerber, deserves a special word of thanks for giving me both useful criticisms and needed psychological support during the early stages of this project. I would also like to express my gratitude to my wife, Louise Katainen, who has been a careful reader and an inestimable help in so many other ways during the last two years.

In addition, my thanks go to Marilyn Bradian and Nikki Matz for their assistance in typing the manuscript and to the University of Arizona History Department for its generous support during my temporary stay in Tucson. Finally, I would like to thank the Mabel McLeod Lewis Memorial Foundation for helping to finance the research necessary for this work.

Grateful acknowledgment is made to the following for their permission to use material from their sources: The Princeton University Library for the Bernard M. Baruch Papers; the Yale University Library for the Henry L. Stimson Papers; the Chicago Historical Society for the Donald R. Richberg Papers; Atlantic Little, Brown and Co. for excerpts from *Roosevelt and Frankfurter: Their Correspondence, 1928–1945* edited by Max Freedman (1967); Harcourt Brace Jovanovich, Inc. for excerpts from *Law and Politics* by Felix Frankfurter, edited by Archibald MacLeish, copyright 1939 by Harcourt Brace Jovanovich, Inc., renewed 1967 by Archibald MacLeish; Harper and Row, Publishers, Inc. for excerpts from ON ACTIVE SERVICE In Peace and War by Henry L. Stimson and McGeorge Bundy. Copyright 1947 1948 by Henry L. Stimson; Doubleday and Company, Inc. for excerpts from THE NAVY AND THE NATION, copyright 1919, renewed by Josephus Daniels.

# The Limits of Liberalism

# CHAPTER I

# The Significance
# of a Liberal Consensus

IN the years following the Second World War, an influential group of historians and social scientists began to portray American history and politics as being characterized by a degree of continuity and stability which was remarkable in comparison to the experiences of Europe. This view departed from the Progressive school of thought which had dominated American historical writing since the First World War. While the Progressives had described American history as an ongoing struggle between sharply contending political and economic forces, the new "consensus" historians and "pluralist" political scientists of the 1950s emphasized the extent to which America had historically been free from irreconcilable ideological and social conflicts.[1]

Daniel Boorstin and Louis Hartz formulated the two most influential interpretations of the American past based on the notion of consensus. In *The Genius of American Politics,* published in 1953, Boorstin argued that from the moment of initial settlement by Europeans, conditions of life in the New World led to the development of a distinctly American "way of life" which became notable for its emphasis on practical values and its disdain for dogma and abstract theorizing. "The unprecedented opportunities" afforded by the American continent and "a peculiar and unrepeatable combination of historical circumstances" produced a people who shared a pragmatic problem-solving outlook and a faith in the utility of democratic institutions. In Boorstin's view, Americans had always been so preoccupied with the task of exploiting the natural bounty of their environment and making their institutions work well in practice that they never became involved in potentially divisive arguments over abstract questions of political or social philosophy. Thus, American society, according to Boorstin, came to be characterized by a unique nonideological consensus which reflected not so much a pervasive agreement over a given set of stated beliefs, but rather a commonly shared approach to living happily in a naturally favorable environment.

In having conceived of the American consensus in this fashion, Boorstin denied the obvious possibility that the pragmatic and democratic attitudes which he described as central to the American way of life could themselves be considered the foundation of a coherent ideology. In fact, one of the purposes of Boorstin's analysis seems to have been the denigration of the role played by ideas and ideology in American history. Americans, as Boorstin portrayed them, appeared typically as "doers" responding to the "givenness" of their surroundings rather than as "thinkers" attempting to impose their vision of what life ought to be on their environment. Ultimately, Boorstin's conception of the American consensus seemed to rely on a form of environmental determinism.[2]

While Boorstin's work provided an initial impetus to the development of consensus history, Louis Hartz's study, *The Liberal Tradition in America,* published in 1955, soon gained greater acceptance as a more satisfactory explanation and description of the origins and nature of an American consensus. In contrast to Boorstin, Hartz argued that American society had been characterized by unity and stability, not because of the absence of political theorizing, but rather because of the almost unchallenged dominance of a single ideology, Lockean liberalism. Although Hartz never spelled out exactly what he meant by the term, Lockean liberalism clearly seemed to include a commitment to the concepts of individualism, property rights, a free market economy, equality of opportunity, and a limited state, which arose in conjunction with the development of capitalism in the Western world. In place of the vague notion of "givenness" offered by Boorstin to explain the origins of America's consensus, Hartz developed the hypothesis that a Lockean consensus attained such a lasting hold on the American mind because of America's lack of a feudal past. Having been "born equal" with no legacy of feudal institutions, the United States developed without either a true conservative tradition attempting to uphold the values of a feudal past or a revolutionary socialist tradition seeking to overthrow both capitalism and the remaining vestiges of feudalism. Hartz, unlike Boorstin, thus clearly implied that the American "way of life" was itself firmly rooted in an ideological tradition.[3]

Political scientists and sociologists in the late 1950s also began to contribute to the development of a picture of American society which emphasized the extent of stability and agreement over fundamental values in the United States. Some social scientists at this time proclaimed an "end of ideology" in America. However, their underlying assumption was not that Americans had no ideology at all, but rather, in the words of Robert Dahl, that Americans were, "a highly ideological people" whose ideology usually went unnoticed because they were "to an astounding extent, all agreed on the same ideology."[4]

A growing school of social scientists, moreover, added to the notion of consensus by focusing on the pluralistic nature of American society and politics. According to the "pluralists," American politics was characterized by the formation of continually shifting loose coalitions composed of many diverse special interest groups. The cross pressures and conflicting loyalties generated by the typical American's membership in a wide variety of interest groups prevented the American electorate from coalescing into permanent clearly polarized political groupings. Politics thus became a matter of compromise and bargaining over specific issues instead of a struggle over fundamental values between bitterly opposed sectarian parties. A widely shared consensus on the basic ideals of "democracy" and an absence of sharply defined class conflict, in other words, were both causes and consequences of the institutional framework in which American political life took place.[5]

By the beginning of the 1960s, consensus interpretations of American history and politics had proliferated, but consensus history soon produced critics as well as followers. Even before the decade of the Fifties was over, consensus history began to be attacked for ignoring or improperly downplaying instances of important conflict in American history.[6] As issues of race, ethnicity, and sex became more prominent and a source of greater divisiveness in American life in the 1960s and 1970s, American historians and social scientists turned increasingly to an examination of the serious conflicts over these questions which had occurred in America's past. Much of the new social and ethnic history of recent years represented a definite departure from the consensus approach which had been so influential in the late 1950s and early 1960s.

The consensus view of American history and politics came to be criticized not only for what it overlooked, but also for the political bias with which it seemed to have been intimately associated. Opponents argued that consensus history and pluralist social science served essentially to reaffirm and justify the political conservatism, social conformity, and Cold War chauvinism which dominated American life in the 1950s. The glorification of American society as being uniquely free from social tensions and ideological conflicts was, according to critics, not so much an accurate descriptive analysis of America's past as it was a prescriptive argument against the legitimacy of contemporary dissent and demands for basic changes in American society.[7]

The Cold War did form an ever-present backdrop to both *The Genius of American Politics* and *The Liberal Tradition in America*. Boorstin and Hartz both explicitly noted the connection between their attempts to analyze America's past and their desire to understand the extent to which that past equipped the United States to fight a Cold War in which combat increasingly took place in the realm of ideology. Their conclusions, like their views on the nature of the American consensus, were by no means the same. However, a pervasive concern about the Cold War, as well as an underlying antipathy to communism, informed the work of both men.[8]

In Boorstin's case, an extremely laudatory description of American society and a refusal to subject the vague notion of an American way of life to serious scrutiny appeared to lend credence to the charge that consensus history and political conservatism were but two sides of the same coin. Boorstin himself proudly proclaimed: "Our history has fitted us, even against our will, to understand the meaning of conservatism." Yet Hartz, in contrast, was generally critical of the Lockean consensus he described. Rather than developing the concept of consensus as a means of avoiding a critical examination of the ideological basis of American life, Hartz concluded from his analysis that America's single-minded commitment to the liberal tradition had frequently been "irrational."[9]

While the consensus approach has often tended to obscure or distort the reality of class divisions and other social conflicts in America, it ought not to be simply discarded as an outmoded expression of 1950s-style political conservatism. Richard Hofstadter, who is frequently credited with having authored the first embryonic statement of a consensus view of American history, has argued, convincingly in my opinion, that:

. . . it is a mistake to assume that the consensus idea is intrinsically a *prescriptive* one which commits us to this or that particular arrangement. It is part of the *descriptive* task of the historian or political scientist to find and account for the elements of consensus in any situation, but he is not required to endorse what he finds. He may analyze society in functional terms, but this does not require him to assume that no arrangements are dysfunctional. If the matter is seen this way, I believe, it will be understood that the idea of consensus is not intrinsically linked to ideological conservatism. In its origins I believe it owed almost as much to Marx as to Tocqueville, and I find it hard to believe that any realistic Marxist historian could fail to be struck at many points by the pervasively liberal-bourgeois character of American society in the past. Many aspects of our history, indeed, seem to yield to a "left" interpretation, and some radical historians have in fact begun to see it that way. Presumably, insofar as the idea of consensus has permanent validity, it will be detachable from any particular political tendency and will prove usable from more than one point of view.[10]

Ideological consensus has been a key factor in American history, and American political life has generally operated within a framework in which conflict over fundamental socioeconomic issues has been excluded. To note the existence of such an ideological consensus and political stability, however, does not necessarily imply either approval of the content of that consensus or a denial of the reality of social injustice and class divisions in America. In fact, in order to understand the course of modern American history, it is, I believe, crucial to analyze the way in which the dominance of what Hartz has called "the

American liberal tradition" has worked to prevent America from coming to grips with the ongoing social and economic problems produced by a highly unequal distribution of wealth and power.

The present study seeks both to identify the defining characteristics of the American liberal tradition and to explore the question of how the existence of a liberal ideological consensus affected the evolution of the American political economy between 1900 and 1940. It was in this period that the foundations of the modern American political economy were established, beginning with the Progressive movement for reform at the turn of the century and culminating in the New Deal of the 1930s.

I

In many ways, life in America changed dramatically between 1900 and 1940. During these forty years, the United States became a truly urban nation, with the number of Americans living in cities and towns increasing from 40 to 57 percent of the population. Along with urbanization came a major transformation of the American labor force. Whereas in 1900, 38 percent of all Americans made a living in agriculture, by the eve of the Second World War this number had been reduced to 17 percent. Conversely, the percentage of American workers in white collar jobs increased from 17 to 31 over this same period. Not only were American workers increasingly better educated and occupying jobs demanding greater skills, but they were also becoming increasingly more organized and better paid. At the turn of the century, only 4 percent of Americans in non-agricultural employment belonged to labor unions; by 1940 this figure had jumped to 27 percent. Average annual earnings for the typical American worker rose from between $400 and $500 in 1900 to $1300 in 1940. This increase in earnings, moreover, was clearly translated into a significantly higher standard of living. While only a tiny number of wealthy Americans owned automobiles or had electricity, telephones, or central heating in their homes in 1900, by 1940 about 80 percent of American families had electricity,

60 percent had automobiles, and 40 percent had telephones and central heating.[11]

While the quality of life and the nature of work changed significantly, the distribution of wealth and power remained essentially the same during the first four decades of the century. Even as overall standards of living improved, American society continued to be characterized by a glaringly unequal distribution of income and wealth and by the persistence of widespread poverty amidst apparent affluence.

Precise figures on the distribution of income and wealth for the turn of the century are not available. However, a rough calculation using income statistics developed by Stanley Lebergott shows that the 7.6 percent of American families whose income was over $1300 in 1900 received approximately 39 percent of the nation's total income. Put another way, this small elite earned as much in 1900 as did the approximately 70 percent of American families constituting the lower end of the income scale. Personal wealth was even more unequally distributed than income. One contemporary observer estimated that in 1890 the wealthiest one eighth of American families owned seven eights of the nation's wealth, and that the richest one percent actually possessed more wealth than the rest of the population combined. These estimates may overstate the case, but there is little doubt as to the great extent of inequality in turn-of-the-century America. Such inequality continued to characterize American society forty years later. On the eve of American entry into the Second World War, the top 5 percent of income recipients earned 26.5 percent of the nation's total income. This was approximately equal to the total earnings of the 60 percent of the population at the lower end of the income scale. As in 1900, the concentration of wealth was even more striking than the concentration of income. In 1939, the richest one half of one percent of the population owned 28 percent of all personal wealth in the United States.[12]

Inequality, in and of itself, does not necessarily indicate poverty or deprivation. If everyone were a millionaire, it would be difficult to argue that the individual who had a million dollars was by definition poor simply because others had even greater wealth. Most economists agree, however, that poverty is a "relative concept—relative to the kind of standard that society is able and willing to provide to the less fortunate at any particular time."[13] What a society defines as a minimally adequate standard of living will undoubtedly change over time as that society's potential for providing food, shelter, and other "necessities" develops.

One careful study of poverty in America has calculated that for a family of four in 1905 to have lived at a level of "minimum adequacy" (as judged by the standards of the time rather than of today), a budget of $625 would have been necessary. Using this standard, approximately 37 percent of the American people at the beginning of the century lived in poverty. By 1941, according to this same study, the "minimum adequacy" budget for a family of four had increased to $1343. Although the onset of the Second World War had already begun to bring an unprecedented degree of prosperity to America in 1941, 32 percent of the American people continued to live below the poverty line. During the depression of the 1930s, the figure had been much higher, nearly 50 percent. Even at the peak of the predepression boom in 1929, over 40 percent of all American families failed to enjoy a minimally adequate standard of living. Thus, during the forty years prior to the Second World War, the United States made virtually no progress in eliminating or reducing the high level of poverty which continued to exist in the world's richest society.[14]

The American economy was also characterized throughout the first half of the twentieth century by a high degree of industrial concentration. A relatively small number of huge privately-owned corporations, exercising "monopoly power" over prices and production in many key industries, dominated the American economy during these years. At the beginning of the century, America's first great wave of industrial mergers left slightly over 300 firms in control of about 40 percent of all manufacturing capital in the United States. One or two giant corporations were responsible for at least half of the output in each of 78 different industries. By 1939, corporate concentration had become even more pronounced. In that year, America's 250 largest manufacturing firms owned 65 percent of the nation's productive capacity, and oligopoly was the dominant form of economic organization in such industries as steel, automobiles, cigarettes, cement, cans, copper, and iron ore. The classical model of a decentralized competitive economy had lost much of its relevance for twentieth-century America. Economic power, as well as income and wealth, continued to be very unequally distributed in America throughout the period from 1900 to 1940.[15]

In other Western nations, the combination of rapid social change brought on by the industrial and technological revolutions and the continuing existence of a maldistribution of wealth and power led either to revolutionary political upheavals, or, at a minimum, to the rise of powerful political parties calling for the institution of a socialist order. The United States experienced neither revolution nor the development of a socialist party of lasting importance. It is true, however, that the first four decades of the twentieth century did witness a tremendous growth in the size and functions of government.

At the beginning of the century, government at all levels provided only a limited range of social services and played only a minimal role in the nation's economic life. Slightly over one million Americans (about 4 percent of the work force) were employed by local, state, and federal government in 1900. Of these, less than 200,000 were civilian employees of the federal government which had an annual budget of only one half billion dollars. By the end of the New Deal, government had begun to play an important role in the overall performance of the economy and in providing a significant array of social welfare programs. In 1940, nearly four million Americans were government employees (over 8 percent of the work force), one million of whom were civilian employees of the federal government whose budget had increased to nine billion dollars a year. The growth of government could also be measured by the fact that the share of the nation's nonmilitary capital assets owned by all levels of government had risen in this period from 6.6 percent to 13.3 percent.[16]

A greatly expanded role for government and the persistence of inequality and poverty seem to present an anomaly. Certainly most liberals who supported the expansion of government powers and responsibilities between 1900 and 1940 did so with the stated intention of reducing injustice and inequality in American society. In order to understand the failure of liberal reform efforts to bring about a greater measure of social justice and equality during the first half of the twentieth century, it is necessary to examine both the ideological framework within which proposals for reform were devised and the way in which such proposals were actually put into effect. In seeking to explain *how* the existence of a liberal ideological consensus shaped the evolution of the American political economy, I must disclaim, at the outset, any intention of fully exploring the related, but conceptually separate, question of *why* most Americans, including those who never completely shared in the enjoyment of the American dream, remained at least passively loyal to the liberal tradition in spite of that tradition's limitations. For the moment, I leave this question to other scholars.[17]

While the tremendous expansion of the role of government obviously reflected an important evolution in American political attitudes and expectations, I hope to show not only why the persistence of certain fundamental liberal beliefs ought to be considered more significant than the changes in liberal ideology which took place in this period, but also how the continued dominance of a liberal consensus placed limits on the ability of liberals to analyze adequately the basic sources of America's social problems. In examining the course of liberal reform from Progressivism through the New Deal, I believe one can discern a distinct and recurring pattern of development. Generally speaking, agitation for the establishment of new political mechanisms initially came from middle class reformers, or from others outside the ruling elites of the time, who were motivated by a desire to curtail the powers of existing elites or, at least, to impose upon those elites a greater degree of social responsibility. However, for reasons I hope to explain in the body of this work, the reform movements of the first half of this century were eventually co-opted by the dominant elites of the time. In the long run, those who benefited the most from the expansion of the powers of government were the wealthy and the privileged, not the poor and the powerless. Rather than serving as a means of eliminating the root causes of America's social ills, liberal reform actually took place in such a way that it helped sustain a social system which was in many ways unjust.

## II

The following study examines the careers and ideological development of a variety of individuals who thought of themselves as representatives of the liberal tradition and who participated in the evolution of that tradition during the first half of the twentieth century. Josephus Daniels, Henry Stimson, Bernard Baruch, Donald Richberg, and Felix Frankfurter all entered public life by the early years of the twentieth century and had some association with the progressive movement which sought to bring liberalism into line with the needs of a growing urban industrial society. Subsequently, each man remained a public figure at least until the end of the Second World War. At some time during this period, moreover, each man was in a position of significant responsibility in government. Although these men did not form an identifiable group, their individual paths crossed frequently, and, more importantly, they expressed a concern with and had an involvement in the major social, economic, and political developments which shaped the course of American twentieth-century history.

By examining the lives of individuals of various backgrounds whose active public careers spanned the entire period from progressivism through the end of the New Deal, I believe it is possible to identify those concepts and values which served as the core of an ongoing liberal consensus throughout this period. In addition, the choice of individuals who not only wielded political power, but also who left an extensive written record of their ideological development, provides an excellent opportunity for analyzing the way in which ideology influenced the evolution of the American political economy. The five men in this study are of particular interest, not because they were necessarily creative or influential in the realm of thought, but rather because their lives reflect the crucial point of intersection between ideas and action. These men were concerned with questions of ideology, but they tended to conceive of ideological problems in relation to concrete decisions or specific policy alternatives rather than in more abstract terms. By analyzing both the ideological development and political careers of these five men, I hope to shed light on the close relationship between the intellectual and political history of the first forty years of the twentieth century.

The organization of this study reflects my desire to explore the significance of the liberal tradition both as it has been expressed in the lives of individuals and in the collective history of the United States. My work is thus divided into two sections. The first considers the five men to be discussed on an individual basis. Its primary purpose is to examine the social and intellectual forces which shaped the ideological commitment each man carried into public life at the start of the twentieth century. This section serves as a means of introducing the reader to the cast of characters who are subsequently joined together in the narrative which follows in the second section. At the same time, the examination of the social and intellectual backgrounds of these men also enables me to describe the defining characteristics of the liberal tradition as it existed at the turn of the century.

The second section is organized chronologically and traces the development of the careers and thought of these five men over the first four decades of the twentieth century. Their public actions and ideological evolution in response to important events and trends are analyzed and compared. The chapters in this section do not consider everything of significance that happened in the life of each individual, but they do explore the common patterns of experience which shed light on the historical era in question. The chapters in this section, therefore, examine the relation of each of these men to the progressive movement, the First World War, the 1920's, the onset of the Great Depression, and the New Deal.

## CHAPTER II

# Coming of Age
# in the Traditions
# of Nineteenth-Century
# Liberalism: Josephus Daniels,
# Henry Stimson,
# and Bernard Baruch

JOSEPHUS Daniels, Henry Stimson, and Bernard Baruch were all born in the decade following the start of the Civil War. They came of age in a world characterized as much by the rapidity and exuberance of its economic growth as by the confident innocence of its moral values. When these three men embarked on public careers, the social and intellectual traditions in which they were raised exerted a continuing influence on their thoughts and actions. In spite of obvious differences in background, Daniels, Stimson, and Baruch each acquired an essentially similar commitment to the American liberal tradition.

I

Josephus Daniels' career as a public figure spanned nearly three-quarters of a century. Beginning as the editor of a small town North Carolina newspaper, Daniels subsequently became North Carolina's Democratic National Committeeman in the 1890s, Secretary of the Navy during the First World War, and Ambas-

sador to Mexico in the 1930s. Throughout his career, Daniels'
liberalism always bore the imprint of the moral and political values which dominated the nineteenth-century rural environment
in which he was raised. Daniels' twentieth-century commitment
to liberalism was grounded in a faith in evangelical Methodism
and Jeffersonian Democracy.

The Civil War had been raging for just over a year when
Josephus Daniels was born on May 18, 1862 in the North Carolina port town of Washington. Daniels' parents could both trace
their family origins in America back at least to the time of the
Revolution. However, the Daniels family was far from prosperous. Josephus' father was a shipbuilder whose only property was
a modest family home which he had built with his own hands.
During the Civil War, not only was Daniels' father killed, but
the family's house in Washington was also destroyed. When the
Confederate armies surrendered in 1865, Daniels' mother found
herself alone and nearly penniless. With three young sons to
care for, Mary Daniels decided to begin life anew by accepting
an invitation from her sister to settle in the village of Wilson in
the eastern plains of North Carolina. Mary Daniels soon became
postmistress of the town and was thus able to support her family
while her sons grew to manhood.[1]

The influence of Mary Daniels on her son Josephus was
profound. In his autobiography, Daniels observed: "If I could
worship at the shrine of any mortal, my devotions would be at
an altar erected to my mother." A faith in God and the Methodist church was the most important legacy Daniels inherited
from his mother. "Churchgoing," Daniels later recalled, "was
the chief interest and diversion in our family." In addition to
regular church attendance, each morning began, and every day
ended, with a family prayer and the reading of a chapter from
the Bible. At the age of thirteen, Josephus' religious fervor was
reinforced when an old-time religious revival swept through
Wilson. A comforting faith in evangelical Methodism remained
an essential element of Daniels' outlook on life until the day he
died.[2]

Of all the Protestant sects, Methodism was one of those
least concerned with theological doctrine. As Daniels himself
put it: "From the beginning Methodism was a *life* rather than a

*creed."* This life, however, embodied certain values which had great ideological significance. Daniels' religious faith was marked, first of all, by its egalitarian ethos. According to Daniels, Methodism was peculiarly a religion for the common man. It had flourished in America because its ministers had been willing to "live the life of the people" instead of preaching down to the masses "from an elevation of ease and comfort." Daniels always felt that any true religion had to be equally accessible to all who sought its solace. As we shall see, the belief that all persons had an equal opportunity, before God, to seek salvation complemented and reinforced Daniels' conviction that equality of opportunity was also desirable in the realms of politics and economics.[3]

Another characteristic of Daniels' religious upbringing was its stress on a stern, almost rigid, code of personal behavior. Daniels was a lifelong abstainer from alcohol and tobacco, and also made a point of being plain in both dress and manner. He even doubted the propriety of theater-going. Proudly referring to the ethical climate of the state in which he was born and raised, Daniels once said:

I love to think of North Carolina as standing apart from the richer and more showy commonwealths, setting an example of frugality and simplicity in an age of luxury and display. I love to think of its people keeping the faith of the fathers, untarnished by the gilt and glitter of fashion, unseduced by the restless ambition of place hunters and by the vices of pleasure seekers; and untouched by the skepticism and irreligion which endanger the strength and permanence of home and government.[4]

While Daniels' religion taught him to shun ostentation and vice, it also instilled in him a deep seated faith in the importance of thrift, perseverance, and hard work. Idleness was as much a sin as conspicuous consumption. Daniels, in other words, was raised to be a firm believer in the Protestant work ethic. The individuals who held the highest positions of respect in Daniels' moral universe, therefore, embodied what Max Weber has called the "spirit of capitalism." Daniels' moralistic individualism was an egalitarian social ethic, but at the same time, it idealized the type of frugal hard-working individual who was necessary to the expanding marketplace economy of the late nineteenth century.[5]

Although Daniels adhered to a very strict code of personal morality, his religious faith helped give him an outgoing personality and infused him with a joyful sense of optimism. He explained to his wife, shortly after their marriage, that:

. . . when I think of you and my mother, & your religion & your trust in God, they are proofs of the truth of Christianity, stronger than Holy Writ. In your lives I see daily the *living* of Christianity—& the sunshine gospel—that is worth a thousand arguments. I could not believe the Bible if all Christians wore long faces. But I believe in the religion that you live, & it helps me every day to be strong & to look at life bravely and cheerfully.[6]

Daniels' religious faith not only assured him of the essential moral goodness and order of the world in which he lived, it also gave him a lasting confidence in the conviction that "the best is yet to be." Such confidence often sustained him in the political struggles of his later career. At the same time, however, his faith in the basic rightness of the world made it difficult for him to challenge the fundamental economic and political assumptions upon which his world was based.[7]

Daniels believed that the moral order created by God centered in the institution of the family. He felt that it was the "better influences of our mothers and of the women of our families which uphold and make us strong." The influence of women and the family, in Daniels' view, kept society from reverting to "the savagery of old." Believing that "Love and Marriage and the Family" would always be a "trinity" without rival, Daniels came to oppose divorce except on Biblically sanctioned grounds. He became, however, an early convert to the cause of women's suffrage and did not oppose the efforts of women to enter the work force. While he generally associated women with matters of the spirit and men with questions of politics and economics, Daniels' faith in the natural attractions of home life, and his commitment to the ideal of equality of opportunity, led him to support the view that women, too, deserved a free choice in determining their own lives. "In the long run," he once argued, "it makes for the progress of the world that the door of opportunity should be opened to them."[8]

In addition to deriving certain moral and social values from his Methodist upbringing, Daniels also chose a career that had an at least implicit religious significance. When, at the age of sixteen, Daniels began to edit his first newspaper, it was clear that he had experienced nothing short of a religiously-inspired calling. For the rest of his life, the only years in which he was not an editor of a North Carolina newspaper were those in which he served as Secretary of the Navy and Ambassador to Mexico. Daniels was obviously speaking from experience when he told a gathering of Georgia schoolboys that:

. . . heavenly visions come to all youths . . . If your ear is attuned to the heavenly flashes, the clear call will come early, and it will come in one's teens if not before. . . . I verily believe that at this period there comes to youth the clearest, holiest, supremest visions vouchsafed in any period of life. If heeded, the years to follow are crowned with usefulness and glory and honor. If a deaf ear is turned, then Opportunity and Duty, having knocked, never come again.[9]

In one of his earliest recorded speeches, "The Three Repositories of Power—the Pulpit, the Bar, and the Press," delivered when he was twenty-five, Daniels explained that the calling he had taken on was one of great responsibility. He believed that, in his day, the editor had succeeded the priest and the lawyer as the most important molder of public opinion.

It is a great thing to be at the head of a newspaper and place ideas before thousands and millions—great in opportunity and great in responsibility. Unless the editor feels the burden of the responsibility and makes his paper a stupendous engine for good and for all that is useful and ennobling, and places himself firmly against all that is debasing and injurious, his multiplied power degrades and turns women's lives to shame and men's to dishonor. A paper can do the Lord's own work in the broadening and betterment of mankind. It can serve the Devil with equal efficiency and fidelity.

Throughout his life, Daniels continued to use the press as a secular pulpit from which he preached a gospel of social and political morality.[10]

During his formative years, Daniels was as much influenced by the social and political values of the community in which he grew up as by the religious and moral beliefs he learned at home and in church. When the Daniels family moved to Wilson, it was a village of less than one thousand inhabitants in the center of a sparsely populated rural county. Although King Cotton ruled in Wilson, the town was located just outside North Carolina's black belt, the area which, before the Civil War, had been characterized by concentrated land ownership, large plantations, and a dense slave population. Daniels thus grew up in a region dominated by yeoman farmers. He later recounted himself fortunate to have been raised in "a community free from caste or social chasms" where "democracy prevailed and snobbishness was put in its place." Daniels, in fact, claimed that his native state generally provided an environment hostile to any "spirit of exclusiveness" or class prejudice, since North Carolinians were "fond of personal liberty and individual manhood" and did "not relish organizations or associations intended to elevate one class of people above another." Hence, "the equality of all men or personal superiority based entirely upon merit," Daniels argued, could "be called North Carolina's faith and practice."[11]

Like most Southern communities in the years after the Civil War, however, Wilson was not free from racial divisions and hatreds. Race was a critical dividing line in the political life of Daniels' native environment, and it later became a significant issue in Daniels' own career. Yet Daniels' commitment to the yeoman ideal was strong enough to cause him to wonder, during his youth, and in later years, whether it would not have been a good idea for the federal government to have given the freed slaves forty acres and a mule after the Civil War, so that they, too, could have been afforded the opportunity of developing the virtues attendant upon yeoman life.[12]

While the community of Wilson was dominated by the hardy individualistic and democratic spirit of the yeoman farmer in its social life, the Democratic party had an equally strong hold on its political life. According to Daniels, "almost every white man in Wilson belonged to the Democratic party as had their fathers from the time of Jefferson." He once wrote to his mother that "next to my faith in God & I say it reverently is my faith in pure Democracy." There was no question that for Daniels, "pure Democracy" was best expressed in the philosophy and example of Thomas Jefferson. Just as Methodism was Daniels' touchstone in religion, so was Jeffersonian Democracy his byword in politics. So consistently did he claim that the teachings of Jefferson, when correctly understood, fit the needs of "every age and every change and chance," that his wife supposedly once told him: "When you die . . . you will not want to go to Abraham's bosom as do most of the faithful, but you will ask St. Peter to take you to Jefferson's wisdom."[13]

Daniels frequently referred to the Jeffersonain dictum of "equal rights to all and special privileges to none" as the best summation of his idol's philosophy. As Daniels understood this credo, there was but one economic system capable of fulfilling its promise. Capitalism, in Daniels' view, was built upon the same concept of equality of opportunity which was also at the heart of the Jeffersonian vision. The marketplace of capitalism had as its guiding premise competition under equal conditions for all who wished to enter its sphere. "With its safety valve of Free Competition and destruction of Privilege," Daniels argued, capitalism was "based upon the instinct of family preservation, of rewards for toil and thought, and recognition of man's freedom and independence." It was pre-eminently the economic system designed to utilize and reinforce the moral and social values to which Daniels was so firmly attached. For when "given free course," capitalism "encouraged industry, thrift, and initiative." The institution of private property itself seemed to Daniels to be an expression of a person's individuality and a necessary safeguard of both personal liberty and the sanctity of the home. The marketplace, in turn, was a perfect model of a non-coercive and equitable mechanism for ordering relations among individuals. Competition was a fair and impersonal means of protecting men from the subjective and arbitrary control of other individuals.[14]

Daniels' belief in a system of free enterprise and private property was born in the rural nineteenth century world of the yeoman farmer. Throughout his life, he always harbored suspicions about the immoral ways of the city. Still, Daniels' optimistic faith in the future extended to a confident attitude toward the ultimate merits of industrial progress. As the youthful editor of the Wilson *Advance* in the 1880s, Daniels was a strong supporter of the movement for a New South and encouraged and personally participated in the econonic growth of his own home town. Industrial advance, he believed, was a potential boon to civilization so long as it was not allowed to overwhelm society. Economic development was an essential element of progress, although it was necessary to guard against the vices which all too often accompanied such development.[15]

One danger of economic growth which Daniels learned to fear was the rise of monopolies which threatened to undermine the rule of competition. The Jeffersonian tradition taught Daniels to oppose undue concentrations of either economic or political power. At one time, late in his life, he even mused whether "bigness" itself was not "our greatest foe." Daniels' commitment to industrial development, however, remained firm from the beginning to the end of his career. But as society progressed and became economically more complex, the small entrepreneur and urban working man came to embody for Daniels many of the virtues which had formerly been associated with the yeoman farmer. Daniels' son Jonathan once observed of his father.

Though he had never tilled an acre, he liked to regard himself from his shining square-toed shoes to his round black hat as one of those yeoman in the services of Jefferson's radicalism still.[16]

While the political philosophy Daniels was schooled in reflected the uncomplicated individualistic society in which it originated, Daniels' Jeffersonian creed was not based on the simple notion that that government which governed least governed best. He always felt that government was under a positive injunction to implement the ideal of "equal rights to all and special privileges to none." Government was "not something far removed from us," but rather an agency for "promoting our own welfare." Although the conception of the state which he inherited from nineteenth-century Jeffersonianism by no means justified any widespread intervention in, or regulation of, the nation's economic life by the government, it did lead Daniels to make the cause of publicly supported education an enduring crusade. As far back as 1886, he advocated federal aid to education, contending that it was a necessary and desirable means of giving substance to the ideal of equality of opportunity for all citizens. Many years later, he declared:

Every child born into this world has the inalienable right of an opportunity to go to a school supported by public taxation, so that he may
burgeon out all that is in him. . . . Experience has taught that the only
guarantee of education of all the people is the operation of public
schools as the essential factor of democratic government.[17]

The idea that government should serve the interests of all
the people, and not just a single class or group, was central to
Daniels' conception of the proper role of the state. He felt that
no class, whether it be the rich and powerful or the laboring
masses, ought to seek to use government as an instrument to
further its own special interests. Although Daniels himself acquired a suspicious attitude toward the wealthy, he opposed any
approach to politics based on "class hostility" or "envy of the
prosperous" which would have attempted to pit one segment
of society against another.

Even as he came to be critical of the efforts of powerful
capitalists to gain special favors from government, he still seemed
to deny the possibility that permanent class divisions were, in
fact, a distinctive feature of late nineteenth-century American
society. Having been raised in an environment which was relatively free of class barriers, and having been instilled with a confident faith in the moral order of the world in which he lived, it
was difficult for Daniels to conceive of America becoming a
society built on the distinctions of class. Capitalism, as Daniels
understood it, was an economic system which was a respecter
of individuals, not social classes; just as Jeffersonianism in politics, and Methodism in religion, were grounded in a perception
of all human beings as individuals, rather than as members of a
social group. Whatever problems might arise, Daniels learned,
early in life, that any appeal to class interest represented a denial of the traditions which he treasured.[18]

While Daniels learned to oppose the idea of class government, he found no similar injunction against party government
in the political philosophy of Jefferson. Growing up in the South
during Reconstruction, Daniels acquired a lasting loyalty to the
Democratic party, believing it to be the party which stood for
"purity, good morals," and "decency." Partisanship always remained a powerful consideration for Daniels. Even when "our

parties make mistakes," he once wrote, "in the long run we can serve our state better . . . by staying in our own party than by . . . going across the line when our party runs contrary to our views." Although Daniels believed that a government had to reflect, throughout its ranks, the partisan identity of its leaders in order to "function well," he did not wish to see a Democratic government become a vehicle for handing out "favors, subsidies" and "immunities" to the nation's "farmers, laborers," or "consumers." The ideal of party government was not to be confused with the threat of class government. The Democratic party, as Daniels saw it, was simply the most effective political instrument for implementing the Jeffersonian philosophy of "equal rights to all and special privileges to none."[19]

By the end of the nineteenth century, Josephus Daniels' ideological outlook had been well established. Raised in the traditions of evangelical Christianity and Jeffersonian Democracy, Daniels adopted an outlook which was at once moralistic, individualistic, and egalitarian. No person could be guaranteed salvation or material success, but everyone, in Daniels' view, was equally entitled to a fair chance of trying to attain these goals. A partisan Democrat in politics, Daniels was a firm believer in the justice and efficiency of a private enterprise economic system and looked with optimism to the years of progress which surely lay ahead in the twentieth century. He realized, however, that, as always, vigilance on the part of the faithful would be necessary in order to guard against what he described to his fellow North Carolinians as the possible corruption of "the religion of your mother and politics of your father."[20]

## II

Like Josephus Daniels, Henry Stimson had a lengthy and distinguished career in public life. He was a federal attorney in the administration of Theodore Roosevelt, Secretary of War under both William Howard Taft and Franklin Roosevelt, and Secretary of State in Herbert Hoover's Cabinet. Born only five years after Daniels, Stimson, too, was very much a product of the nineteenth century. In contrast to Daniels, however, Stimson grew up in a Northern, urban, upper middle class home. As a consequence, Stimson's thinking was shaped by religious and political traditions which, at least in form, differed from those which influenced the ideological development of Daniels. Stimson's life-long commitment to the Presbyterian church and the Republican party was as much a reflection of his privileged social origins as was Daniels' faith in Methodism and Jeffersonian Democracy a reflection of his less favored social position. In spite of differences in background between the two men, however, Stimson's ideological inheritance was essentially similar to Daniels'.

Henry Lewis Stimson was born in New York City on September 21, 1867. His forebears had come to America from England in the first half of the seventeenth century and were, as Stimson put it, part of "the God-fearing, the Puritan stock of this country." Henry's father, Lewis Atterbury Stimson, was a member of the fledgling New York Stock Exchange at the time of his son's birth. He had only recently embarked on a career in finance, joining with his own father, Henry Clark Stimson, to form the Wall Street firm of Stimson and Son. The elder Henry Stimson had come to New York just before the start of the Civil War and had quickly succeeded in establishing a name for himself in the stock market. Young Henry's mother, Candace Wheeler Stimson, had grown up in a respected New York home to which literary figures such as Washington Irving, Mark Twain, and Walt Whitman were frequent guests. She had been well trained in the arts and had traveled abroad before marrying Lewis Stimson. Although not extremely wealthy, the Stimson family enjoyed a solid sense of economic security. Property and social standing were almost taken for granted.[21]

There were, however, other sources of disruption in the Stimson family during Henry's boyhood. In 1871, Lewis Stimson chose to give up his promising career in order to become a doctor. During the next three years, Stimson moved his family around Europe while he studied to prepare himself for his new profession. Within two years of the family's return to New York, Henry's mother died. Lewis Stimson then decided to send Henry, who was eight years old at the time, to live with his grandparents. Henry stayed with his grandparents in New York until he was thirteen, at which time he was enrolled in Phillips Academy in Andover, Massachusetts. Later, Henry continued his education at Yale, and, in 1890, received a law degree from Harvard.[22]

In the comfortable late nineteenth-century world of his youth, Stimson learned to accept, just as firmly as did Daniels, the certainty and permanence of moral and religious values. Stimson's greater social status, though, was reflected in the fact that for generations members of the Stimson family had been either Presbyterians or Congregationalists, denominations which traditionally had a greater appeal to persons of high social standing than did Daniels' Methodist church. While, as Stimson put it, enough Stimsons had been "clergymen and deacons . . . to keep up fairly well the moral standards of the stock," by the 1870s, the Stimsons' Presbyterianism had become little more than a rationalistic and secularized faith in Victorian morality. Young Henry's mother, shortly before her death, ruefully observed that the family was "so American and Presbyterian" that it "did not go to church at all on Christmas day." The religious faith which was instilled in Henry, both at home and later in the classrooms of Phillips and Yale, can best be described as the secularized version of Christianity which has come to be known as the Genteel Tradition.[23]

Stimson learned to believe, as did Daniels, that there was a moral order to the world God had created. Stimson never in his life doubted the existence of "a Power in the universe that makes for righteousness." This "Power," he felt, guaranteed the "inevitable progress of our race towards civilization." Though he admitted that "the sunshine of Christianity may have pierced through the clouds of our human nature in apparently unrelated spots of light," his confidence in the "growth and permanence of these spots of light" allowed him to make an abiding faith in "the reality and continuance of progress" an essential feature of his outlook on life. Stimson, like Daniels, was thus buoyed throughout his career by the belief that "the man who tries to work for the good, believing in its eventual victory, while he may suffer setback and even disaster, will never know defeat."[24]

Stimson also came to share with Daniels a strong commitment to a stern standard of personal behavior which embodied the values of the Protestant work ethic. In his autobiography,

Stimson revealingly chose the adjectives "sturdy, thrifty, religious, energetic, middle class," to characterize the "Puritan stock" out of which he sprang. Stimson's own upbringing, though it took place in a setting of relative comfort, implanted in him a high regard for the value of hard work, individual responsibility, and self-discipline. He learned, as he once said, that the road to freedom and salvation "was no easy highway of license, but the stern path marked by the milestones of courage, discipline, and persistent effort." While his Presbyterian religion permitted him to enjoy a wider range of entertainments than were allowed to Daniels, Stimson was brought up with an attitude toward vice and self-indulgence which was essentially similar to Daniels'. Like Daniels, he abstained from alcohol throughout most of his life.[25]

Stimson may well have developed an even greater preoccupation with the problems of self-control and self-discipline than Daniels. For while Daiels was raised in a religious home with very strict standards, the religion of his mother and the mores of the community in which he lived allowed, and even encouraged, the open expression of his faith and emotions. The influence of Stimson's homelife and social background was quite different in this regard. Although Henry left his father's home at the age of eight and did not return to live in it until after graduation from law school, he still considered his father "the greatest influence upon the ideals and purposes of my adolescent life." During Henry's three years at Phillips Academy, Lewis Stimson did not once visit his son, but, instead, sent occasional letters containing advice such as: "do nothing of which you are ashamed and show no shame on account of any honest thing you do;" and "always try to deserve success for success without deserving may easily prove a calamity."[26]

The distance in personal relations between Henry and his father was undoubtedly a factor in the development of Henry's aloof character. While he was an undergraduate at Yale, Henry began to court Mabel White. The young couple soon agreed to marry, but Lewis Stimson convinced his son to postpone the move until Henry had securely established himself in his chosen profession. The marriage was consequently put off for over five years. During this time, Henry made no attempt to rebel against the restraining hand of his father, in whose house he was living for the last three of those years. Instead, Henry seemed to make his father's point of view his own, accepting the long wait as a necessary exercise in self-restraint and prudence. While both Stimson and Daniels acquired highly moralistic outlooks which stressed the need for strict standards of personal conduct, Stimson, unlike Daniels, also learned to shy away from overt expressions of emotions to others. He thus developed a staid personality which was a reflection of the upper middle class Victorian society in which he was raised.

Stimson also came to share with Daniels the essentially individualistic outlook which went hand in hand with a Puritanical attitude toward morality in late nineteenth-century America. A Christian upbringing, according to Stimson, reinforced an individualistic orientation by its "emphasis on the sanctity of each human soul." Stimson was taught, at home and in school, that moral questions revolved around the "responsibility of the individual man." As an adult, Stimson once told Theodore Roosevelt:

When I am in doubt as to what to do in a confused situation I very often find help in trying to reduce it to its simplest terms according to the relations between man and man.

This tendency to analyze situations in terms of individuals was deeply ingrained in Stimson's way of thinking. It applied to his conception of social and political questions as well as to personal matters.[27]

While Stimson learned to accept the "Christian principle of the equal value of all human personalities," in his social environment this ideal came to be interpreted primarily as a requirement for every individual to live up to a standard of moral responsibility, rather than as a claim which every person had to certain universally shared rights and privileges. Although, as we shall see, Stimson, like Daniels, believed in the economic and political principle of equality of opportunity, his individualistic faith was not complemented by a deep seated sense of social egalitarianism as was Daniels'. In fact, Stimson's conception of a morally responsible individual was grounded in a class-based ethnocentric outlook.[28]

For Stimson, moral integrity required more than simply following a strict code of personal conduct. It called for an almost intangible quality which could only be described as "character." Stimson never explicitly defined this concept, but he did once say that "character" was "social" in nature, and he pointed to institutions like Phillips Academy and the "public schools" of England as "essential training grounds" for its development. Stimson thus apparently had in mind the development of those traits and manners which only a "general education" could produce. "Character," in other words, required the possession of the social graces which one needed in order to move in the upper crust circles in which Stimson was himself raised. Throughout his life, it was always easiest for Stimson to recognize "character" in a person with whom he shared a similar social background. Philosophically, Stimson believed that all people deserved to be considered as individuals. In practice, however, he seemed unable to resist assuming, at least unconsciously, that the development of individuality was dependent on the enjoyment of certain class privileges.[29]

In the Genteel Tradition in which Stimson was nurtured, character was not only associated with social class, it was also associated with sex. The terms "character" and "manhood" frequently appear in conjunction with one another in Stimson's writings. In praising the "individualistic activities of manhood," Stimson particularly valued what he considered to be the manly virtues of courage, endurance, and self-discipline. He had a lifelong attraction to the military life and, from the time of his youth, took regular yearly outings in the mountains and wilderness areas of North America. He explained that "the effect" of these wilderness experiences on his "physical, mental, and moral" condition was "great."

Not only is self-confidence gained by such a life, but ethical principles tend to become simpler by the impact of the wilderness and by contact with the men who live in it. Moral problems are divested of the confusion and complications which civilization throws around them. Selfishness cannot be easily concealed, and the importance of courage, truthfulness, and frankness is increased. To a certain extent the effect is similar to the code of honor learned by the soldier in the field.[30]

Stimson identified the idea of individual responsibility itself with the concept of manhood. In learning to view the institution of the family as the "fundamental assumption upon which modern civilization rests," Stimson concluded that life in the family necessarily excluded women from taking on independent responsibilities outside the home. This, he believed, made women incapable of undertaking the full burdens of citizenship. Unlike Daniels, Stimson thus opposed women's suffrage right up until the adoption of the Nineteenth Amendment, arguing that:

Almost every man, even before he becomes of age, has had some experience in taking care of himself and others. "To be the man of the family" means learning the hard lessons of self-support and protection of others which are the foundation of government. With such hard lessons the majority of women are entirely unacquainted.[31]

In the genteel world of Stimson's youth, the world of responsibility and work was seen as an almost exclusively male preserve which existed outside the secure and morally pure confines of the home.

The influence of the Genteel Tradition was also apparent in the racial attitudes which formed an important part of Stimson's conception of character. His model of a morally responsible individual was quite clearly white and Anglo-Saxon, as well as middle class and male. Stimson firmly believed that the Anglo-Saxon peoples were peculiarly blessed as a result of "their customs and tradition," in that they, more than other peoples, had developed a culture which fostered individual responsibility and initiative. Stimson was so steeped in the Anglo-Saxon bias of the Genteel Tradition that it was difficult for him to view non-white non-Christian races as having the "initiative and persistence of effort" which were the hallmarks of character. In effect, Stimson judged the level of development of a nation or a race in terms of the extent to which it made individualism, self-discipline, and competitiveness basic cultural values. For Stimson, racism and an ethnocentrically based individualism were but two sides of the same coin.[32]

Stimson's racial outlook differed in this regard from Daniels'. Stimson's racism was grounded in his fundamental conception of character and culture. His racial views were, in essence, a complement of his attitudes about class. Daniels' racism, however, was rooted in the specific political, and, to a lesser degree, social, problems involved in the tragedy of white-black relations in the South. It did not extend, as did Stimson's, to practically all non-white non-Christian peoples.[33]

In analyzing Stimson's ideological heritage, it is impossible to draw a fixed dividing line between the influence of religion and the Genteel Tradition, on the one hand, and the economic and political philosophy of nineteenth-century Republicanism, on the other. Both were pervasive and complementary ideological forces in the world of Stimson's youth. He was raised in a "Republican family," and except for a brief attraction to Grover Cleveland in the early 1890's, he remained a Republican for the rest of his life. While Presbyterianism and the Genteel Tradition affirmed the moral value of individual initiative and self-discipline, the Republican Tradition taught Stimson the importance of these virtues for a nation's economic and political life.

The late nineteenth-century Republicanism which dominated the world in which Stimson grew up, no less than the Jeffersonianism of Daniels' world, was based on the belief that capitalism was pre-eminently the economic system which rewarded individual initiative and hard work and made possible the enjoyment of personal freedom. Stimson believed that capitalism represented the culmination of the Anglo-Saxon people's steady movement toward the creation of a more fully individualistic society. The "American system of business and government," he once said:

. . . is not an accident but an evolution. It is based on ideas which permeate our whole life and methods of thought. It is the result of the migration of a virile pioneer race into a new continent, bringing with them the English conception of individual rights and the English system of common law, and building up in their new home an individualistic form of government and an individualistic habit of life and business. We have left the development and conduct of our industries to the initiative of the private citizen and our conception of the relation of government to business has been in the main the simple one that government existed merely to prevent the rights or activities of one man from encroaching upon the equal rights of another.[34]

Freedom itself, Stimson believed, could in large part be defined in terms of the "freedom of human enterprise," the freedom of the individual to develop his "natural capacity to its uttermost no matter how far beyond his competitors it might place him." "The cardinal test of democracy," according to Stimson, "was simply that . . . in the race for pre-eminence, there should be no distinctions of wealth or locality; no test . . . save the test of brains and character." Liberty and equality of opportunity were, therefore, as closely linked in Stimson's ideological outlook as they were in Daniels'. He, too, unquestioningly learned to accept the idea that the decisions of a freely operating marketplace economy were the most efficient and equitable means of distributing a society's resources. Not only did a private enterprise system materially reward those individuals who possessed the morally desirable traits of initiative, self-discipline, and persistence, but it also provided a mechanism which seemed to substitute an objective form of authority for the dangers of subjective and coercive decision-making.[35]

Stimson learned to believe that moral and political progress went hand in hand with economic progress and the development of a capitalist form of economic organization. The "development of business and commerce" was critical to the growth of "individual liberty and free institutions," he argued, because it brought about the creation of a substantial "middle class or bourgeoisie." Effective representative government, he felt, was possible only in a society which had a "well-developed middle class," since it was the individualistic self-disciplined bourgeois who was best able to practice the "eternal vigilance" and "organized self-control" which were the "price of liberty" and "self-government." Growing up in the dynamic economic environment of the post-Civil War Northeast, Stimson came to identify the moral order of the Genteel Tradition with the expanding capitalist economic system of the Gilded Age. In both, the bourgeois, the independent man of property, served as the model of virtue. While Stimson and Daniels thus shared a faith in industrial development and entrepreneurial values, Stimson unlike Daniels, had no vestigial attachment to the rural world of the yeoman farmer. Neither did he share Daniels' sympathy for the working man.[36]

Stimson's social origins also shaped his lifelong commitment to the Republican party. Stimson's support for the GOP became almost as important a feature of his political life as loyalty to the Democratic party was in Daniels'. Party loyalty, Stimson once claimed, was an essential element in "the political character of Anglo-Saxon countries." A country with a two-party system, moreover, had, in Stimson's opinion, reached "a higher degree of progress in the line of self-government" than one in which the electorate tended "readily to fly into factions on many issues." Stimson believed that the differences between the Republican and Democratic parties were significant, but he acknowledged that "true party government" was "easiest where people are homogeneous and divide politically merely upon issues of policy or principle." He thus recognized that an underlying consensus was a fortunate stabilizing feature of American political life.[37]

Once Stimson became active in politics, he frequently explained his commitment to the Republican party by citing its historic role as the "party of progress." He increasingly came to identify himself with the Hamiltonian tradition of Republicanism and declared that his party:

. . . stood for efficiency in government; that it has never regarded government as a mere organized police force—a sort of necessary evil, but rather an affirmative agency of national progress and social betterment.

Stimson argued that compared to the "critics" who were attracted to the philosophy of Jefferson, the followers of Hamilton had always been "doers." Still, in the late nineteenth-century political environment in which Stimson first developed his loyalty to the GOP, there were few substantive policy differences distinguishing Republicans from Democrats. It seems clear that the main attraction of the Republican party for Stimson was the character of the party's membership. Within its ranks were found the "richer and more intelligent citizens of the country," Americans who, in Stimson's view, stood apart from the "foreign elements" and less educated persons who belonged to the Democratic party. If the function of government was to provide the country with leadership, it was not surprising that Stimson looked to the party which historically attracted the nation's men of "character" to supply that leadership.[38]

Stimson's Republicanism, though, entailed no more activist

a theory of government than did Daniels' Jeffersonianism. It simply put a much greater stress on the importance of moral leadership and efficient administration. Responsible government, as Stimson understood it, was totally compatible with a free market economy; for he believed that the marketplace offered a fairer and more efficient means of allocating the nation's resources than could any political method of decision-making. Stimson's Hamiltonianism did, however, lead him not only to emphasize the importance of running the government on sound business principles, but also to speak far less often than Daniels about the necessity of infusing government with a democratic ethos. Stimson even once complained that the notion that "any American, trained or untrained, was fit for any position in public life, has been productive of more bad government in our country than almost any other political error." [39]

Stimson's concern about character and responsibility in government reflected a commitment to the idea of noblesse oblige. Men of character had an obligation to serve society by giving direction to the nation's political affairs and also by contributing, in private life, to the "good of the community" in which they lived. Stimson himself eventually adopted the practice of hosting an annual Thanksgiving festival at which he provided food, drink, and entertainment for as many as one thousand of his neighbors. [40]

Moral leadership and sound administration were necessary elements of good government. The extensive use of government power to compel certain types of behavior was not. In the economic sphere, the impersonal marketplace was more to be trusted than the interfering hand of government. Even in the sphere of moral behavior, Stimson felt that the "minute you introduce the principle of compulsion, the moral effect of example" was "destroyed." The essential spirit of Stimson's Hamiltonian philosophy is summed up by his biographer, Elting Morison:

What his generation called the better element had neither the right nor the privilege of seeking by compulsion and restraint to make all men better in the same way. This element had, however, the obligation to demonstrate wherein it was better, to prove its truth by its endeavor, and it had the positive duty to strive to make a world that others would find better than the one they were living in. In private and in public, this is what the life of Henry L. Stimson was all about.[41]

While Stimson's attitudes about morality and politics had a clear class bias, he still learned to oppose the concept of class government as strongly as did Daniels. Direct appeals to "class feeling" or to action in behalf of the "special interests and vested property rights" of certain groups in society were antithetical to Stimson's idea of statesmanship. "The best political leadership," in his opinion, "was that which appealed not to class against class or to interest against interest, but above class and beyond interest to the good of the whole community of free individuals." Even as he generally looked to members of his own social class to provide the nation with this leadership, in his own mind, he viewed such potential leaders not as representatives of a given class, but rather as individuals who had most fully developed the traits of initiative and responsibility which were as necessary in government as they were in social and economic life. America was to Stimson, as it was to Daniels, a "community of free individuals," not a society of fixed social classes. "There is no older lesson taught by history," Stimson once proclaimed:

. . . than that in a great self-governing commonwealth like ours, either we must all rise together towards happiness and prosperity or we must all sink down together towards failure and misfortune. There is no such possibility as having one class of the community climb to permanent welfare or success by tearing down and trampling on the welfare of another class. And the only result of such an attempt would be to bring disaster upon all.[42]

Although Stimson and Daniels differed in social origins and in their subsequent partisan allegiances, they nevertheless came to share a similar individualistic non-class oriented view of American society and politics. Both learned to believe that a capitalist organization of society did not necessarily produce social divisions along class lines, and that government ought not to be regarded as a proper instrument for the advancement of class interests. Stimson may have had strong personal and social prejudices stemming from his own class background, but he would have vehemently and sincerely disavowed the notion that such attitudes led him to adopt a philosophy which favored the use of government power for the advantage of the socially privileged.

By the last decade of the nineteenth century, Henry Stimson had acquired a well defined ideological outlook. His Presbyterian and Republican background had instilled in him a deep respect for the importance of individual initiative and responsibility in the realms of morality, economics, and politics. A faith in private property, competition, hard work, and a limited, but responsible government, was a natural product of Stimson's privileged upbringing in post-Civil War America.

## III

Bernard Baruch belonged to the same generation as Josephus Daniels and Henry Stimson. Though he entered public life when he was already in his forties, Baruch went on to become head of the War Industries Board during the First World War and subsequently served as an unofficial but highly influencial adviser to a long line of Presidents. After the Second World War, he was entrusted with the critical responsibility of devising an American plan for the international control of atomic energy. The brand of liberalism which Baruch espoused during his career, like that of Daniels and Stimson, had its origins in the late nineteenth-century world in which he was raised. Unlike Daniels and Stimson, however, Baruch did not have solid roots in a long established, well defined American community. Though Baruch was imbued with an ideological faith which was essentially similar to that of Daniels and Stimson, as a Jew, and as a man who was neither fully of the South nor of the North, Baruch acquired his liberal faith more as an isolated individual than as a man enjoying a natural sense of identification with any long standing American political or social tradition.

Bernard Baruch was born on August 19, 1870 in Camden, South Carolina, a rural town with a population of about two thousand. His father, Simon Baruch, had come to America from Prussia at the age of fifteen. Seven years after his arrival, Simon Baruch graduated from the Medical College of Virginia and be-

gan a career as a doctor. Baruch's mother was a seventh generation American whose family had been well-to-do planters
before the Civil War. At the time of Bernard's birth, the Baruch
family lived in comfortable, though not elegant, fashion. As a
doctor, Simon Baruch was a man of some social standing in his
community. He served as head of both the South Carolina Board
of Health and the state's Medical Association before deciding,
in 1881, to move his family to New York in order to pursue his
interest in medical research and to provide his children with
greater educational opportunities. Subsequently, young Bernard
attended the public schools of New York and graduated from
the City College in 1888. In his formative years, Baruch thus
lived in two very different social environments, one similar to
the community in which Daniels was raised, and one much like
the setting in which Stimson grew to manhood.[43]

One consideration set Baruch apart from either world,
however. In a society which was predominantly Protestant, Baruch was a Jew. His father was far more interested in Judaism's
ethical and historical teachings than in its strictly religious doc-
trines and rites; but Baruch's mother saw to it that her son was
raised as a practicing Jew. Still, Baruch grew up without strong
religious convictions and, in his autobiography, described himself as a man "not given to any creed." He married an Episcopalian and was content to see his daughter raised in the religion
of his wife. Nevertheless, Baruch's Jewish origins clearly left their
mark on the development of his personality and outlook.[44]

As a Jew, Baruch was often perceived both by others and
by himself as an outsider, as a man who did not fully belong in
the society in which he lived. Baruch recalled that while growing up in Camden, a small town with only a handful of Jewish
families, he experienced no sense of religious prejudice. The
situation changed, though, once the Baruch family moved to
New York. There Baruch personally felt the "difficulties" of "in-
tolerance and bigotry." He was particularly affected by his exclusion from fraternity life at college. Growing up with the sense
of being an outsider permanently influenced Baruch's thinking
in several important ways.[45]

First, Baruch always felt a special need to prove his own
Americanism. According to his biographer, Margaret Coit, Bar-

uch saw himself "always as first a Southerner and an American [and] could never understand those who insisted on considering him primarily a Jew," including those fellow Jews who could never "quite understand that when he said 'my people,' he meant his fellow Americans and South Carolinians." Baruch never explicitly renounced his identity as a Jew, but as late as 1940, while Hitler was threatening the very existence of the Jews of Europe, Baruch adamantly refused to associate himself with a proposed Jewish encyclopedia, explaining:

I have no desire to be a part of any hyphenated-encyclopedia, or party, or organization. If it were something like Who's Who—all right, but I cannot see any reason for giving anything to the Jewish Encyclopedia. It is about time we thought about America and nothing else.[46]

While continually affirming his own Americanism, Baruch learned to stress the importance of being considered as an individual, rather than as a member of a religious, racial, or social group. "The key to progress in racial and religious understanding," he once argued, "lies in the recognition that the individual gains for his or her own attainments." Thus, he claimed that in his own life he came to understand that the way to meet the "problem of prejudice" was "to take these discriminations as spurs to more strenuous achievement." An essentially individualistic outlook, in other words, became not only an antidote to prejudice when adopted by others, but also a way for Baruch to loosen his ties to his own Jewish identity. As we shall see, even after Baruch achieved a large measure of material success and public acclaim, his own sense of himself as an outsider continued to play an important part in his career. Having experienced the pains of social exclusion, he always remained hesitant to risk further chances for rejection. He thus learned to treasure the independence which he came to associate with being a "lone eagle."[47]

While specifically religious values did not have as great an impact on the formation of Baruch's ideological outlook as they did in the cases of Daniels and Stimson, Baruch, too, was influenced by the confident moral universe of the late nineteenth-century. Like Daniels and Stimson, he learned to accept, almost unquestioningly, that "everything would be reduced to a cynical zero'' if the certainty of Victorian moral values was ever challenged. He also developed a faith in progress, the inevitable march of all nations "towards a better life and increased freedom for the individual." In contrast to Daniels and Stimson, however, Baruch's conception of what constituted proper individual conduct was, as we shall see, much more thoroughly a product of the secular influences which affected his outlook than of his religious upbringing.[48]

Not only was Baruch an outsider in terms of his religious identity, but he also experienced the disruption of moving, as a boy, from a rural Southern community to the largest city in the nation. Although Baruch was educated in New York, made his fortune on Wall Street, and maintained his business headquarters there for his entire adult life, he never came to see himself as a Northerner. His parents never forgot their love of the South, and they passed on this feeling to their son. Simon Baruch had been a doctor in the Confederate army during the Civil War and had even been a member of the Ku Klux Klan during Reconstruction. Bernard Baruch's parents harbored no ill feeling toward the North, but his mother made her son promise that he would never "lose touch with the land" of his forebears. Baruch faithfully fulfilled this promise. Twenty-five years after having moved to New York, he purchased a huge tract of land, known as Hobcaw Barony, in his native state of South Carolina. This estate then became Baruch's winter home and vacation refuge. More importantly, it allowed him to feel that he had reaffirmed his original identity as a Southerner.[49]

Baruch's Southern identity was thus largely the result of a conscious choice made as an adult. He was too much a city boy by upbringing and by early avocation to be as thoroughly associated with the rural South as a Josephus Daniels. Baruch's attachment to the South, however, was an expression of important practical concerns and deep seated psychological needs. Jordan Schwarz argues that Baruch's identification with the South was a product of "national ambitions." While a career in Wall Street would be the source of Baruch's wealth and power, a home in South Carolina would make that power "respectable" by creating the impression that "neither New York nor Washington had corrupted him." It would give him "another identity

with which non-New Yorkers" could be "more comfortable."
While Schwarz is undoubtedly correct in viewing Baruch's cultivation of a Southern identity as being at least partially the product of political calculation, Baruch's decision to purchase Hobcaw Barony antedated his interest and involvement in public
life. It might also be understood as an attempt on Baruch's part
to establish, in his adult life, a sense of belonging by reconnect-
ing with the roots of his childhood. In addition, Baruch's desire
to create an image of himself as an hospitable Southern country
squire may well have been a means of creating for himself, as
well as for others, an alternative to his identity as a money conscious Jewish speculator. Baruch's own ambivalence about his
Jewishness thus may have contributed, perhaps unconsciously,
to his choice of a Southern identity.[50]

While Baruch remained in touch with the rural South of his
childhood, he grew up as a boy of the city. Early in life, he
developed an ambition to own a railroad; and by the time he
was ready to set out on a career, the world of Wall Street
beckoned to him. Baruch, no less than Daniels or Stimson, accepted the faith in economic and industrial development which
dominated late nineteenth-century America, and he decided to
seek his fortune in the New York financial world which helped
to make that development possible.

Baruch's identification with the South helped determine his
political loyalties. The memory of the "debaucheries of carpet-
bag rule" was kept alive in the Baruch family, so that Baruch
grew up thinking of himself as a "Southern Democrat." He recalled that in 1896, when he considered voting for McKinley,
his great uncle tried to dissuade him from that course by re-
minding him of the "Lost Cause and Reconstruction," and warning him that his "arm would surely wither" if it "marked a Republican ballot." Doubts about the ability of William Jennings
Bryan and then sympathy for Theodore Roosevelt led Baruch to
abandon temporarily the Democratic cause; but by the time he
was himself ready to embark on a public career, loyalty to the
Democratic party would become a key aspect of his political
outlook. Like Daniels and Stimson, he came to believe in the
desirability of a stable two-party system, arguing that "to be effective, a citizen must choose one of the two major parties as
the instrument through which he will try to work."[51]

Baruch's commitment to the Democratic party, however, differed from Daniels' in that it was not based on a belief in a clearly defined ideological tradition. Baruch recalled that as late as 1910 he "had no well-developed political philosophy." Not having firm roots in a stable community, Baruch grew up without the strong commitment to a well established American ideological tradition which both Daniels and Stimson had. This is not to say that Baruch reached maturity without a discernible ideological perspective. Rather, the ideology which he adopted was more directly a reflection of the economic concerns which dominated the post-Civil War age of enterprise. In substance, Baruch's outlook was very much like those of Daniels and Stimson, but his liberalism was much more obviously an elaboration of the assumptions upon which late nineteenth-century laissez-faire capitalism was built. In contrast to Daniels and Stimson, Baruch did not conceive of liberalism in terms of any religious or political traditions of long standing. The essential basis of post-Civil War American liberalism, a faith in an individualistic, free market, private enterprise economy thus appears in clearest form in the outlook adopted by Baruch.[52]

Recalling his days in college, Baruch singled out a professor of political economy, George B. Newcomb, as the one teacher whose influence proved to be of lasting importance. Baruch actually claimed that "much of my later success can be attributed to what I learned from him." Newcomb's presentation of classical economics was persuasive to Baruch because it combined "philosophy, logic, ethics, and psychology" and economic theory into one grand synthesis. This ideology upheld the fairness and efficiency of a private-enterprise, free-market economy on the basis of certain critical assumptions about both human nature and the proper role of government.[53]

Baruch learned unquestioningly to believe that:

The moving forces of mankind are acquisitiveness, the urge to function as an individual, a yearning for freedom in mind and body, and above all the constant quest of opportunity to advance. These are the attributes of individualism and the man without them is not worth his salt. Indeed, he is not a man at all.

The human "desire to function" was itself synonymous, in Baruch's view, with the "desire to profit," so that a "concern for money" was a "very human" trait and not something "immoral."[54]

In a society made up of acquisitive and competitive individuals, hard work and self-discipline were essential not only for individual success, but also for the stability and progress of the community as a whole. "Work," Baruch once exclaimed, "is the cure for envy, hatred, malice, avarice and general dissatisfaction. It is the talisman for contentment, comfort, self respect, and, above all, peace." "The man who really works," Baruch concluded, "is too busy looking after himself and his family to engage in bitterness toward others." Baruch was thus the equal of Daniels and Stimson in his praise of the values of the Protestant work ethic. He also spoke of "self-discipline" and the "control of our emotions and appetites" as the "strong backbone" of "morality." For Baruch, however, these traits were important primarily as the source of worldly success and social order, rather than as the source of spiritual salvation.[55]

During the early part of his career, success was clearly the focus both of Baruch's own life and of his ideological outlook. He may have felt that, on a personal level, success was a possible road to social acceptance. Thus, he once acknowledged: "Whatever I saw others accomplish, I was driven to try to do myself." In the highly competitive economic world of the 1890's, Baruch learned by experience, as well as in theory, that perseverance, self-control, and individual initiative were needed by the man who wished to get ahead.[56]

Baruch's acceptance of the view of human nature posited by classical economics caused him to become perhaps even more individualistic in outlook than Daniels and Stimson. According to Baruch, "the incentive of the hope of individual gain and advancement" was the dynamic force behind "all our progress." Moreover, he contended that the "individual" was "the first fact of liberty" and that "reason" and "freedom" had meaning only in individual terms. It naturally followed that Baruch held an unquestioning faith in the institution of private property, both as a means of tapping most effectively the human quest for "personal advance" and as a means of safeguarding the integrity and personal freedom of the individual. Baruch even preferred to describe the American political economy as an "individualistic system" rather than as a "capitalistic" system in order to highlight his belief in the central role of individualism in American society.[57]

The natural complement to Baruch's faith in the profit motive and private property was his belief in the fairness and efficiency of a free market economy. Baruch learned to regard the "law of supply and demand" as the basis of all economic wisdom. He was deeply impressed with the view that "we cannot free ourselves from the ultimate workings of natural economic forces or the inevitable human equations which govern mankind." A free market system, he believed, was founded on a proper respect for the "natural laws" of economics because it allowed for a natural balancing of the forces of supply and demand. Most importantly, it represented an essential safeguard to individual liberty because the marketplace could determine an efficient and equitable distribution of resources without relying on the use of "coercion." In his autobiography, Baruch summed up the lesson he had learned from classical economics on this point:

What are the alternatives to the profit system? What incentives for work can be put in its place? One alternative would be to have men work for the love of their labors, or out of a sense of service to others. Some persons do find happiness in living altruistically. But I know of no community which has ever been able to hold together for long behind this ideal.

The other alternative to the incentive of profit is to force men to work by order of some higher authority, as in the Soviet Union. Wherever it has been applied, it has meant a loss of some freedom. At times, it has reduced men to slavery.

The profit motive, however, offers a form of incentive that does not rest on coercion. In this respect, it is a vital mechanism of personal freedom.[58]

The power exercised by a free market on the lives of individuals was thus not seen by Baruch as the product of any personally identifiable "higher authority." Having learned to view the market as a meetingplace for separate individuals seeking their own ends, Baruch came to assume that the decisions rendered by the market were objectively and impersonally determined by the force of "natural law." Freedom was not endangered so long as one could feel that the power controlling one's life was not being exercised by other identifiable individuals.

Baruch, like Daniels and Stimson, was instilled with the belief that in America no such identifiable class or group of individuals controlled the nation's economic or political life. That there were rich and poor in late nineteenth-century America was simply a reflection of the fact that "neither God nor Nature intended" that all individuals could or should be "equal in the results of their efforts." A capitalist economy, however, was, in Baruch's view, best designed to foster the "opportunity of being able to better oneself through one's own striving" without being subject to the arbitrary coercive control of someone else. Capitalism, in other words, maximized the extent of liberty and equality in society.[59]

While Baruch's initial political views were not "well-developed," his political attitudes stemmed directly from his faith in the theories of classical economics. His Southern background largely determined his allegiance to the Democratic party, but he also came to explain his loyalty to the party because:

> I believe that the Government should mind its own business. I believe that the people who are least governed are best governed. . . . The people should be free to work out their problems. The only thing that good government can do is to see that everyone has equally easy access to the door of opportunity.[60]

Baruch's conception of government responsibility was similar to that of Daniels and Stimson. He adopted a laissez-faire attitude, but he was not committed to a literal version of the doctrine. While Baruch favored government action to assure citizens an equal opportunity in the race to get ahead, he opposed any attempt to use government to further the interests of "classes or groups that come together for special purposes." He thus learned to abhor laws whose effect would be:

> . . . to shackle personal initiative or to be catspaws to serve envy directed toward those who are willing to subdue their emotions and appetites and use their time and activity vigorously to achieve success.[61]

When Baruch criticized the dangers of individuals relying too heavily on government, he frequently referred to government in the image of a mother. He once asserted that "there are three mothers in a man's life," his natural mother, his religion, and his government. Men turned to one of these mothers, he commented, when they were afraid or helpless. Baruch contrasted the modern tendency of men to look toward "Mother Government" with the "self-sufficiency, courage, and independence" of America's forefathers, whose behavior had been guided by the desire "to pit unaided strength against the world."

Thus our fathers . . . were strong. Faced with every economic hardship, they looked to government for nothing and left to each man or business the working out of salvation. But, by this very device, they bequeathed prosperity. Their inheritors grew fat and flaccid. Where the fathers relied on themselves, their sons, like children crying for mother at every perplexity and disappointment, have acquired a habit of looking to political government for a solution to all their major problems.[62]

Baruch, like Stimson, and to a lesser degree Daniels, developed a view of the world in which the values of individualism and manhood were closely linked. Personal autonomy was to be sought as a goal and made into a principle of economic and political life, even if such autonomy meant sacrificing the comforts of love.

Bernard Baruch's background instilled in him a deeply felt though simplistic faith in the individualistic values of late nineteenth-century America. A belief in the "natural laws" of economics which he learned in his youth, moreover, would continue to provide the foundation for Baruch's ideological outlook throughout his life. Developments in the twentieth century, and particularly his own experiences in public life, however, would pose a severe challenge to those economic "laws." Baruch's ideological response to this challenge, as we shall see, often proved ambiguous and even contradictory. This was especially true because Baruch, unlike Daniels and Stimson, had no well established religious or political tradition upon which to fall back.

## IV

By the beginning of the last decade of the nineteenth century, Josephus Daniels, Henry Stimson, and Bernard Baruch had each acquired the foundations of the ideological outlooks they would carry with them into their later public careers. Coming from different social and intellectual backgrounds, they nevertheless shared a common set of assumptions and ideas which formed the basis for an identifiable American liberal tradition. The variety of influences shaping the ideological outlooks of these men may seem disparate, but, in effect, evangelical and genteel Christianity, Jeffersonian Democracy and Hamiltonian Republicanism, as well as classical economics, were complementary currents in the mainstream of American liberalism.

At the center of this liberal tradition was an unquestioning faith in capitalism. All three men learned to view private property as an institution which was both an essential expression of human individuality and a necessary safeguard of personal freedom. All three firmly believed that a private enterprise economy operating on the basis of the profit motive was not only the most efficient economic system possible, but also the most equitable means of allocating a society's resources and rewards. Each man came to view the marketplace of capitalism, with its rule of open competition, as the model for a just form of authority; for the market seemed to them to be both impartial and essentially non-coercive when it rendered its decisions. When functioning properly, the market appeared to be a mechanism for giving expression to the natural laws of supply and demand rather than to the subjective or self-interested desires of a single class or group in society. Each accepted the profit motive as the necessary driving force in economic life. All three men also welcomed the industrial development of the late nineteenth century as an important element in the inexorable march of human progress, although Daniels, at least, inherited a deep seated fear of the dangers of monopoly which accompanied that development.

The view of government which all three acquired was primarily a reflection of the conception of economic life they held. In spite of their partisan differences, all three defined the function of government in remarkably similar terms. They all believed that the major responsibility of the state was to insure all of its citizens an equal opportunity to enter into the competition for personal advancement which went on in the private enterprise economy. While none of them was instilled with an ab-

solutist commitment to laissez-faire or social Darwinism, neither
did any of them envision a significant role for government in the
operation or direction of the nation's economic life. A free market, not the political power of the state, was, in their view, the
most reliable and equitable means of determining the allocation
of economic resources.

Complementing their concern that government protect the
integrity of the market and thereby assure everyone equal opportunity, was their belief that in those instances where government action was necessary, it ought not to favor one class or
group at the expense of another. Government action, they felt,
ought to apply equally to all citizens as individuals, just as the
market theoretically gave equal treatment to all who sought to
enter its sphere. These men did not fear government per se, but
they did fear the use of government as a coercive force to guarantee a politically pre-determined outcome in the competition
for individual gain. They conceived of liberty itself as the right
to be subject only to those supposedly imparital groundrules
which were needed to provide a fair framework for competition
between individuals. To have one's destiny determined by the
subjective decisions of another individual, a ruling class or the
state, was, in their view, to be denied one's freedom.

None of these men, however, acknowledged the possibility that the social order which had arisen during the second half
of the nineteenth century under the aegis of a supposedly impartial market system was, in fact, based on the existence of
class domination. Nor did they realize that a government which
attempted only to uphold the theoretically objective decisions
of the marketplace was, in essence, functioning as a de facto
protector of such a social system. These men learned, in other
words, to see neither the class basis of the society in which they
had been brought up, nor the true nature of the authority exercised by the market. For the laws of the market were no less a
product of the economic and political power wielded by certain
individuals than were the laws of the state.

The inability of these men to come to grips with the issue
of class was due, in large part, to their strongly individualistic
outlook on life. Their deeply entrenched individualism was reflected in their tendency to equate liberty with equality of individual opportunity. An acceptance of the work ethic led each of

these men to believe that every individual was ultimately himself or herself responsible for the extent to which he or she
gained worldly success or spiritual salvation. The virtues which
they most highly valued, self-discipline, self-reliance, individual
initiative and perseverance, were all the virtues of the independent individual. Even Stimson, who, of the three, was most obviously affected by a class-based perception of others, felt that
a person ought to be judged as an individual and not as a member of a class or group. They all thus learned to think of America
not as a society of classes, but rather, as Stimson put it, as a
"community of free individuals."

Each of these men also learned to associate, to some extent, the virtues of individualism with the demands and prerog-
atives of manhood. Their concept of individualism, and consequently their view of society, was, in a sense, hardened by their
tendency to identify as tough masculine traits those characteristics which were needed to succeed in the worlds of business
and politics. In separating, either consciously or unconsciously,
the world of women, the family, and the home, from the world
of men, business, and government, these men came to define
individuality in terms of a sense of harsh aggressiveness which
seemed necessary in the competitive world of the marketplace.
In the economic and political arenas, men had to stand alone
without either the support of a group or class identity or the
love of the women they had left at home.

The liberal faith which these men all shared was, however,
suffused with a confident belief in the moral order and goodness of the world in which they lived. While they were growing
up, they learned to have an almost absolute faith in clearcut
moral standards of right and wrong. This sense of moral and
ethical certainty helped give added support and justification to
their social, political, and economic ideas, and to their faith in
the basic goodness of the American social order. While they
believed that moral perfection was out of the reach of human
beings, they still were certain that continued moral progress was
not only possible, but inevitable. As these men reached maturity, they all looked optimistically to the future, possessing an
almost naive confidence in the sufficiency of the American liberal tradition in which they had been raised.

# CHAPTER III

# The Shaping of Two Twentieth-Century Liberals: Donald Richberg and Felix Frankfurter

IN their careers in public life, Donald Richberg and Felix Frankfurter were practically contemporaries of Josephus Daniels,
Henry Stimson, and Bernard Baruch. Yet they belonged to a different generation. Although Daniels, Stimson, and Baruch were
nurtured in the liberalism of the nineteenth century, Richberg
and Frankfurter came of age and had their ideological outlooks
shaped just as the twentieth century was beginning. They, too,
became adherents of the American liberal tradition, but their
conception of liberalism was clearly marked by its twentieth-
century origins. Having graduated from college shortly after 1900,
both Richberg and Frankfurter acquired a faith in liberalism
which, in large part, reflected their schooling in a newly emerging conception of social science. In contrast to the previous
generation, Richberg and Frankfurter developed a liberal perspective which seemed more modern and intellectually sophisticated. But if the mode of expression was different, the substance of their ideological inheritance was still remarkably similar
to the one passed on to Daniels, Stimson, and Baruch.

I

While Donald Richberg held public office for only a brief time
during his life, he was active in public affairs for more than fifty

years. Starting out as a municipal reformer in Chicago in the first decade of the twentieth century, Richberg first entered the arena of national politics as an officer in Theodore Roosevelt's short-lived Progressive party. In the 1920s, as counsel for the nation's railway workers, he became one of the country's leading labor lawyers. During the 1930s, Richberg joined Franklin Roosevelt's New Deal as General Counsel for the National Recovery Administration and became one of the most influential figures in the government. In the later years of his life, Richberg became a noted defender of conservative causes, writing extensively on issues of public concern, helping to draft several important pieces of legislation, and teaching law at the University of Virginia.

During the course of his lengthy career, Richberg supported a variety of movements and causes whose goals were seemingly contradictory. Richberg, however, maintained a basically consistent outlook throughout his public life, remaining faithful to the fundamental tenets of the liberal ideology he adopted at the beginning of his career. Richberg's ideological commitment to liberalism, though, was grounded in a sense of pragmatic scepticism which contrasted sharply with the unquestioning faith of Daniels, Stimson, and Baruch. For Richberg's liberalism was shaped both by his own early experiences with an unstable world of personal and family relationships, and by his exposure to an emerging conception of social science which challenged the confidently moralistic foundation of late nineteenth-century liberalism.

Donald R. Richberg was born in 1881 in Knoxville, Tennessee, but grew up in Chicago. His father's family had emigrated to America from Germany following the unsuccessful revolution of 1848. Richberg's grandfather, who was of middle class Lutheran background, settled in Chicago and soon established one of that city's first profitable meat packing plants. Richberg's father subsequently became a respected lawyer and civic leader in Chicago, serving at one time as President of the city's Board of Education. Richberg's mother came from a family of Vermont Yankees which traced its roots in America back to the time of the Revolution. Before her marriage to John Richberg, Eloise Randall had been a principal of a Chicago public school. Donald Richberg was thus raised in a family which enjoyed material wellbeing and social status in a city which was rapidly becoming one of the nation's major metropolises.[1]

Richberg's comfortable middle class background was, in many respects, similar to Henry Stimson's. There were, however, certain factors at work in Richberg's family life which caused him to grow up without Stimson's almost unquestioning belief in the certainty and permanence of Victorian social conventions. To begin with, a pattern of non-traditional marriage and family relationships characterized the history of the Richberg family. His father had been married, had three children, and then been divorced, before marrying Eloise Randall. Richberg's maternal grandparents had also been divorced. Their marriage had broken up because Richberg's grandfather had become unable to accept the outspokenness and independence of mind of his wife, who was both a physician and a militant suffragette. Richberg's own mother was also an unusual woman. After having retired from a career in education in order to marry and raise a family, she decided at the age of fifty-five, just as Donald was finishing law school, to follow in the footsteps of her mother by entering medical school and becoming a doctor. John Richberg took pride in his wife's accomplishments in school, but objected to her actually practicing medicine in Chicago on the grounds that it would appear as if he were unable to support his own family. As a result, Richberg's parents separated. His mother moved to San Francisco, practicing medicine there for several years before returning to Chicago in 1909 in order to care for her ailing husband.

Richberg's own family experiences thus brought into question the traditional conceptions of marriage and sex roles which had been an important part of the nineteenth-century upbringing of Daniels, Stimson, and Baruch. Richberg continued, as an adult, to be affected by the unstable and changing patterns of personal and social relationships which became characteristic of life in the twentieth century. For while Daniels, Stimson, and Baruch all had conventional marriages lasting nearly fifty years, Richberg suffered through two unsuccessful marriages ending in divorce before finally establishing a stable home life with his third wife.

As a result of his family background, Richberg developed a

greater sensitivity to the stifling effect of Victorian social conventions than did the three older men discussed in the last chapter. He gave expression to this sensitivity in several novels which he wrote before deciding to commit himself fully to a career in public affairs. In *A Man of Purpose,* Richberg created a semi-autobiographical story about a Chicago lawyer who loves a woman unhappily married to another man. At one point in the novel, this woman exclaims:

Think of it! The world talks and talks of freedom as the most priceless thing in life, freedom to develop one's own life, to live out one's ideals; and yet a man or a woman can use marriage as a chain with which to hold another person in slavery—and do it in the name of morality—and worst of all, in the name of love!

In another novel, *In the Dark,* Richberg also has the heroine of the story deliver a protest against the treatment of women by society. She observes that "the world is used to the man without money or friends, and gives him a few rights of brotherhood," but a woman, she complains, "must have money or have rights upon some man's money" since "there's no right of sisterhood for her."[2]

Although Richberg learned to question some of the social conventions of late nineteenth-century America, he was still never fully liberated from Victorian morality. In his autobiography, he admits that the success of his third marriage was due to the fact that he had at last found a woman who, though having a "mind of her own and ample ability to take care of herself," still considered it her principal duty "to encourage her husband in his ambitions and not allow him to feel that her own ambitions required any particular consideration or sacrifice on his part." Moreover, Richberg, like Daniels and Stimson, tended to see women as the source and "motive power" of religious inspiration. They remained the special guardians of spiritual values. While Richberg learned from experience to doubt the inevitability or necessity of many of the social conventions of the world in which he was raised, he nevertheless could not break away completely from a lingering belief in their utility.[3]

Richberg's religious upbringing was also unorthodox. In the realm of religion, as in the realm of social convention, Richberg grew up without an unquestioning faith in the forms and institutions which were taken for granted in the world of Daniels and Stimson. Neither of Richberg's parents belonged to an organized church. Although Donald was sent, as a child, to several different Sunday schools, he grew up without any attachment to organized religion. He was taught to respect the importance of religious and spiritual values, but, as an adult, he found himself unable:

. . . to take part in the forms of worship prescribed by any particular church, since in so doing I should be attempting to formulate, and thus to delimit by narrow human ideas that which I believe surpasses human imagination.

Richberg consequently came to see the "formalism" of "orthodox Christian churches" as "more disturbing than satisfying to my religious yearning."[4]

Although Richberg learned to be skeptical about the merits of organized religion, his intellectual outlook still came to be grounded in an essentially religious faith. He believed that "there is a reason for everything," and that a "faith" in such a belief was "the only basis upon which existence is intelligent." Without a "simple faith in the reason and purpose of living," Richberg once noted, human beings could not escape from "the emptiness and despair of a struggle that has no meaning and no end." Richberg, like Daniels, Stimson, and Baruch, thus came to accept the idea that there was a moral order and purpose to life, but Richberg's faith lacked the sense of confident optimism which characterized the faiths of these older men. It is difficult to imagine any of them observing, as Richberg once did, that:

On any other basis [than faith] the failure to commit suicide is mere cowardice; and yet in that cowardice there must be an instinct of faith, a belief that one must go through or offend some higher law than he is able to understand.

Richberg, it seems, felt compelled to consider the alternatives to a life without faith, but found them both rationally and emotionally untenable. Daniels, Stimson, and Baruch, in contrast, probably never even questioned their faith in the moral order of the universe.[5]

Richberg's conception of moral order and his belief in the importance of spiritual faith, however, still had a significant effect on his political and social outlook. For he learned to view an active commitment to an ethical standard which he called the "ideal of service" as the most satisfactory means of giving expression to his spiritual yearnings. Richberg believed that Christ himself embodied the principle that "we are put here to *give* to life, not to *take away,*" even though this great ideal had become "hidden" in the "dogmatic teachings" of his ministers. Participation in public affairs became for Richberg a means of expressing his "faith in the divinity of life," since it offered him the opportunity to combat the "thief ideal" that the man who "gets the most and gives the least is the biggest success." The "ideal of service" to others, he contended early in his career:

. . . is taking the place of the old puritan notions of sin and virtue that are written through our laws and were preached to the people, until the people stopped going to church . . . [and] began to systematically disobey the laws that they didn't believe in. The lawless, godless epoch is passing and the newer spirit is demanding ethical principles instead of legal prohibitions; and a religion for workdays as well as Sunday.[6]

While Richberg developed what his biographer has described as a "moralizing style" in his approach to ethical issues, in his code of personal behavior he was less puritanical than either Daniels or Stimson. His unorthodox religious upbringing seems to have entailed less emphasis on self-discipline and the avoidance of self-indulgent vices than did the training of the Methodist Daniels or the Presbyterian Stimson. Richberg did not grow up with a lax standard of personal morality, but compared to Daniels or Stimson, or even Baruch, he was distinctly less old-fashioned in his conception of vice and virtue. This contrast in attitude was subsequently reflected in the fact that Richberg became much less inclined to utilize the rhetoric of the Protestant work ethic or to accept unquestioningly the moral individualism which was implicit in that ethic.[7]

Richberg's initial conception of political and economic issues was related to the attitude of skepticism toward Victorian moral and social conventions which he acquired in his formative years. For Richberg developed an ideological outlook which led him to be as mistrustful of the exercise of orthodox or unchallengeable forms of authority in economic and political life as he was skeptical about conventional forms of authority in the realm of religion and morals. Not only did he come to reject any form of authority which demanded unquestioning obedience, but he also came to be particularly wary of any type of authority which sought to enforce its claims through the use of coercion. Richberg's exposure to the new conception of social science which was emerging just as he was coming of age reinforced his fears of orthodoxy and made him especially apprehensive about the use of coercive power by those in positions of social authority. He came to feel that the exercise of such power created a dangerous means of compelling obedience to moral conventions and social standards which had no claim to absolute validity. The use of coercion also threatened to undermine the spiritual efficacy of the voluntaristic ideal of service to others which was so important to Richberg.

The turn-of-the-century movement in social thought which contributed significantly to the shaping of Richberg's ideological outlook did not represent a fully articulated political or economic tradition in the sense that Jeffersonian Democracy, Hamiltonian Republicanism, or classical economics represented such a tradition. The newly emerging conception of social science questioned many of the premises of the ideological traditions which provided the foundation for the nineteenth-century liberalism of Daniels, Stimson, and Baruch. However, it did not itself constitute an ideological tradition which was substantively different from that liberalism. Richberg's early exposure to the developing discipline of social science was important primarily because it provided him with a well developed rationale for questioning the validity of moral conventions and social institutions whose permanence and inevitability his own personal experiences had caused him to doubt. But the new social science furnished Richberg only with a mode of social analysis, not with a fixed set of conclusions about the way in which society ought to be organized. Richberg could not accept on faith, as could an older generation of Americans, the values and institutions of his society. Yet, since the new social science offered him no substantive alternative, he still grew up holding essentially the same political and economic beliefs which Daniels, Stimson, and Baruch had earlier inherited.

Although Richberg completed his formal education less than fifteen years after Stimson and Baruch had finished college, the intellectual climate in the country's academic community had markedly changed during these years. By the time Richberg graduated from the Harvard Law School in 1904, the American academic and intellectual environment had been significantly transformed by a new movement in social thought which Morton White has characterized as a "revolt against formalism." When Stimson and Baruch entered college in the 1880s, the modern conception of social science had only just begun to be formulated. Social questions were still usually approached on the basis of a priori assumptions which were supported primarily by orthodox authorities and the conventional wisdom of the day. Social thought was largely divorced from actual experience and remained generally unresponsive to the needs of a society which was rapidly changing as a result of industrialization. When Richberg entered the University of Chicago in 1897, however, a revolt against this outmoded type of formalistic thinking was well under way. Men such as Oliver Wendell Holmes, Thorstein Veblen, and John Dewey had by this time begun to develop a new approach to the study of social questions which emphasized the importance of examining the historical and cultural context of actual processes of social development. Abstract theorizing on the basis of dogmatic moral assumptions was thus giving way to a more scientific analysis of how individuals and institutions actually functioned.[8]

From the outset of his career, Richberg's thought showed an affinity with the outlook embodied in the revolt against formalism. Even though he was not, by his own admission, a serious student in college, and did not apply himself to the study of the social sciences, the intellectual ferment at the two institutions of higher learning which Richberg attended seems to have left its mark on his thinking. The University of Chicago and the Harvard Law School were both strongholds of the newly emerging scientific approach to the study of society. The University of Chicago, which opened its doors only five years before Richberg became a student there, was, in fact, the first university in the United States to be founded with "a full complement of academic departments for graduate instruction and research in all the social science disciplines," including the nation's first-ever department of sociology. Harvard also had come under the influence of the new movement in social thought by the turn of the century. Two of the major figures in the revolt against formalism, Oliver Wendell Holmes and William James, exercised great influence over the intellectual life of the Harvard community, and the law school became a pioneering institution in the development of a more scientific and practical method of studying law.[9]

The major legacy which Richberg gained as a result of his early exposure to the revolt against formalism was a belief in the importance of adopting a scientific attitude in approaching questions relating to man and society. The conception Richberg came to hold of human nature is perhaps the best illustration of this legacy. Whereas Daniels, Stimson, and Baruch all learned to accept unquestioningly the assumption that human nature was an unchanging given, Richberg came to believe that:

Human nature is not the unchangeable quality assumed by those whose vision is limited to a few generations. Human nature is a persistent development, wherein dominating motives and purposes are transformed in strength and direction from day to day under pressure of living conditions that are undergoing changes through the increasing exploitation of natural power by man power.[10]

Just as the perspective of science required Richberg to reject any fixed definition of human nature, so, too, did it lead him to the conclusion that it would be unscientific to try to establish eternally valid laws for society on the basis of either abstract logic or moral absolutes. Echoing the legal philosophy of Holmes, Richberg once said:

We cannot build as the natural scientist may—laying one truth upon another—because we do not quarry truths in the work of lawmaking. The law is the temporary expression in a temporary pattern of the ever changing ethics of the human will behind the law. The rules whereby men may live together in comparative peace and for mutual advantage are set forth in the law, and as the conditions of living change it is obvious that the law must change.[11]

The emerging concept of science, as Richberg came to understand it, was primarily a method of examining social problems on the basis of observable facts and within the context of their historical evolution. He realized, though, that science could be a potentially destructive force. For the development of science "undermined the authority of many institutions" and "moral standards" whose permanence had once been taken for granted. Science, Richberg recognized, brought forth "a mass of undeniable facts that have swept away the assumptions upon which we have built our ethical, our social, and our legal codes." Although social science could not, and ought not, in Richberg's view, be used to erect a new set of moral and social beliefs into an unchallengeable orthodoxy, the scientific method did hold out the best hope for "the re-creation of effective moral standards" and rationally defensible "social and political institutions." [12]

During his career, Richberg frequently called upon those who had been scientifically trained in the study of social problems to provide leadership and direction for society, believing that these "incorruptible searchers for truth" would be best equipped to demonstrate the possibility of making the "ideal of service" a rational standard of social responsibility. This emphasis on the scientific foundation of ethical standards differentiated Richberg's conception of service from Henry Stimson's view of social responsibility. While Stimson perceived the responsibility to serve one's community largely as an obligation stemming from one's social position, Richberg saw a commitment to service growing out of a rational education based on a scientific understanding of the needs and problems of society. [13]

Richberg's scientific perspective thus caused him to approach questions relating to economics and politics differently than Daniels, Stimson, or Baruch. He became as unwilling to accept, on faith, the inevitability of economic and political institutions and laws as he was unwilling to assume the immutability of moral and social conventions. Yet, if Richberg learned to examine the economic and political beliefs of his day with a more critical eye, he still developed a lasting commitment to the fundamental tenets of America's liberal tradition. Richberg grew up with a more qualified faith in the ideal of individual competition than the previous generation of liberals, but like that generation, he came to believe that economic life could best be organized around the institutions of private property and a free market.

Richberg learned to reject the idea that eternally valid "natural laws" governed the sphere of economic activity. He once noted that "in the history of civilization," "natural forces" had never by themselves automatically "produced an economic system." The law of supply and demand, which Baruch had come to accept as the essential foundation of all economic wisdom, was, for Richberg, dependent upon certain social and historical circumstances. Yet the concept of a self-governing market still became central to Richberg's economic outlook.[14]

The idea of a market economy was particularly attractive to Richberg because of the form of authority it embodied. Richberg was raised in an intellectual and social environment which made him mistrustful of established forms of authority. Any type of authority which resisted questioning or rigidly opposed change represented a kind of absolutism or formalism which ran contrary to the spirit of science. This applied not only to the world of ideas, but also to the worlds of economics and politics. It is clear that Richberg developed a fear of any form of authority which combined rigidity with the power to enforce its views or decisions by coercion. In economics and politics, Richberg thus came to see decentralized and impersonal mechanisms of decision-making as preferable to centralized forms of authority controlled by identifiable individuals. The marketplace, consequently, seemed to provide a means of avoiding, in economic affairs, the problem of concentrated and personalized authority. At the same time, the market also had the advantage of being continually open to new input and to changing priorities. From the outset of his career, Richberg felt that a market economy provided a model system of authority. It was based, in his view, on a pattern of voluntaristic relations which maximized not only individual freedom, but also the flexibility and adaptability of society as a whole.

Richberg also learned that "the rights of property" were not the product of "any everlasting principle," but rather depended "upon the economic conditions which prevail" in any given society. Richberg therefore insisted that the rights of property necessarily entailed certain social "obligations" and "responsibilities." A belief that the institution of private property was "essential to individual freedom" was, nevertheless, ingrained as deeply in Richberg's thinking as it was in the thinking of Daniels, Stimson, or Baruch. Richberg may not have been taught to place as much emphasis on the institution of property as a desirable means of encouraging and rewarding the development of hard-working, self-denying, competitive individuals, but he did learn to see property as an important bulwark of individual independence in the face of external authority.[15]

Even though Richberg developed an abiding commitment to the concept of a market economy, he did not come to see individual competition in quite the same light as the older men discussed in this study. Having come of age in an era which was already dominated by large-scale business enterprise, Richberg was less imbued with the entrepreneurial perspective of the nineteenth century. By the time Richberg set out on his career, he had come to understand that the marketplace was no longer an arena of competition between isolated individuals, and that cooperative enterprise, as well as competition, was important to the efficient operation of the economy. Richberg thus came to the conclusion that labor unions and large corporations would both have a constructive role to play in the evolution of the nation's economy.

Similarly, Richberg came to be aware of the possible conflict between his belief in an ethical ideal of unselfish service to others and an unqualified acceptance of the profit motive. But if he came to maturity having a greater sensitivity to the problems of a capitalist economic system than Daniels, Stimson, or Baruch, there is still no evidence that he ever seriously considered possible alternatives to a private enterprise market economy. Capitalism was not, for Richberg, a preordained economic system, but it still represented in his mind the only practicable means of ensuring individual freedom and social progress.

The legacy of political beliefs which Richberg inherited was, of course, closely related to his economic ideas. In politics, as in economics, Richberg was little influenced by the dogmas of laissez-faire. He rejected any faith in the "law of the survival of the fittest," and recognized that government should not be limited in its functions to the "mere maintenance of law and order." The proper functions of government could not be fixed according to some abstract logic, but rather had to be determined according to the evolving needs of society. Richberg's schooling in social science made him generally receptive to the idea that government could be used as an effective forum for scientific efforts to improve society.[16]

Although Richberg developed a conception of government which stressed its potential as an instrument of experimentation, he still learned to accept certain critical limitations on the exercise of authority by the state. While Richberg thought that government provided an appropriate means for encouraging the development of socially beneficial forms of behavior and institutions, his fear of coercive authority affected his view of the state. Government could be active and vigorous, but it ought to use compulsion on its citizens as infrequently as possible. On this crucial point, Richberg was essentially in agreement with Daniels, Stimson, and Baruch. He, too, rejected the idea that the power of government could be used successfully "to compel men to do right." The state could use its authority in the "prevention of what is clearly wrong," that is, in the restraint of "evils of a positive and proved character," but it ought not to attempt to establish a single standard or fixed ideal of the good which it might then try to force upon its citizens. No "human beings" had "ever exhibited" the "godlike wisdom and ability" which would be required of those in power if government attempted to impose on its citizens a single system of morality or a planned economy. Government, as the "organized force" of society, might become the most terrible of all forms of absolutism if it was entrusted with the power to establish and enforce by coercion fixed standards of what was morally right and socially desirable.[17]

While Richberg grew up with an ideological outlook which was less individualistic in orientation than that of the three older liberals previously discussed, his attitude toward political and economic institutions was still guided by the belief that "the supreme function of social organization" was to "create freedom" for the "individual." At the height of his career, Richberg aptly described himself as a "reconstructed individualist." He became sensitive, early in his life, to the fact that nineteenth-century liberalism exaggerated the extent to which any given individual controlled his or her own destiny. However, he retained a fundamental commitment to the liberal idea that the satisfaction of individual, rather than collective, goals was the ultimate purpose of both economic and political life.[18]

Richberg also acquired an enduring suspicion of any attempt to turn government into an instrument of class interests. Richberg, like Daniels, Stimson, and Baruch, became imbued with a feeling that, in America at least, any single-minded pursuit of class interests represented a form of "anti-social" behavior which threatened the harmony and stability of society. Richberg once observed: "So long as the governing class has no solid class support, but must satisfy many conflicting interests, the people remain free." Should government come under the control of a single class, the likelihood would become great that the open and continuous debate over the proper means of encouraging social progress, which was essential to both individual freedom and scientific advance, would be replaced by an absolutist attempt to impose a single standard of values on society.[19]

Although Richberg shared with Daniels, Stimson, and Baruch an antipathy toward the idea of class government, he grew up with a different attitude toward party government and political partisanship. Unlike the three older men, Richberg was raised in a family which did not have a long tradition of partisan allegiance to either the Democratic or Republican parties. Although Richberg's father was politically active, he had shifted his party affiliation in the Reconstruction era from the GOP to the Democratic party, so that young Donald inherited no strong sense of party identity. In fact, Richberg developed an attitude of skepticism toward the institution of the political party which was comparable to his attitude toward the moral and social conventions of late nineteenth-century America. He never denied the utility of political parties, but throughout his life he always remained skeptical of accepting a permanent commitment to any one party. In adopting the attitude of a scientist in his approach to social and political problems, Richberg seemingly rejected the idea that

partisanship could rightfully play a significant role in government. In contrast to Daniels, Stimson, and Baruch, who remained lifelong members of a single party, Richberg became a
political maverick, jumping back and forth between the Republican and Democratic parties, and also becoming involved in
the Progressive parties which were established in 1912 and 1924.

By the time Donald Richberg was ready to embark on his
career, he had already acquired the basic framework of the ideological outlook he was to carry with him for the rest of his life.
His personal and intellectual background had taught him to adopt
a flexible and pragmatic view of social institutions and values.
The skeptical attitude toward authority and unchecked concentration of power which resulted, however, became the basis of
a commitment to a private enterprise market economy and a
state of limited powers which was distinctly similar, in substance, if not in tone, to the liberalism of Daniels, Stimson, and
Baruch. The mistrust of self-seeking power which made Richberg, throughout most of his career, a critic of the exploitative
practices of corporate America, was, in later years, redirected
toward the increased power of government and labor. Yet Richberg remained, as we shall see, a basically consistent advocate
of the liberal ideology he had adopted in the formative years of
his life.


## II


Felix Frankfurter has been described by one legal historian as
"the single most influential figure in American constitutional law"
of his era. Appointed to the Supreme Court in 1939, Frankfurter's tenure on the bench extended from the close of Franklin
Roosevelt's New Deal to the beginning of John Kennedy's New
Frontier. Even before taking a place on the nation's highest court,
Frankfurter had been an important figure and had contributed
significantly to the shaping of American law for over thirty years.[20]

Frankfurter began his career in 1906 as an assistant to U.S.
Attorney Henry Stimson and continued to work under Stimson
when the latter became Secretary of War in Taft's Cabinet. During the First World War, Frankfurter served in Wilson's adminis-

tration as a special adviser on labor problems, eventually becoming chairman of the War Labor Policies Board. Following the war, he returned to the Harvard Law School, where he had first been made a faculty member in 1913. As a professor at Harvard for the next two decades, Frankfurter pioneered in the development of administrative law and influenced the careers of many men who went on to become prominent figures in American public life. During these years, he also followed in the footsteps of his mentor and friend, Louis Brandeis, by acting as a volunteer counsel in numerous public interest legal cases. In the 1930s, as one of Franklin Roosevelt's most intimate advisers, Frankfurter helped to shape the New Deal before finally being named to the Supreme Court.

Frankfurter, like Richberg, was a thoroughly twentieth-century liberal. His ideological outlook was affected by a similar exposure to the turn-of-the-century revolt against formalism and was, if anything, even more modern and scientific in its mode of expression than Richberg's. For Frankfurter had practically no ties to the society and traditions of nineteenth-century America. He acquired his commitment to the American liberal tradition within the context of America's emergence into the twentieth century.

Felix Frankfurter was born in Vienna on November 15, 1882. At the time of his emigration to America with his family in 1894, Frankfurter had never even heard a word of English spoken. Like many other German-Jewish immigrants, the Frankfurters settled in New York. In previous generations, the Frankfurter family had included among its members several learned rabbis, and Felix's own father had at one time studied to pursue such a career. In the United States, however, Leopold Frankfurter had to struggle to make a living by selling linens out of a shop in his own home and from door-to-door. Frankfurter's formative years in America, consequently, were spent not only in humble surroundings, but also in an environment which must have at first seemed alien. Frankfurter thus grew up as one of America's "new men." His American identity would be formed not through any ties to the American past, but rather by the future which America held out before him.[21]

Frankfurter's religious upbringing was, in many ways, similar to Bernard Baruch's. He was raised in a Jewish family which was "observant" but not "orthodox" in matters of religion. Like Baruch, Frankfurter ceased to be a practicing Jew by the time he graduated from college and later married a Christian. H. N. Hirsch argues that Frankfurter, too, was never totally comfortable with his own Jewishness because he never felt "completely accepted" by the Protestant "establishment" in America. As a result, according to Hirsch, Frankfurter "continually tried to resolve the question of whether he was an insider or an outsider" throughout his career, without ever fully succeeding. Yet Frankfurter clearly related to his Jewishness differently than did Baruch. While drifting away from a religious involvement with Judaism, Frankfurter became an active Zionist early in his career and maintained that commitment for the rest of his life. Frankfurter was much more willing than Baruch to proclaim publicly the sense of "fortifying pride" he felt in being a Jew.[22]

Two factors may account for this difference between Frankfurter and Baruch. Since Baruch decided early in life to make his fortune in business, he may have felt, at least unconsciously, threatened by the possibility of being identified with the negative sterotype of the Jew as greedy money lender. Frankfurter, in contrast, was, by his own description, "bookish," even as a boy. He may, therefore, have more easily seen himself identified with the positive stereotype of the Jew as intellectual or learned professional. In his own family, Frankfurter's uncle was a model of such learning, being not only a linguist and an archaeologist, but also librarian-in-chief at the prestigious University of Vienna.

Even more importantly, however, Frankfurter developed a conception of "Americanism" which made it easier for him to retain his Jewish identity without alienating himself from his ideal of what it meant to be an American. Baruch, as a native-born American and Southerner, seems to have associated the idea of Americanism with attachments to the nation's past, to a particular region, and to the dominant Anglo-Saxon culture of the country. Frankfurter, on the other hand, adopted a more pluralistic conception of Americanism which focused on the unifying significance of an ideological consensus among Americans rather than on historic, ethnic, or geographical bonds. An immigrant himself, Frankfurter argued that since the United States was "the only country without a racially homogeneous population rooted to a particular soil," the only force which truly united all Americans was a common faith based on "our belief in the moral worth of the individual whatever his race, color or religion." Whereas Baruch wished to be viewed as an individual as a means of blotting out his religious and ethnic identity, Frankfurter found it possible to think of himself as an individual who could be equally an American and a Jew. In so doing, he never doubted that he remained fully committed to Americanism, and, in fact, noted about himself: "It is well known that a convert is more zealous than one born to the faith." Ironically, it was thus Frankfurter, the immigrant, rather than Baruch, the native-born American, who became more secure in his identity as an American and ultimately less of an outsider in his relationship to American society.[23]

In moving away from any involvement in the practice of organized religion, Frankfurter claimed that he had "disassociated" himself "from all the forces of the past through which belief in supernatural forces appear as belief in some form of God." Frankfurter developed a religious outlook which was even more skeptical of the practices of formal religion than that of Richberg. He became, in his own words, a "reverent agnostic" or "believing unbeliever." Ethical and moral standards were always of great importance to Frankfurter, but his spiritual faith took the form of an intellectual humanism which required no formal institutional outlets for expression and which depended on no assumptions about the existence of either a hereafter or a transcendent power in the universe. Of all the men discussed in this study, Frankfurter was thus the most secular in his attitude toward religion and in his conception of spiritual values.[24]

Frankfurter's religious agnosticism was but one aspect of the pervasive attitude of skepticism which came to characterize his entire intellectual outlook. For Frankfurter was affected, even more than Richberg, by the turn-of-century revolt against formalism which sought to bring all dogma into question. By the time he graduated from the Harvard Law School two years after Richberg, Frankfurter had already developed what was to become an enduring commitment to the methods and perspective of the newly emerging social science. Frankfurter may have had little direct exposure to the new currents of thought as a student at the City College of New York, since that institution lagged behind in the developments which were transforming American education. However, his own extensive reading at the Cooper Union and the New York Public Library, his three years at Harvard, and his subsequent close personal associations with Oliver Wendell Holmes and Louis Brandeis, eventually made him an influential exponent of the new approach to social science, in general, and to a scientific conception of the law, in particular.[25]

Frankfurter contended that since "life" was "too big, too vital an enterprise to forecast the issues, to know the detailed trend of things—or to care," it was necessary to accept the fact that "you must make up your mind to go to sleep on a pillow of doubt." In rejecting all "closed systems" of thought as incapable of comprehending an "illimitable" universe, Frankfurter learned to develop a "conception of the world for which no absolute" was "adequate." This meant, for example, that Frankfurter, like Richberg, considered "any suggestion of the fixity of human nature" to be unthinking dogmatism. To understand human nature, or any other aspect of human existence, it was necessary, in Frankfurter's view, to examine not only what it had been in the past, but also what it could "be made to be" in the future. Frankfurter thus developed an intellectual perspective in which the empirical method of science became central.[26]

Frankfurter always proclaimed himself a "great believer in reason," arguing that reason alone made civilized life and orderly progress possible. He recognized, however:

. . . how slender a reed is reason—how recent its emergence in man, how powerful the countervailing instincts and passions, how treacherous the whole rational process. But just because the effects of reason are tenuous, a constant process of critical scrutiny of the tentative claims of reason is essential to the very progress of reason.

In stressing the importance of a conception of reason which was based on a "tentative, groping, obscure empiricism," Frankfurter clearly reflected the perspective of the revolt against formalism. Reason, for Frankfurter, was by no means identical to "formal logic," since in his view "logical coherence unchecked by actuality" led only to "sterile dogma." So long as the fruits of reason were "verified all along the line by" their "correspondence with facts," however, it was possible to maintain a "positive faith" in the potential of reason and science to "pierce nature's mysteries." The development of social science, Frankfurter believed, held out the hope of the "conquest of knowledge leading" to "the good life of society." [27]

Although Frankfurter, like Richberg, adopted a faith in science which was accompanied by a rejection of formal religion, he, too, recognized certain limits to the role that could be performed by science. He once warned Walter Lippmann:

To treat science as a religion is to pour new wine into old bottles that can't hold it. No doubt, the advance of science compels a shift in the religious argument and withdraws from it some ancient support. But no amount of "science" replaces the need that devotees of "religion" feel. The mystic desires may be differently expressed, but they are there when they *are*, regardless of the farthest reaches of scientific equipment. [28]

Frankfurter's commitment to the intellectual outlook embodied in the revolt against formalism affected his approach to social questions in much the same way that Donald Richberg's conception of science affected his social philosophy. It produced in Frankfurter a "temper of mind" and an "intellectual procedure" which endured throughout his life; but as in the case of Richberg, it caused him to think of "liberalism" not as a "body of economic or social doctrine," but rather as an "attitude of the spirit." "A liberal attitude," Frankfurter explained, implied "tolerance and resort to reason rather than force in the adjustment of human difficulties" and had "nothing to do with one's views of policy in concrete problems." Frankfurter, like Richberg, thus learned to question many of the assumptions of nineteenth-century liberalism. However, he, too, embarked on his career with an ideological outlook which was little different in substance from the outlooks of Daniels, Stimson, or Baruch. In his fear of centralized or coercive forms of authority in economic and political life, and in his belief in the desirability of a private enterprise market economy, Frankfurter demonstrated a fundamental commitment to the essential elements of the American liberal tradition. [29]

Coming to intellectual maturity at the beginning of the twentieth century, Frankfurter never developed any faith in the rigid laissez-faire economic theories of the age of enterprise. To Frankfurter, the system of ideas built upon the concept of the "economic man" represented a set of "false abstractions" and "artificial simplifications." Frankfurter, however, like Richberg, continued to uphold the idea of a competitive market economy on utilitarian grounds. He recognized that a private enterprise system was neither divinely ordained nor the only form of economic organization which was possible, but he still came to:

. . . believe in competition, in the excitement of conflict and the testing of man against man in a fair fight. We not only like these things for themselves as the spontaneous expression of personality in a free society; we also depend on them to get things done. At least in our economic system the dynamo is self-interest—a self-interest which may range from mere petty greed to admirable types of self-expression.[30]

Frankfurter shared Richberg's feeling that a market system constituted the most effective means of guarding against the establishment of any form of absolute authority in economic affairs. Fearing any "concentration of power" as a "standing threat to liberty," Frankfurter learned to conceive of a market mechanism as a desirable method of decentralizing decision-making, and, in effect, depersonalizing the exercise of authority in the realm of economic life. For Frankfurter, the "opportunity" a "private enterprise" system created for a few individuals "to make fabulous or unearned fortunes" was not so important as "the encouragement and freedom of action" such a system gave "to men to shape their own lives and to plan their own destinies."[31]

From the outset of his career, however, Frankfurter was well aware that the marketplace was no longer, if it had ever been, an arena of competition among discrete or totally independent individuals. The America in which both he and Richberg came of age had already gone too far along the road of economic consolidation for either man to hold onto such an outmoded conception of economic life. Frankfurter, though, like Richberg, still came to believe that a market economy, even if it operated on the basis of competition between large-scale enterprises and cooperating or consolidated groups, held out the best hope of preventing the development of an authoritarian economic system. Frankfurter thus learned, early in life, to accept the inevitability of the growth of large corporations, but he also came to favor the development of labor unions as a necessary balance to the rise of such large-scale enterprises. All the while, however, he remained fearful of entrusting any one group of individuals, whether democratically elected or handpicked by a few powerful special interests, with the authority to dictate to society on basic matters of economic policy.

While Frankfurter did not idealize or identify with the old style individualism associated with the yeoman farmer or the struggling entrepreneur, he, like Richberg, learned to stress the importance of maximizing the independence and autonomy of the individual within an increasingly complex and interdependent society. It is for this reason that Frankfurter became a firm believer in the advantages of private property. He, like Richberg, learned to emphasize the need to attach certain social responsibilities to the enjoyment of property rights, but he consistently maintained that:

. . . in some of its aspects property is a function of personality, and conversely the free range of the human spirit becomes shrivelled and constrained under economic dependence. Especially in a civilization like ours where the economic interdependence of society is so pervasive, a sharp division between property rights and human rights largely falsifies reality.[32]

Believing that the institution of property served as an important bulwark of individual freedom, Frankfurter came to see a seriously uneven distribution of property as a threat to liberty. Having witnessed as a boy the stratified society of late nineteenth-century Vienna, Frankfurter was impressed both by what he perceived as the great extent of social mobility in the United States, and by the widespread distribution of property among Americans. He came to feel that these conditions provided the foundation for American democracy and freedom. Frankfurter thus developed a commitment to the ideal of equality which was stronger than that of any of the other men discussed in this study except Daniels. For Frankfurter's conception of equality was not totally encompassed by the notion of equal opportunity. He realized, as he once put it, that "there is no greater inequality than the equality of unequals." While Frankfurter never in his career advocated any simple leveling of incomes or wealth, he became more sensitive than such older liberals as Stimson and Baruch to the close relationship between economic inequality and the denial of meaningful freedom.[33]

Although Frankfurter and Daniels were the most egalitarian in outlook of the five men being discussed, there was a certain contrast in emphasis in their conceptions of equality. Daniels' nineteenth-century rural upbringing and his consequent identification with the simple yeoman farmer caused him to stress the social aspects of equality. A strong dislike for any form of social snobbery was a pervasive influence on Daniels' egalitarianism. Frankfurter, on the other hand, thought of equality primarily in economic and political terms, and showed far less emotional attachment to the ideal of the common man. In spite of the fact that he was himself a member of an ethnic group which suffered from social prejudice, Frankfurter seemed to derive his attitude toward equality more from a "scientific" examination of the problem of individual freedom in an industrial society than from a personally felt dislike of social discrimination.

Frankfurter's conception of the proper role of government also reflected the direct influence of the revolt against formalism. His political views complemented his economic outlook in that he learned to reject a "laissez-faire" approach to "law" just as he rejected "the laissez-faire of economics." From the outset of his career, Frankfurter came to see government as a particularly important vehicle for "experimentation" in the attempt to improve society. "There is no royal road to governmental effectiveness," he once observed, "except trial and error." In Frankfurter's opinion, "inertia and a priori planning" were each "the enemy of wisdom" in matters of public policy.[34]

Frankfurter naturally argued that the experimentation which was essential to government had to be grounded in a "critical knowledge of past experience." Possessing a strong faith in science, Frankfurter came to emphasize the necessity of having government utilize the services of scientifically trained experts in its tackling of social problems. This was especially necessary,

Frankfurter contended, because in the twentieth century, "modern politics" was becoming "largely economics," so that the "staples" of political life were becoming ever more "deeply enmeshed in intricate and technical facts." Political questions, therefore, had to be "extricated from presupposition and partisanship" since their solution required "systematic effort to contract the area of conflict and passion and widen the area of accredited knowledge as the basis of action."[35]

Frankfurter, consequently, developed an abiding faith in the necessity of maintaining "a highly trained and disinterested" body of permanent civil servants. He became a great admirer of the British civil service system and learned to rue the fact that in the United States a variety of factors operating throughout the nineteenth century had "combined against" the development of comparable "scientific standards of government." He thus became critical of the "easy-going, loose-jointed, and unprofessional" standards of administration which dominated American public life. His own exposure to the newly emerging discipline of social science led him to believe that:

If . . . democracy is to work, we must in the future, more than ever before, temper the romantic American political tradition that everyone is competent for everything with the common sense of John Stuart Mill's observation. "Mediocrity ought not to be engaged in the affairs of state."

"Without a permanent and professional public service, highly trained, imaginative, and courageously disinterested," Frankfurter felt that "the democratic aims" of society could not "be achieved." It would be through the development of this type of civil service that the scientific spirit embodied in the revolt against formalism would be infused into government; for scientifically trained public servants would best be able to deal with social problems "not dogmatically, but pragmatically, empirically, by trial and error, distrusting all absolutes."[36]

Henry Stimson also attacked, in similar terms, the spoils system which had become a tradition in American politics. In emphasizing the scientific training of administrators, however, Frankfurter differed from Stimson, who, although believing in efficient administration, put a much greater stress on qualities of moral leadership and integrity. Stimson did not so much envision "scientists" as the backbone of government, but rather "gentlemen," properly raised and of respectable social origins. This contrast in emphasis clearly reflected the differences in social and intellectual background between the two men. As an immigrant without the social ties or standing of Stimson, Frankfurter more naturally looked to the cultivation of intelligence through rigorous academic training, rather than breeding, as the necessary preparation for public service. Frankfurter's faith in "scientific expertness" was thus much closer in spirit to Richberg's outlook than to Stimson's.[37]

Never having developed an absolutist faith in the notion of a self-regulating political economy, Frankfurter looked to "wise statesmanship" on the part of a government aided by experts trained in "social engineering" to determine at precisely what points the cost of competition might become "too great" and the pursuit of "self-interest" harmful to society. Yet, while Frankfurter was by no means nurtured on a philosophy of laissez-faire, he still developed a strong antipathy to the idea of government using extensive powers of coercion upon its citizens. In his fear of coercive authority, Frankfurter closely resembled Richberg.[38]

Frankfurter once referred to "government" as "the largest club to which we all belong." Government, and especially democratic government, provided the ultimate forum for "the free exchange of opinion regarding the wisest policy for the life of society." As such, it established "the political framework within which reason" could "thrive most generously and imaginatively on the widest scale." The great advantage of democracy, in Frankfurter's view, was that it had the potential for most fully embodying a non-coercive and rational method for arriving at public decisions. The "basis" of "democracy," according to Frankfurter, was "reason not authority."[39]

Frankfurter envisaged the state taking an active role both in suppressing certain forms of socially harmful behavior and in assisting the performance of "those tasks of mutual aid which must be done communally." Still, Frankfurter's basic skepticism about the ability of "poor fallible man, however great, wise and deep his insight," to come up with "ultimate wisdom" made

him wary of entrusting the individuals who made up government with the power of forcing men to live up to any one fixed
ideal of the Good. In his emphasis on the importance of a scientific basis for government experimentation, Frankfurter saw
persuasion and example, not coercion, as the appropriate tools
of government. "There are just two ultimate forces in government," Frankfurter once wrote:

You can wrap them around with names, with institutions and use a lot
of words, but it comes down to two great forces. One is talk and the
other is force. There are no two other ways of governing human
beings.[40]

In stressing the importance of maintaining a continual process of "give and take," and study and discussion, if government
was to remain both effective and fair, Frankfurter saw that the
"clash" of "interests" was a necessary aspect of democratic
government. While government served as a forum for the "mediation of class and group and regional interests," Frankfurter's
fear of concentrated power and the development of absolute
forms of authority led him to conclude that it was essential to
individual freedom that no one interest or class ever gain complete supremacy over the other interests in society. Frankfurter
thus grew up with a hostility toward the idea of class government which was similar to that of each of the other men discussed in this study.[41]

As an immigrant, Frankfurter saw the United States as being
particularly fortunate in terms of its freedom from the class distinctions and class consciousness of the European society into
which he was born. The existence of widespread social mobility and the "freedom from past caste" in America, Frankfurter
argued, made Americans less likely to think of government in
strictly class terms. This served as an important deterrent to the
development of a class-based conception of politics which
would have threatened both liberty and progress. Thus Frankfurter proudly proclaimed of his adopted country:

Our recent origin has saved us from those tenacious resistances to
political adaptations which come from a system of rigid social stratifi-
cations. It has given us a fluid society. To the bounteous economic

resources of the country must be added this freedom from the undue weight of the past to help us in working out a civilized and humane society.

Frankfurter was never completely oblivious to the existence of class differences in the United States. Neither did he view social and economic issues in such individualistic terms as the older generation of liberals discussed here. However, he, too, learned to be wary of utilizing a strictly class analysis of social problems and to fear the use of government for class conscious purposes.[42]

Frankfurter, like Richberg, did differ from Daniels, Stimson, and Baruch in the conception he developed of the place of partisanship and party loyalty in politics. Frankfurter, of course, had no history of family allegiance to any one party. It is interesting that the first political heroes in the young immigrant's life, William Jennings Bryan and Abraham Lincoln, represented both of the nation's major party traditions. The importance Frankfurter attached to a disinterested, non-partisan approach to social issues obviously conflicted with the emphasis such nineteenth-century liberals as Daniels, Stimson, and Baruch put on party loyalty as a prerequisite for effective political action. Frankfurter thus came of age without any strong commitment to either the Democratic or Republican parties. His initial attraction to the Democratic party of Bryan was soon followed by an identification with the Republican party of Theodore Roosevelt, and for the rest of his life, Frankfurter found little difficulty in shifting his partisan allegiance. Although he learned to appreciate, early in his career, the stabilizing effects of America's two-party system, like Richberg, he became willing in 1912 and 1924 to support third party Progressive movements which he saw as embodying a dispassionate and scientific approach to public issues.

Felix Frankfurter acquired a commitment to the American liberal tradition which reflected not only the new trends in social thought at the turn of the century, but also the aspirations of an immigrant who looked with hope to a future which his own intelligence and education could make possible. Frankfurter's liberalism, with its emphasis on a dynamic and open society utilizing the skills of those scientifically trained in the handling of social problems, was not a negation of the older liberalism of such men as Daniels, Stimson, and Baruch. It did, however, seek to extend that liberalism to meet the needs of both twentieth-century life and a newly arising segment of the American middle class.

## III

Coming of age after the beginning of the twentieth century, Donald Richberg and Felix Frankfurter derived their commitments to American liberalism from different intellectual sources than Daniels, Stimson, and Baruch. They were both significantly influenced by the revolt against formalism which resulted in the rise of a new conception of social science around the turn of the century. Not only did both men grow up placing far more emphasis on the importance of utilizing the methods of science in dealing with the complex issues facing society, but both men also developed a far more critical and skeptical attitude toward existing institutions and values than the three older liberals who were raised in the intellectual climate of the nineteenth century.

While the span of years separating the generation of Richberg and Frankfurter from that of Daniels, Stimson, and Baruch was not great, by the time the two younger men were growing up, the simpler, more clearly individualistic world of the nineteenth century was rapidly giving way to the more complicated and interdependent world of the twentieth century. Both Richberg and Frankfurter continued to accept the fundamental tenet of the liberal tradition that the freedom and well being of the individual were the ultimate purposes of social organization, but in contrast to the three older men, they were brought up with a clearer understanding of the intricate web of associations and organizations upon which the individual necessarily relied in modern industrial society. It would be an exaggeration to state that Richberg and Frankfurter were nurtured in a full-blown intellectual tradition of "pluralism," in the sense that that term eventually came to be used. However, their intellectual upbringing well prepared them to adopt a more explicitly pluralistic perspective later in their careers. For the relative freedom

Richberg and Frankfurter enjoyed from the stricter individualism in which Daniels, Stimson, and Baruch were raised allowed them to adopt more easily the growing emphasis on the importance of group identities which later came to characterize liberalism. Group identifications of various kinds, whether with one's occupation, ethnic background, or local community, eventually offered an apparent alternative to a class consciousness which liberals of both generations had learned to fear.

Richberg and Frankfurter's skepticism and lack of unquestioning faith in the institutions of nineteenth-century America, as well as their belief in scientific methods of dealing with social problems, also contributed to their less partisan approach to politics. Unlike Daniels, Stimson, and Baruch, they never developed a lifelong commitment to the political party of their fathers. In other important respects, however, the attitude of doubt which stemmed from their exposure to the revolt against formalism simply provided a new foundation for a conception of economics and politics which was essentially similar to the outlooks Daniels, Stimson, and Baruch had come to adopt in their early years.

If there were distinct differences between the nineteenth-century liberalism in which Daniels, Stimson, and Baruch were reared and the twentieth-century liberalism in which Richberg and Frankfurter were raised, the extent of essential ideological agreement between the two was, nevertheless, far more important. The central tenet of both versions of the liberal creed was a faith in a free market private enterprise economy. All five liberals examined in this study grew up believing that a market mechanism, in combination with the institution of private property, provided not only the most efficient means of organizing economic activity, but also the best safeguard against the development of a centralized or authoritarian system of decision-making which would threaten their most cherished ideal, individual freedom.

The marketplace became, for all five men, the model upon which they constructed their concept of authority. For at the heart of the liberal tradition was a fear of coercion being exercised directly upon an individual by another identifiable individual or group of individuals. Felix Frankfurter once claimed that the "reconciliation of authority with liberty" was "the priceless heritage of the Anglo-Saxon peoples." Yet it is clear that in adopting the model of a market as the source of authority in economic life, liberalism, even as it was understood by the generation of Richberg and Frankfurter, resolved the conflict between liberty and authority by creating a myth about the nature of market relations. The image of the marketplace as a source of essentially non-coercive and impersonal decisions was, at bottom, more a reflection of liberal fears and desires than of actual reality.[43]

Still, it would be misleading to label the liberalism which either generation inherited as strictly laissez-faire in orientation. Both generations learned to fear the use of coercive power by the state as an improper exercise of authority and as a threat to individual liberty, but neither generation learned to disparage an active or constructive role for government. The faith which Richberg and Frankfurter acquired in the uses of social science led them to accept a conception of government as a forum for experimentation which was undoubtedly even further removed from the laissez-faire ideas of the nineteenth century than the conception of government which was adopted by Daniels, Stimson, and Baruch. All five men, however, shared a recognition of the necessary role government had to play, both in protecting the right of every citizen to enjoy an equal opportunity to realize his or her own potential and in checking the socially harmful excesses of irresponsible individuals.

Richberg and Frankfurter may have accepted more readily the inevitable evolution of large-scale organizations and group interests, but they, as well as Daniels, Stimson, and Baruch, inherited a liberal antipathy to the use of government as an instrument for furthering the interests of any single group or class in society. Moreover, regardless of the realities of American society and politics at the beginning of the twentieth century, all five men were nurtured in the belief that America remained an essentially classless society.

The ideological inheritance of these men has thus far been discussed in general terms and with little reference to the specific policy issues which were the principal subjects of controversy in American politics during the late nineteenth century.

For only after the beginning of the twentieth century, when all five of these men had become active public figures, would the practical significance of their ideological inheritance become clear.

As we shall see, the liberal ideology which was passed on to these men would not remain unchanged over the course of the next half century; nor would the generational differences in their conceptions of liberalism be insignificant in shaping their reactions to the major social and economic developments of the years to come. The narrative examination of the careers and ideological development of these men which follows will trace not only the way in which their conceptions of the liberal tradition evolved, but will also seek to demonstrate how their continuing commitment to the basic framework of liberalism served as a fundamental limitation on their ability to transform America into a truly free and democratic society.

# CHAPTER IV

# The Rise of Progressivism 1900–1914

IN 1901 two events occurred which symbolized the arrival of a new era in American history. The nation's first billion dollar corporation, United States Steel, was organized, and young, vigorous, reform-minded Theodore Roosevelt became President. The trust had become a focus of public concern, and progressivism had become a major force in national politics. Before the Progressive era came to an end with the outbreak of the First World War, Josephus Daniels, Henry Stimson, Bernard Baruch, Donald Richberg, and Felix Frankfurter had each become associated with the movement for reform in America.

During this period, these men, and many other Americans, responded to the basic changes in the structure of the American economy which were taking place by coming to accept the need for an expanded role for government in the nation's economic life. They realized that the nineteenth-century ideal of an open and competitive market economy had become threatened by the growth of corporations and trusts of unprecedented size. Consequently, a new breed of progressives looked to government to take a more active role in policing the operations of the economy in the hope that the nation's free market system could be made to continue functioning fairly and efficiently. The groundswell of support for a new conception of government culminated in the election of 1912 and bore fruit in the legislative accomplishments of the administration of Woodrow Wilson. Progressivism thus marked a new departure for American liberalism. Yet progressivism remained a grossly inadequate response to the economic and social challenges which confronted America at the beginning of the twentieth century.


I


The spirit of reform did not spring up overnight in 1901. The decade of the 1890s had been one of severe economic depression and intense political agitation resulting in the rise of the Populist party. Of the five men being considered in this study, three were old enough to have been politically active during the 1890s. A review of the careers of Baruch, Daniels, and Stimson, however, indicates that important differences characterize their attitudes and actions before and after the turn of the century. The reform movement to which they gave their allegiance in the years after 1900 was a new departure for them as well as for American liberalism.

Bernard Baruch graduated from the City College of New York in 1888. He soon went to work for the brokerage firm of A. A. Housman, rising from the position of errand boy to partner by the mid-1890s. He rapidly gained a reputation on Wall Street as an expert on the nation's railroads, and by the end of the Spanish-American War he had already become a wealthy man. Before reaching the age of thirty, Baruch had purchased his own seat on the New York Stock Exchange and often dealt directly with financial giants such as Thomas Fortune Ryan. He had also married into a well-to-do Episcopalian family. Baruch was thus a man on his way up whose primary concern at this early stage of his career was making money. It is not surprising, therefore, that he was not involved with the political protests of the Populist era. Brought up to identify with the conservative wing of the Democratic party, Baruch found the choice between Bryan and McKinley in 1896 a difficult one to make. He later recalled that "I was so mixed up in my thinking that I can't remember for whom I voted," though Baruch claimed it was likely that he had followed his father's lead by voting for John Palmer, a gold Democrat. At least by 1900, however, Baruch had become either sufficiently disenchanted with Bryan's seeming radicalism or attracted to McKinley's brand of Republicanism to vote for the Republican ticket.[1]

The careers of both Josephus Daniels and Henry Stimson in the years befor 1900 present a sharp contrast to that of Bernard Baruch. Both men had been active in political affairs before Theodore Roosevelt entered the White House. Daniels, in fact, had experience in North Carolina politics dating back to 1880, when, at the age of eighteen, he had become editor of the Wilson *Advance,* a strongly partisan weekly newspaper. Even before he was able to vote, Daniels had already made his first political speech and participated in his first election campaign. As an active figure in the North Carolina Democratic party, the young editor was rewarded with the job of State Printer in 1887. In 1893, he went to Washington to serve for two years as Chief Clerk to Secretary of the Interior Hoke Smith. By 1896 he had been elected Democratic National Committeeman from North Carolina and had attended his first national party convention. Daniels thus participated directly in the political struggles of the 1890s.[2]

The desire for reform was not at all alien to Daniels during these years. As early as 1886, he wrote to his mother that he would refuse to:

. . . sell myself to these railroad corporations which are eating out the best life of the State and standing in the way of all real progress. The great fight coming is monopolies & corporations against the people & in that fight men who stand by the people will receive no quarter from the money power of the country. I shall give them all the fight that is in me & of course win their eternal hatred.[3]

Daniels subsequently helped lead a campaign in North Carolina for the creation of a state railroad commission with power to set rates and prohibit rebates. This campaign came to fruition in 1891 when such a commission was finally established. Daniels was critical of the excessive powers being acquired by other large corporations, as well, calling special attention to the growth of the North Carolina-based Tobacco Trust (the American Tobacco Company) which was formed in 1890. He supported the passage of strong state anti-trust laws and helped lead the crusade which in 1899 resulted in North Carolina becoming the first state in the Union to create a corporation commission. Daniels was also an ardent advocate of a number of other reforms in the early years of his career, most particularly, increased public support for public education and state-wide prohibition.[4]

Henry Stimson graduated from the Harvard Law School in 1890 and then joined Elihu Root's highly respected New York law firm. Although his family had traditionally been Republican, Stimson supported Cleveland in 1892 because of the Democratic candidate's stand on the tariff. At about the same time, Stimson became a member of a non-partisan Good Government Club in New York. By 1895, however, largely as a result of the influence of Root, who was one of the leaders of the New York Republican party, Stimson returned the the GOP in order to participate in the movement to reform the party from within. He later observed:

I could not live and work in those early years in such an office as that of Root and Clarke without learning the importance of the active performance of his public duties by a citizen of New York.[5]

When Stimson entered politics, he began at the bottom, serving as captain of his own small election district and then working his way up to become head of his Assembly District's Republican club in 1901. Stimson's concern for reform in the 1890s focused on the issue of bossism in New York. During this period, Thomas Platt was the undisputed boss of both the Republican party and the government of the state. In a letter to Root, written in 1901, Stimson summed up the major purpose of the "revolt made by our Club against corrupt party methods:"

Its aim has been to have the district controlled according to the wishes of the voters of the district rather than according to the wishes of county leaders outside the district; it holds that district leaders should be chosen from within rather than from without. And if I am not much mistaken, this issue which has been a burning one between us and the County Organization is the issue which at bottom determines the differences between true party leadership and mere bossism.[6]

Stimson's efforts at grass roots political reform helped produce two concrete achievements in the 1890s. First, in 1897 Stimson and his supporters were able to defeat the machine candidate for the State Assembly and to elect one of their own

men in his place. Second, Stimson and his fellow insurgents succeeded in getting the state legislature to pass a primary election
law in 1898 which was intended to reduce the power of the
political bosses of the state.[7]

While Daniels and Stimson were interested in various reform issues before 1898, their efforts to better society in this
period contrasted significantly with their reform activities following the turn of the century. During the 1890s, both men focused mainly on state and local issues; whereas after the turn of
the century they increasingly turned their attention toward national problems and looked to the federal government for possible solutions to those problems.

Although Daniels held a minor post in the Cleveland administration and subsequently gained membership on the Democratic National Committee in 1896, the focus of his reform activities in the 1890s was almost exclusively on the state level.
His campaign against the railroads centered on an attempt to get
state legislation to deal with these problems. Even when he was
living and working in Washington as Chief Clerk in the Interior
Department, he continued to edit a North Carolina weekly and
maintained his position of influence in state affairs. Moreover,
the single issue which generated the most intense concern and
ultimately had the highest priority in Daniels' mind was the relation of the race problem to state politics.

Stimson's concentration on local issues is even more striking in that his reforming energy was focused almost exclusively
on a single New York Assembly district. In neither case did these
men identify with a strong national reform movement. Before
1896, the only national issue which seems to have seriously
attracted the attention of either Daniels or Stimson was the tariff.
Subsequently, free silver and the Spanish-American War aroused
their interest, but throughout this period the political battles in
Raleigh or New York always took precedence for them over
those taking place in Washington.[8]

Most students of progressivism agree that it emerged as a
national movement only after the reform impulse had first been
stirred by the type of city and state level political struggles in
which Daniels and Stimson were involved in the 1890s. Yet there
is a disagreement among historians as to the exact relationship

between the political ferment of the depression years of the 1890s and the subsequent development of national progressivism in the decade before the First World War. David Thelen argues that the depression of 1893–1897 was crucial in forcing people "to build bridges over the social chasms" which had previously divided them and in bringing about "a spirit of cooperation across class lines to solve problems that were being seen for the first time as mutual problems."[9]

The depression of the 1890s did stimulate a widely shared perception of the need for political and economic change in the United States. However, the careers of Daniels and Stimson illustrate the ways in which the crisis of the Nineties also created deep seated fears among middle-class Americans of the possibility that demands for change might get out of hand and lead to socially and politically radical consequences. The reactions of both Daniels and Stimson to the Populist party reveal the extent to which the depression of the 1890s deepened, rather than eased, the racial and class divisions which characterized American society. So long as the crisis atmosphere of the depression persisted, Daniels and Stimson could not support the cause of reform with single-minded purpose because of their fear that a movement for change might ultimately destroy, rather than improve, the existing social order.

For Daniels, the path to reform was blocked by the all-important question of race. The economic upheavals of the 1890s shook the racial order of the South to the point where a new political party threatened to break down the color barrier in Southern politics. Daniels found himself cut off from the major vehicle for reform in this period, the Populist party, primarily because of his belief in the doctrine of white supremacy and the necessity of working for change only through the medium of a white Democratic party. He was sympathetic to many of the reform proposals put forth by the Populists but ended up vigorously opposing the new party on the grounds that it posed the threat of "negro rule." Daniels was able to reduce the issues involved in the 1896 state elections to the simple statement that what was to be decided was "whether North Carolina" was "to be governed during the coming years by the white man or the black man and his tools." Daniels' opposition to Populism on racial grounds reached a peak in 1898 when he served as the editorial spokesman for the state Democratic party in a virulent white supremacy campaign which destroyed the power of the Populist party in North Carolina. This was followed in 1900 by the enactment of an election law, which Daniels helped prepare, designed to eliminate, once and for all, black participation in the state's electoral politics.[10]

Daniels' career in the 1890s thus illustrates a point made by C. Vann Woodward: "The Populist party, bearing the odium attached to any threat to white solidarity, had in large measure constituted an obstruction of the spread of reform in the South." Daniels' own biographer has observed that "what Daniels was saying, in effect, was that North Carolinians had to remove the Negro as an element in politics before any real progress or reform could be realized."[11]

Of lesser weight in Daniels' opposition to Populism, but still of significance, was his concern about the potential influence of "socialists and anarchists" in the movement. He feared that these extremists were fostering a "spirit of distrust, of class hostility, and of envy of the prosperous" which represented "a blight and a disgrace to our civilization, and . . . an impediment to action looking to better laws and better conditions." He felt such measures as the abolition of national banks, government ownership of public utilities, and the sub-treasury plan went too far to be acceptable measures of responsible reform. To be sure, Daniels' concern over political polarization along class lines also expressed itself in criticism of the opponents of reform. He strongly condemned Republican businessmen for using economic coercion against their employees in an attempt to influence the national election of 1896, because such action made the "campaign assume a shape of the masses against the classes."[12]

This same fear of rising class antagonisms also made Stimson draw back from the Populist brand of reform. In contrast to Daniels, however, Stimson blamed William Jennings Bryan, not Republican businessmen, for abandoning the attitude of a "statesman" by his efforts "to stir up class feeling." In a letter written during the peak of the 1896 campaign, Stimson clearly expressed his concern that any movement for change not be allowed to challenge the foundations of the social order.

I was a Democrat myself at the last Presidential Election and voted for the Democratic candidate, but in common with a great many other former Democrats, I do not consider Mr. Bryan to be a true Democratic candidate and I am going to vote against him this Fall. I believe his election would cause a greater panic among business circles and more suffering and distress among the wage-earners of the community than has been experienced by the United States since the Civil War and I think it is the patriotic duty of everyone, Republican and Democrat alike, to bury the Chicago platform with its planks in favor of free riot, free silver and the overthrow of the Supreme Court so deeply that no one hereafter will ever try to gain votes at the expense of honor, law and order.[13]

Stimson and Daniels may have differed strongly on the candidates in the election of 1896, since Daniels was one of Bryan's early backers. However, for both men, hostility to the Populist party reflected deeper underlying concerns which, at the time, tempered their support for reform. In a period of economic dislocation and social upheaval, their fears about the stability of the major supports of the social order oftentimes were stronger than their hopes for the possibilities of peaceful and constructive change. Even those who were sympathetic to reform in the 1890s frequently felt the need to rein tightly the impulse to reconstruct society in order to make certain that it did not lead uncontrollably to racial or social revolution.


## II


The end of the depression and the rapid decline of the Populist party after 1896 thus set the stage for the emergence in national politics of a reform movement with which Americans as diverse as the five men considered in this study could wholly identify. The return of prosperity and the consequent easing of social tensions and fears made it possible for middle class Americans to view efforts at change with less ambivalence. Increasingly, after 1900, Daniels and Stimson, along with Baruch, Richberg, and Frankfurter, who became politically active before the outbreak of the First World War, came to see attempts at political reform as a hopeful and necessary means for strengthening the bonds holding American society together.

The development of the progressive movement after 1900, of course, cannot be understood simply as the product of the onset of prosperity. On a more fundamental level, progressivism must be seen as America's political response to the emergence of a radically new economic order. The rise of large-scale corporate capitalism at the turn of the century was the key force behind the development of a nationwide movement which for a variety of purposes and in a variety of ways sought to mitigate at least some of the effects of the new economic order.

What Alfred Chandler has termed "modern business enterprise," huge corporations "managed by a hierarchy of salaried executives" and containing "many distinct operating units," first appeared in the United States in the 1850s and 1860s in the burgeoning railroad industry. By the 1880s what the progressives themselves would call "trusts" had developed in several other industries. Popular fears of the growing power of trusts and railroads in this period led to the passage by Congress of two generally vague and ineffective regulatory statutes, the Interstate Commerce Act and the Sherman Antitrust Act. However, it was not until after the depression of the 1890s that an intensive consolidation movement brought about a basic transformation of the structure of the American economy.[14]

Economic historian Thomas Cochran states that the period from "1897–1903 was the most important for industrial mergers and consolidations in United States history." When U.S. Steel was organized in 1901, it had an initial capitalization of nearly one and a half billion dollars, more than that of the twelve largest American firms of 1893 combined. By 1904 the three hundred largest industrial corporations owned twenty billion dollars in assets. This represented more than forty per cent of the nation's industrial wealth. Thus, the problems posed by the growth of trusts, while first arousing concern in the 1880s, appeared in much sharper focus after the turn of the century.[15]

A number of factors accounted for the development of huge firms, in general, and the burst of consolidations at the turn of the century, in particular. Roughly, they can be divided into two categories: those relating to the maximization of efficiency in production and distribution, and those relating to the maximization of profit through the manipulation or control of the marketplace. The trend toward large units of production can be explained, in part, as a result of the pressure to achieve economies of scale in the use of existing technologies of production. By the turn of the century, however, the desire to reduce production costs in this way was not a crucial factor in the merger movement, since in many cases the individual units of production involved in the consolidations were already large enough to benefit fully from the economies of scale which were then technologically feasible. Chandler argues that the merger movement can better be understood as a means of maximizing efficiency by more effectively coordinating the high volume of production already made possible by technological advances with the rapidly expanding mass market for industrial goods in the United States. Through vertical integration and the internalization within a single administrative structure of a wide range of business transactions, from the purchase of raw materials to the mass marketing of finished products, modern business enterprise "was able to coordinate supply more closely with demand, to use its working force and capital equipment more intensively, and thus to lower its unit costs."[16]

A socially beneficial quest for greater efficiency and higher productivity, however, was not the only factor involved in the growth of big business in America. A desire to achieve monopoly power over markets was also a factor which was especially important in the early stages of the trust movement. For industrial giants such as John D. Rockefeller, James Duke, and Henry Havemeyer, combination was a means of eliminating competition in order to establish not only a better position for themselves in negotiating over costs with suppliers, but also to make themselves less subject to the rigors of the laws of supply and demand when setting prices for consumers. While the huge firms growing out of the merger movement at the turn of the century could not hope to charge any price they wanted, Robert Heilbroner concludes that "above all, *the aim of consolidation was to remove the threat of the unrestricted price compeition that proved so dangerous for a world of large-scale enterprise* (emphasis in original)."[17]

The consolidation movement also generated profits for those who issued and marketed the securities of the newly formed industrial combines. Without the development of an immense pool of available capital which a relatively small number of investment bankers could exploit in the organization of mergers, the wave of consolidations at the turn of the century would have been impossible. The profits created by the initial organization of these consolidations were not necessarily related to any real increases in efficiency or productivity. In fact, there was actually a decline in this period in the rate of growth in the capital goods industries of the country, since the post-Civil War era of great geographical expansion and extensive building had finally come to an end. As a result, the demand for capital for productive purposes at last began to decrease. The return of prosperity following the depression of the 1890s, however, meant that funds were rapidly accumulating in the nation's financial institutions: trust and insurance companies, commercial and savings banks. This capital was then available for the nation's financiers to use for speculative purposes. Since, as Cochran and Miller put it, "mergers proved the simplest way to create speculative opportunities, these funds began to find their way into the securities of new combinations instead of into their plants." In addition, the incredible size of the mergers contemplated after 1897 required those companies which were combining to seek aid from the nation's newly powerful financiers to market their securities. J. P. Morgan's intervention in the formation of U. S. Steel was a perfect example of this phenomenon. Only finance capitalists such as Morgan had the facilities to market the four billion dollars worth of new securities produced by the merger movement between 1898 and 1904.[18]

By the early years of the twentieth century, the American economy had assumed the basic shape it still retains today. American industry had become dominated by a few hundred firms, and the economy as a whole had become increasingly integrated as a result of the establishment of close ties between a select group of bankers directing the flow of investment capital and a small elite of industrialists directing the output of the nation's factories. Some sectors of the economy did remain fully competitive, and out-and-out monopoly was extremely rare. Nevertheless, oligopoly, the control of a dominant share of a particular market by a handful of firms, had become characteristic of most key industries. The American economy at the turn of the century was a marvel of production unmatched anywhere in the world, but the new corporate order was by no means free of fundamental defects.

Perhaps the most obvious abuses stemming from the new industrial order involved the conditions in which millions of workers were forced to toil. No labor organizations matched the power of the great industrial firms which had arisen by the beginning of the twentieth century, so that workers were relatively powerless in securing decent working conditions. At the turn of the century, the average work week for non-farm labor was sixty-two hours. Safety was so low a priority for management that 35,000 workers died in industrial accidents and 500,000 more were injured each year. Such working conditions might conceivably be seen as the temporary excesses of an economy rushing headlong into industrialization, rather than as inevitable and permanent features of the new system of economic organization. However, there was nothing accidental or temporary about the detrimental impact the growing concentration of control in industry had on the functioning of the price system and the distribution of wealth in the United States.[19]

The emergence of oligopoly in industry did, in fact, result in a reduction in price competition. This, in turn, had a distorting effect on the American economy. The introduction of what economists would later call "administered prices," prices established by oligopolistic understandings rather than strictly in accordance with market conditions, made prices generally less responsive to downward market pressures. America's industrial giants did not become immune from market forces or the influence of the business cycle when determining prices. However, an inflationary bias did become built into the American economy since oligopolies not only could set prices somewhat higher than justified by market conditions in times of high demand, but also because they tended to respond to decreases in demand not by lowering their pre-determined prices but by reducing production. While the turn-of-the-century merger movement was certainly not the only factor involved, it very likely contributed to the inflationary trend which developed in the United States after 1897. Whereas prices moved steadily downward in the period of intense industrial competition between 1865 and 1897, from 1897 to 1914 the cost of living went up 39 per cent.[20]

In addition, as William Comanor and Robert Smiley have demonstrated, the power to charge prices above those which would have been possible under fully competitive conditions meant, in effect, that "a stream of excess payments by consumers" occurred which the owners of industry were able to capitalize, thus contributing significantly to the "degree of inequality in the distribution of wealth." The rise of large-scale industrial enterprise at the turn of the century was accompanied between 1896 and 1914 by what one economic historian has termed "the last great surge in American inequality." It is not coincidental that only after the emergence of the new corporate order did concern about the growing degree of inequality in America inspire the first scientific studies of the nation's distribution of wealth and income. From data gathered since then, it is clear that a tiny minority of Americans came to enjoy the lion's share of the benefits of the new economic order. In 1900 the top 7.6 percent of the population had a larger total income than did the 70 per cent of the population at the lower end of the income scale. Wealth was undoubtedly even more unequally distributed.[21]

The development of an economy in which tremendous resources of collectively accumulated capital were allocated by a small economic elite raised other questions as well. In theory, market forces were supposed to determine the most efficient overall allocation of resources. Yet, as Chandler notes:

In many sectors of the economy the visible hand of management replaced the invisible hand of market forces . . . modern business enterprise took over the functions of coordinating flows of goods through existing processes of production and distribution and of allocating funds and personnel for future production and distribution.

Although Chandler contends that "the market remained the generator of demand for goods and services" and thus the ultimate determinant of the flow of capital, the growth of oligopoly and the replacement of the market mechanism in the internal workings of most key industries inevitably had a distorting effect on the market's hypothetical efficiency in allocating resources throughout the economy. Certainly the flow of capital into the mergers of the turn of the century could not be fully justified in terms of overall productive efficiency. Many of the consolidations at that time attracted capital not because they required or could use additional funds to improve productivity or to increase production in response to market demand; rather, many combinations occurred because of the speculative opportunities made possible by the issuance of new securities or because of the promise of excessive profits resulting from the market control exercised by the recently formed oligopolies. In addition, the purity of market forces would soon be further undermined as America's giant firms developed mass-marketing techniques, especially advertising, which could be used to create and manipulate consumer demand.[22]

Even in theory, a reliance on the incentive of private profit as a means of allocating resources depends upon the highly questionable assumption that profitability and social utility are virtually identical. Yet not all profitable ventures necessarily serve the common good; nor will all projects beneficial to the community return a profit in a conventional sense. The accumulation of a large reservoir of capital in the United States by the turn of the century had been made possible by the collective efforts of millions of Americans. Those funds, however, had come under the control of a relatively tiny minority which allocated them with the purpose of maximizing their own personal gain instead of seeking to insure the well being of the entire nation. It is ironic that while America's industrial and financial leaders increasingly sought to substitute planning and coordination for market forces in the internal operations of their integrated firms, they continued to deny the possibility that anything other than a market system based on the quest for private profit could serve as an efficient means of allocating resources in the economy as a whole.

## III

During the early years of the twentieth century, all five of the men examined here reacted to the economic developments of the period by singling out the trust question as the central public issue of the day. Well before the climactic election of Woodrow Wilson in 1912 made possible the enactment of a full slate of progressive legislation, the men discussed in this study had concluded that the federal government's power to oversee the operation of the nation's private enterprise economy would have to be strengthened so that the benefits of the new industrial order might be preserved and the dangers minimized.

As early as 1886, Josephus Daniels realized that the rise of "monopolies and corporations" and the "money power" would be at the center of future political struggles. Daniels' concern about the growing power of trusts was largely a product of his Jeffersonian faith in a system of free enterprise based on the ideal of "equal rights to all and special privileges to none." Although he welcomed the benefits of industrialization and "rejoiced at the prosperity and growth" of the large tobacco industry in his native state of North Carolina, he began fighting against the corrupting economic and political influence of the railroads in the 1880s and warned of the dangers posed by the formation of the Tobacco Trust in 1890. Such trusts, he argued, would use their monopoly power to drive smaller competitors out of business so that they could then charge artificially high prices to the unprotected consumer and use their political influence to secure special favors from government. Thus the development of unchecked corporate power threatened both the nation's system of free enterprise and its system of political democracy.[23]

Because of the divisive nature of party and racial conflicts in the 1890s, however, Daniels did not focus on the trust problem as the central campaign issue in a Presidential election until 1904. In 1896, Daniels concentrated on the issue of free silver as the best means of uniting Populists and Democrats behind Bryan; while in 1900, he favored making imperialism the major issue of the campaign. Ironically, Daniels' effort to appeal directly to anti-trust sentiment in 1904 was in support of a Democratic conservative, Alton Parker. However, the rapid expansion of trusts, which, in Daniels' view, were assuming "all the tyranny, corruption and insolence of the Greek oligarchy without their just sense of responsibility," and Roosevelt's growing reputation as a trustbuster, made such a campaign emphasis both necessary and desirable in 1904.[24]

Daniels' response to the trust question between 1900 and 1912 grew out of his commitment to Jeffersonianism; for his belief in the ideals of equal opportunity and a competitive market system caused him to emphasize the need for vigorous action to break up the rapidly expanding trusts which were coming to dominate the nation's economic life. Not only did he support the passage of an anti-trust law "with teeth" in his home state to reduce the power of the Tobacco Trust, but he also called for much stricter enforcement of the Sherman Anti-Trust Act by the federal government. Daniels hailed the federal government's first-ever anti-trust suit, brought against the Northern Securities Company in 1902, but he became increasingly disenchanted with the Roosevelt administration's failure to follow through on its anti-trust prosecutions. He wanted to see:

As much money as may be needed . . . appropriated for this purpose, and the President given ample power to enforce the laws. If he will employ lawyers of the first order of ability, and give them instructions to send even Rockefeller to prison for violating the anti-trust laws, the Standard Oil and other monopolies will be broken up. But they can not be destroyed by mere small fines upon the corporation.

Daniels later criticized lenient court rulings which allowed trusts to divide themselves only to the extent that "the hand divides into fingers."[25]

While trust-busting to insure effective competition was crucial to Daniels' thinking, it was not his only proposal for dealing with corporate power. He had long been a supporter of governmental regulation in the form of a state corporation commission which was to have the power to regulate railroad rates and unfair business practices. He supported specific state legislation to compel the railroads to respond to public needs, such as laws requiring the erection of passenger depots wherever "practicable and necessary" and establishing mandatory compensation for shippers suffering losses due to delays or damages of goods transported. Daniels came to favor government regulation of all public utilities, and by 1905 he was even editorializing in support of the idea that municipal ownership of public utilities was "right in principle and . . . necessary to secure cleaner politics."[26]

On the national level, Daniels vigorously backed efforts to increase the powers of the federal government's principal regulatory agency, the Interstate Commerce Commission, and strongly criticized Roosevelt for compromising the effectiveness of the Hepburn bill by agreeing to an amendment which made ICC rulings on railroad rates subject to the delays and interference of judicial review.[27]

Daniels felt that existing violations by the government of the Jeffersonian creed of "special privileges to none" had contributed to the rise of monopolies. He argued, therefore, that the power of trusts could be reduced simply by restoring a government policy of equal treatment for all business concerns. Daniels thus continually pressed for the elimination of the protective tariff and, in his own state, called for tax reform to end the special favor of allowing corporations, especially railroads and public utilities, to have their holdings assessed at well below their market value. Only then would the state's corporations be made to pay their fair share of taxes.[28]

Complementing Daniels' proposal for reducing the power of trusts was his support for measures to improve the conditions of labor. He approved of labor organization and was himself an honorary union member. He consistently opposed the use of sweeping injunctions to put down strikes and favored legislation both to prohibit child labor and to set maximum hours for women workers. Daniels clearly expressed his sympathy for labor in the Presidential campaign of 1908 when he not only enthusiastically backed a proposal for the creation of a separate Department of Labor headed by a labor man, but also claimed that: "For the first time in the history of American politics, the interests of labor are bound up with the success of one political party."[29]

Henry Stimson was slower than Daniels to appreciate the political and social ramifications of the trust movement. Only after he became a federal attorney for the Southern District of

New York in 1906 did his political perspective begin to expand beyond a rather provincial concern for clean government. He was then confronted, for the first time, with the problem posed by unchecked corporate power and manipulation. As U.S. Attorney, his three most important cases all involved abuses of economic power. Two concerned the Sugar Trust, American Sugar Refining Company: one for violations of the recently passed Elkins Act which outlawed rebates by railroads; the other dealing with the fraudulent avoidance of import duties. The third case focused on the manipulative financial dealings of Charles W. Morse of the Bank of North America, a man whose banking practices were partly responsible for bringing on the panic of 1907. After leaving the federal attorney's office, Stimson pursued his new found interest in the trust issue while campaigning for Governor of New York in 1910, and while serving as Taft's Secretary of War.[30]

Stimson believed that the "growth and consolidation of capital" was "economically justifiable and necessary," but that the development of large concentrations of capital created a major political problem:

How to preserve these real benefits of size and consolidation—of union—and yet protect the public (including both the consumer and the competitor) from the evils of monopoly—i.e., arbitrary prices and unfair or oppressive competition.

In responding to this problem, Stimson, like Daniels, considered the possible effectiveness of both trust-busting and government regulation, but, in contrast to Daniels, he found the balance to weigh heavily in favor of regulation. As he explained to a friend in 1910:

I have always believed that the Inter-State Commerce Law in its enforcement of *equal* rates between shippers successfully struck one of the most effective blows against monopoly.

I never felt that the Sherman Law was as perfect or effective an effort of legislation as the other . . . I have come to the conclusion that, while the Sherman Law is, in my opinion, effective and final legislation as to those so-called "loose" combinations represented by agreements between competitors and unincorporated associations, there is nevertheless required a different and more effective treatment of the modern corporate *monopoly*. Although a skeptic at first, I have come to the conclusion that the only effective remedy for the modern corporate monopoly engaged in interstate commerce is some system of federal regulation such as could be obtained by federal incorporation or federal license, preferably the former. And I think that that is what we will come to sooner or later.[31]

As a member of Taft's Cabinet, Stimson tried, for the most part unsuccessfully, to push the Taft administration into supporting legislation which would have specifically enumerated those practices to be considered unfair methods of trade and set up a federal administrative agency to oversee the activities of businesses engaged in interstate commerce. Stimson wanted such an agency to be given power to answer authoritatively all questions regarding the legality of particular business practices. A federal incorporation law would then become part of a comprehensive effort by the government to deal with the trust problem. From his experience as a U.S. Attorney, Stimson had come to believe in the importance of an informed and aroused public opinion. He thus felt that the publicity resulting from federal licensing or incorporation could serve as an added check on corporate abuses.[32]

Stimson also contended that the growth of the "tremendous structure of modern incorporated business" had occurred while the organization of government had remained "faulty" and "inefficient." It was only natural, therefore, that in any contact between business and government, business, with its more scientific organization and greater efficiency, would dominate. Consequently, Stimson argued that all levels of government had to be restructured so as to "make them conform more nearly to the system of administration which has been found effective in our big business corporations." This entailed drawing clearer lines of responsibility, developing sounder budget mechanisms, and, in some cases, simplifying the machinery of government.[33]

Stimson was not oblivious to the hardships of labor under the new economic order. While campaigning for Governor of New York, he supported the idea of improved workmen's compensation laws. In the wake of the infamous Triangle Shirtwaist Company fire of 1911, he chaired, for a short time, a highly respected citizens' committee which sought to raise safety standards in places of work in New York. Nevertheless, Stimson was much less interested in the cause of organized labor than Daniels. He never made it a point either to praise the efforts of unions or to defend them against unfair treatment by management or the courts.[34]

Felix Frankfurter graduated from the Harvard Law School in 1906, the same year in which Henry Stimson became a U.S. Attorney. By the end of that year, Frankfurter's career had become closely linked to Stimson's. Upon the recommendation of Dean James Barr Ames of Harvard, Stimson hired Frankfurter as one of a number of young assistants in his reorganization of the federal attorney's office. Soon, a close personal and professional relationship developed between the two men. Frankfurter worked under Stimson during the latter's three year tenure in office as U.S. Attorney and then followed Stimson into private practice in 1909, joining the elder man's New York law firm. When Stimson ran for Governor of New York in 1910, Frankfurter remained at his side in the capacity of private secretary. A year later, when Stimson went to Washington to become Secretary of War, he invited Frankfurter to serve under him as a law officer in the War Department.[35]

It is not surprising, therefore, that Frankfurter's views on the trust question in these years closely paralleled those of his mentor. He experienced the same firsthand exposure to the abuses of corporate power while working in the U.S. Attorney's office. Afterwards, Frankfurter helped to write some of Stimson's most important public speeches on the trust issue. In the Fall of 1911, when Stimson was preparing a major policy address on the subject, Frankfurter summed up his own views on the issue when he suggested that Stimson incorporate into his speech the following statement: "In these days governmental activity must be productive not merely prohibitive." Frankfurter was in full agreement with Stimson that the problem confronting the nation was not finding means of opposing "inevitable industrial expansion," but rather finding ways of "controlling those forces" unleashed by the new economic order. In 1912, Frankfurter observed that his own experience in government had convinced him of "the utter hopelessness" of trying to use law suits to establish a dividing line between "monopoly" and legitimate "big business." Instead, he favored setting up a "permanent administrative tribunal that, by the accumulation of experience, would evolve proper standards, and, above all, secure the permanent light of publicity that is the first essential to healthfulness." [36]

Frankfurter also supported efforts to enact minimum wage and maximum hours laws in order to establish decent working conditions for workers who were virtually impotent in the face of the massive power of huge corporate enterprises. "More and more," he argued, "we realize that there is no greater inequality than the equality of unequals." In defending the use of government power to provide the economically powerless with some protection, Frankfurter claimed:

Our whole evolutionary thinking leads to the conclusion that economic independence lies at the very foundation of social and moral well-being. Growing democratic sympathies, justified by the social message of modern scientists, demand to be translated into legislation for economic betterment, based upon the conviction that laws can make men better by affecting the conditions of living. We are persuaded that evils are not inevitable, and that it is the business of statesmanship to tackle them step by step, tentatively, experimentally, not demanding perfection from social reforms any more than from other human efforts.

Frankfurter, however, did not explicitly advocate any measures beyond the moderate social justice laws then being enacted in states throughout the country. In calling for "legislation for economic betterment," he meant only that recent developments in social science had made it both possible and desirable for government to establish, scientifically, minimum labor standards below which work itself might prove unhealthful. Frankfurter thus did not propose that government attempt to force a significant redistribution of wealth. [37]

Donald Richberg graduated from the Harvard Law School two years before Frankfurter. Returning to Chicago in 1904, Richberg joined his father's law firm. Because this firm numbered among its clients the City Treasurer and Board of Assessors, Richberg quickly gained an appreciation of the corrupt relationship between business and the city's government. Offended by what he saw, he publicly supported a reform candidate for mayor in 1905 whose major issue was the municipal ownership of the city's traction system.[38]

In 1906, only two years after leaving law school, Richberg put forth his own novel proposal for dealing with the trust problem. In an article published in the Chicago *Tribune,* entitled "Why Should Not Corporations Be Imprisoned," Richberg argued that the only effective means of putting an end to corrupt and illegal business practices would be to have offending firms put into government receivership until such abuses were halted. During its period of "imprisonment," any profits accruing to a corporation would become public revenue. Richberg went to Washington in 1907 to discuss his plan personally with Attorney-General William H. Moody. In 1911, he published another, somewhat more detailed, version of his proposal. He made it clear that he believed that the development of large corporations had brought with it many advantages, but he argued that no single corporation ought to be allowed to control more than 50 percent of the business in any given industry. He proposed, therefore, to have the government place into receivership any company which either engaged in specific types of unfair trade practices, or which surpassed the 50-percent limit and thereby entered into the area of monopoly control.[39]

The issue of corporate corruption was also the central theme of a novel by Richberg, *The Shadow Men,* published in 1911. The book dramatized Richberg's contention that the prosecution of individuals, or the levying of relatively insignificant fines on corporations, had proven inadequate as methods of dealing with the problems of the new corporate era. The novel made clear Richberg's view that a change in the popular conception of morally acceptable standards of behavior was essential if reform efforts were to be successful.[40]

Thus, in the first decade of the twentieth century, a deepening concern about the potentially dangerous political and economic consequences arising from the growth of large-scale corporate capitalism led at least four of the five men studied here to adopt what John W. Chambers has felicitously called the "interventionist" conception of government developed by the progressive movement. These men realized that the Gilded Age view of the proper role of government would have to be expanded in response to the tremendous changes taking place in American society. Yet, it is important not to exaggerate the extent to which progressive ideology evolved beyond the liberal consensus of the late nineteenth century. Chambers correctly observes that the progressives "modified the philosophies of laissez-faire, an unregulated marketplace, and unrestricted individualism." However, these philosophies, as noted in the preceding chapters, were never absolute to begin with; nor, in the years before World War One, did progressives such as those discussed here completely reject the key assumptions upon which these philosophies were based.[41]

Certain common themes emerge from the foregoing examination of the responses of Daniels, Stimson, Frankfurter, and Richberg to the developing trust issue. While all four men came to believe in the necessity of strengthening the powers of government vis-a-vis the powers of the great new corporate enterprises, none of these men yet looked to government as a substitute for market forces in the operation of the economy. Whether focusing primarily on the need for government to break up monopolies, as was generally the case with Daniels, or whether focusing on the need to modernize government so that it could more effectively oversee the conduct of big business, as was the case with Stimson, Frankfurter, and Richberg, all four men shared the view that the function of government was essentially to police the marketplace so as to guarantee its supposed efficiency and fairness as an allocator of resources. In responding to the problems posed by the development of corporate capitalism, all of the men considered in this study rather narrowly concentrated on the most obvious and blatant excesses of the new economic order.

They opposed the tactics of "cutthroat competition" which enabled certain large firms to drive their competitors out of business through clearly manipulative and unfair practices, and they worried about the growth of outright monopolies which would be able to exercise sole control over the marketing of particular products to consumers. They were concerned with the corrupting influence corporate money too often exerted on government, especially at the local and state level, and also found distasteful the shocking treatment sometimes afforded workers under the new industrial order. Their solution for these problems, though, was only a limited expansion of government power. Regardless of the different emphases in their proposals, all four men sought only to give government the power to establish and enforce clearer guidelines as to proper conduct in the marketplace. The game would remain basically the same, but the referee would take a more active role in trying to make certain that the players adhered to certain minimal standards of decency while playing.

The men examined here did not, in other words, recognize or confront many of the basic issues raised by the growth of corporate capitalism in the United States. While fearing monopoly, they failed to comprehend fully the nature of the oligopolistic economic structure which was emerging in America. In spite of increasing disparities in the distribution of income and wealth, they largely ignored this problem in their proposals and continued to view America as essentially a classless society. Even though they recognized that growing concentration in industry and finance gave great potential power to a tiny minority of Americans, they refused to consider seriously the possibility that some form of public control of key resources might be more socially desirable. They persisted in believing that even in an economy dominated by huge privately controlled accumulations of capital, the investment of resources and the distribution of wealth should be left to the supposedly impersonal determination of the market rather than to the conscious decisions of representatives selected by the people.

## IV

Liberal fears of the economic and political power of trusts provided progressivism with much of its motive force. However, the progressive movement was also inspired by a growing concern among middle class Americans that the new corporate society threatened to rob them of a sense of meaning and satisfaction in their personal lives. While the economic revolution of the era was the crucial underlying factor in the rise of progressivism, the reform movement reflected not only a commonly shared ideological concern about the consequences of the new economic order, but also a widespread and deeply felt personal dissatisfaction with the values associated with that order. The kind of personal concerns which helped bring many Americans over to the cause of reform appear quite clearly in the life of Bernard Baruch in this period.

In contrast to Daniels, Stimson, Frankfurter, and Richberg, Baruch had little involvement in public affairs or reform before 1912. From his vantage point on Wall Street, however, he was in an excellent position to observe the inner workings of the consolidation movement which was occurring at the turn of the century. Baruch may well have understood its underlying significance more clearly than the other men considered here. He later recounted his admiration for J. P. Morgan's attempts "to achieve . . . the economic unity and stability of the country."[42]

At the same time, Baruch generally sympathized with the "policies" of President Roosevelt. He apparently appreciated both the constructive possibilities of finance capitalism and the need to give government limited powers to police the operations of the economy so that the new order would be created with due regard for the public welfare. Still, Baruch himself acknowledged that he had no well developed political philosophy in this period, let alone a fully thought out position on the trust question.[43]

While an active interest in public affairs became a central feature in the lives of the other men discussed here, Baruch remained preoccupied with more strictly personal concerns during the early years of the twentieth century. By the turn of the century, Baruch was beginning to express discontent over the lack of personal fulfillment in his own life. As noted previously, Baruch may have pursued a career in business because of a feeling that the accumulation of wealth offered the most likely means of overcoming the social stigma attached to his Jewish origins. While Baruch's mother supported her son's desire to seek his fortune in the business world, his father hoped that Bernard would become a doctor like himself. Simon Baruch, however, did not attempt to interfere with his son's plans for a career.[44]

After little more than a decade on Wall Street, Baruch was able proudly to proclaim to his father (probably in 1900) that he had amassed a fortune of one million dollars. In his autobiography, Baruch recalled that his father's reaction to his news was, at best, one of indifference. This caused Baruch to begin:

. . . reflecting along lines that had disturbed me more than once before. Of what use to a man are a million dollars unless he does something worth while with them.

Able to buy anything I wanted that was for sale, I realized how much there was that could not be bought for money. I found myself contrasting my own career with that of Father's—my moneymaking against his accomplishments in medicine and hygiene and in helping his fellow man.

From that point on, Baruch began to give financial support to his father's medical research as one means of rendering his "money making" more meaningful.[45]

In addition, within a few years he started to concentrate his investments in "companies which sought to develop new sources of supply for such varied materials as copper, rubber, iron ore, gold, and sulphur." He was able to feel that such ventures, by "wresting new resources from the earth and putting them at the disposal of mankind," helped to create "true wealth" and not just "money." Still the outsider, however, Baruch retained his independent position as a speculator by usually selling out his interests in these enterprises as soon as they reached the dividend-paying stage.[46]

During these years, Baruch also began to dream of becoming associated with J. P. Morgan in the latter's efforts to bring "unity" and "stability" to the nation's economy. Baruch's admiration for a man whom he considered to be a "master" stemmed from his perception of Morgan as a man who "cared little for the possession of money." Bringing order, stability, and integration to the nation's economy were, in Baruch's view, objectives of far greater purpose.[47]

Baruch's failure to develop a lasting association with the House of Morgan was a product of circumstances and of his own ambivalence about surrendering the independence he enjoyed as a lone operator. During the panic of 1907, Morgan personally organized a fund to save the country's financial institutions. Baruch, at one point, decided upon the "dramatic gesture" of going to Morgan in person to contribute one and a half million dollars in "cold cash" in order to "impress Mr. Morgan with my faith in his leadership and in my own ability to discern the essential soundness of the country." At the last moment, however, some feeling of inner doubt and insecurity overcame Baruch, and for reasons he could not himself explain, he just "couldn't go through with it." He ended up making his contribution anonymously. Two years later, another opportunity arose for establishing a connection with Morgan through a proposed joint investment in the development of sulphur resources in Texas. Baruch met personally with Morgan to discuss the venture, referring to it as a "good gamble." Morgan responded curtly by saying that he never "gambled," and Baruch thus lost his last chance to establish a lasting link to the House of Morgan.[48]

Baruch's need for meaning in his life was finally fulfilled when he committed himself wholeheartedly to the Presidential candidacy of Woodrow Wilson. As a potential campaign contributor, Baruch was introduced to the Democratic Presidential candidate by fellow City College of New York trustee, William McCombs. Baruch was sympathetic to Wilson's political views, but the special attraction he felt toward the former college president was largely a result of Wilson's stand against the social exclusiveness of Princeton's eating clubs. Baruch must have interpreted Wilson's stand as a defense of those who, like Baruch himself, did not enjoy the special privileges and status attendant upon social position. While Baruch's involvement in the 1912 campaign was limited to a financial contribution, psychologically, his support for Wilson supplied the purpose in life he had long been seeking. His biographer, Margaret Coit, notes:

For Baruch more than his money was at stake. All his awakened idealism was in his struggle. "If Wilson is defeated, I don't know what I shall do," he told Garet Garrett, who had watched him in his long search for a consuming purpose. He supposed that he would have "to go back to Wall Street and play the game."[49]

Baruch's reasons for turning to the cause of reform, as it was personified by Woodrow Wilson, were thus more personal or psychological than political or ideological. Yet this type of motivation was by no means unique to him. Each of the other men discussed here also experienced comparable feelings as to the need to engage in a personally meaningful and socially responsible career. They all rejected the idea of pursuing a career whose primary goal would have been financial gain and believed that the new economic order gave undue emphasis to selfishness and materialism. In their view, the new corporate system threatened to undermine American society morally, as well as economically and politically, by making monetary gain, rather than personal satisfaction and social well-being, the aims of life. Each experienced this problem as a moral challenge which was directly related to his own choice of career. For all of them, consequently, involvement in the progressive movement represented a means of infusing meaning and purpose into their own lives, as well as a way of defending America's traditional economic and political values.

Upon graduation from college, Henry Stimson was still uncertain about the career he wished to pursue. He considered becoming a minister, a doctor, or a lawyer, sure only that he wanted "to do good in some way." Finally, he accepted what he described as "the course which I think my father desires for me," though it was "precisely the one in which I stand in most deadly horror, viz that of a successful New York lawyer." Henry's father, Lewis Stimson, had himself given up a financially promising career on Wall Street in order to enjoy the greater personal satisfaction of a life devoted to medicine; yet he was intent on seeing his son attain both social and material success. Henry thus attended the Harvard Law School and subsequently, through his father's connections, obtained a position in the prestigious law firm of Elihu Root. At this time, young Henry was anxious to marry, but again he acceded to his father's wishes and postponed his plans for marriage for over five years until he had established himself professionally and assured himself of an income adequate to meet the demands of married life in respectable New York society.[50]

Only after Stimson entered public life as a U.S. Attorney did he acknowledge the discontent he had felt earlier as a Wall Street lawyer. Speaking to the twentieth reunion of his Yale class, Stimson observed:

The last two years of my life have represented a complete change in my professional career. The profession of the law was never thoroughly satisfactory to me, simply because the life of the ordinary New York lawyer is primarily and essentially devoted to the making of money—and not always successfully so. There are some opportunities to do good in it . . . [but] it has always seemed to me, in the law, from what I have seen of it, that whenever the public interest has come into conflict with private interests, private interest was more adequately represented than the public interest. . . . [After leaving corporate practice and entering government service] the first feeling was that I had gotten out of the dark places where I had been wandering all my life, and got out where I could see the stars and get my bearings once more. . . . And it has made a tremendous difference and a tremendous change in the satisfaction of my professional life. There has been an ethical side of it which has been of more interest to me, and I have felt that I could get a good deal closer to the problems of life than I ever did before, and felt that the work was a good deal more worth while. And one always feels better when he feels that he is working in a good cause.

Stimson's involvement in the "good cause" of reform thus represented not only an attempt to curb the power of trusts, but also a personal breaking away from an unsatisfying career whose principal aim had been making money.[51]

There is a distinct parallel between Donald Richberg's early experiences in the legal profession and those of Stimson. Richberg, like Stimson, became a lawyer largely due to the urgings of his father, who was himself a prominent Chicago attorney. Richberg once complained that a boy's education rarely gave him the ability "to choose his career intelligently rather than" simply adopting "the trade of his father," and cited, as an example, the case of someone becoming a lawyer only because that had been the profession of his father. Even after Richberg had himself graduated from law school, he still had hopes of making a living as a writer. However, he eventually yielded to his father's pressure and returned to Chicago to join his father's law practice. Richberg followed his father's advice largely because he wished to marry, and he recognized the wisdom of his father's view that it was necessary to have a secure income with which to meet the financial obligations of marriage. In contrast to Stimson's experience, however, Richberg's father did not also advise his son to postpone his marriage for years until he had gained professional security.[52]

Having become a lawyer, Richberg found little personal satisfaction in his career, stating that the practice of law "was my livelihood and not my ambition." He later referred to the early years of his practice as "the dullest in my life" and unhappily contended that:

. . . the modern practice of law, which calls principally for mental ingenuity to help a client do anything he wants to do, seemed to me intellectually one of the most degrading occupations in the category of respectable employments. I began to believe that the superlawyer should have the brains of a Machiavelli; the hide of a walrus, and no moral convictions.[53]

Richberg sought more uplifting experiences in his support for municipal reform causes and in his writing. He criticized the "commerical" values which were the "dominating ideals of our generation," calling them a "thief ideal" which lauded the "man who gets the most and gives the least" as "the biggest success." Richberg's desire to act upon the belief that "our best service to ourselves lies in giving our best service to others" was not fully actualized until he was able to devote his full energies to the progressive crusade. When he did join the movement on a full-time basis, it was clear that his battle against the corrupting influences at work in America was a campaign for personal, as well as political, regeneration.[54]

Felix Frankfurter also sought a career which would prove to be a meaningful vocation rather than simply a means of making money. In Frankfurter's view, the law represented just such a career. Unlike Stimson and Richberg, Frankfurter had always "wanted to be a lawyer." He was attracted to the law both because of its intellectual challenge and because of its potential as an instrument for social improvement. Frankfurter thus recalled that, although becoming a lawyer had been his only boyhood ambition, he had never pictured himself as a lawyer with "clients."[55]

Upon graduating from law school, Frankfurter did work briefly in a large New York firm in which he was the first Jew ever to be hired. He soon gave up that job, however, and took a cut in salary in order to accept Stimson's offer to become an assistant in the U.S. Attorney's office. Frankfurter found great satisfaction in public service, and especially in being associated with Stimson. After subsequently joining the Harvard Law School faculty, Frankfurter wrote to Stimson:

So much of what I am, the spirit which I carry into work, the significance I endeavor to find in life, are things we wrought out together. You see all my non-school life has been lived with you and the wrench has been none too easy. Well—in purpose, in aims, even in a good deal of detail I *know* our collective work will continue. Cambridge, and what it should mean, will in no rhetorical sense, be a continuation of all these years.[56]

On the other hand, Frankfurter held in contempt lawyers who pandered to the desires of their wealthy clients in order to become rich themselves. While working in the federal attorney's office, Frankfurter attended proceedings before the Interstate Commerce Commission in which lawyers for E.H. Harriman defended their client's attempts at railroad consolidation. Immediately afterwards, Frankfurter concluded:

If it means that you should be that kind of a subservient creature to have the most desirable clients, the biggest clients in the country, if that's what it means to be a leader of the bar, I never want to be a leader of the bar. The price of admission is too high.[57]

Josephus Daniels never doubted that the primary purpose of any career ought to be doing "the Lord's own work in the broadening and betterment of mankind." Daniels' newspaper profession, as we have seen, seemed to represent for him a religious calling in which he felt himself able to combat the corrupting ideals of greed and materialism. He vowed early in life that he would never "sell" himself to the monopolies or to the "money power" which were threatening to undermine the moral character of American society. The career of a crusading editor was thus a perfect means for Daniels to advance the cause of reform and, at the same time, satisfy his own deeply felt need to do the work of the Lord.[58]

Progressivism thus arose as both a personal and a political response to the new social order which had evolved by the turn of the century. Richard Hofstadter and Robert Wiebe have offered two influential, though contrasting, explanations of the socio-psychological dynamic which produced the progressive mentality. Hofstadter argues that the leadership of the progressive movement was drawn primarily from "the old gentry, the merchants of long standing, the small manufacturers, the established professional men, the civic leaders of an earlier era." These men "suffered from the events of their time not through a shrinkage in their means but through the changed pattern in the distribution of deference and power." For the most part white Anglo-Saxon Protestants, they experienced the psychological trauma of a "status revolution" resulting from recent changes in the economic and social structure of the country. Having seen their wealth and influence come to pale in comparison to that of the heads of America's new corporate institutions, they sought to restore their previous position of moral and political leadership by heading a reform movement against the trusts. Wiebe, on the other hand, claims that progressivism was led by members of a "new," rather than an "old," middle class. He argues that the economic revolution of the period created a newly self-conscious class of professionals, administrators, and technical experts which saw a chance to establish itself as an indispensable element in America's increasingly complex industrial society. "The heart of progressivism," Wiebe concludes, "was the ambition of the new middle class to fulfill its destiny through bureaucratic means."[59]

While both views contribute to our understanding of progressivism, neither ought to be accepted without qualification. First, it is impossible to distinguish absolutely between the old middle class and the rising corporate elite. Hofstadter himself acknowledges that many of the new industrialists came from well established and privileged families. Moreover, it is impossible to draw a definitive dividing line between the old and the new middle classes, since many reformers who came from old middle class backgrounds subsequently adopted the scientific outlook which characterized the new middle class. Donald Richberg, for one, can easily be classified as either a member of Hofstadter's old middle class or Wiebe's new middle class.

Differences in social origins within the middle class do not adequately account for the development of the progressive mentality in particular individuals. It is, therefore, more helpful to focus on the common discontent which members of both the rising and declining middle classes felt with the new economic order and values which were emerging at the end of the nineteenth century. For among the men considered here, all five, in spite of differences in social background, came to share a similar dissatisfaction with the emphasis on materialism and personal gain which dominated the new economic order. While they upheld the value of the work ethic, they feared that work might lose its meaning if it became disassociated from a sense of social responsibility.

It is interesting that for Henry Stimson and Donald Richberg, the two men examined here whose backgrounds most clearly identify them as members of the old middle class, dissatisfaction with the new corporate order reflected not so much a reaffirmation of the values of their fathers, but rather a symbolic rejection of paternal authority. Stimson and Richberg had both been pressured by their fathers into becoming lawyers primarily for financial reasons. Both men, consequently, experienced a lack of personal satisfaction early in their careers and undoubtedly bore an at least unconscious resentment toward their fathers as a result. When Stimson and Richberg were able finally to devote themselves to public service, they had found a means not only of furthering their ideological beliefs, but also of breaking away from the influence of their fathers. While Lewis Stimson and John Richberg had imparted to their sons a sense of idealism and social responsibility, they may have compromised themselves, in their sons' eyes, by forcing their own children to put a greater emphasis, in practice, on financial security. Thus, the progressivism of men like Stimson and Richberg was not so much a product of a "status revolution," as it was an indirect indictment of their fathers' accommodation to the corrupting values of the new economic order.[60]

Felix Frankfurter, of course, most clearly fits the description of a new middle-class progressive offered by Wiebe. Lacking either established roots in America, or a background of financial security, Frankfurter found education the path to personal advancement. Early in his career, Frankfurter concluded that training in the law would enable him to participate in the development of the "organized scientific thinking" required by "the modern state." As a new American, Frankfurter's identification with the progressive cause represented a means of upward mobility rather than a defense of previously enjoyed status privileges. Frankfurter himself felt that his career was neither an identification with, nor a rejection of, his father's life and values. For he once observed that "the greatest debt I owe my parents is that they left me alone almost totally."[61]

The common bond linking new middle-class progressives such as Frankfurter with old middle-class progressives such as Stimson is symbolized by the relationship which developed between these two men. If any one person served as a father figure for Frankfurter during his adult life, it was Stimson. From the moment they first worked together in the U.S. Attorney's office, the two men developed a close professional and personal relationship which had its foundation in a common commitment to the ideal of disinterested public service. Their views were never identical. Yet, in spite of contrasting social and intellectual backgrounds, they both shared a common sense of concern about the values of the new economic order and a common desire to contribute to the development of a government which would be able to instill a greater degree of social responsibility into that order.[62]

Several important works of recent scholarship have challenged the view that progressivism can be understood as essentially a middle-class movement. John Buenker and David Thelen have both argued that progressivism emerged as a result of a "series of interacting and shifting coalitions" of various socioeconomic groups. Buenker, in particular, claims that the "urban new stock working class" played as important a role in the progressive movement as any sector of the middle class. It is significant, however, that both Buenker and Thelen focus almost exclusively on the state and local level in their analyses of the origins of progressivism. The inspiration and leadership for progressivism in the arena of national politics undoubtedly came from middle class reformers (albeit of differing backgrounds) like the men examined here. It was the concerns of men like Daniels, Stimson, Baruch, Richberg, and Frankfurter, rather than the concerns of the poor, of oppressed minorities, or of recent working class immigrants, which figure most prominently in the crucial election of 1912 and in the reform proposals enacted into law in the early years of the Wilson administration.[63]

## V

The progressive movement significantly influenced American political life between 1901 and 1912, but its greatest impact was felt in the period between 1912 and the beginning of the First World War. The three-way Presidential contest between William Howard Taft, Theodore Roosevelt, and Woodrow Wilson served as a dramatic focus for the political debates which had been raging during the previous decade. Progressives throughout the country, including the men discussed here, believed that the election might result in the final fulfillment of the promise of the progressive movement.

Most progressives in 1912 believed that either Roosevelt's New Nationalism or Wilson's New Freedom represented the culmination of progressivism. To contemporary observers, the two programs embodied conflicting approaches to the problem of what to do about the trusts. Wilson's New Freedom seemed based on the belief that large-scale enterprise was neither inevitable nor desirable and apparently called for a vigorous government effort to break up the nation's trusts through a stricter enforcement and strengthening of the anti-trust laws. Roosevelt's New Nationalism, in contrast, was widely viewed as an opposing philosophy based on an acceptance of huge corporations as an inevitable and highly efficient form of business organization. TR's Progressive party thus seemed to advocate increased government regulation of the trusts, rather than an attempt to recreate an atomistic economy.

Bernard Baruch, as we have seen, strongly supported Wilson in 1912 and became one of the New Jersey Governor's major financial backers. Baruch's commitment to Wilson, however, was a highly personal one. Unlike the other men considered in this study, he apparently had no clear-cut ideological preference for either the New Freedom or the New Nationalism.[64]

Josephus Daniels, on the other hand, was both an ardent political supporter of Wilson and a firm believer in his New Freedom ideology. Daniels corresponded with Wilson as early as 1886 and first met him in 1909. From the time of that meeting, Daniels thought of Wilson as the next President and helped to secure the Democratic nomination for him in 1912. During the campaign, the North Carolina editor served as chairman of Wilson's publicity committee. Daniels was, of course, attracted to Wilson as a fellow Southerner, but he also felt that the former college president would be the strongest possible Democratic candidate because of his potential appeal to Mugwump Republicans. In addition, Daniels was enthusiastic about Wilson's New Freedom, believing that a Wilson administration would bring a return to Jeffersonian principles of government. He was convinced that Wilson intended to take vigorous action against the country's trusts. At the same time, Daniels criticized Roosevelt for having used only rhetoric in his attacks on the "lawbreakers of great wealth" when, as President, he had had the power to take far more effective action.[65]

Donald Richberg and Felix Frankfurter supported TR's Bull Moose party crusade in 1912. As firm believers in the necessity of adopting a scientific approach toward the problems of government, both men rejected the notion that unquestioning loyalty to one of the two major parties was required for effective political action. Since Richberg and Frankfurter each thought that Roosevelt's Progressive party offered the best hope for instilling a scientific spirit into the operations of government, both men were willing to support the cause of the third party.

Richberg not only served as legal counsel in the new party's effort to win a place on the Illinois ballot, but he also was the party's candidate for State's Attorney. While Richberg had long respected Roosevelt, he was initially sympathetic to the candidacy of Wisconsin Senator Robert La Follette. He threw his support to TR, though, because he finally concluded that the former President would be the most effective spokesman for the "mass sentiments and yearnings of my generation." Roosevelt embodied for Richberg both the spiritual "revolt of youth against age, of idealism against materialism," and the rational belief in the necessity of having the government regulate the power of trusts through the use of modern expertise.[66]

Frankfurter also admired Roosevelt as a man "genuinely stirred to the new social function of government." He thought that the former President best understood that it was the "business of statesmanship to effect by policy what revolution effects by force." In contrast, Frankfurter attacked Wilson's New Freedom for its "invocation of the golden past" and for its emphasis on the Sherman Law, which, in Frankfurter's view, reflected either a lack of "frankness or perception" on Wilson's part. Worst of all was "Wilson's sneer against government by experts," which Frankfurter considered to be "vicious, because we are singularly in need in this country of the deliberateness and truthfulness of really scientific expertness."[67]

Unlike Richberg, however, Frankfurter had some qualms about openly joining the Progressive party crusade. Although he had no strong ties to either major party, Frankfurter felt constrained in his support for TR because of his professional and personal relation to Henry Stimson. Stimson had joined Taft's Cabinet in 1911 and was thus a member of the incumbent's Republican administration during the campaign of 1912, as was Frankfurter, who served as an aide to Stimson in the War Department. As a member of the incumbent's administration, Stimson felt duty-bound to support his chief.[68]

Personal loyalty, though, was not Stimson's only consideration in backing Taft in 1912. Stimson had long been closely associated with Roosevelt and had, in fact, been regarded as TR's hand-picked candidate for Governor of New York in 1910. He was in basic agreement with Roosevelt on the trust question and had praised TR's initial statement of the New Nationalism at Osawatomie, Kansas, in 1910, informing Roosevelt at the time of how "pleased" he was that "you enumerated a definite and constructive radical platform." Yet, even in 1910, Stimson expressed what proved to be a telling reservation:

The only thing I wished to say particularly is that it seems to me vitally important that the reform should go in the way of a regeneration of the Republican party and not by the formation of a new party. To me it seems vitally important that the Republican party, which contains, generally speaking, the richer and more intelligent citizens of the country, should take the lead in reform and not drift into a reactionary position. If, instead, the leadership should fall into the hands of either an independent party or a party composed, like the Democrats, largely of foreign elements and the classes which will immediately benefit by the reform, and if the solid business Republicans should drift into new obstruction, I fear the necessary changes could hardly be accomplished without much excitement and possibly violence.

Although Stimson remained frustrated by his inability to get Taft to move in the direction of Roosevelt's New Nationalism, his sense of party loyalty and personal duty still caused him to vote for Taft in 1912.[69]

Frankfurter, in the Fall of 1911, agreed with Stimson that the "Republican Party, in its essentials, satisfies or is capable of satisfying" the "essential prerequisites" for a "progressive" party, but he explained to his mentor that party loyalty could not be a deciding factor for him.

I have had to work out with no little mental travail these years my own bearings in these transitional days of parties; and my gropings of hope for and loyalty to the Republican party as the party that ought to be the liberal party and largely tends that way, are perhaps valuable as reflecting the rather troubled viewpoint of not a few of the younger generation.

Although Frankfurter strongly favored Roosevelt in 1912, he followed Stimson's advice to refrain from campaigning openly for the Progressive party so that it would be politically possible for him to remain as Stimson's assistant in the War Department.[70]

## VI

The early years of Wilson's administration not only proved to be the culmination of the progressive movement; they also demonstrated that the differences between the New Freedom and the New Nationalism had, in fact, been more rhetorical than substantive. Before examining some of Wilson's major legislative accomplishments, however, it will be helpful to consider the activities of the five men discussed here during the final years of the Progressive era. With the exception of Baruch, each of these men exercised a degree of public responsibility in this period which was as great or greater than any he had ever before enjoyed.

Although Baruch had been an important financial contributor to Wilson's campaign, when Wilson took office, Baruch remained aloof from the Democratic administration's efforts to implement the New Freedom. Baruch's special relationship with President Wilson was not to become a factor in Baruch's transformation into a public figure until after the outbreak of war in Europe.[71]

Daniels, on the other hand, was rewarded for his role in Wilson's Presidential campaign by being named Secretary of the Navy. For the first time in his life, Daniels thus found himself in a position to put into practice his vision of Jeffersonian Democracy. Two aspects of Daniels' administration of the Navy Department in the years before American participation in the First World War are of particular interest. He attempted both to extend democratic opportunity within the Navy and to protect the Navy from exploitation from without by the large corporations which were its major suppliers.

Daniels quickly learned that "the most serious defect in the Navy was the lack of democracy." Committed to the idea of equal opportunity, Daniels soon instituted a number of policy changes designed to democratize the Navy. He ordered officers and enlisted men housed under the same roof; extended the already existing ban on liquor to officers, as well as ordinary sailors; put up to a referendum certain minor changes in the Navy uniform; and set a precedent of treating enlisted men with respect, rather than as objects of disdain. Most important of all, Daniels took steps to strengthen the Navy as an "educational institution" by establishing "schools on every ship" at which attendance was compulsory for those deficient in rudimentary skills. This was part of a general attempt by Daniels to make it possible for any Navy man to gain advancement by his own effort. He opened the Naval Academy to a select number of enlisted men, admitted by competitive examinations, so that it became theoretically possible for an enlisted man eventually to rise to the rank of admiral. To implement the principle of equal opportunity and open competition from the top down, as well as from the bottom up, Daniels issued orders making advancement in the officer ranks dependent on merit and service at sea, rather than on seniority and political connections in Washington. While Daniels did not try to do away with the hierarchical structure of the Navy, he did try to establish greater possibilities for upward mobility within the existing structure.[72]

Having long been a critic of monopolies and trusts, Daniels found himself, as Secretary of the Navy, confronted with the problem of how to deal with the large corporations which were the Navy's chief suppliers. Competition under free market conditions had always been Daniels' ideal. Yet, only a few months after taking office, he learned how difficult it would be to enforce such a principle in the administration of Navy contracts. The Navy's call for competitive bids on one particular contract produced three identical proposals from the country's only three armor-plate producers, Carnegie, Bethlehem, and Midvale, and an explanation that it was accepted practice for such contracts to be equally divided among the three companies. This marked only the beginning of what proved to be an eight year struggle between Daniels and the Navy's major suppliers of steel, oil, and smokeless powder, over prices and competitive bidding procedures. In this instance, Daniels refused to accept the bids, insisting that "competition would be the rule of the Navy Department" while he was in charge, since that was the only way to be certain that the government was paying a "fair price" for its purchases. In subsequent years, Daniels continued to turn down bids which he felt were unacceptable. He also sought to inject competition into the assignment of contracts by seeking offers from foreign producers and by reducing the size of individual Navy orders so that smaller companies could bid on contracts too.[73]

Daniels' frustration at trying to foster competitive bidding in industries controlled either by a single trust or by a handful of colluding firms led him to the conclusion that government-owned plants ought to be built to serve as a "yardstick" by which to measure the fairness of prices charged by non-competitive private companies. In admitting that it might become necessary for such publicly-owned plants to supply all of the government's demand for a particular product, Daniels argued that he would "not call a monopoly anything that the government owns."[74]

As Navy Secretary, Daniels also engaged in an ongoing fight over the control of the government's oil reserves. He sought to keep the government from leasing its resources to private developers and to block the attempts of certain companies and individuals to collect on claims which supposedly antedated the withdrawal of the public lands from general use. Daniels criticized many of the nation's major corporate interests, claiming at one time that "history does not warrant an assumption that the patriotism of these companies would prove superior to their desire for profits." Daniels not only strongly supported maintaining government control over its oil reserves, but he also approved of the idea of having the government withdraw from public use other government-owned lands containing minerals and ores needed by the military. Discussing the tungsten deposits of Colorado at a Senate hearing in 1916, Daniels engaged in the following exchange:

Daniels: I think if we had public lands there that we could use for the Government service, and for the betterment of the Government service, I think we ought to do it [have them withdrawn from public use by the President].

Sen. Thomas: But let us go a step further. Would it not be equally consistent to make reserves of deposits of iron ore to be converted into pig and afterwards into steel for the use of the Navy?

Daniels: You carry me along to a position that I have long favored. If we had a new country here and were not embarrassed by private claimants, I should say we ought to reserve the oil, the coal, and iron.[75]

Daniels' actions in his first years as Secretary of the Navy reveal his continuing commitment to the ideals of equal opportunity and free market competition, but they indicate also his growing realization that the public interest could not be protected solely by relying on a strict enforcement of the anti-trust laws. The problems posed by the existence of monopoly power in certain key, defense-related, industries even led Daniels to consider, on a limited basis, government ownership or control of vital resources. Yet Daniels still rejected any attempts at radically altering the structure of the American economy. He could not bring himself to admit the possibility that a system based on the private ownership of the means of production could produce a society divided into classes, the very nature of which made the ideal of equal opportunity a myth rather than a potential reality. While Daniels was frequently critical of individual businessmen and individual firms, he failed to view corporate behavior as the logical and necessary outcome of an economic system based on the pursuit of profit. Daniels' attitude toward the disposition of land still in the public domain shows that he was not totally insensitive to the deeper issues raised by the development of corporate capitalism. However, the "embarrass[ment]" caused by the existing pattern of private ownership, and his continuing belief that the marketplace of supposedly open competition offered the optimal means of determining the distribution of resources and wealth, prevented Daniels from breaking out of the confines of his inherited liberal world view.

With the change of administrations in Washington in 1913, Henry Stimson returned to New York to resume his law practice. Now a leading figure in the state's Republican party, Stimson came home committed to the task of seeing his party "reorganized on a progressive basis." When the voters of New York decided, in 1914, to elect delegates to a Constitutional Convention to be held the following year, Stimson saw an opportunity to have his party push for a thoroughgoing effort to reform the state's government in accordance with the lessons of the previous decade. Stimson was chosen by the Republican state organization in 1914 to chair a committee which was to draw up proposals for the coming convention. In the election of delegates later that year, he received one of the highest vote totals for an at-large candidate. With the Republicans in control of the convention, Stimson's long time friend and former associate, Elihu Root, was made chairman of the gathering which assembled in 1915. As a result, Stimson was given his choice of committee assignments and opted for the chairmanship of the Finance Committee. Stimson's role in the New York Constitutional Convention reveals the practical priorities he assigned to the reform proposals of the Progressive era.[76]

Two years before the convention was convened, Stimson had begun to push for a reform program centered around two basic ideas, the executive budget and the short ballot. Stimson had been the most important influence in converting Root to a strong belief in these two proposals. As head of the Finance Committee, Stimson took the lead in getting the convention to approve an amendment giving the Governor sole power to propose government expenditures, subject only to the power of the legislature to reject or reduce his recommendations. Stimson believed that the executive budget encouraged sounder financial practices because it tied expenditures directly to expected revenues. He also felt that it rectified one of the "inherent weaknesses of a legislative body," its inability to put the general interest ahead of local interests. Stimson thus argued:

Each representative comes from a single district. He is responsible to the district and not to the state at large. If the interests of the state come into conflict with those of the district, and he sides with the state, the district can put him out of public life. . . . And so legislative action, when left to itself without the leadership of the executive who represents the entire state or nation, necessarily and inevitably tends to sink into a series of log-rolling deeds between the various members, acting in the interests of their respective districts, and often quite oblivious to the interests of the state at large.[77]

During the convention, Stimson also devoted significant attention to the short ballot, that is, a reduction in the number of officials elected in state-wide voting, and to a consolidation of the number of bureaus, agencies, and departments in the government. Stimson claimed that the short ballot would bring about effective reform through the "concentration and coordination of the functions of government rather than by a further diffusion of them." He contended that the proposed reform rested on "the principle that before you can hold a man or a government responsible for doing wrong you must first give him adequate power to do right."[78]

Presented with the opportunity to redesign the fundamental law of the state of New York, Stimson put the highest priority on reorganizing the government according to the organizational principles of modern business. He did not take this opportunity to press for any important social or economic reconstruction because he acted upon the belief that the political problems of the Progressive era resulted not so much from the dangerous development of huge concentrations of private economic power, but rather from the fact that government had failed to keep pace with business in terms of efficiency and organization. Only the existence of "weak government" had stood as "an open invitation to private despotism." Thus, Stimson concluded:

Much of the difficulty of our present time has come from the fact that our age is getting more and not less complicated, and that the representative system which we have is being overloaded by the pressure of new burdens. We shall not cure his difficulty by going back to the obsolete machinery of a simpler age.

. . . with that development into what we call collectivism, the dependence of the people upon government and necessity of more expert and more intelligent government is becoming more pressing every day.[79]

Both Felix Frankfurter and Donald Richberg embarked on their careers believing that scientifically trained social servants had an essential role to play in public life. During the final stages of the Progressive era, both men were offered the opportunity to assume such a role for themselves. For a brief time after Lindley Garrison succeeded Henry Stimson as Secretary of War in the new Cabinet under Wilson, Frankfurter stayed on as an assistant in the War Department in order to continue the pioneering work he had already begun in the field of federal regulation of water power. Soon, however, Frankfurter was extended an offer to join the faculty of the Harvard Law School. Never having considered a career in teaching, Frankfurter gave the offer a great deal of thought before arriving at his decision, seeking the advice of those whose opinions he most respected. Henry Stimson advised Frankfurter to decline the offer, arguing:

I have no doubt that you would do a very good and useful work and quite likely a uniquely useful work in such a chair in the Law School. You have certainly the ability and the exceptional experience. But I question whether it would afford you scope for some of your abilities which to my mind are more exceptional than even your legal ability— and practical experience in criminology. You have the greatest faculty of acquaintance—for keeping in touch with the center of things—for knowing sympathetically men who are doing and thinking, of almost all men—certainly all young men that I know. I query whether that most valuable faculty would not be to a great extent lost at the Law School. To me you seem a man whose place is at the center of the great liberal movement which [is] now going on in national and industrial life, and you have already had unusual opportunity for making a circle of acquaintance upon which your future work will be based. As Mrs. Stimson said, "The law school will be a side track," and I am inclined to agree with her.[80]

After consulting with others, Frankfurter decided to write out for himself a memo setting forth the pros and cons of going to Harvard. He observed that the "Rooseveltian decade of excoriating protest" had come to an end, and that what was now needed was to give "direction" to the "social passions" which had already been aroused.

All along the line we propose, determine, legislate—without knowing enough. Empiricism of the worst sort is abroad—in administration and legislation of necessity. To be stable, to meet our realization of the need and capacity for conscious readjustments, requires data, and correlated, persistent, prophetic thinking. Largely that cannot be done in office. It must be done from the outside and translated by those in office with all the risks and limitations of translation, or have been done before men come to office. There should be a constant source of thought for the guidance of public men and the education of public opinion, as well as a source of trained men for public life. The problems ahead are economic and sociological, and the added adjustments of a government under a written constitution, steeped in legalistic traditions, to the assumption of the right solution of such problems. To an important degree, therefore, the problems are problems of jurisprudence . . . In the synthesis of thinking that must shape the Great State, the lawyer is in many ways the coordinator, the mediator, between the various social sciences.

. . . Others think, above all, office for me. I have now no additional aim than the realization of ideas. But even if—I am not sure that Harvard isn't as good a ticket to draw in the lottery of chances as the other routes, either sticking it out here or New York practice. So far as one can tell, the trend is bound to be more and more toward drawing officials who are presumably thoroughly trained.[81]

Frankfurter decided, therefore, to accept the Harvard offer. His long career as a law professor began in the Fall of 1914. At Harvard, he joined with Roscoe Pound in the development of "sociological jurisprudence," specializing in the new areas of administrative and public utilities law which had arisen as a result of increased government regulation of industry. By trying to aid the development of "scientific thinking" for the "Great State," Frankfurter hoped to inspire his students to become more than "skillful practitioners" or "clever pleaders." He hoped to lay before them the "glorious vision of the law . . . as a vital agency for human betterment." Being at the nation's most prestigious law school, Frankfurter saw himself as helping to shape specially skilled, socially conscious, lawyers and administrative technicians who would become America's future leaders. Frankfurter, moreover, began to set a personal example for his students by succeeding Louis Brandeis in the role of "people's attorney." Soon after going to Harvard, Frankfurter became a frequent defender of progressive legislation which was being challenged in the courts.[82]

At almost the same time that Frankfurter was invited to join the faculty of Harvard, Donald Richberg was offered a full-time job with the Progressive party national organization in New York. In the wake of the election of 1912, the Progressive party leadership hoped to expand the traditional conception of party functions. A Progressive National Service was, therefore, established to educate the public on important issues and to act as a reference service for Progressive officeholders. Richberg was asked to become Director of the Legislative Reference Bureau, and he eagerly came to New York in the Spring of 1913 to begin work. During the year he spent in New York, Richberg's responsibilities consisted primarily in helping to prepare legislation to be proposed by the handful of Progressive party members in Congress. He assisted in the writing of an anti-child labor bill, an anti-convict labor law, a workmen's compensation act for federal employees, a women's eight-hour-day law for the District of Columbia, and bills to establish commissions on social insurance, naturalization, natural rivers, and the tariff. Most important of all, he helped to prepare three separate pieces of legislation dealing with the trust problem.[83]

Richberg's work as head of the Legislative Reference Bureau enabled him to feel that he had transformed his own "practice of law from a petty service for private interests into a service enhanced by the public interest." Just as Frankfurter hoped to contribute to the effort to turn the law into an agency for reform, so did Richberg believe that he was helping to establish a new role in which legal "technicians" could serve the cause of constructive change. Commenting in 1914 on the future possibilities of legislative reference bureaus, Richberg expressed a hope in the development of a new type of lawyer which closely paralleled Frankfurter's thinking on the subject:

Outside of its immediate practical uses there is a part in more distant changes which may be played by legislative reference bureaus for political parties. There is in the work that combination of law and politics and social science which is rapidly creating a new profession, which might be termed that of social counselor. It may be regarded as one of the large divisions into which the profession of law is separating.

. . . The corporation lawyer is more of a business man than a lawyer. There are lawyers engaged in real estate business whose legal knowledge is specialized and usually far from profound. The bank attorney is more than half banker. The lawyer politicians who dominate our legislatures and fill a large part of our executive offices are not lawyers—let it be said to their credit—they are engaged in useful occupations.

Richberg believed, however, that the creation of legislative reference bureaus at all levels of government would help to produce many "earnest young men devoted to the ideal of helping the law to keep pace with the giant strides of social and industrial needs."[84]

Stimson, Frankfurter, and Richberg all realized that the developmernt of a complex industrial economy made necessary the modernization and professionalization of all levels of government. Scientific and professional training in the skills of administration and information gathering and analysis had already become required for those managing the great new modern business enterprises, and Stimson, Frankfurter, and Richberg recognized that without the development of a corps of similarly trained public officials, government would become a virtually irrelevant and powerless institution. However, even in supporting the creation of a professionalized government bureaucracy, these men did not yet envision such a bureaucracy as exercising any controlling or directing power over the economy. Frankfurter and Richberg, in particular, may have wished to see government experts given responsibility for establishing minimum standards of healthfulness for working conditions and minimum standards of fairness to serve as ground rules in the corporate quest for profit. Prior to World War One, however, none of the men discussed here thought that administratively determined decisions, whether arrived at by a government bureaucracy or by the new corporate bureaucracies operating in the private sector, could or should substitute for the decisions of a free market as to the overall allocation of resources.

## VII

The men discussed here thus contributed, in various ways, to the attempt to implement the progressive ideal of a strengthened and modernized state. Progressivism, however, culminated not in such individual efforts, but in the enactment by Congress of Woodrow Wilson's New Freedom program in 1913 and 1914. An examination of some of Wilson's major legislative accomplishments, and of the reactions of the men considered here to them, is thus a fitting way to conclude the present discussion of progressivism.

During the campaign of 1912, most Americans believed that the rhetorical differences between Wilson's New Freedom and Roosevelt's New Nationalism reflected a basic contrast in philosophy and program. That view was seriously challenged by Wilson's actions once he took office. Even during the campaign, however, a close examination of the ideas of the principal formulator of the New Freedom would have revealed the large measure of agreement between the two positions. Louis Brandeis is described by Arthur Link as the "chief architect of Wilson's New Freedom," and as "Wilson's only really important adviser during the campaign of 1912." It is noteworthy that both Josephus Daniels and Felix Frankfurter, two men who stood on opposing sides in the contest between Wilson and Roosevelt, greatly admired Brandeis for his contributions to the progressive movement. Brandeis may have appeared, at first glance, to have been an advocate of a simplistic anti-monopoly policy designed to recreate a "golden past" of small-scale competitive enterprise. Yet Brandeis, like Daniels and Frankfurter, and the other progressives considered here, supported a far more complex role for government in the new industrial order. Frankfurter, in particular, should have realized that Brandeis' position was not basically in conflict with his own or with TR's New Nationalism.[85]

From the time he had been a law student at Harvard, Frankfurter had respected Brandeis because of the "people's attorney's" commitment to the public interest. Before the election year of 1912, the two men had become good friends, and Brandeis had begun to exert an important influence on the younger man's conception of the law. Brandeis had by then already pioneered in the introduction of sociological evidence into judicial decisions in the famous case of Muller v. Oregon. He had also helped to create what Samuel Haber has called an "efficiency craze" in America through his use of scientific management studies in the Eastern Rate case.[86]

Frankfurter, nevertheless, complained during the 1912 campaign that Brandeis' position that "big business should be allowed to *grow* but not be *made*" was not a "very helpful generality." Frankfurter was also disappointed that Brandeis seemed "rather rigidly against administrative regulation" of business. Still, it is surprising that during the heat of the campaign Frankfurter apparently lost sight of the fact that he considered Brandeis to be perhaps the nation's leading exponent of a scientific approach to social problems. The most important lesson Frankfurter claimed to have learned from Brandeis was the necessity of relying on the "logic of facts" and on the aid of scientifically trained experts in the conduct of economic and political affairs. Even Daniels, who admired Brandeis primarily for "his royal fight against Privilege," felt that one of Brandeis' greatest strengths was his ability to back up "every statement or position with such an array of facts and logic as to make his positions impregnable."[87]

When put into practice, Brandeis' philosophy did not differ significantly from Roosevelt's New Nationalism. Haber persuasively argues that while Brandeis' outlook was based on a reaction against "mere money-making" and the growth of powerful trusts, it represented not so much a desire to recreate the dominance of the "old ways and old families," but rather an attempt to establish a sense of "professionalism" and rule by the "competent" in both business and government. The rhetoric of the New Freedom and the New Nationalism may have appealed to different groups. However, Brandeis' conception of government constituted a perfect blend of the concerns felt by all the progressives examined in this study. This became clear when the New Freedom actually became the basis for the Wilson administration's legislative program.[88]

Under Wilson's leadership, Congress in 1913 and 1914 enacted three major pieces of legislation apparently designed to strengthen the government's ability to prevent abuses of private economic power. First, widespread public concern about the development of a "money trust," i.e., concentration of control over the nation's investment capital in a few New York financial institutions, helped spur the Wilson administration to push for the enactment of legislation creating the Federal Reserve Board. Many historians regard the Federal Reserve Act as the "most important and enduring legacy of the New Freedom and Woodrow Wilson's presidency." The landmark law established a Federal Reserve System composed of eight to twelve districts and capped by a Federal Reserve Board appointed by the President. The act gave the Federal Reserve System the responsibility for issuing currency and made Federal Reserve notes the obligation of the United States Treasury. The measure was thus intended, in Arthur Link's words, "to establish a workable reserve system, destroy the concentration of credit in Wall Street, and give the country an elastic currency suited to expanded business needs."[89]

While public demands for government intervention in the investment banking industry made banking reform politically popular in 1913, the major impetus behind the specific proposal for a federal reserve system had, in fact, originally come from the banking community itself in the wake of the financial panic of 1907. Congress did make some changes in the original proposal put forward by the nation's leading banking interests, most significantly, by creating a Presidentially appointed governing body rather than one selected by the bankers themselves, and by establishing a district system rather than a single central bank.[90]

These changes were hailed at the time as a triumph of democracy over Wall Street. Yet, as Bernard Baruch later observed, the New York bankers who voiced opposition to the law as enacted in 1913 "lived to value and praise it." In the view of one leading historian of the subject, "the ties between big business and Wall Street [were not] significantly loosened." Banker influence became pre-eminent within each of the Federal Reserve districts and on the Federal Reserve Board itself. Moreover, the new system did nothing to diminish the concentration of credit and reserves in New York. If anything, the Federal Reserve Act may have worked indirectly to strengthen New York's position as the nation's banking center. Even while the debate over the Federal Reserve Act raged, Josephus Daniels admitted that the Wilson administration "would be stupid to try to injure the greatness of New York" because it "could not end New York's lead in finance if it would and would not if it could."[91]

The Federal Reserve Act was a representative expression of the general thrust of progressive thinking on the subject of government regulation. It in no way envisioned public control or direction of the investment process as a proper function of government. Rather, the legislation was designed simply to rationalize the system by which currency was issued and to give the banking community itself more effective tools for responding to short-term shortages of liquid reserves. In other words, the power of government would be invoked only to make the operation of the existing banking system more fluid and not to reconstruct that system or infuse it with a sense of public purpose.

In 1914 Wilson successfully directed through Congress both a bill establishing the Federal Trade Commission and the Clayton Act which amended the Sherman Antitrust law by setting restrictions on interlocking directorates and by clarifying what practices constituted an illegal restraint of trade. Although Link observes that the legislation setting up the FTC ran "counter to Wilson's original plan" regarding government regulation of business, he also notes that it was Brandeis who "almost single-handedly persuaded the President" to support such legislation. Brandeis' backing for the creation of an administrative tribunal to oversee the operations of big business was wholly consistent with his emphasis on the need to utilize scientific expertise in the government's handling of economic and political problems. Taken together, the enactment of the FTC and Clayton bills represented a legislative climax to the progressive movement's response to the emergence of corporate capitalism.[92]

Progressives as seemingly diverse as Daniels and Stimson hailed the legislation dealing with the trust issue which Wilson was able to steer through Congress. Daniels supported the creation of a FTC which could tell businesses "what they could do and could not do" as "a more prompt, a more direct method" of government regulation than the "long and tedious" process of court suits. He still claimed, however, that the "guiding principle" in the President's antitrust program was that "private monopoly" was "indefensible and intolerable," so that what remained "to be regulated" was "competition, to prevent such unlawful oppression of the weaker by the stronger as tends to the creation of the monopoly." Stimson, too, was pleased with Wilson's antitrust program. He noted in his diary in 1913 that he believed that Wilson's program reflected "essentially the same position" which he had himself recently developed. Stimson expressed the same basic view of the trust question as Daniels:

We cannot legalize monopoly without bringing on State regulation of prices. . . . If therefore we are unwilling to accept State regulation of prices, we must accept the only other regulation which is possible— that of competition, actual or potential.[93]

Donald Richberg was much more critical of Wilson's initial antitrust proposals than any of the other men considered here. As Director of the Progressive party's Legislative Reference Bureau, Richberg had helped draft competing legislative proposals for the establishment of a FTC and for the clarification of what constituted unfair trade practices. Richberg had even succeeded in getting the Progressive party leadership to incorporate his plan for the imprisonment of criminal corporations into its legislative program. He acknowledged at the time that both Wilson and the Bull Moose Progressives shared a:

. . . common recognition of the need for governmental action
—(1) to remove the protections of secrecy from illegitimate business;
(2) to eradicate unfair trade practices; and (3) to destroy monopoly.

Richberg also admitted that both reform approaches recognized "the necessity for a body of experts to examine business activities and enlighten the public as to actual conditions."[94]

Yet Richberg denounced the Democratic antitrust program in 1914 as still reflecting the view that big corporations were "artificial and anti-social" institutions. Moreover, he claimed that Wilson considered the proposed FTC as only "an aid to the Legislature and the courts in their task of reforming the abuses brought to light," rather than as the type of government agency "most fitted" to exercise "the power of reformation" over irresponsible business concerns. Even as he attacked the Democratic proposals, however, Richberg admitted that the differences in emphasis between the Democratic and Progressive approaches might have reflected only a "temporary shyness" on the part of the Democrats as a result of the recentness of their acceptance of the idea of regulation by federal commission. Richberg may also have attacked Wilson's program out of a certain sense of personal disappointment, since the trust legislation sponsored by the Progressive party, which he had helped draft, was made irrelevant by the Democrats' similar proposals. Looking back at this period later in his life, Richberg recognized that the New Freedom, in practice, differed little from the New Nationalism he had supported in 1912.[95]

## VIII

Almost fifty years after the enactment of the New Freedom program, Bernard Baruch claimed that Wilson had successfully "launched a vigorous attack against special privileges and monopoly," and, in so doing, had finally brought the workings of government up to date with "the new social, economic, and political conditions" of industrial America. Baruch praised Wilson, moreover, because he felt that this had been accomplished with reforms which:

. . . were not intended to remake the American political and economic system, but to strengthen, preserve, and protect it (from itself, in many respects) by correcting and eliminating the abuses which had grown up about it.[96]

Baruch was correct in claiming that the progressive movement helped modernize and professionalize government in the United States by making the organization of the government's bureaucracy more closely parallel the lines of organization previously adopted by large scale business enterprise. He was also correct in asserting that progressivism, as embodied in the program of the Wilson administration, worked to preserve rather than "remake" the existing socio-economic structure. Did progressivism, however, effectively eliminate the major "abuses" which had arisen as a result of the development of corporate capitalism? Was the movement successful in ending or significantly reducing "special privilege" and in providing institutional mechanisms for adequately representing the public interest in the new economic order? How did the progressive movement actually affect the functioning of the nation's political economy?

The progressives discussed here all accepted the inevitability and desirability of large scale corporate enterprise, but they drew the line at outright monopoly. They all agreed that government ought to prohibit predatory behavior by firms which sought to use "unfair" methods to achieve monopoly control in any industry. In fact, the federal government in this period did act to break up several powerful trusts (most notably Standard Oil). Yet, because the progressives focused almost exclusively on the dangers of monopoly while virtually ignoring the problems of oligopoly, and because the courts narrowly interpreted the antitrust laws to apply only to firms using "unreasonable" means to monopolize an industry, the ultimate impact of government antitrust action was to sanction and, in effect, encourage the development of oligopoly as a substitute for the pattern of single firm dominance which otherwise might well have emerged under unrestrained market conditions. The pace of industrial combination, which had rapidly accelerated around the turn of the century, did slow in the decade before the First World War. However, this period still witnessed the consolidation of a new economic order in which power rested in the hands of a small elite.[97]

The impact of progressive supported federal regulation of business was hardly very different than the impact of government antitrust action. In its first years of operation, the Federal

Trade Commission's most important activity was its sponsorship of legislation exempting from the antitrust laws industrial combinations formed to stimulate exports abroad. Even in its efforts to restrain fraudulent and unfair business practices, the commission saw its task essentially as cooperating with the business community in the elimination of the kind of destructive competition which threatened the stability of the new economic structure. The FTC did virtually nothing to challenge the rise of an economy dominated by oligopolies. Nor did the commission seek to develop any means for ensuring that in the major economic decisions affecting the entire nation, the needs of the public would be taken into consideration.[98]

While the progressives may have taken pride in their efforts to modernize government and restrain monopoly, they made no serious attempt to counter the growth of inequality and poverty which occurred in America between 1900 and 1914. The gap dividing rich and poor widened in these years, since increases in wages not only lagged behind the increases in returns going to capital, but even failed to keep up with increases in the cost of living. Real annual earnings for urban unskilled workers actually decreased, on average, by one quarter of one percent each year between 1896 and 1916. In 1913, the share of total national income going to the top one percent of income recipients rose to 15 percent. Inequality in the distribution of wealth, as opposed to income, rose more dramatically, reaching what may have been its all-time peak in American history on the eve of the First World War. According to Williamson and Lindert, the wealthiest one percent of households in 1912 may have owned roughly half of all the nation's personal wealth.[99]

Even more striking than the growth of inequality during the Progressive period, is the fact that in this era of apparent prosperity there was actually an increase in the number of Americans living in poverty (whether measured by an absolute standard or by a relative standard taking into consideration changing social expectations and living conditions). According to one calculation utilizing an absolute standard, the percentage of Americans living in poverty, which had dropped significantly between 1870 and 1900 from nearly half to a little less than one third of the population, rose slightly during the years before the

First World War, so that the percentage of Americans in poverty again rose above one third. Another measure of the increase in poverty in this period can be obtained by examining the relationship between average annual earnings for those employed in manufacturing and the minimum adequacy budget required by a family of four. In 1905 (the earliest year for which Ornati presents budget figures), the average factory worker's earnings of $494 represented 79 percent of the budget needed to maintain a family of four in minimally adequate living conditions. By 1914, average annual earnings for blue-collar workers had risen to $580, but by then this amounted to only 77 percent of a minimum adequacy budget. In other words, a factory worker with a wife and two children could not earn enough money at his regular job to keep his family out of poverty.[100]

Many progressives, including most of the men discussed here, wished to see government take some steps to improve working conditions, but not one of the progressives examined in this study directly challenged the root causes of inequality in America. The maldistribution of wealth was, in large part, a product of a system in which the ownership of the nation's capital resources was concentrated in the hands of a small class. The rich became richer because their ownership of income producing assets gave them far greater earning capacity than the overwhelming majority of Americans who had to live off the meager income generated by their own labor. The progressives may have worried about high prices and the excessive profits generated by monopoly. However, they still did not view the maldistribution of wealth and the persistence of poverty as the products of a class based economic system which clearly favored the interests of the few over the interests of the many.

None of the progressives considered here challenged the crucial assumption that the pursuit of private profit was the only fair and rational basis upon which to build a healthy economic system. Yet all of these men personally rejected the idea that money-making should govern the conduct of their own lives. In addition to expressing dissatisfaction with greed and materialism as personal values, they also recognized, at least implicitly, that the pursuit of profit as a corporate ideal had led to the rise of trusts and the potential collapse of the nation's free market system. These men came to extol the personal satisfaction they experienced as a result of their own unselfish commitments to public service. However, they never seriously questioned the desirability of having private profit serve as the basis for the nation's economic life because they never acknowledged the possibility that economic activity on a societal level could be sustained by any motivation other than the desire for personal gain. They thus continued to assume that, for most individuals, the virtues of the Protestant ethic, discipline, responsibility, and perseverance, had to be imposed from without, and looked to the "carrot and stick" of the marketplace as the best means of enforcing these values. At least for themselves, though, they apparently believed that they could forego the incentive of personal profit because their commitments to self-discipline and social responsibility were sufficient to inspire them to constructive and unselfish service to society.

Recently, a number of historians have argued that progressivism laid the intellectual foundation for what would eventually be called "pluralism" or "interest group democracy," i.e., a system of political economy based on controlled competition between government supervised organizations of businessmen, workers, farmers, and other groups in society. David Thelen, for one, seems to bemoan what he describes as a trend in progressivism away from an initial "insurgent" quest to create a consumer movement uniting all Americans across class and ethnic lines toward a more "modernist" approach relying on a less publicly spirited pursuit of group self-interest.[101]

The examination of the ideological development of the five men discussed here reveals that consumerism was an important element in progressivism. Thelen apparently believes that such a consumer oriented movement, had it continued, held out the promise of effectively advancing the common interests of all Americans. However, it would be more accurate to conclude that consumerism represented an essentially middle-class perspective which virtually ignored the problems faced by millions of Americans whose poverty severely limited their roles as consumers. By focusing on the way in which every American, as a consumer, seemed to be equally affected by the changes taking place in the structure of the economy, progressives managed to hold onto their long cherished view of America as a society free from the class divisions of the old world. Yet, it was the intensification of class disparities resulting from the different relation workers and capitalists had to the means of production which was the crucial fact of the Progressive era.

While the progressives discussed here all came to accept large scale corporate enterprise and the need for bureaucratic expertise in the public, as well as the private, sector, one must not exaggerate the extent to which they had developed either a theory of interest group politics or a conception of government as a positive force in the nation's economic life. They could not yet be accurately described as "pluralist" or "corporatist" thinkers before 1914. For the most part, they still conceived of government in negative terms exercising only a limited policing power over the marketplace. Even the newly established or strengthened regulatory commissions, the FTC and ICC, made no effort to establish the government's right to participate in any kind of economic planning in behalf of publicly determined goals. Bureaucracy, in other words, was needed to complement, not replace, the workings of the market. Nor did the liberals considered in this study put great emphasis on the importance of encouraging the growth of organizations among workers, farmers, or other groups in society to serve as a countervailing force to the power of business. At this stage in their evolution, their primary organizational interest was to bring government into the twentieth century. Only when confronted with the task of fully mobilizing the nation for war would progressives turn toward more advanced ideas regarding the proper role of government and interest group organization in the private sector.

Most historians examining progressivism have viewed the movement primarily as an attempt to eliminate abuses in the new industrial order and to curtail the unrestrained power of the trusts. In contrast, Gabriel Kolko contends that the establishment of "business control over politics" so that business could utilize "political outlets to attain conditions of stability, predictability, and security—to attain rationalization—in the economy" was the "significant phenomenon of the Progressive era." Kolko argues that the drive for "reform" in the early part of the twentieth century was spearheaded not by a declining old middle class or a rising new middle class, but rather by the "major economic interests" in American society. He contends, moreover, that "it was not the existence of monopoly that caused the federal government to intervene in the economy, but the lack of it." For in Kolko's view, it was the failure of the merger movement at the turn of the century to establish a fully stabilized monopolistic economic order which led the nation's industrial and financial leaders to seek such stabilization through the agency of government. Kolko thus concludes:

There were any number of options involving government and economics abstractly available to national political leaders during the period 1900–1916, and in virtually every case they chose those solutions to problems advocated by the representatives of concerned business and financial interests. Such proposals were usually motivated by the needs of the interested businesses, and political intervention into the economy was frequently merely a response to the demands of particular businessmen. In brief, conservative solutions to the emerging problems of an industrial society were almost uniformly applied. The result was a conservative triumph in the sense that there was an effort to preserve the basic social and economic relations essential to a capitalist society, an effort that was frequently consciously as well as functionally conservative.[102]

Kolko makes an important contribution to our understanding of the way in which progressive sponsored reforms actually affected the evolution of the American political economy. However, in analyzing the origins of the progressive movement, he exaggerates both the degree to which America's leading corporate interests remained subject to the unwanted rigors of competition after the turn-of-the-century wave of mergers, and the role played by those interests in initiating the movement to strengthen the powers of government. Those taking the lead in initiating the progressive movement were middle-class Americans like the men considered in this study, individuals who were concerned about the economic and political implications of the rise of unrestrained corporate power, the corruption of moral and spiritual values associated with the new industrial order, and the seeming impotence and inefficiency of government in the face of the tremendous social changes taking place. The movement for change instigated by these middle-class reformers was, however, in effect, co-opted by the very interests whose power the progressives sought to limit. As Robert Wiebe observes, the "progressive movement . . . changed businessmen considerably less than they had the movement."[103]

The failure of the progressive movement to institute a more egalitarian and democratic social order was due not only to the economic and political strength of the nation's dominant interests, but also to the progressives' inability to transcend their own liberal ideology. The progressives' continued acceptance of long-standing liberal assumptions regarding the lack of class divisions in America, the importance of the profit motive, the objectivity of market forces, and the dangers involved in political direction of the economy, made it virtually impossible for them to move the nation toward the elimination of poverty and the establishment of a more equitable distribution of wealth and power, or toward the development of an economic system in which the public interest might play a role at least equal to the pursuit of private profit. As a result of their ideological limitations, these men supported measures which, at best, only lessened some of the most obvious excesses of the new economic order. At worst, these measures created new agencies of government which were used to further consolidate and strengthen the power of America's dominant economic interests. To a large extent, the reforms of this era simply postponed any serious consideration of the basic problems confronting the nation. The coming of war would soon give added emphasis to these contradictions.

# CHAPTER V

# The Impact of War 1914–1920

THE First World War broke out in Europe just as progressivism in America had seemingly reached its peak. When the fighting started in the Summer of 1914, Josephus Daniels, Henry Stimson, Bernard Baruch, Donald Richberg, and Felix Frankfurter were all preoccupied with issues of domestic reform raised by the progressive movement. None could envision the tremendous impact the distant war would ultimately have on the problems which were then the focus of their concern. The war and its immediate aftermath, however, would significantly affect the careers of most of these men, as well as their thinking about the proper organization of the nation's political economy. In addition, it would, in the words of Murray Rothbard, prove to be "the critical watershed for the American business system."[1]

The outbreak of war in Europe came as a shock to men who were committed, at the time, to the peaceful reform of their own society. Frankfurter later recalled that in 1914:

One had high hopes that by the steady progress of free inquiry you could remake the world. It never dawned on anybody that a war like the great World War in 1914 was still possible—you know, "We've gotten beyond that. This is the age of reason."

Richberg, in his autobiography, expressed a similar attitude, stating that on the eve of the fighting he had been "convinced that the time of great wars was ended" because modern warfare "would be too destructive and too costly for any large nation seriously to consider going to war with another."[2]

Before the war came to an end in 1918, four of the men

considered in this study had been totally involved in America's war effort. Only Donald Richberg's career remained virtually unaffected by the conflict. He continued practicing law in Chicago throughout these years, his sole contribution to the national crusade consisting of occasional patriotic speeches in behalf of the Illinois Council of National Defense. In contrast, Henry Stimson threw himself wholeheartedly into the campaign for military preparedness during the period of American neutrality. After America's declaration of war, Stimson, who saw himself as "much more naturally a soldier than a lawyer," entered the army. Though forty-nine years old at the time, Stimson spent nine months on active duty overseas and left the service after the Armistice with the rank of colonel. Although the war thus had a significant impact on Stimson's life, his decision to seek battlefront duty removed him from any possible role in the formulation of government policy at home.[3]

Josephus Daniels, Bernard Baruch, and Felix Frankfurter, on the other hand, did significantly influence government domestic policy during the First World War. Daniels was Secretary of the Navy throughout the war and a member of the Council of National Defense which Wilson created in 1916 to administer and plan the military and industrial mobilization of the country. While neither Baruch nor Frankfurter were members of the government when the war began in 1914, each of them attained a position of leadership in the war administration which gradually evolved during the next four years. By the end of the war, Baruch, as Chairman of the War Industries Board, and Frankfurter, as Chairman of the War Labor Policies Board, had become the primary government policy makers in the areas of industry and labor, respectively.[4]

America's involvement in the First World War required an unprecedented collective effort to mobilize the nation's industrial, scientific, and human resources for a common purpose. As a result, the war experience raised the question of whether it would be possible to achieve such an all-encompassing national objective by relying on the automatic functioning of a private enterprise, free market economy. In the decade which preceded the war, reformers such as those examined here had already begun to call for government to take on increased responsibilities in relation to the nation's economic life. For the most part, however, they simply wanted government to take a more active role in establishing and enforcing guidelines which would restrict or eliminate unfair, illegitimate, or socially harmful forms of economic behavior. They did not envision government as a significant agency of public planning attempting to establish specific economic objectives according to a publicly defined conception of the national interest. They still relied upon the marketplace as the fairest and most impersonal means of determining the proper distribution of goods and services. Progressives did come to appreciate the importance of utilizing experts, technicians, and administrators to deal with the complex problems raised by life in industrial society, but because of their still limited conception of the role of government, they did not foresee the necessity of developing a massive public bureaucracy to operate, control, or even supervise the major economic institutions of the private sector. America's experience in the First World War, however, compelled men like Baruch, Daniels, and Frankfurter to consider seriously the possibility not only of active government planning and coordination of the economy, but also of government encouragement and sponsorship of the activities of the new organizational elites which had just begun to emerge in the years before the war.[5]

I

During the Progressive era, an expanding elite of managerial experts, engineers, and scientists experienced a steadily growing sense of professional self-consciousness and ambition. In 1915, however, there were still no existing institutional mechanisms through which the expertise of these professionals could be effectively put to work in the event America had to mobilize its resources for war. Ironically, the government official who took the first steps to remedy this situation was Secretary of the Navy Josephus Daniels.

While Daniels himself had little in common with the technically trained elite which had recently arisen in the United States, he realized that the country would need to utilize "the inventive genius" of America's technical experts "to meet the new conditions of warfare." Since the Navy did not have within its own ranks the scientific personnel necessary for the task which might lay ahead, Daniels decided in 1915 to seek the voluntary cooperation of experts in the private sector. He called upon America's most famous inventor, Thomas Edison, to serve as head of a newly established Naval Consulting Board which was to be composed of technical experts willing to volunteer their services for the good of the country. As a result of a suggestion by Edison, Daniels staffed the new Consulting Board with volunteers selected by the nation's leading professional societies of engineers and scientists. Most of the experts named, in fact, not only had technical training, but also had risen to important managerial and executive positions in some of the country's largest industrial firms. Their outlook, in other words, was shaped as much by the demands of business as by the demands of science. Thus, at the outset of the mobilization effort, Daniels acknowledged the government's dependence on expertise provided by the private sector and gave official recognition and status to organizations representing key segments of the nation's new managerial elite.[6]

Once the board was established, Daniels allowed its members great leeway in examining technical problems which the experts themselves considered potentially important in the event of war. One of the engineers named to the board, Howard Coffin, a vice-president of the Hudson Motor Company, quickly created a Committee on Industrial Preparedness. This committee conducted, in 1916, a pioneering nation-wide survey to determine the country's potential for war production, including the possibilities which existed for plant convertibility, standardization of products, and the use of scientific management techniques. Both the form of organization utilized by the Navy Consulting Board, volunteer representation from established associations and institutions in the private sector, and the actual work performed by the board, served as models for the government's subsequent war-time mobilization program.

While Daniels was not troubled by the fact that the Navy had to rely on private citizens and professional societies to deal with the scientific and technical problems of war, he was concerned about the implications of the Navy's dependence on a handful of corporations for the supply of needed war material. Almost from the moment he had become Secretary of the Navy, Daniels had been involved in continuous disputes with important corporations over prices being charged to the government for such essential products as armor-plate, smokeless powder, and refined oil. Daniels frequently proclaimed his belief in the necessity of competitive bidding on government contracts in order to insure fair prices. Frustration with the collusive practices of certain industries, however, had led him in some cases to call for the building of government-owned plants as a means of guaranteeing the competitiveness of bids from private companies. Even as prices shot up in the United States in 1915 and 1916 in response to war orders from abroad, Daniels continued to insist on open bidding, occasionally refusing all bids when he felt competitive offers were not being honestly made. This procedure at times resulted in the Navy falling behind in filling its orders. In Congressional testimony in the Spring of 1916, Daniels rejected a plan calling for the Federal Trade Commission to establish fair prices for steel supplied to the Navy, arguing that the government would have a difficult time determining the actual cost of production for a single item coming out of a factory which turned out a multitude of products. In addition, he simply did not feel that the government ought to put itself in the position of telling companies "what their profits should be." In Daniels' opinion, only the open market could do that fairly.[7]

In less than a year, Daniels was forced to reconsider his position on the subject of government price-fixing. In the early months of 1917, America's imminent entry into the war further drove up prices on the open market and made delays in the Navy's obtaining of needed supplies extremely dangerous. The Navy had very few factories of its own in which to produce war material. Daniels, therefore, was compelled to acknowledge the necessity of establishing the "closest co-operation between the manufacturers and the Government." In the extraordinary conditions created by war, Daniels had to admit that the open market could no longer consistently be counted on to determine fair and reasonable prices. Daniels, though, remained doubtful that the country's businessmen would unselfishly answer the "call of patriotism" and thus "be willing to overlook the opportunity of abnormal profits." Consequently, he came to accept the need for some kind of negotiated agreement between the government and industry regarding production and prices so that procurement delays could be minimized and profits kept within reasonable bounds.[8]

As early as March, 1917, Daniels agreed to a contract with a group of shipbuilders calling for the construction of battle cruisers according to a cost-plus formula which allowed the contracting firms a profit margin of 10 percent above their costs of production. Throughout the war, Daniels regretfully accepted the necessity of a number of similar arrangements. From the start, he "hated to do this, knowing the danger of overhead and rental being fixed at too high" a figure, but he acknowledged that in the "emergency" there was "nothing else to do."[9]

Perhaps the most important price negotiations undertaken by Daniels in 1917 involved the steel industry. Along with Baruch (whose role will be discussed below), Daniels became a key figure in the government's effort to convince the leaders of the steel industry, most particularly Elbert Gary of United States Steel, to establish a fixed schedule of prices below the inflated levels reached by March in anticipation of America's entry into the war. Gary's initial refusal to cooperate with the government not only reinforced Daniels' belief in the desirability of constructing a government-owned armor plate factory as a yardstick by which to measure the reasonableness of prices; it also led him to support unilateral price-fixing by the government. Only two months after America's declaration of war, Daniels had concluded that it had become necessary to fix the price of such essentials as steel, copper, coal, and oil. He even asked himself: "Why should we not fix the price of money?"[10]

Eventually, threats of government commandeering of steel plants convinced industry leaders to accept a form of negotiated price-fixing which became more prevalent during the course of the war than the use of cost-plus formulas. A single price to be paid by the government for a given product was established through discussions and bargaining between representatives of the affected industry and representatives of the government. All producers, large and small, subsequently received the same price from the government, regardless of production costs. While the prices finally set for steel were below the peak levels reached earlier in 1917, they were intentionally set high enough to make the production of steel profitable for practically every company in the industry. This was done in order to stimulate total output as much as possible.[11]

As the war continued, Daniels became increasingly unhappy with this approach to price-fixing, feeling that it gave too great a profit to the huge corporations which had the lowest production costs. Although Daniels was especially concerned that small independent businesses not be excluded from obtaining government contracts, he did not wish to see the government, in effect, subsidize big business in order to accomplish this goal. Instead, by the end of the war, he was arguing for a policy of lower fixed prices, but with the addition of mandatory pooling arrangements to spread around government contracts to all competent producers. Any losses suffered by high-cost producers would be made up, in Daniels' plan, by subsidies drawn from the excess profits of the most efficient low-cost producers in the industry. Still, Daniels realized that no matter what pricing policy was adopted by the government, some companies would inevitably reap extremely high profits from war-related orders. Consequently, he supported the enactment of an across-the-board excess profits tax as a means of returning to the public treasury any unwarranted gains resulting from the war.[12]

At about the same time in 1915 that Daniels first set in motion the government's mobilization of scientific and technical experts by creating the Naval Consulting Board, Bernard Baruch was considering a similar effort in the area of industrial preparedness. He foresaw a variety of supply and transportation problems arising in the event of a full-scale production effort and personally recommended to President Wilson, in September, 1915, the establishment of a volunteer commission of businessmen to formulate plans for the possible mobilization of industry. In August, 1916, Wilson responded to this suggestion, and to the advice of others, including Howard Coffin of the Naval Consulting Board, by supporting legislation creating a Cabinet level

Council of National Defense, to be assisted by a Presidentially appointed Advisory Commission. Baruch was one of the seven men named to the Advisory Commission.[13]

While Baruch had always been a firm believer in the efficacy of the laws of supply and demand, he quickly realized that war created a type of demand which differed "in its essential nature from the normal demands of peace."

In peacetime the free working of the market place can be trusted to keep the economy in balance. The law of supply and demand has *time* in which to operate. But in war that equilibrium must be achieved by conscious direction—for war, with its ravenous demands, destroys the normal balance and denies us time. And time means lives.

In order to achieve the "conscious direction" of the economy which he believed would be critical in any full-scale mobilization, Baruch initially envisioned a friendly and cooperative effort between representatives of government and the leaders of American industry.[14]

Before working with Daniels to secure a price agreement for steel, Baruch, as a member of the CND's Advisory Commission, had already set the precedent for such negotiations by meeting with the leaders of the copper industry. These men, not coincidentally, were former business associates and personal friends of Baruch. In early 1917, Baruch and the copper barons had amicably agreed upon what they all considered to be fair and potentially stable prices for copper. The steel negotiations proved to be more difficult though. Baruch even found it necessary to threaten Judge Gary with the possibility of a government takeover of the industry to win his acceptance of a price agreement. However, the underlying assumption upon which Baruch based his approach to industrial mobilization was that the government would ultimately have to rely on the existing institutional structure of private enterprise. Although relations between representatives of government and business were at times strained during the course of the war, it did not take long for industry leaders themselves to see the advantages of negotiating price and production agreements with government mobilization agencies. For such agreements not only guaranteed high profits, but also helped reduce the degree of economic instability and unpredictability which accompanied America's involvement in the war.[15]

Baruch's dealings with the copper and steel industries convinced him of the importance of establishing ongoing channels of communication through which government and industry could exchange information on war requirements and production capabilities in order to facilitate the smooth flow of needed war material. He thus expanded upon his early mobilization efforts by encouraging the creation of "cooperative committees of industry" for other crucial raw materials, such as tin, lead, oil, lumber, and rubber. These committees functioned like trade associations, serving as:

. . . centers of contact from which the Government's purchasing agencies could get full and authoritative information concerning both immediate and prospective supply capacities and the industries could get information showing immediate and projected Government needs.[16]

Like Daniels, Baruch thus played a crucial role in the government's evolving effort to mobilize the nation for war by encouraging the development in the private sector of voluntary organizations of administrative and technical experts which would wield governmental authority. As was the case with Daniels, however, Baruch did not see his task as creating a large or permanent government bureaucracy. The two leading students of Baruch's role in the industrial mobilization of the First World War agree that Baruch relied principally on his own personal contacts in the business world and on informal arrangements, rather than on formalized procedures and clearly established lines of hierarchical authority. He was, in the words of Jordan Schwarz, "an operator, not an organizer." Still, Baruch's encouragement for the creation of cooperative committees of industry was based on a recognition of the necessity of allowing those with special knowledge and skills to use the mantle of government authority for the purpose of managing the nation's war-time economy.[17]

Baruch's activities as a member of the CND's Advisory Commission were carried over into the War Industries Board which Wilson created in July of 1917. By this time, though, Baruch's reliance on informal committees composed largely of executives from the nation's dominant corporations, and his failure to establish clear lines of authority dividing those acting in behalf of the government from those representing the interests of industry, created political problems for the Wilson administration. Baruch himself acknowledged the problem in his initial approach to mobilization:

The unprecedented rapidity with which expansion occurred on every hand was soon accompanied by confusion and overlapping of duties and jurisdiction. Dissatisfaction began to come to light on the part of firms not directly represented on the committees. The possible misconception of the position of the committees in appearing to represent, even in a vague sense, both the buying and the selling interests was very soon felt.[18]

Baruch was convinced of the usefulness of working through cooperative committees of industry, but public and Congressional criticism forced him to create a more formalized structure in which there would be a clear dividing line between the representatives of government and the representatives of business. Baruch subsequently designated a specific individual as the War Industries Board agent for each of more than sixty commodities which were organized as separate sections of the WIB. Distinct, but parallel, War Service Committees of Industry were then created to function in conjunction with these official WIB commodity agents. These committees were, for the most part, set up under the auspices of the United States Chamber of Commerce, which itself had been established in 1912 as an association of business associations to foster coordination and cooperation across all sectors of the economy.[19]

Grosvenor Clarkson, a member and subsequent historian of the WIB, later summed up the results of the new organizational structure:

Businessmen wholly consecrated to Government service, but full of understanding of the problems of industry, now faced businessmen wholly representative of industry as distinct from Government. Cooperative but sharply separated points of contact were thus created.

Although the outward form of the mobilization organization had been modified in the direction of greater bureaucratization, the internal power relations and operating assumptions clearly remained the same. In their reconstituted form, the commodity sections continued to serve as the basic working units of the government's mobilization effort. When the War Industries Board was itself reorganized by Wilson in March, 1918, Baruch was rewarded for his leadership in the evolution of the war-time mobilization organization by being named chairman of a reconstituted and more powerful WIB.[20]

During the course of the war, Baruch came to believe that the government's most important role in the domestic mobilization was the setting of production priorities. He later called a system of priority classification the "synchronizing force" of industrial mobilization. The priority system Baruch and the WIB evolved was designed to curtail production of non-essential goods by insuring that basic raw materials which were in short supply were provided only to producers of needed war materiel. Priorities were also established to regulate access to the nation's increasingly overburdened transportation system in order to speed delivery of immediately needed war goods.[21]

While establishing priorities became the most important feature of the government's attempt to give direction to the economy, Baruch's approach to this task reflected his reliance on the voluntary cooperation of private business. The WIB did not have the staff to impose such a system on industry through compulsory government supervision, nor did Baruch favor the creation of the huge bureaucracy which would have been necessary to undertake such a program. Consequently, the operation of the priority system was left mainly to the discretion of the nation's businessmen, who voluntarily attached priority classifications to their orders according to guidelines set by the WIB.[22]

As a key figure in the government's attempt to stimulate industrial output, Baruch consistently concentrated on production totals, rather than on the fairness of prices paid by the government for needed war materiel. In this regard, his attitude contrasted somewhat with that of Daniels, who found it more difficult to accept what seemed to be excessively high prices and profits. Baruch, like Daniels, did become an early supporter of price controls in order to limit both profits and inflation. However, he felt that the primary objective of the mobilization administration, as he explained to Daniels in June of 1917, was obtaining adequate supplies, not maintaining reasonable prices: "I would rather pay too much now and get these pressing materials, even if I thought I was paying too high a price, than to wait and perhaps not get them in time."[23]

Unlike Daniels, Baruch never entertained serious doubts about the advisability of fixing prices at relatively high levels in order "to keep substantially in full operation every mill and blast furnace which contributed appreciably" to the production effort. He rejected both cost-plus and pooling arrangements as policies which would fail to maximize the incentive for increased production, i.e., the incentive of profit. Baruch also criticized the former proposal because he felt its implementation would have required the creation of a large government bureaucracy of bookkeepers.[24]

## II

While Baruch and Daniels were playing critical roles in the government's dealings with industry, Felix Frankfurter became a key figure in the formulation of government labor policy during the First World War. When Frankfurter left Washington in 1914 to begin his new career as a law professor, he was given a commission in the Army Reserve so that he could continue to give legal advice to the War Department. Shortly after America's declaration of war in the Spring of 1917, Secretary of War Newton Baker called Frankfurter back to Washington to discuss a number of questions concerning the Department's relations with labor. What was originally intended as a brief visit for purposes of consultation became a full-time commitment which lasted for the duration of the war. Frankfurter immediately became Baker's leading adviser on labor policy and, in the Fall of 1917, was named Counsel and Secretary of the President's Mediation Commission. Before the war ended, Frankfurter had become chairman of the single most important government agency dealing with labor policy, the War Labor Polices Board.[25]

From the time Frankfurter originally left the War Department in 1914 to the time he returned in 1917, his own career had brought him into increasingly closer contact with the problems of labor. When Louis Brandeis was nominated to a seat on the Supreme Court, Frankfurter succeeded his friend as counsel for the National Consumers' League. In that capacity, he defended the constitutionality of a number of minimum wage and maximum hours laws before the nation's highest court. Frankfurter had been an early admirer of Brandeis' pioneering efforts to incorporate information derived from the social sciences into legal briefs, and his own work defending laws regulating working conditions led him to become interested in the Taylor Scientific Management movement. He stepped back from a full commitment to Taylorism, however, because of his belief in the necessity of unionization as a means of both protecting the interests of workers and giving them a sense of participation and identification with their work. By 1917, when Frankfurter re-entered government service to help formulate a war-time labor policy, he was already convinced of the desirability of calling upon social scientists, industrial managers, union representatives, and government officials to cooperate in devising scientifically sound solutions to the nation's labor problems.[26]

Frankfurter first assumed significant responsibility in the war administration when he was named Secretary and Counsel of the President's Mediation Commission. In practice, he was in charge of the agency's operations. The commission had been established by Wilson in response to an outbreak of labor disputes in the West which threatened to disrupt the entire industrial mobilization. Wilson hoped that the commission would be able to mediate peaceful settlements in industries then being racked by serious labor warfare and that it would also be able to make recommendations as to how to avoid the repetition of such difficulties in the future. While touring the West, Frankfurter dealt with a variety of explosive situations, including the industrial warfare which was then ravaging the copper mines of Colorado and Arizona. Violent conflicts between labor and management had culminated in the infamous Bisbee deportations not long before Frankfurter arrived on the scene.[27]

Frankfurter's first-hand inspection of the situation in the West reinforced many of his previously held views about the problems of labor. While in Arizona he observed that the "bottom fact" of the problem was that the "men feel they were not treated as men" and that they "were without a share in determining the conditions of their labor." He commented that the workers enjoyed "no fellowship" in "the great industrial enterprise which absorbs them." The underlying issue, he concluded, was "not material but really spiritual." The managers of the mines, he wrote to his fiancee:

. . . are masters of the inanimate forces that are a mine. Mastering a mine they lightly assume that they know how to master men; they control a quarry and forget it's *also* a community. You see I'm getting much absorbed in all this—I hope I face it without prepossessions and I'm confident I haven't too many except—that human beings are human beings, and that even the Slavs and the Mexicans are not too hopelessly different, certainly not in desires and dignities from us who are the aristocrats, the privileged ones, of the world. The whole thing goes pretty fundamentally to what kind of a world we want—towards what kind of a world we want to build.[28]

Frankfurter was even more convinced, after his trip to the West, that unionization and collective bargaining were necessary elements in any resolution of the labor problem. Leaders of the copper industry, however, remained adamant in their opposition to union recognition. As a representative of the government, Frankfurter saw his job as simply restoring peace to the mines so that production could be resumed, rather than trying to bring about a revolution in labor relations in the industry. He was able to win from management a pledge that it would not discriminate against union members in its hiring practices, and he also gained acceptance for the establishment of administrative machinery to adjust grievances and to fix wages. This was as far as the mine owners would go, however. Frankfurter had no power to force them to yield to labor's key demand for union recognition.[29]

The final report of the President's Mediation Commission was written almost entirely by Frankfurter. It presented the President with a list of seven recommendations to serve as a guide for government labor policy during the remainder of the war. Frankfurter's first recommendation, interestingly enough, was the elimination of "profiteering . . . to the full extent that governmental action can prevent it," in order to lay to rest any "sense of inequality" which would "disturb the fullest development of labor's contribution to the war." Frankfurter called for government recognition of the principle of collective bargaining since "modern large-scale industry [had] effectively destroyed the personal relation between employer and employee—the knowledge and cooperation that came from personal contact," so that a "collective relationship between management" and labor had become "indispensable." He also advocated the establishment of the eight-hour day as a general rule and an educational campaign by the government which would portray labor "as part of the citizenship of the state." In all instances where decent working conditions and fair grievance procedures had been assured, Frankfurter asked labor to give up, voluntarily, "all practices which tend to restrict efficiency." Finally, Frankfurter advised Wilson to establish both a "unified direction" for all government dealings with labor during the war, and an ongoing agency, similar in purpose to the temporary Mediation Commission, to deal with future labor problems before they exploded into crisis situations.[30]

Following Frankfurter's suggestion, and advice from others, Wilson created a unified War Labor Administration in early 1918, with Secretary of Labor William B. Wilson serving as War Labor Administrator. As finally constituted, the War Labor Administration operated through two subsidiary bodies, a War Labor Board, chaired jointly by ex-President Taft and Frank Walsh, which mediated specific labor disputes, and a War Labor Policies Board, chaired by Frankfurter, which was designed:

. . . to standardize the rates of wages for similar work, the overtime policy, and the method of dealing with strikes; to act as a court of appeal to hear cases from those adjustment agencies which provided for appeals; to introduce the standard basic eight-hour day for all departments in which it had not been established, to standardize the method of employment by recruiting through the Employment Service of the Department of Labor; and to adopt and enforce uniform policies regarding the revision of government contracts to cover labor policy.[31]

As Chairman of the War Labor Policies Board, Frankfurter concentrated on rationalizing government employment practices and on seeking to establish, to the extent the board's limited powers allowed, fair and reasonable working conditions for all workers employed by firms doing business with the government. While Baruch was attempting to centralize and coordinate the purchasing activities of the government's numerous agencies and departments, Frankfurter made a similar effort to eliminate disruptive competitive bidding for labor among employers fulfilling government contracts. In addition, Frankfurter began to cooperate with Baruch, before the war ended, to develop an overall system of priorities for labor which would serve as a complement to the WIB's priority system for raw materials. Frankfurter's activities on the labor front thus parallelled those of Baruch on the industrial front. Frankfurter and Baruch, in other words, each recognized the need to streamline and coordinate government business practices, and to have the government provide overall direction to the mobilization effort in order to maximize production.[32]

At the same time, just as Baruch and Daniels were concerned with keeping prices and profits at reasonable levels, so did Frankfurter seek to gain industry acceptance of desirable working conditions and fair wages. Frankfurter was a strong supporter of making the eight-hour day a general principle of government labor policy. In his most dramatic experience as Chairman of the War Labor Policies Board, Frankfurter personally confronted Elbert Gary of U.S. Steel over this issue. Frankfurter advocated the eight-hour day both as a measure of equity to labor, and as a means of ultimately insuring greater productive efficiency in the war effort, stating that it was not only:

. . . the best industrial standard, judged by the needs of production carried over an appropriately long time and dealing with industry properly managed, but that such a working day is also essential in order to give opportunities for fruitful leisure, which alone can give us an educated and responsible democratic citizenship.[33]

Frankfurter initiated negotiations with Judge Gary early in the Summer of 1918 to get the eight-hour day adopted by U.S. Steel. Although Gary obstructed and delayed the progress of the discussions, Frankfurter's arguments and threats finally convinced the steel executive to accept the principle of a basic eight-hour day little more than a month before the end of the war. In this important test of wills and power, Frankfurter had won at least a qualified victory. As in the case of his previous experience with the copper industry, however, concessions regarding working conditions were granted by industry not only without the additional step of union recognition, but, in effect, in place of it.[34]

The War Labor Policies Board, under Frankfurter's leadership, also sought to establish a policy of wage standardization. Frankfurter described this program as meaning for workers what "price fixing means for the manufacturer." He explained that while:

. . . the price-fixing committee takes into account the cost of production and proper profits, so wage standardization must be built upon an accurate knowledge of the cost of living and a just estimate of what makes up the right American standard.

However, just as price-fixing was not intended solely as a means of establishing fair prices, neither did Frankfurter's conception of wage standardization represent an attempt to set wages without concern for their impact on the production effort. In fact, the program was designed "to secure the stabilization of employment conditions," whether that meant raising wages to reasonable levels to avoid labor troubles which disrupted production, or preventing employers in non-essential industries from raising wages in order to draw workers away from more vital industries.[35]

Frankfurter was often frustrated by the unenlightened attitude toward labor still held by many leaders of American industry. Like Daniels and Baruch, however, he did not believe that government takeovers of recalcitrant industries were a plausible means of rectifying the problems with which he came in contact. Prior to the creation of the War Labor Policies Board, while Frankfurter was still serving as the Secretary of the President's Mediation Commission, he became involved in negotiations to end a major strike against Pacific Telephone and Telegraph. He quickly came to the conclusion that though the government might use the threat of a public takeover of the telephone system as a means of pressuring company executives to negotiate, the prospects for successful government operation of the system were poor. As a result, Frankfurter was "determined, if possible, to avoid" such a course of action, not only because he particularly doubted Postmaster-General Albert Burleson's ability to head such a takeover, but also because he felt that:

. . . Washington was already taking in more than it could absorb. The general administrative conditions were not all that could be desired; indeed, far short of it, and should the government take over the telephone lines in addition to all else I didn't know who the people would be who were competent to have due regard for the needs of war, the needs of the government and also due regard to the human interests that were involved.[36]

## III

Even this relatively brief review of the ways in which Daniels, Baruch, and Frankfurter responded to the problem of mobilizing America for war reveals the extent to which the war experience stimulated, rather than halted or retarded, the continuing evolution of their thinking about how best to organize the nation's political economy. In this sense, the First World War, far from bringing an end to the ferment of the Progressive era, actually accelerated some of that era's key developments. During the course of the war, all three men came to realize that an effective mobilization effort could not be achieved by relying simply on the ordinary play of market forces. At least for the duration of the war emergency, a conscious attempt to direct and coordinate the nation's economic life would be required in order to stimulate sufficient war production, limit inflation, and promote a reasonably equitable distribution of the benefits and burdens arising from the war effort. The war thus caused these men to consider the possible advantages to be gained from creating a managed economy in which government would play a critical role by establishing overall objectives and priorities.

While Daniels, Baruch, and Frankfurter all came to agree on the necessity of a greatly expanded role for government as a coordinator and sponsor of economic planning in war-time, they sought to achieve such planning largely through the voluntary efforts of organized interests in the private sector. Even as they realized the importance of utilizing the skills of specially trained administrative and technical experts in the government's mobilization effort, they still viewed with fear the possible growth of a large government bureaucracy able to use coercive powers to control the nation's economic life. Hence, as Robert Cuff observes, they accepted as "a fundamental principle of the national war mobilization . . . the development of national policy through the institutional recognition of private individuals and private interest groups." [37]

None of the men discussed here was completely oblivious to the problems created by basing the war mobilization on the voluntary cooperation of private interests. They realized that some individuals and some business firms would seek to exploit the situation for their own selfish ends. At one time or another during the war, each of these men found it necessary to use at least the threat of a government take-over to win the cooperation of recalcitrant industry leaders. Daniels, moreover, came to believe that the progressive principle of public control of natural monopolies ought to be extended to government operation of the vital war-time transportation and communication industries. Still, these men believed that, as a rule, the nation's resources could most effectively be mobilized by relying on private enterprise and the incentive of profit. Their willingness to work through the existing system of economic institutions was due not only to their concern about the practical difficulties and dangerous time delays which would undoubtedly have accompanied any attempt to expand war production by building up the public sector, but also to their continuing faith in the major tenets of liberal ideology. [38]

Because they assumed that capitalism in America created no clear conflict in class interests, they believed that the motives of profit and patriotism could be merged so as to insure both an efficient and an equitable industrial mobilization. Thus even Daniels, who at times vociferously criticized businessmen for trying to profit inordinately from the war crisis, could deliver the following paean to the American Bankers' Association in September 1918 praising the way in which the bankers' contribution to the war effort succeeded in joining the demands of patriotism, profit, and efficiency:

The country is proud of you. You have shown the world that when your country calls, our bankers, like our soldiers and our sailors, have forgotten all selfish interests, all class interests, all interests of every kind, and with no thought of personal advantage or disadvantage, have set out to help win this war as best they can. And if we are proud of the spirit in which you have done this, we are no less proud of the splendid intelligence and the business efficiency with which you have translated your willingness to serve into actual efficient service, the magnitude of which cannot be overstated. . . .

I have spoken, incidentally, of your prosperous condition. It is pleasant to think that virtue is not always its only reward, that in helping your country, I think, perhaps you help yourselves. It is the silver lining to our present clouds, just as our boys will come back stronger, better, more efficient men than they went forth; just as our manufacturers have learned many things which will make them far more efficient as manufacturers than before the war began, just as the whole country will be a stronger, more efficient country than it ever was before, so have the bankers learned by actual experience that in sacrificing much to your country, you have found increased ways of efficiency by which you may also help yourselves.[39]

Rather than focusing on the potential inequities of an industrial mobilization based on the existing system of economic organization, the men discussed here came to feel that the war experience was more likely both to reinforce the nation's already strong sense of unity and to accelerate the country's adoption of even more efficient techniques of organization. Well before the United States entered the war, Henry Stimson contended that American involvement, if it came, would serve to advance the ideals of "nationalism and democracy." An early advocate of universal military training, Stimson viewed the "problem of preparedness" as but one aspect of the larger problem of "national fitness." He believed that the "swift march of civilization" had brought the nations of the world into "sterner and sterner competition," so that a "higher organization and a greater efficiency [was] being demanded in every phase of national activity,—in government, in manufacture, in trade and commerce, as well as in war." Mobilizing for war confronted

America with "the biggest problem" in her history, "whether the individual citizen" would have "the vision and the will to make the sacrifice necessary to create an efficient organization in our democracy equal to the task of meeting its competitors."[40]

Daniels and Stimson shared the belief that no inherent problem of class conflict existed to undermine the unifying "spirit of dominating American nationalism" which the nation's involvement in war only intensified. In fact, Daniels, who more than any other man considered in this study had fervently hoped to avert American participation in the fighting, was able to proclaim in May, 1918:

. . . in the shadow of this great war we say we are all Democrats, we are all Republicans, we are all Americans. . . . We have come to see the day, and I believe it has come forever, when sectionalism is dead and buried in America.

We are getting a new conception of Americanism—that we are all men of the same faith, differing only in opportunities and advantages; and with that spirit enlisted and the Republic mobilized, there is no more doubt that we will win than that God rules in the heavens.[41]

The faith the men discussed here had in the possibility of utilizing the existing system of economic organization to achieve an equitable and efficient war mobilization was further reinforced by their developing belief in the scientific objectivity of the administrative and technical experts who were coming to play an ever greater role in America's economic life. Of the three men being considered, Frankfurter may have been the most ardent advocate of utilizing supposedly impartial scientific expertise to determine optimal standards of industrial efficiency. Yet all three men, by relying upon organizational elites in the private sector to provide managerial leadership for the war mobilization, assumed, at least implicitly, that such experts would be guided by objective considerations of efficiency, whether they operated in the private or in the public sector. The belief that capitalism in America generated no permanent class divisions and no essential conflict of class interests was thus strengthened by a slowly evolving assumption that a growing body of professionally trained experts would help usher in a more highly rationalized form of captalism. The new professionals would provide a corps of impartial experts whose skills could be used to maximize the efficiency of the nation's market economy by directing or managing the way in which the market functioned.

It was hardly coincidental that the earliest support for an expanded role for government as a coordinator and director of the war mobilization came from engineers and professional managers like Howard Coffin. For these members of the nation's growing organizational elite not only believed that an effective mobilization effort required the use of their skills, but they also realized that by seizing the initiative at the outset they had the opportunity to advance their own status and power. As Robert Cuff observes, the new bureaucrats and technocrats who first stepped forward generally "stood apart from the dominant centers of power in American social and economic life." They did not themselves own controlling interests in, or exercise managerial control of, such great firms as U.S. Steel, Standard Oil, or the House of Morgan. These firms remained largely uninvolved with the government's first tentative steps to prepare the country for the economic impact of war. In the first two years of the European War, the House of Morgan itself was actually able to do more than the government to maintain a semblance of economic stability in the country since it acted as the sole purchasing agent in the United States for both England and France. The activities of professionals like Coffin, however, did establish a pattern which was soon followed by representatives of the most powerful institutions in the American economy when those interests began to appreciate the advantages of merging their own efforts at planning with those of the government.[42]

It is important to realize, however, that the outlook of the new professional managers and technical experts was not really as objective and scientific as Daniels, Baruch, and Frankfurter would have liked to believe. In fact, the outlook of this new elite was in no way incompatible with the interests of the nation's great corporate enterprises. David Noble has persuasively analyzed the actual function of the emerging technocratic elite:

Although, in the wake of modern engineering, corporate industry has taken on a scientific aura and capitalism has assumed the appearance of reason itself, the engineers have no more replaced the capitalist than science has replaced capitalism. Whether as managers or technical experts, the engineers have merely continued to serve capital, wittingly or not, their habits of thinking about problems and formulating solutions constituting for the most part a highly refined form of capitalist reason.

Thus, as the government's mobilization organization expanded, the professionals and businessmen who assumed positions of responsibility tended to identify the interests of the nation with the interests of its dominant business firms.[43]

Of course, industry and finance were not the only interests represented in Washington during the war. Labor, too, had its spokesmen in the mobilization administration. Grosvenor Clarkson claims that throughout the war "there were no dealings with 'big business' or any other kind of business in which labor was not consulted and represented." Yet, whereas the Advisory Commission to the Council of National Defense had a single union representative among its seven members, and the War Industries Board had a solitary union man on its executive committee; the War Labor Board included equal representation for management and labor, and the War Labor Policies Board headed by Frankfurter was composed solely of officials from the various purchasing agencies of the government. Thus, it did not include anyone to represent directly the interests of organized labor. Clarkson himself admits that Hugh Frayne, the union man appointed to the WIB, was chosen not "to represent labor, but to manage it." In addition, the practice of relying on "Dollar-a-Year-Men," who volunteered their services to the government meant, as Daniels later realized, that only those who were wealthy would be able to afford government service.[44]

Was America's liberal approach to mobilizing for war as effective and equitable, in fact, as the liberals discussed here believed, in theory, it could be? In order to answer this question, one must examine the extent to which the war economy was successful in accomplishing the three major goals established by those in charge of the war mobilization: adequate war production, stable prices, and a fair distribution of the benefits and burdens accompanying the war effort. First, though, it is necessary to review the state of the American economy on the eve of the First World War.

Although the years immediately preceding the start of World War One are usually characterized as a period of prosperity, the American economy experienced a significant degree of stagnation between 1907 and 1915. Unemployment in 1914 averaged 8 percent, and the initially unsettling effect on America's export trade resulting from the outbreak of war abroad helped drive the figure up to an annual average of nearly 10 percent for 1915. The manufacturing and transportation industries were especially affected by the stagnation of America's prewar economy. Unemployment in these industries was 13 percent in 1914. In this same period, it will be recalled, inequality in the distribution of wealth may have reached its all-time peak in American history. The maldistribution of wealth in prewar America held down the potential growth of demand which would have been necessary to achieve full employment; while, on the supply side, the concentration of control in industry, which tended to keep prices artificially high, limited industry's need to make full use of its productive capacity. In sum, the American economy in 1914 was not performing at anywhere near its potential.[45]

After initially creating a temporary damper on economic activity, the European war soon proved to be a tremendous boon to the American economy. War orders from England and France quickly provided the demand for American goods which the American economy had been unable to generate internally. Before the United States had itself entered the war, the Allies had injected about five billion dollars into the American economy. By the end of 1916, manufacturing output had increased 39 percent, mining output had gone up 26 percent, and activity in the railroad industry had risen 24 percent. As a whole, the Gross National Product had increased 14 percent in two years. The slack which had existed in the economy was more than taken up, so that unemployment had practically been eliminated before the United States entered the war.[46]

After 1916, in spite of the efforts of agencies like the Council of National Defense and the War Industries Board, additional stimulation to the nation's industrial output proved to be much more difficult. In fact, during America's actual participation in the war in 1917 and 1918, there may have been a slight decrease in the total physical output of the nation's manufacturing plants. The system of priorities created by the war administration, and the lure of high prices for needed war materiel, did succeed in shifting the prewar distribution of production, so that the performance of war industries was generally better than that of manufacturing as a whole. However, even in the critical steel industry, total output actually declined in the last year of the war. While Baruch, in particular, later expressed great pride in the accomplishments of American industry in the war, it is clear that the government's policies to stimulate production were not an unqualified success.[47]

More than anything else, the problem of controlling war-inspired inflation forced Daniels, Baruch, and other liberals to support an expansion of the government's power over the economy. In the sixteen months before Baruch initiated, in 1917, the policy of government negotiations with certain industries to establish supposedly reasonable prices, the nation experienced a rapid inflationary surge which raised the average price of all commodities nearly 50 percent. The average price of metals, in fact, skyrocketed by July 1917 to a level three-and-one-half-times higher than it had been in 1913.[48]

Following its creation, the WIB was successful in at least curbing inflation. During the last eight months of the war, while Baruch was WIB chairman, inflation slowed to an annual rate of roughly 10 percent. Not surprisingly, inflation was most effectively reduced in those sectors of the economy over which the government's mobilization agencies exercised greatest control. Price "fixing" was generally limited to raw materials, especially metals. For these materials, prices increased only 8 percent in 1918. However, in the same period, both the price of manufactured goods, and retail prices as a whole, rose 17 percent. Grosvenor Clarkson observes that price-fixing, "contrary to popular notion," was not intended to be "primarily the champion of the oppressed people against extortion and profiteering." It was designed to spur production. The WIB's lack of personnel and its failure to establish a comprehensive price-control system, thus limited the effectiveness of the government's ability to maintain a stable overall price level. While the war mobilization agencies were partially successful in controlling inflation, their success was a result not of their reliance on voluntary cooperation and restraint, but rather of their willingness to use the threat of government coercion.[49]

In analyzing the effectiveness of the liberal approach to war mobilization, assessing the mobilization's degree of success in ensuring a fair distribution of the benefits and burdens accompanying the war effort presents the greatest difficulties. There is, of course, no absolute standard of fairness by which to measure the equitability of the war mobilization. The war, in fact, left what might be described as an ambiguous legacy. In some respects, the mobilization clearly benefitted those who had been at the bottom of the social ladder in 1914. Not only did the war virtually eliminate uinemployment, but it also had the effect of improving working conditions by fostering greater acceptance of the eight hour day and by encouraging the growth of unionism. In large part because of sympathetic government policies, labor union membership increased from 2.7 million in 1914 to 4.2 million in 1919, though this still represented only one eighth of the wage earning population.[50]

Moreover, the First World War, according to Williamson and Lindert, "had a remarkable egalitarian impact" on the distribution of income and wealth in America. The nature of war production resulted in a heavy increase in the demand for unskilled labor, at the same time that the raising of a large army and the halt in immigration served to restrict the supply of such labor. Wages for unskilled labor consequently rose in relation to wages for skilled labor and to the cost of services by professionals. This decline in wage differentials became a crucial factor in an overall reduction in income and wealth inequality. The share of total income received by the top one percent of the population went down from 15.6 percent in 1916 to 12.7 percent in 1918. Looked at from another perspective, real wages for unskilled workers increased by almost ten percent between 1914 and 1919. The war, however, did not have an equally beneficial impact on all workers. While the unskilled improved their position, skilled workers and those on fixed salaries saw their positions deteriorate significantly. Skilled workers experienced a decline of 11 percent and those on fixed salaries a drastic reduction of 25 percent in real wages between 1914 and 1919.[51] The figures on the reduction of inequality in the distribution of income during the war are somewhat misleading for another reason as well. They measure income received by individuals, but not all the gains made by corporate enterprises, since they reflect only those corporate profits distributed as dividends and not those retained as undistributed surpluses.

Baruch, Daniels, and Frankfurter all opposed war "profiteering," but they also accepted the profit incentive as the best means of stimulating production. Consequently, they all agreed that it was necessary to impose an excess profits tax on business so that unwarranted corporate profits could be recaptured by the public treasury. The tax which was adopted in 1917 subsequently raised $2.25 billion in federal revenues in the fiscal year ending June, 1918, and it helped make total after-tax corporate profits lower in 1918 than they had been in either 1916 or 1917. Even with price controls and an excess profits tax, however, corporate earnings in 1917 and 1918 increased significantly over their prewar levels. George Soule notes that 46 typical manufacturing corporations increased their dividend payments from $209 million in 1913 to $384 million in 1917 and $343 million in 1918. In his study of the steel industry, Melvin Urofsky concludes that "at no time in its history" did the industry enjoy "higher profits than during the First World War."[52]

Yet the greatest corporate gains were reflected not in dividends paid out to individual stock holders, but rather in surpluses retained as corporate savings. The war experience, in fact, demonstrated the tremendous difficulties inherent in any effort by the government to recover excess profits once such profits entered the treasuries of American corporations. The imposition of an excess profits tax not only encouraged corporations to develop cost accounting methods which could be used to understate taxable profits, but it also acted as a stimulus to the accumulation of undistributed surpluses which could then be used to finance corporate expansion. In 1918, the undistributed surplus of U.S. Steel was nearly half-a-billion dollars, considerably more than twice the amount of the firms net earnings. For the 46 typical manufacturing corporations cited by Soule, corporate savings also significantly exceeded corporate dividends during the war. Ironically, the war thus had the effect of reducing the power of America's finance capitalists by making the nation's large manufacturing corporations less dependent on external sources of investment capital.[53]

The war mobilization may appear, at first glance, to have benefitted labor and capital in roughly equal proportions. In retrospect, however, it can be seen that most of the gains made by labor proved to be temporary, while those made by capital were longer lasting. The leveling trend in income distribution not only came to a halt with the end of the war, but was, in fact, reversed in the years which immediately followed. By 1929, inequality had again reached the peak levels of 1914. The movement toward greater equality in the distribution of income during the war was only the temporary product of an exceptionally heavy demand for an unusually restricted supply of unskilled labor. It was not the result of any permanent change in the structure of the American political economy. While labor union membership increased during the war, the major industries utilizing factory labor successfully resisted labor efforts to win union recognition. In the years following the end of the war, union membership declined significantly.[54]

In contrast, America's great corporate enterprises continued to capitalize on their war-time gains even after the war had ended. The huge surpluses accumulated during the war helped make possible the expansions and mergers of the 1920s which further consolidated power within the American economy. In addition, the war mobilization not only stimulated continuing industry attempts to standardize and rationalize production; but it also served as a model and precedent for subsequent efforts by America's corporate leaders to utilize the legitimizing power of government to sponsor or sanction forms of industrial planning and coordination which served, in effect, to enhance the position of dominance already enjoyed by the nation's largest firms.

The same pattern of development which characterized the reforms implemented in the Progressive era thus also characterized the war-time mobilization process. Agitation for an expanded role for government began outside the major centers of power in the country, largely among an aspiring group of technically trained professionals and among a more established group of patriotically motivated Americans such as Henry Stimson. Before long, however, the nation's most powerful economic institutions began to react to the potential dangers and benefits to their own interests entailed in an expansion of the government's functions. Several factors then worked together to enable these dominant institutions not only to protect their own interests in the face of such agitation, but even to exploit this agitation for their own ends by coordinating their activities with those of the state.

There was, of course, no immediately available institutional alternative to basing the war mobilization on the existing organization of the nation's political economy. However, the fact that individuals in positions of power such as Daniels, Baruch, and Frankfurter operated on the basis of a set of assumptions which did not fundamentally challenge the legitimacy of that organization was also an important factor in the ultimate outcome of the war mobilization. These men attempted to develop government policies which would have insured a fair distribution of the burdens and benefits of the war effort. Yet their continuing belief in the greater efficiency of private, as opposed to public, enterprise and in the importance of the profit motive as a spur to economic activity, and their desire to avoid the creation of a large government bureaucracy, combined to make it virtually impossible for them to accomplish the goal of an equitable mobilization. The enactment of a radically different mobilization policy may have been a practical impossibility given the immediacy of the country's production requirements and the lack of an already existing government bureaucracy to run or closely supervise American industry. Still, as a result of their wartime experiences, liberals such as Daniels, Baruch, and Frankfurter should have at least gained a better understanding of the inherent contradictions between their ideals of justice and equality and their ideological commitment to American capitalism.

## IV

With the end of the war, American liberals were immediately confronted with the question of whether the government ought to continue in peace-time its newly developed role as a central agency for economic planning and coordination. Bernard Baruch took great pride in the accomplishments of the War Industries Board. It was only natural that he would consider the possibility of continuing the system of WIB economic controls after the Armistice, at least in order to ease the transition from a war-time to a peace-time economy. A number of important business and financial leaders, moreover, favored such a move because they feared the destabilizing effects of a rapid end to government regulations once the war ended. As late as November 12, 1918, Baruch was sending out trial balloons in the press to test public reaction to the continuation of controls. President Wilson, however, was firmly opposed to the idea of a post-war extension of the war-time mobilization agencies' authority. Wilson had had misgivings, all along, about the government's cooperation with big business and the virtual suspension of the antitrust laws which that cooperation entailed, fearing that private industry was taking advantage of the situation for its own benefit. Once Wilson's desire for a quick dismantling of controls became apparent, Baruch followed the President's lead and gave up the idea of continuing the WIB into peace-time. Baruch thus reported to Wilson on November 27, 1918:

The work of the War Industries Board is actually over with the exception of closing up the details. The American people would resent, I believe, the continuance of apparent war powers; and further continuance of the War Industries Board, shorn as it is of its powers, would create a lack of respect for the government which sought to maintain unenforcible regulations. Therefore, I think the sooner it closes up its work and leaves, the better it will be for all concerned.

I think it would be a great lesson to the world if the citizen soldiers, be they industrial or military, who responded to the call of the Government, shall as the need passes, be mustered out.[55]

Baruch's final decision in favor of abandoning controls as quickly as possible was a product of a number of factors. First, it is unlikely that he would have pushed too hard for a course of action opposed by Wilson, since such persistence might have endangered the special relationship with the President he had developed. Even judging the case strictly on its merits, Baruch must have had mixed feelings about giving the War Industries Board continued life. On the one hand, he had learned to appreciate what could be done when the government intervened to give coordination and direction to the economy. On the other hand, he undoubtedly feared that once the fighting stopped the unity of purpose which had been essential to the operation of the war-time system of controls would quickly disappear. Moreover, the WIB would have been without legal power after the Armistice. It would, therefore, have required a renewed mandate from either the President or Congress to continue operating. Such a mandate would have necessitated a revision of the anti-trust laws, which, at the time, was probaby politically impossible.

In addition, Baruch had not abandoned his faith in a market economy. He was not himself sure how he felt about establishing, on a permanent basis, the government's right to intervene in the economy on an extensive scale. Baruch had, after all, justified the government's war-time intervention in the economy by viewing the war as an exceptional emergency situation requiring a response by the government which might not have been appropriate in peace-time. Still, a tension had been created in Baruch's mind between his ideological commitment to a free-market economy and his practical experience with the possible advantages of business-government cooperation and joint planning. This tension was to remain a significant factor in his thinking about the political economy for the rest of his life.

Baruch also had personal reasons for going along with Wilson's wishes to end the board's life. At the time of the Armistice, Baruch had received a position of great public acclaim for his war-time services, and there can be no doubt that he would have been hesitant to become involved in a post-war experiment in economic planning and government regulation which might have endangered his public image. Calling for the permanent suspension or modification of the anti-trust laws, or failing to maintain stable economic conditions after the war if controls had been continued, might have put Baruch's entire WIB experience in a bad light and thus undermined the position of public esteem that Baruch had finally achieved. In the end, therefore, Baruch was willing to let the WIB die after the Armistice, but that did not mean that he wished either to give up the personal satisfactions and rewards of public life or to see the government fail to capitalize on the lessons of the war mobilization. As he later said:

The WIB experience had a great influence upon the thinking of business and government. WIB had demonstrated the effectiveness of industrial cooperation and the advantages of government planning and direction. We helped inter the extreme dogmas of laissez-faire, which had so long molded American economic and political thought. Our experience taught that government direction of the economy need not be inefficient or undemocratic, and suggested that in time of danger it was imperative.[56]

Baruch's final report on the accomplishments of the War Industries Board was published in 1921. In this document, he recommended that the WIB's most significant institutional innovation, its system of cooperative committees of industry, ought to be preserved and expanded on a permanent basis. He argued that "these associations" were "capable of carrying out purposes of greatest public benefit" and explained that they could help "eliminate wasteful practices" in industry by encouraging standardization of products and the localization of production "in places best suited economically for it." As centers for the "exchange of trade information," they could also contribute to greater industrial efficiency by more effectively bringing together producers and purchasers, so that "supply and demand" could "be more economically balanced."[57]

Baruch recognized, however, that such business "combinations" were also capable "of carrying out purposes of greatest public disadvantage," because they would have the power to regulate production and prices and to favor "one type of buyer over another." Consequently, Baruch claimed:

The question, then, is what kind of Government organization can be devised to safeguard the public interest while these associations are preserved to carry on the good work of which they are capable. . . . the experience of the War Industries Board points to the desirability of investing some Government agency, perhaps the Department of Commerce or the Federal Trade Commission, with constructive as well as inquisitorial powers—an agency whose duty it should be to encourage, under strict Government supervision, such cooperation and coordination in industry as should tend to increase production, eliminate waste, conserve natural resources, improve the quality of products, promote efficiency in operation, and thus reduce costs to the ultimate consumer.

. . . The purpose contemplated is not that the Government should undertake any such far-reaching control over industry as was practiced during the war emergency by the War Industries Board; but that the experience of the war should be capitalized.[58]

Felix Frankfurter also felt that there were lessons to be learned and applied from the war-time mobilization. Like Baruch, Frankfurter at one time gave serious thought to the possibility of continuing government controls on the economy into the immediate post-war period in order to smooth the nation's transition from war to peace. As early as June, 1918, though, he seems to have been aware that continued post-war controls were likely to meet opposition both from within and without the Wilson administration. At that time he asked Professor Walton Hamilton to "formulate a quiet, unostentatious, scientific program" for reconversion. Frankfurter was careful, though, to make the request on a personal and confidential basis, rather than in his official capacity as head of the War Labor Policies Board. Frankfurter wished to see the government continue its war-time policy of insisting that certain minimum standards for wages and working conditions be written into all contracts to which it was a party, but by the end of the war, he, like Baruch, recognized the impossibility of extending the life of the mobilization agencies into peace-time. At a conference on demobilization held in late November, he called upon the government to continue serving as a "clearing house of knowledge and information" relating to industrial relations. He also expressed the hope that the government would continue to "furnish instruments of arbitration where there is difficulty." Frankfurter admitted, however, that:

. . . our traditions of laissez-faire are tremendous, and the direct participation of the government is likely to be a meager one in the next few years. The dominant hope to one who has watched as closely as he could, is not in government, but in the consensus of public opinion that must assert itself in industry.[59]

Frankfurter came out of the war with an increased appreciation of the need for American industry to avoid the "chaos of unbridled competition." Since he believed that in the forseeable future the use of government power to accomplish this end was impracticable and undesirable, he counted on the ability of social scientists and professionally trained experts like himself to convince the American people, in general, and America's business leaders, in particular, that improved working conditions and a more scientific approach to industrial problems would improve productivity and thereby increase profits, so that ultimately all of American society would benefit. In 1919, in an article discussing the future of industrial relations, he noted the importance of applying the insights of scientific management to entire industries, and not just to individual factories. In the following year, he supported the concept of an industry-wide "representative committee" to deal with the problems then besetting New York's clothing industry. Frankfurter's interest in industrial cooperation thus paralleled Bernard Baruch's post-war concern for a more rationalized economy. Frankfurter, however, went beyond Baruch in that he explicitly favored the inclusion of representatives of labor and the public, as well as management, in such industrial organizations. Cooperative efforts by the owners of American industry would be beneficial to the nation as a whole, in Frankfurter's view, only when workers and impartial experts participated in determining the direction of those efforts.[60]

Josephus Daniels had only grudgingly accepted the need for government to develop a cooperative relationship with business in order to facilitate the planning and coordination necessary for an effective war effort. Consequently, he was less enthusiastic than either Baruch or Frankfurter about the possibility of continuing into peace-time the corporatist approach utilized in the war mobilization. Reviewing the nation's war experience, Daniels reiterated his belief in the desirability of a competitive free enterprise economic system:

Looking back at it now, the mere suggestion of waiving competition— and thereby striking at the very foundation of the system—brings a smile of incredulity. But it was no joke at the time. Scarcely had war been declared when requests came from a number of quarters for authority "to cut red tape" by doing away with competition, the argument being advanced that deliveries could thereby be expedited and important work accelerated. The idea was not easy to suppress, because its many advocates really believed they were right and insisted upon convincing superior authority. The answer was that competition was bound to speed things up rather than retard them and that, in any event, the responsible officials in Washington had given the matter due consideration and decided definitely and finally that competition must continue uninterruptedly, as to everything except where demand so largely exceeded the supply as to compel priority orders.[61]

The war mobilization did, nonetheless, affect Daniels' thinking about the economy. It served at least to bring into question the validity of many of his liberal assumptions concerning the relationship between politics and economics. Just before the Armistice, Daniels proclaimed that the war experience would prove to be "fundamental" and that "its effect will be to change everything." "We will not be afraid in peace," he said, "to do revolutionary things that help mankind, seeing we have become accustomed to doing them in war." He was particularly concerned with the fight to keep radio communication, which had been developed by the Navy during the war, under public control. The war, he believed, had also demonstrated the advantages of public control of the telephone, telegraph, railroads, and even shipping.[62]

Daniels clearly revealed the unsettling effect the war had on his thinking in a speech delivered at the University of California in 1919. He told his audience that it was essential to remain "open minded" when considering "the best way of making democracy safe for the world."

The old-time economic doctrine of supply and demand must be reopened. Is it able to prevent monopolization of the necessities of life? Or does it only secure competition in labor while combinations control the price of food and clothing? Can legislation destroy the weights which hamper its working or must government in peace as in war fix the price of commodites to protect the public and prevent profiteering? How can capital and labor work without strikes and lockouts? That is a question of transcendent interest and importance. To its study the wisest men must devote themselves.[63]

V

Although Donald Richberg and Henry Stimson were not directly involved in the government's war-time mobilization of industry, their views as to the proper organization of the nation's political economy were also influenced by the war and its immediate aftermath. In fact, the chaotic transition from war to peace and the accompanying labor strife produced by the quick ending of war-time controls caused all five men discussed here to give closer attention than ever before to the role of labor in a liberal economic order.

In the months immediately following the end of the war, unemployment soared to approximately 7 percent. The economy soon recovered, but with recovery came severe inflation. The consumer price index in 1919 rose 15 percent above its 1918 level. As a result, millions of workers were forced to resort to strikes in an effort to gain wage increases so that they could avoid suffering a decline in their standard of living. While organized, skilled workers were actually able to recoup some of the losses in real wages they had experienced during the war, unskilled workers saw their real wages decline in 1919. The year after the Armistice proved to be one of the most turbulent years in the history of American labor relations.[64]

The nation's war experience and difficult transition to a peace-time economy had a profound impact on Richberg's thinking about the role of labor in American society. From the outset of the war, Richberg took seriously the rhetoric of democracy which was used to justify America's participation in the fighting. One month after America's declaration of war, he argued in the New Republic that in order to "defend and perpetuate our political democracy," it was necessary to "establish democracy in the commercial government" which was "the real government of the nation." Richberg contended that labor had to be given a voice in the direction of industry and that management recognition of unions afforded the most effective means for achieving such "democratization of industry."[65]

Several months later, Richberg took it upon himself to approach J. Ogden Armour, a leading figure in Chicago's meat packing industry, to discuss the abysmal working conditions in the stockyards. He asked Armour: "How can I talk about democracy when you make a mockery of the word in the yards?" Richberg went on to claim that a successful war effort depended on the "whole-hearted, voluntary support of labor," and that unionization represented the "most efficient way" of securing such cooperation.

If labor is to do its part in this war, labor must be organized thoroughly in order that its responsible representatives may meet, as the responsible representatives of the employing interests meet, and plan with government officials to give the greatest amount of service possible, while at the same time protecting themselves against carrying an unequal share of the national burden.[66]

Richberg later recalled that the "hardest of all problems" for him to understand during the war was why it should have been deemed "noble and just" for labor to work "without adequate compensation" in behalf of the war effort, while, at the same time, it was considered "necessary and righteous to offer extraordinary rewards to persuade men to contribute their property to the same great cause." In the midst of the war, Richberg warned Armour that if America's business leaders persisted in their "arrogant methods" and "short-sighed" selfishness, they might ultimately create a sense of "class consciousness" among American workers which could produce a "revolutionary" movement in the United States seeking to "destroy every personal and property right which the class conscious capitalist holds so dear." Richberg believed it was fortunate that American workers had not yet become "fully class conscious" because they still hoped to become the "capitalist[s] of tomorrow." However, he concluded that the lesson of the war was that America would suffer from alternating periods of "war with profiteering and peace with poverty" until the nation succeeded in democratizing its industrial life. Looking to the future, neither "Roosevelt progressivism," nor the "barren dogmatism of state socialism" were adequate, in Richberg's view, to the challenge which faced the nation.[67]

The labor turmoil of 1919 reinforced Richberg's belief in the necessity of incorporating organized labor more fully into America's economic life. Early in 1920, in a letter to Herbert

Hoover, the man Richberg hoped would soon become the Republican presidential nominee, Richberg spelled out a general plan for reforming the nation's industrial order. The underlying cause of the "industrial sickness" then plaguing the United States, Richberg argued, was the "unnatural competition" between labor and capital which had come to characterize American industry. Not only did the owners of individual industrial enterprises maintain a state of "warfare between themselves and those whom they employ[ed]," because they sought "to obtain the labor investment at the lowest rate of interest in order to pay the highest rate of interest on the capital invested;" but there was also industry-wide cooperation between all the "capital controllers" on one side and all the "labor controllers" on the other, which further reinforced the unnatural sense of competition between capital and labor. Richberg claimed that the nation's experience in the First World War, when "natural co-operation" between all those involved in the same enterprise had become "necessary for self-preservation," had proved how "unsound" the system of "unnatural competition" was. "The industrial problem," according to Richberg, was thus "to establish co-operation inside industrial units and permit the free action of supply and demand and regulation of competition to govern industry as a whole." [68]

Richberg contended that the public had the right to insist that industry be organized in such a way as "to eliminate the necessity or desirability of strikes," since industrial warfare menaced the "prosperity and the actual security of the community." Because a corporation existed "by will of the State," it was, in Richberg's view, "wholly within the power of the State to refuse to permit a corporate organization" to create an "economic autocracy" which would undermine "the political ideals of democracy itself." [69]

Richberg thus asserted the government's responsibility to guarantee the right of workers, who "invested" their "entire capital in [an] enterprise by devoting their services to it," to share in the "control of the enterprise" in which they were involved. The result, Richberg was certain, would be beneficial to all concerned:

Clearly the capital investors and the labor investors in an individual unit have joint interests to make the business as profitable as possible, to compete with other industrial units and thereby promote their personal interests. Having thus joint interests they should be joined in the control and join in sharing the profits of the enterprise. As such cooperation in industrial units increases, the cost of obtaining capital will necessarily diminish because the risk of capital invested in an enterprise, free from internal dissension, must be much less than the risk of capital invested in an enterprise constantly involved in civil war.[70]

The war years obviously marked an important evolution in Richberg's thinking about the political economy. Certain previously held assumptions, however, continued to provide the basic framework for his approach to the subject. To begin with, Richberg's proposal for restructuring American industry reflected a strong belief in the underlying community of interest between labor and capital. Competition was natural between firms engaged in the same line of business, not between owners and workers involved in the same company. Class conflict, in other words, was not necessarily a product of capitalism. In fact, Richberg advocated an expanded role for organized labor within the nation's private enterprise system as a means of averting the development of class consciousness among workers.

In addition, while Richberg favored increased cooperation within individual industrial enterprises, he continued to rely on the marketplace to govern relations between business firms and to regulate the operation of the economy as a whole. He still feared the possibility of government developing coercive powers so great that it would be able to dictate to private industry on the basis of politically determined economic goals. Even in calling for government to require corporate enterprises to adopt a more democratic form of organization, Richberg insisted that he did not see the problem as "one of passing laws to compel men to do right," but rather as one "of creating conditions under which a man's individual interest will be found in rendering his best service to the community." By 1920 Richberg had come to the conclusion that the American economic system as it then operated had serious defects. However, he still believed that a competitive private enterprise system was a solid foundation upon which to build a just economic order. All that needed to be done, in his view, was to bring labor more fully into the existing system.[71]

Of the five men discussed here, Henry Stimson was furthest removed from the problems arising from America's war-time mobilization of industry. Yet when Stimson returned home following the Armistice, he, too, concluded that the war had demonstrated the need for certain organizational reforms. He perceived an increase in support among many of the nation's "most prominent business men" for the kind of governmental reforms he had advocated before America's entry into the war, since these business leaders had themselves now witnessed first-hand "the unbusinesslike methods of our central government" during their service as volunteers in the government's war mobilization. Already, he noted, many of these war-time "dollar-a-year-men" were "going through the country preaching the necessity of a federal budget," one of Stimson's pet pre-war reforms. Daniels, incidentally, also supported a new budget system. He noted that with "the steady improvement in management of public business," the need for "experts in commercial methods"would increase so that soon "none except these experts will be able to carry on the Government's fiscal and business affairs."[72]

The upsurge of social unrest which occurred during the first year of peace gave added impetus, in Stimson's mind, to the necessity of bringing greater efficiency and accountability to the practices of government. Writing to Giffort Pinchot in December, 1919, Stimson observed:

I disbelieve more than ever in dislocated machinery and checks and balances which diffuse responsibility and prevent the machinery from going on. The more complicated and difficult our social situation becomes, the more imperative it is that we should have such a responsible government.

It is idle, and in a sense unfair to tell our laboring classes that they must refrain from direct action and resort to the methods of democracy when the methods of democracy seem to be skillfully arranged so as to thwart the enactment into law of the wishes of an intelligent majority.[73]

The problems of labor had never been of central concern to Stimson, but, as in the case of the other men discussed here, the events of 1919 compelled him to take a closer look at the situation of American workers and to consider their proper role in the industrial order. In the Summer of 1919, Stimson affirmed his belief in the right of labor to strike "as the most effective weapon now in the hands of the working man for bettering his industrial condition." However, he went on to warn that the use of strikes not "be allowed to cross over into the . . . sphere of political contests." He argued that if the "principle of using industrial force in politics becomes recognized, political democracy is doomed."[74]

By the end of the year, Stimson's thinking on the problems of industrial relations had further crystallized. In a letter intended for publication, he commented:

In my opinion, the question between labor and capital in this country will not be solved by solutions which come from the top. At the present there is over-organization on the side of labor, just as in the past there has been over-organization on the part of capital. By this, too much power has been concentrated in the hands of leaders without attendant responsibility. This produces a top-heavy situation by which strikes are called by those leaders without a sufficient sense of responsibility. The situation is analogous to the over-organization of capital in the shape of trusts and holding corporations. The evolution of time has made those forms of over-organization by capital illegal, and has thrown capital organization back to a more respresentative form. I think the same evolution must take place in labor. The relations between capital and labor must be solved by a more human and cooperative relation in the lower units.

To put concretely what I mean, I think the solution must be in some form of relation between the employer and the laborer in the respective shops . . . The laborer must be given an interest in the profits resulting from a diminished cost of production, and he must be given a greater voice in shop management through a more democratic system. By this building up from the bottom, upon a cooperative and democratic foundation, we will eliminate most of the issues which now lead to industrial warfare upon a national scale.[75]

Stimson was more wary of the labor movement than the other men considered in this study. Like them, however, he had been forced to give more thought to the necessity of incorporating workers more fully into the decision-making processes of American industry. In certain important respects, Stimson's thinking was evolving in a direction similar to Donald Richberg's. Like Richberg, Stimson hoped that relations between capital and labor within individual units of industry could be improved by reinforcing the sense of common interest between the two groups. As we shall see in the following chapter, however, Stimson's perception of the nature of this common interest, and his assumption that the problem of "over-organization of capital" had already been solved by the reforms of the Progressive era, allowed him to be more sympathetic than Richberg to the development of company unions which took place in the next decade. Finally, in spite of Stimson's call for a more active and better organized government, he, like Richberg, still wished to maintain a clear dividing line between the processes of economic and political decision-making. Government might have an increased role to play, but not at the expense of undermining the nation's system of private enterprise.

Felix Frankfurter's participation in the war mobilization only confirmed his belief in the necessity of allowing organized labor to play a greater role in America's industrial life. Like Richberg, Frankfurter realized that "you cannot preach those glorious calls, liberty and justice and democracy" as a justification for war "without having the workers translate democracy in terms of their industrial experience." He attributed the labor turmoil which occurred right after the war to the nation's "faulty organization of industry." In Frankfurter's view, "the chief reason for the social unrest" was the "disparity" which the "masses of workers" increasingly felt "between their political and economic existence." While workers enjoyed the opportunity to participate in and influence the workings of the nation's political system, "the masses of men" exercised "no control," or at least "felt" they had no control, "over their lives" in industry.[76]

Frankfurter argued, therefore, that it was necessary to "constitutionalize industry." In language quite similar to that used by Donald Richberg, he claimed that collective bargaining had to be the "starting point" for any solution to the country's social and economic problems, since such a step would be:

. . . nothing but belated recognition of economic facts—that the era of romantic individualism is no more . . . We are confronted with mass production and mass producers; the individual, in his industrial relations, but a cog in the great collectivity. The collectivity must be represented and must be allowed to choose its representatives. And it is through the collectivity, through enlisting its will and its wisdom, that the necessary increase in production alone will come.[77]

The events of 1919 also forced Bernard Baruch to give serious thought to the problems of labor for the first time in his career. In June, Baruch proclaimed to the press that labor would "never again . . . be satisfied with" the conditions under which it had toiled before the war. Workers, Baruch argued, had to be given a "proprietary share" in what they produced, and they had "to be taken into the management of the corporations by which" they were employed. "Capital instead of hanging back and passively resisting," had to support such changes "or else labor may not be satisfied with what it is entitled to and may demand more than its share."[78]

In the Fall of 1919, President Wilson convoked a National Industrial Conference with the hope that selected representatives of labor, management, and the public might come together to devise a way of putting an end to the industrial strife which was then disrupting the American economy. Wilson chose Baruch to head the supposedly impartial public delegation at the conference. Only days before the conference was to convene in early October, the American Federation of Labor called a long threatened strike against the steel industry, taking nearly 300,000 workers off the job. When the conference began, Samuel Gompers insisted on making a settlement of the steel strike the paramount issue of the meetings which were to follow.[79]

Baruch entered the conference feeling sympathetic to labor's demands for an eight-hour day and the recognition of its right to collective bargaining. He did not believe, however, that a meaningful system of collective bargaining excluded either open shops or company unions. He hoped that such an approach to union recognition might provide the basis for a compromise settlement of the steel strike, and he actively sought to convince Judge Gary and other industry leaders of the wisdom of accepting such a compromise. Gary and his colleagues, though, remained adamant in their opposition to unionization, so that the Industrial Conference quickly became deadlocked and ended without having accomplished anything. Not long afterwards, the steel strike was so thoroughly broken that the industry remained unorganized until the 1930s. Commenting on the outcome of the strike, the leading student of government relations with the steel industry in this period concludes:

During the war, industry had been willing to concede minor points for government sanction of co-operative activities; when it came to yielding on something important, such as union recognition, the steelmakers had refused to budge. If price fixing was the greatest success of the entente, it is a measure of the triumph of business over government that the great failure of the entente was labor. Federal agencies had proclaimed great principles, but the Administration had not been willing to employ the necessary coercion to enforce awards. The hopes raised during the war made the strike possible; the nature of the entente made the strike's failure inevitable.[80]

A month after the collapse of the Industrial Conference, Baruch outlined his views on the labor problem in a letter to William Jennings Bryan. He observed that "all fairminded thinking people" agreed that "the unrest, distrust, and dissatisfaction" then being manifested by American workers was justified, and that "the injustice involved must be found and eradicated." Thus, he favored the "recognition of the rights of those who labor not alone with their hands," but also of "that great mass of salaried employees, private and official, who have had little opportunity to voice their difficulties." Baruch reiterated his support for the eight-hour day, collective bargaining, and the right to strike "with such limitations and safeguards as would be found necessary and proper in the interests of workman, employer, and public."[81]

Like Richberg and Stimson, Baruch believed that both employer and employee had "an obligation to the consuming public to keep the output of the necessaries going at as full capacity as possible." Consequently, he advocated the creation of a voluntary board of mediation and arbitration within the Labor Department. Baruch did not wish to give such a board the power to compel labor and management to accept its decisions, but he did claim that the publicity resulting from the announcement of the proposed board's findings would create a sanction of "public opinion" which would "carry such weight" that, in practice, the board's "findings would be taken as final."[82]

Josephus Daniels had long been sympathetic to the cause of labor. Shortly before the Armistice, he hopefully prophesied that in the wake of America's successful effort to make the world safe for democracy, the "large returns from farm and factory will not go to the few, but will be apportioned to men of brain and brawn in proportion to the value of their contributions." When labor was forced to resort to strikes to defend its position in the period of postwar reconversion, Daniels acted as a defender of the rights of labor within the Wilson Cabinet. He argued that the National Industrial Conference being held in October be empowered to compel Judge Gary and the steel industry to accept a labor offer of arbitration. In heated Cabinet discussions on the subject, Daniels rejected Secretary of State Lansing's contention that the "right of property" entitled the owner of a business "to conduct it as he pleases." Daniels claimed that the "public" also had "rights" which were in fact superior to "employe [sic] or employer" rights, and that these public rights also had to be considered.[83]

In spite of his recognition of the necessity of granting labor a more representative role in industry, Daniels still made it clear that he opposed any "riotous Bolshevism" which sought to overthrow the "rights of property." In calling for the purging of all forms of "class domination," Daniels attacked both radicals on the left and reactionaries on the right for departing from the principles of "Americanism," including the ideal of a competitive private enterprise economic system. "Class domination," he contended, would never "flourish on this continent," so long as "copious draughts of Americanism" continued to be recognized as the proper prescription for a healthy body politic.[84]

## VI

Until fairly recently, most historians had assumed that the coming of the First World War brought an end to the preoccupation with domestic reform which characterized the Progressive era.

Such a view is no longer tenable. In fact, as we have seen, the war and its immediate aftermath greatly accelerated the evolution which had previously begun to take place in the thinking of progressives about the proper organization of the nation's political economy. If controlling the power of trusts and safeguarding the free play of the marketplace were the central themes of the Progressive era, then encouraging cooperation and coordination throughout the economy and giving labor a greater voice in the nation's industrial life were the major themes of the war era.

Only when confronted with the challenge of mobilizing the nation's resources for war did the men discussed here begin to consider the advantages inherent in what would later be called a managed market economy. The economic planning and coordination required by the demands of modern war forced these men to experiment with governmental and quasi-governmental mechanisms which would have been virtually inconceivable to them just a few years earlier. The war not only compelled liberals such as Daniels, Baruch, and Frankfurter to view the economy as an interrelated whole, rather than as the sum of many independent markets; but it also encouraged them to explore corporatist approaches to the problems created by the emergence of an industrial society. Thus, the men examined in this study all came out of the war with an increased appreciation of the need to utilize bureaucratic expertise and of the benefits to be gained from greater cooperation and standardization throughout the economy.

It is important to note, however, that the corporatist ideas generated by the war developed within the already existing framework of liberal ideology. While these men understood the need for economic planning and coordination in wartime, they still believed that a successful mobilization effort could be, and ought to be, conducted largely on a voluntary basis in order to avoid the creation of an overblown government bureaucracy. The fear and distrust of coercive state power, in other words, remained strong. In addition, these liberals believed it was possible to rely on the organizational activities of individuals and groups in the private sector because they continued to assume that capitalism in America had produced no basic conflict of class interests. Individual businessmen or firms might be short-sighted or greedy, but there was nothing inherent in the operation of American capitalism which would make it impossible to achieve an equitable and efficient mobilization by relying on the country's existing business and professional elites. In fact, an increasing faith in the impartiality and professionalism of America's growing number of technical and organizational experts helped reinforce this willingness to base the war mobilization on the organizational initiatives of those in the private sector.

The degree to which these liberals accepted as permanent the need for a bureaucratically managed economy should not be exaggerated. None of these men rejected his faith in the desirability of maintaining a market mechanism as the ultimate allocator of economic resources because of the nation's war experience. They may have looked forward to the more extensive use of voluntary planning and cooperation within American industry after the war, but they did not envision the visible hand of management taking over most of the crucial functions traditionally performed by the laws of supply and demand in peacetime. All of them remained firmly committed to private enterprise and to the incentive of private profit as the keystones of a fair and productive economic system.

The war, and especially its immediate aftermath, also caused all five men to pay greater attention than ever before to the problem of how labor ought to be integrated into the industrial order. Whereas the organization of labor had been only a minor concern for these men during the Progressive era, by 1920 they had all come to the conclusion that industrial peace, and hence social stability and national prosperity, depended upon the recognition of labor's right to participate more fully in American industry's decision-making process. All five men had come to realize that for labor to achieve its demands for a more meaningful role in the nation's industrial life, it would have to be more effectively organized.

The men discussed here came to support the organization of labor not as a means of encouraging worker solidarity and class consciousness, but rather as a means of reinforcing America's liberal consensus. Greater participation by the representatives of organized labor at the grass roots level in industry would foster a spirit of cooperation between workers and management and would bring to the fore a mutual recognition of the under-lying community of interest which liberals believed existed be-tween labor and capital. While the liberals considered in this study saw labor organization, in part, as an instrument of self-protection for workers, their conception of labor organization at this point could be labelled more corporatist than pluralist in orientation. In supporting the organization of labor, they hoped to achieve not so much a balance, but rather a community, of interests. Yet, just as their ideas about the extent to which it would be appropriate to apply the organizational lessons of the war mobilization to America's peace-time economy were sketchy and uncertain, so, too, were their ideas about the proper role of labor still in a state of development and flux at the end of the war era.[85]

Even as they came to see the need to "democratize" or "constitutionalize" industry, Richberg and Frankfurter remained ambivalent about how best to bring about such a change. Rich-berg may have considered the possibility of having the govern-ment insist on a democratic form of organization as a require-ment for incorporation. However, Richberg, as well as Frankfurter, Baruch, Stimson, and Daniels, continued to hope that government coercion would not be necessary to convince industry leaders of the advantages to be gained by granting labor a greater voice in the nation's economic life. It was certainly not their desire to see government overturn the foundation of America's private enterprise economy. Labor was simply to be incorporated more fully into the existing system.

The existing structure, though, was itself far more inequita-ble than American liberals were prepared to admit. To rely pri-marily on the voluntary actions of the private sector was to ac-cept, in practice, the continuation of a system which inevitably worked to the advantage of those already in positions of power. The American working class not only remained largely unorga-nized (union membership reached a temporary peak in 1920 when it represented approximately 13 percent of the labor force), but it also continued to suffer from an inadequate level of in-come. In spite of the gains made by the unskilled during the war, the average annual earnings of an American worker in 1919 were still not sufficient to keep that worker's family above the poverty line. While a family of four at that time needed a budget of $1,422 to maintain a minimally adequate standard of living, the average worker's earnings for that year amounted to only $1,201. The decade ahead would prove to be a critical testing period for the voluntaristic approach to organization and planning which had emerged from the nation's experience in the First World War.[86]

# CHAPTER VI

# The Growth of Voluntarism 1920–1929

**A**FTER two decades of progressive agitation for reform at home and crusading for democracy abroad, America was ready in 1920 for the "return to normalcy" promised by Warren Harding. Normalcy, however, did not entail a return to the laissez-faire liberalism of the late nineteenth century. Recently, historians have begun to appreciate the extent to which the Twenties witnessed significant new developments in the evolution of America's political economy. A growing body of literature, focusing in particular on Herbert Hoover's activities as Secretary of Commerce, has challenged the traditional view of the 1920s as a period of political retrenchment harkening back to an earlier conception of a strictly limited role for government. Ellis Hawley, for one, argues that the "story of America" in the Twenties was at least in part the story of the ongoing development of "new managerial designs reflecting the continuing search for a 'new liberalism' and foreshadowing the 'modern capitalism' of a later era."[1]

While Hoover's contribution to the formulation of a new conception of corporate liberalism during the 1920s has received considerable attention, it would be misleading to regard him as a solitary figure acting in isolation from a broader movement for change within the American liberal tradition. An examination of the careers and ideological development of the five men considered in this study reveals that they, too, were involved in this period in the development of what Hawley describes as an "associational" version of liberalism. They realized that American liberalism would have to continue to evolve beyond its original conception of individualsim and reliance on the untrammeled operation of a free market. As Felix Frankfurter put it, the time had come to admit once and for all that the era of "romantic individualism" in America had come to an end. Liberals increasingly had to adjust to the realization that the group and the organization had replaced the individual as the basic units of social and economic life. "Modern life," Henry Stimson proclaimed in 1929, was "a life of organization," and it became the task these men set for themselves in the Twenties to encourage the growth of organizations in the private sector which could contribute to the development of what Bernard Baruch referred to as a more efficient and "more orderly market" system. In the decade following the First World War, the liberals examined here focused primarily on the development of voluntary interest group organizations and the increasing use of scientific methods of decision-making as the best means for bringing about a more rational and more equitable economic system.[2]

The experience of the first two decades of the twentieth century had forced liberals to support the creation of a more powerful state. As the 1920s began, none of the men discussed here wished to see the role of government cut back to what it had been before the advent of progressivism. Yet, they had always believed that the private sector had to be relied upon as the principal source of initiative and direction in the nation's economic life. Especially in the wake of the First World War, liberals had both an increased realization of the importance of greater coordination and scientific planning in industry, and a reluctance to have the government use its powers of coercion to achieve such economic rationalization. The result, in the 1920s, was an emphasis on voluntary action in the private sector. While the federal government played a role in stimulating such action, it was symbolic of the era's preoccupation with developments in the private sector that the five men considered here generally remained outside of government during the Twenties.

After having served eight years as Secretary of the Navy, Josephus Daniels went home in 1921 to resume active direction of the Raleigh *News & Observer*. As editor and publisher of North Carolina's leading Democratic newspaper, Daniels remained involved in politics, but he was not to return to government service for another twelve years. Bernard Baruch emerged from the war with a national reputation and a taste for public life. Although much of his time would subsequently be spent overseeing his extensive financial interests, he decided against resuming his career as a full-time Wall Street speculator largely because he did not wish to endanger his recently acquired reputation as a disinterested public servant. Baruch stayed in the public eye during the 1920s since he was a man whose advice on public issues was frequently in demand, but he held no government office. Felix Frankfurter went back to Harvard in 1919 with the understanding that his responsibilities as a faculty member would allow him sufficient free time to engage in extracurricular activities involving various public causes. Above all else, however, Frankfurter was a teacher and scholar throughout the Twenties. Donald Richberg was the only man examined here not to have left private life during the First World War. Since 1913 he had practiced law in Chicago in partnership with fellow progressive and future Secretary of the Interior Harold Ickes, a partnership which continued until 1923. Throughout the decade, Richberg continued to practice law. While he became involved in a number of labor and public utilities cases that had important political overtones, Richberg, like Daniels, Baruch, and Frankfurter, never wielded the power of government office in this period.[3]

Henry Stimson left the army after the war to resume his career as a corporate lawyer in New York. He soon became a wealthy man, earning about $50,000 a year from his law practice and also reaping the profits from a trust fund established by his father. In contrast to the other men being discussed, Stimson did return to public life before the end of the Twenties. In 1926 and again in 1927, Stimson was called upon for temporary diplomatic assignments. In the first instance, Stimson was asked to write an advisory brief for the State Department on a border dispute between Chile and Peru which the United States sought to mediate. The following year, Stimson went to Nicaragua as President Coolidge's special representative seeking to end that country's civil war. In 1928, Stimson returned to government service on a full-time basis when he was appointed Governor-General of the Philippines. Newly elected President Herbert

Hoover then selected Stimson to become Secretary of State. However, before Stimson became increasingly involved in foreign affairs during the last years of the decade, he, too, had been preoccupied as a private citizen with developments of public importance taking place in the private sector.

It is highly significant that during the Twenties four of the five men examined in this study became directly involved in the efforts of specific segments of American society to reap the benefits of voluntary interest group organization. Only Josephus Daniels, whose life in this period is described by his biographer as a "decade in obscurity," failed to participate in an important way in the development of associational institutions which took place in the 1920s. Like Herbert Hoover, the liberals considered here believed that the growth of voluntary organizations in the private sector and the greater use of scientific and managerial expertise in economic life held out the hope of fulfilling the promise of a liberal social order. Voluntarism, in their view, represented a necessary antidote both to the possible development of class consciousness and class conflict, and to the rise of an arbitrary and coercive state.[4]

I

Before analyzing the ways in which the men considered here participated, during the 1920s, in the development of voluntary associations in the private sector, it will be useful to examine their views on the presidential campaign of 1924. This election is particularly significant because of the Progressive party candidacy of Robert La Follette. A brief review of the positions taken by these five men in the election of 1924 provides an interesting comparison to their positions in the crucial election of 1912 and sheds light on their attitudes toward the American political system.

As the campaign of 1924 approached, none of these men were enthusiastic supporters of the incumbent Republican administration. While such key figures in the Harding-Coolidge administration as Hoover, Secretary of Agriculture Henry Wallace, and Secretary of State Charles Evans Hughes initiated important policies and programs based on their belief in "a positive role for government . . . as a catalyzer and coordinator of private endeavors" to rationalize the economic life of the nation, normalcy also came to be characterized by a downplaying of the government's function as a watchdog over business and by a series of scandals involving the venal use of high public office. In his memoirs, Henry Stimson, the only regular Republican among the five men considered in this study, diplomatically observes that he believed Calvin Coolidge was a "wholly satisfactory chief," but not "one of the oustanding presidents of his time." There was, however, never any doubt that Stimson, as a loyal Republican, would back the incumbent candidate of his party in 1924, especially since he found Coolidge's prudent leadership and concern for fiscal restraint congenial to his own outlook.[5]

Josephus Daniels and Bernard Baruch, as partisan Democrats, were naturally more critical of Republican rule than Stimson. Yet, by focusing almost exclusively on the issues of corruption, prohibition, and the League of Nations, they failed to offer a thoroughgoing critique of or comprehensive alternative to the politics of normalcy. In early 1924, both Daniels and Baruch looked to William McAdoo to restore Wilsonian idealism to the White House. The deadlocked Democratic convention's compromise choice of John W. Davis was a bitter disappointment to both men. Neither, however, considered abandoning the nominee of his party. Baruch, who had become by this time one of the Democratic party's few important financial backers, ended up contributing over $100,000 to Davis's campaign. Two years earlier, Baruch had explained his commitment to the Democratic party, and abhorence of "splinter parties," in a letter to Daniels. He noted that "talk about a third party" was "ridiculous" and an exercise in futility which simply represented a "way of cheating the people out of what they are entitled to." Daniels was personally on very good terms with Robert La Follette, particularly since the two men had worked together in 1922 in an early effort to uncover the Teapot Dome scandal. He had even been sounded out as a possible running mate for the Wisconsin Progressive in 1924. Daniels, like Baruch, however, was willing to support the lackluster candidacy of Davis because he remained committed both to the Democratic party and to the idea of a two-party system.[6]

As in 1912, only Felix Frankfurter and Donald Richberg were willing, in 1924, to go outside the established political system to support a third party ticket. Members of a younger generation, Frankfurter and Richberg always felt less bound by traditional party loyalties than did Daniels, Stimson, or Baruch; and, in 1924, they were clearly more frustrated by the lack of a meaningful political choice between the candidates of the two major parties. Richberg and Frankfurter, therefore, both publicly supported La Follette's candidacy. Richberg played a prominent role in the Progressive party convention, chairing the committee on resolutions.[7]

Both Frankfurter and Richberg saw La Follette's candidacy as a symbolic alternative to what Frankfurter described as the "crass materialism" of the times. It is striking that Richberg used almost identical language in complaining about the "cynical materialism that dominates the Democratic and Republican parties." La Follette won the support of Frankfurter and Richberg not so much because he offered a fully worked out set of reform proposals, but rather because his campaign held out the hope of initiating a broad renewal of spiritual and political idealism. Neither Frankfurter nor Richberg found it necessary to be very specific in defining the policies La Follette might adopt if elected. The Progressive party platform itself, which Richberg helped to write, included little more than a rehash of old progressive proposals.[8]

In terms of symbols and an overall sense of direction, one particular aspect of La Follette's candidacy had particular importance for Frankfurter and Richberg. As products of the twentieth-century revolt against formalism, both men put a greater emphasis on the prospect of dealing with social problems according to the impartial methods of science than did the three older liberals considered in this study. The test of a true progressive, in Richberg's view, was a willingness to rely on a "consensus of scientific opinion as to the most desirable course of experimentation" in solving society's problems. In a manuscript entitled "Where Are the Progressives Going—and How," written some time after the 1924 campaign, Richberg observed:

It may well be that science must accept its share of responsibility for breaking down the moral standards of previous generations. Science has increased the quantity and quality of material pleasures available to most people. Science has undermined the authority of many institutions that have given to spiritual ideals a power over masses of human beings. But it is to science that we must look for guidance in the recreation of effective moral standards. Scientific men must be relied upon to demonstrate the value of moral principles in the control of individual lives and in the direction of social and political institutions.[9]

In 1924, Frankfurter and Richberg both agreed that La Follette was the Presidential candidate most devoted to the use of scientific methods in political life. La Follette, Frankfurter argued, had clearly demonstrated his belief in the use of "organized intelligence" by his long time associaton with the University of Wisconsin. "Probably no other man in public life today," Frankfurter claimed, "compares with La Follette in the extent of his reliance on disinterested expertness in the solution of economic and social" problems. There were other factors which also accounted for Frankfurter and Richberg's support for La Follette, but none was more important than their belief that he represented the best hope of impressing upon the American people the realization that the:

. . . men who devote their lives to the study of social forces in history, economics, sociology or natural philosophy, are better fitted to guide human thought and to shape moral tendencies than men who devote their lives to making money and to acquiring industrial power so great as to overstrain human capacity.[10]

Daniels, Stimson and Baruch had also increasingly learned to appreciate the fact that the growing complexity of industrial life required a greater reliance on professionally trained and supposedly impartial experts and administrators. After the First World War, Daniels used the language of science when he noted the need for testing all proposed solutions to social problems "under the glass and the spatula and the retorts" of the laboratory. Baruch's war-time experience had convinced him of the need for an expanded government role in the collection and dissemination of statistical information relating to industry. Organization, he realized, went hand in hand with increasing specialization of function and a consequent reliance on technicians and administrators. Modern industrial organization, he claimed, required the creation of a "thinking machine made up of a number of individual thinking units."[11]

Frankfurter and Richberg's perception of La Follette's candidacy, however, was but one indication of the greater emphasis the two younger men placed on a scientific approach to social issues. Both men agreed that the lack of "scientific organization" in industry was at the heart of America's social and economic problems. Thus, the "theorist" and the "intellectual" had a special role to play in the field of industrial relations, since, as Richberg put it, "the practical men" in the field had been so "arrogant and incompetent" in trying to solve the "common problems" of labor and management. Frankfurter and Richberg were confident that the advances in the social sciences in the 1920s were contributing to the development of what Richberg called "a scientific creed of right and wrong—a good and bad political economy" which would make possible the growth of a more and more humane society. Just as natural scientists were called upon to treat biological disease, so, Richberg argued, was it now possible to call upon social scientists to "analyze" and "prescribe a remedy" for societal diseases. During the Twenties, Frankfurter pioneered in the scientific study of the law and the courts, utilizing the techniques of statistical analysis to examine what seemed to him to be the problems of "social sanitation and social engineering" which were involved. He believed that the "objective" spirit of "scientific detachment" would have to become the basis for rational and equitable decision-making processes in institutions as diverse as the courts of criminal justice and the nation's factories.[12]

Both Frankfurter and Richberg believed that the "methods of science" would increasingly replace the use of "fists" and partisan arguments in the resolution of social problems. Their optimism was based, in large part, on the liberal faith that no fundamental conflict between class interests existed at the center of the nation's social system; for they assumed that the judgments of science would eventually be voluntarily, and even eagerly, accepted by all groups in American society. The development of scientific methods of social analysis, they believed, would make it unnecessary for the government to impose politically determined decisions on the private sector. Rather, scientific standards would increasingly be integrated into the private sector's own decision-making processes. The use of such standards, Frankfurter and Richberg believed, would be of benefit to all concerned. It not only would allow for the continued existence of the nation's private enterprise system, but it would also make that system more efficient and more humane in its operations. Approaching the problems of industrial life in a "scientific manner," Richberg contended, was the only way to avoid the "great economic losses and serious social conflicts" which otherwise would "persistently recur." Frankfurter, in particular, acknowledged that "to treat science as a religion" was to "pour new wine into old bottles that can't hold it." He realized that the "final determination of large policy" would have to remain in the hands of the "direct representatives of the public," rather than in the hands of "experts." Yet Frankfurter and Richberg's great faith in science as an objective, essentially nonpartisan method of dealing with social problems was an important indication of their belief that American society could be reformed without exacerbating latent social conflicts, and without politicizing the nation's economic system.[13]

## II

Frankfurter and Richberg may have used the language of science more readily than Daniels, Stimson, and Baruch, but the prospect of making the nation's private enterprise system function more rationally and more equitably, without resorting to an increased use of the state's coercive powers, was the dominant theme in the careers of all five men during the 1920s. In this period, the development of voluntary interest group organizations among workers, businessmen, and farmers became a primary focus in the efforts of these men to further the cause of liberal reform.

The issue of labor organization, as we have seen, had been brought to the fore by the First World War and its immediate aftermath. In the Twenties, however, the union movement became a central concern in the careers of both Richberg and Frankfurter. These men shared the view that the voluntary organization of labor was essential not only to protect the interests of workers, but also to encourage the development of a more rational basis for the nation's economic life.

Donald Richberg's outspoken concern for labor was first expressed in 1917, when he called for the "democratization of industry." During the 1920s, Richberg's own experience with the problem of labor-management relations in the railroad industry served to clarify his views on the role of unions, as well as to give him the opportunity to test his ideas in practice. Richberg became associated with the nation's railway unions as a result of his pre-war acquaintance with Glenn Plumb. Plumb had become legal counsel for the railway shop craft unions and author of a post-war plan for the reorganization of the country's entire railroad system. Richberg began doing legal work for the railway shop craft unions in 1920 on the recommendation of Plumb; and after Plumb's death in 1922, Richberg took over as the unions' chief legal adviser and representative.[14]

Richberg assumed these duties at a time when the shopmen were involved in what labor historian Irving Bernstein has called the "greatest strike of the decade." The lengthy strike, affecting 400,000 workers, ended in defeat for the unions, but Richberg's experience in the dispute intensified his commitment to the cause of organized labor and led him, along with the leaders of the railway unions, to look for some means of establishing a more equitable and harmonious basis for labor-management relations in the industry. With the support of Secretary of Commerce Herbert Hoover, the efforts of Richberg and the railway unions culminated in the adoption by Congress in 1926 of the Railway Labor Act. According to Bernstein, this act was "the only federal labor statute of significance" passed during the 1920s. Richberg was a driving force behind the enactment of the law and played an important role in its drafting. He proudly described it as "fundamentally the most enlightened labor legislation ever enacted" and believed that it could serve as a model for other major industries.[15]

The law empowered the President to appoint a standing five-person Mediation Board to assist in the settling of contract disputes in the railway industry. Management and labor were each required to give thirty days written notice to this board prior to any attempt to bring about a change in contract terms. The board was to mediate in any disputes which arose, and, if necessary, encourage the parties involved to submit to a carefully spelled out process of voluntary arbitration. In the event of a complete breakdown in negotiations, the President was enabled to create an ad hoc emergency panel which was to investigate the situation and then publicly report its findings within thirty days. During this time, management was denied the right to change the conditions of employment; while, for a period of sixty days, labor was not permitted to strike. There was no provision in the law, however, for the enforcement of the ad hoc panel's findings, nor was there any attempt to impose compulsory arbitration on the industry. The act also called for the creation, through the joint agreement of the carriers and their employees, of adjustment boards for the settlement of grievances arising under existing contracts. Finally, the law apparently guaranteed the right of workers to form indpendent unions, since it contained a clause stating that both labor and management were to be allowed to choose their own representatives "without interference, or coercion by either party over the self-organization, or designation of representatives, by the other."[16]

Richberg had long been a critic of American industry's "autocratic" form of organization and single-minded pursuit of profit rather than service. However, in approaching the problem of reforming the railway industry, Richberg operated on the assumption that it was "impractical to offer as a peaceful solution of industrial warfare an arbitrary reorganization of industry" which would seek to "destroy the product of centuries" of social evolution. Any attempt to establish an altogether "new machinery for organizing and utilizing human energies," he contended, would be "dangerous business," since "human beings" could not "play God very successfully."[17]

Richberg's scepticism about the ability of human beings to "play God" reinforced his reluctance to see government unilaterally mandate a solution to the problems of the railroad industry. Richberg and Herbert Hoover worked for the passage of the Railway Labor Act because they saw it as a perfect embodiment of the philosophy of voluntarism to which they were both committed. According to Richberg, the law was designed to leave labor and management "free to work out their differences together" through a mutually agreeable framework of "self-government." The government was given the task of creating a mechanism and an established set of procedures to enable the two sides to "get together," but it was given no power to impose on industry the specific terms of contract settlements. The law made no effort even to hint at the possibility of "socializing" the railroad industry, nor to give the state the power to "determine the responsibility of an industry to society." The only provision in the Railway Labor Act involving the possibility of government coercion of industry was found in the section permitting the President to impose a temporary cooling-off period. Richberg made it clear that the act was in no way designed to equip the government with a "political club" which could be used to "put the force of Government behind one party in an industrial controversy." He pointed out to the unions he represented that, on the basis of past history, labor had more to fear than capital from the possible use of such a club.[18]

More importantly, Richberg believed that any attempt to allow the government to fix wages or other terms of labor contracts, whether through compulsory arbitration or unilateral government fiat, would necessarily lead to government price-fixing, and, eventually, to the almost total control by the state of the nation's economic life. This Richberg firmly opposed. The "sense of freedom" of both employees and employers would be destroyed, he argued, if the government intervened to such an extent in the economy. Richberg thus feared the possibility of too great an expansion of the coercive power of the state even more than he objected to the existing reality of autocratic control of industry by capital. Political coercion, in his view, was ultimately a greater threat to liberty than economic coercion. While contending forces in the private sector could balance each other, the power of the state, if used to the fullest, could not be matched by any other force in society. Once, in expressing his opposition to the development of a "class-conscious, paternalistic state," Richberg contended that both "industrial autocrats" and socialists shared a "mental kinship" in their "desire to exercise coercive power over their fellow men." A democratic state, he believed, had to be essentially non-coercive and built on the principle of cooperation.[19]

Richberg thought that the type of voluntary organization of labor which the Railway Labor Act encouraged and legitimized would eventually lead to the formation of "industrial republics." Richberg's conception of these "industrial republics" clearly reflected the growing appeal of the emerging corporatist version of liberalism with which Herbert Hoover became closely identified. According to Richberg, unions had initially developed because they had been "essential to protect the workers against ruthless injustice arising from the organization of industry on a purely profit making basis." However, Richberg envisioned labor organization as subsequently playing a broader role in the reform of America's political economy. In the future, labor organization would become a means for fostering greater efficiency and cooperation within industry. As the representatives of a more thoroughly organized work force learned to work together with the representatives of organized capital within a framework of "self-government in industry," workers and management would develop a sense of common enterprise and common purpose. Richberg even hoped that eventually labor and management would come to take such pride in the quality of the product of their joint endeavor that the idea of service to the community might gradually supplant a single-minded concern with profit as the standard by which the performance of industry would be measured.[20]

It is important to note that the "industrial republics" envisioned by Richberg were not to be created by consolidating all the firms of a given industry under a centralized form of "self-government." Richberg was calling for the democratization of each company within a given industry, not the establishment of centralized all-encompassing industrial empires. Richberg was instrumental in the creation of a Railway Labor Executives' Association which brought together representatives of all the shop craft organizations and transportation brotherhoods to facilitate the unions' "uniform, or at least harmonious handling of disputes and litigation" arising under the new Railway Labor Act. However, as he explained to a convention of railway workers shortly after the Railway Labor Act was adopted:

I want to make the plea to every single one of these organizations, every time I get a chance, that to the fullest extent they pool their information, they pool their economic strength, not by amalgamation, not by making smaller organizations into great big organizations, no, but by federating the strength of one union with another . . . I don't believe in centralization or concentration of power until you get big unions so large they don't function or represent the men who belong to them. I would not like to see a single union of the railway men of this country. I believe in strength of small organizations, small units, autonomous organizations, federated together.[21]

Richberg opposed such centralization, in part because he believed it would be inimical to the creation of an effective spirit of corporate identity and harmony. Workers and management within a single company could develop a sense of common enterprise and common interest which would be impossible to achieve in an industry-wide organization. Moreover, while Richberg wished to see the principle of cooperation become the basis for labor-management relations within individual companies, he still assumed that relations between firms operating in the same industry ought to be governed by the rule of competition. For the economy as a whole, Richberg remained strongly opposed to any notion of corporatism which sought to substitute comprehensive centralized planning for the operation of market forces.

To the extent that Richberg supported the growth of voluntary labor organization as a means of fostering the development of a community of interest and a common sense of corporate identity between labor and capital, his conception of "industrial republics" may usefully be described as "corporatist." Yet, Richberg's view of the function of labor organization also had another dimension to it. At times, he fell back on what could more accurately be called a "pluralist" conception of unionism based on the idea of a balance, rather than a concert of power between workers and management.

Although Richberg often denigrated bread-and-butter unionism for the narrowness of its focus, in his actual work on the railway unions, he operated on the assumption that "the practical and dominating purpose of any labor organization is to increase wages and to improve working conditions." In urging railway workers to unite in "autonomous organizations federated together," Richberg proclaimed that such organizations were necessary in order to "bring the pressure of a massed strength, massed authority, and massed information against the opposition, which is thoroughly organized for that purpose." Richberg, in fact, at one time argued that the Railway Labor Act was based on the belief that:

. . . organizations and combinations of all forms of self-interest in industry should be encouraged so that organizations of economic power may provide natural balances of power and may deal freely with each other, each conscious of its strength in what the members have to give and conscious of its weakness in what they must seek from others.[22]

This conception of voluntary organization as necessary for the creation of a mechanical balance of power in society is seemingly incompatible with Richberg's conception of labor organization as a step toward the establishment of an organic harmony of interests in industry. That both views could co-exist in Richberg's mind in the 1920s is a reflection of the transitional nature of his thinking during this time. For, ultimately, one view would have to triumph over the other. Yet, in this period, both corporatism and pluralism appealed to Richberg for many of the same reasons. He understood the need to develop a modernized version of liberalism which would not only take into account the fact that organized groups, rather than individuals, had become the basic units of economic life, but which would also prevent America from developing into a class conscious society divided between a monolithically organized labor force and a monolithically organized capitalist class.

Corporatism, at least in theory, obviously represented an alternative to the possible growth of class consciousness, but so, too, did pluralism. The more thoroughly every particular interest group in society became organized, the less likely it would be that Americans would identify themselves soley as members of a broad social class. Here, Richberg's emphasis on the importance of decentralization is crucial. Moreover, Richberg's vision of the possibility of achieving and maintaining a balance of power through interest group organization was predicated on the assumption that the groups contending with one another would not see themselves as locked into a winner-take-all struggle. Decentralized bargaining and negotiation would eventually be productive of a spirit of compromise, not a sense of intractable class conflict.

Richberg's conception of pluralism was still only embryonic in form during the 1920s. In looking to the future, Richberg usually thought more in terms of the promise inherent in the growth of a corporatist version of liberalism. However, the significance of Richberg's approach to the problem of labor organization in this period cannot be fully understood if one ignores the extent to which it reflected an inner uncertainty on his part as to what kind of society America ought to become.

In the years after the passage of the Railway Labor Act, Richberg continued to praise the measure as a model piece of labor legislation. The cooperative effort between the carriers and the unions which had made the law's adoption possible, and the lack of strikes or other publicized labor disputes in the railroad industry in the first years after its enactment, seemed to justify Richberg's enthusiasm for the law. However, the reality of the deep seated conflict of interest between labor and management reasserted itself as soon as the Railway Labor Act was passed. The unions and the railroads were never able to agree on a basis for establishing the grievance boards provided for in the law. In spite of Richberg's misgivings about centralization, it was his position, as well as that of the unions he represented, that grievance boards ought to be organized on a national, or at least regional, basis, rather than along the system lines which the carriers proposed. Although the law had seemingly banned company unions, no method for enforcing this ban had been included in the act. As a result, the unions feared that the initial creation of system boards would allow the railroads to gain recognition of company unions already in existence. The carriers, however, refused to agree to the formation of national or regional boards. One important section of the Railway Labor Act was thus practically nullified. In the late 1920s, while Richberg was publicly praising the constructive precedent established by the passage of the law, a backlog of thousands of unsettled workers' grievances was building up in the industry.[23]

In addition, the supposed success of the act in averting strikes was, in Bernstein's words, "as much shadow as substance." The unions, whose position in the industry had been weak ever since the disastrous strike of 1922, had not been strengthened by the new law, since no attempt had been made to throw the weight of the government behind them. The general absence of strike activity in the railroad industry was actually more a reflection of the lack of strength of the unions, and of their inability to press for higher wages or other demands, than of the success of the Railway Labor Act in creating more equitable conditions for the nation's railway workers.[24]

Felix Frankfurter also became closely associated with the union movement in the Twenties. In 1920, he successfully defended Sidney Hillman's Amalgamated Clothing Workers' union against a potentially precedent-setting suit which threatened to have the garment workers' organization declared an illegal conspiracy. Frankfurter and Richberg's growing interest in the labor movement, as well as their common Harvard and Bull Moose party backgrounds, caused their paths to cross in these years. In 1923, in fact, largely upon the recommendation of Frankfurter, Richberg took into his law firm a young Harvard graduate, David Lilienthal, who was later to become head of the TVA.[25]

On one particular issue, the effort to put an end to the use of labor injunctions, Frankfurter and Richberg worked closely together during the 1920s. The two men proved to be effective allies in the fight against the use of sweeping injunctions in labor disputes, a problem which Bernstein has called the "leading issue of labor policy" in this period. No injunction had ever been more sweeping than the one issued by Judge Wilkerson during the railroad shopmen's strike of 1922. Under its terms, Richberg, as counsel for the unions involved, had even been prohibited from conferring with his clients. Following this strike, Richberg became an important advocate of eliminating the power of judges to enjoin union activities on the basis of the anti-trust laws; while Frankfurter, by the end of the 1920s, had become perhaps the nation's foremost legal scholar on this subject. In 1928, Senator George Norris brought together Richberg and Frankfurter, and two other authorities in the field, to draft a law which finally put an end to the unjustified use of labor injunctions. Their efforts led directly to the eventual enactment of the Norris-La Guardia Anti-Injunction Act of 1932.[26]

Frankfurter's analysis of the injunction issue grew out of a conception of labor organization which closely paralleled Richberg's views on the subject. First, Frankfurter shared Richberg's faith in voluntarism. Although both men supported an act of Congress to resolve the problem posed by labor injunctions, the effect of the law which they helped to write was not to increase government's role in industrial life, but rather to reduce it. Frankfurter contended that since the 1890s, the injunctive process had developed as a one-sided means by which government put "all the coercive powers of society" at the disposal of capital. Josephus Daniels, incidentally, used a similar line of reasoning in a series of editorials written in response to the events surrounding the railway shopmen's strike of 1922. His newspaper described the Wilkerson injunction as "the most drastic judicial crime against free speech in the annals" of American law and defended the right of labor to strike as the workers' only effective weapon against oppressive conditions. The court order by Judge Wilkerson, the paper proclaimed, ought to have been labeled a "rule to destroy labor unions and punish men for belonging to them."[27]

By removing the power of judges to enjoin legitimate strike activities, Frankfurter argued that it would be possible to end the "attitude of hostility towards labor generated by the injunction," so that "the conditions for voluntary negotiation and cooperation" between organized labor and organized capital would be created. In his book, *The Labor Injunction,* published in 1930, Frankfurter approvingly quoted Hoover in support of the concept of voluntarism.

Self-government does not and should not imply the use of political agencies alone. Progress is born of cooperation in the community—not from governmental restraints.[28]

Frankfurter was not, however, a doctrinaire opponent of all forms of government regulation of industrial relations. He had long been a critic of the "liberty of contract" school which denied the state practically any right to regulate the conditions under which labor toiled. In fact, as counsel for the National Consumers' League, Frankfurter went before the Supreme Court in 1923, in the Adkins case, to defend the right of the federal government to establish a minimum wage for women in the District of Columbia. Frankfurter was thus involved in what Bernstein describes as "perhaps the most important" judicial decision of the Twenties affecting the interests of labor.[29]

Frankfurter, though, defended government regulation on quite narrow grounds. In the case of the women workers of the District of Columbia, he argued that their lack of organization, as well as their ignorance, was partly responsible for the fact that some of them were being paid a wage which was not sufficient to afford them "the means necessary to keep their labor going," that is, to live at a minimally decent standard of living. Given such conditions, Frankfurter claimed that it was a reasonable exercise of the police powers of government to protect society from the pauperization of these women by establishing a minimum wage standard. The law entailed no attempt to establish the principle that the government had the right or the ability to fix a fair wage for all workers. It simply set a minimum standard for those unable to protect themselves by bargaining on an equal footing with their employers. In 1916, the Supreme Court had accepted essentially the same argument when Frankfurter had used it in defense of the right of a state to establish a maximum hours standard for women workers. The Supreme Court of 1923, however, no longer found Frankfurter's logic convincing.[30]

Frankfurter's approach to the problem of child labor demonstrated that he did not envision the creation of federally mandated standards for working conditions. He naturally supported the movement to put a stop to the practice of employing children in the nation's factories, but he advised the National Consumers' League against any attempt to accomplish this goal either by constitutional amendment or by federal statute. Frankfurter's objections to seeking action on the federal level were in large part tactical, but he also felt that the power to regulate working conditions ought to be left to the individual states in order to encourage a feeling of "local responsibility" in such matters.[31]

Frankfurter did acknowledge the need for government, at least at the state level, to protect the most unfortunate workers in society by establishing an enforceable standard of minimally decent working conditions. Still, he was more concerned with putting an end to government intervention in labor disputes on the side of capital than he was with finding a way of using the power of the state to support the demands of workers for a larger share of the nation's wealth and a greater voice in running the nation's industries.

Like Richberg, Frankfurter hoped that the voluntary organization of labor would itself enable American industry to operate on a more efficient and rational basis. Yet Frankfurter, too, was not always clear in his own mind whether the organization of labor would contribute to the development of a pluralistic society in which a peaceful and stable equilibrium would be established through the creation of a balance of power or whether it would foster the development of a corporatist society in which all interests would be harmonized. On the one hand, Frankfurter based his approach to the problem of labor organization on the explicit assumption that since large aggregations of capital were "inevitable and socially desirable," it was equally necessary and desirable that "industrial workers" combine in order "to achieve the possibility of free competition with concentrated capital." In opposing government intervention in labor-management disputes, Frankfurter claimed that if labor's right to organize were recognized as a legitimate means of balancing the power of capital, then there would have to be an "acceptance of the economic and social pressure that can come from united action by trade unions." Such language would seem to indicate a pluralist, rather than a corporatist perspective.[32]

However, Frankfurter also argued that unionization, by equalizing the relative power of workers and management, would be an important step toward a recognition of the "principle of joint control" of industry by labor and capital. Ultimately, Frankfurter hoped to see industrial life move "more and more within the area of collaborative enterprise." In this regard, Frankfurter shared Richberg's preference for organization on the basis of "smaller units." Although he appreciated the need for cooperation and coordination on the widest possible scale in industry, he was as opposed to overcentralization as Richberg. Not only did Frankfurter feel that there were limits to the efficiency of overly large organizations, but like Richberg, he also wished to encourage a greater sense of identity of interest between workers and management within individual business concerns. He, too, wanted to avoid the development of an industrial system based upon a monolithic division between an organized working class and an organized capitalist class.[33]

Henry Stimson did not identify with the cause of labor as easily as Richberg or Frankfurter. Early in the Twenties, though, Stimson personally confronted the question of labor organization as a result of being hired to represent the Bituminous Coal Operators' Association before the United States Coal Commission. The commission had been created by the federal government as part of the settlement which had put an end to the nation-wide coal strike of 1922. Before accepting the offer from the operators, Stimson sought assurance from his prospective clients that they would be willing to support a "constructive solution for all" the parties involved. After gaining such an assurance, Stimson undertook an exhaustive six-month study of past and present conditions in the coal industry. One of the first things Stimson did as part of his study was to seek the advice of his friend and former colleague, Felix Frankfurter. The two men exchanged a series of letters over a period of months which revealed both a common interest in finding a sound basis for a revitalization of the industry and certain differences over the role to be played by labor in such a revitalization.[34]

Even before becoming involved in the coal industry investigation, Stimson had acknowledged the need to "salve" the "discontent" a worker felt as a "subordinate" to capital by in "some way" giving him a "voice in the management of his life in the industry to which that life is devoted." While recognizing the need for labor organization, Stimson explained to Frankfurter that he was beginning his investigation of the coal industry with the "prior impression" that:

. . . organization has gone too far geographically and that the only real solution of most of our industrial problems should come from a closer personal touch between employer and employee, which is obtainable only in smaller units.[35]

Stimson also embarked on his own study with a long standing inclination to question the ability of working class people to demonstrate the "self-restraint" which the responsible exercise of power required. From the outset, therefore, Stimson tended to be much more fearful of the potential dangers of unionism than Frankfurter or Richberg, and he was thus more concerned with the necessity of maintaining checks on the possible abuses of power resulting from the organization of labor. In one of his first letters to Frankfurter on the subject, Stimson not only disagreed with his friend's position on the use of labor injunctions, but also expressed his support for the idea of requiring the incorporation of unions as a means of encouraging labor to act responsibly.[36]

In many respects, Stimson approached the problem of unions much as he had approached the problem of trusts twenty years earlier. Both, in his view, seemed to be necessary institutional developments in an industrial society. Both, however, needed to be watched and, at times, regulated by government in order to guard society against their potentially harmful effects. That Stimson could fear the unions of the Twenties, weak as they were, as much as he had once feared the trusts, was a reflection of his social and intellectual background.

Stimson's study of the situation in the coal fields served to confirm his previous suspicions of organized labor. He became more opposed than ever to the "one big union idea," in general, and developed a strong dislike for John L. Lewis' United Mine Workers, in particular. He argued that the country's largest union was trying to "fasten an irresponsible class supergovernment upon American political institutions" with its attempt to "monopolize mine labor throughout the United States." The UMW's use of "the potent engine of the check-off," and its resort to physical violence, Stimson claimed, was "inconsistent with the standards of enlightened and liberal unionism." He later recalled in his memoirs that his investigation of the coal industry "showed him that on both sides of the fence" there had been a "history of ruthlessness," and that:

. . . in a sense the irresponsibility of capital struck him as the more culpable, because he continued to believe that men of wealth and power had special obligations to the community.

Still, at the time, Stimson's most passionate criticisms were directed at the UMW, which he described to Frankfurter as "an arrogant and confident opponent." [37]

When it came time to make recommendations to the Coal Commission, Stimson proposed what he thought was an even-handed approach based on the belief that:

In order to preserve our democracy this nation must ultimately find a solution for our present armed status in labor relations and our present methods of solving labor controversies by industrial force. Our present methods lead directly down the road to larger and larger organizations on both sides,—to the "one big union" idea; to "direct economic action" instead of the reason and persuasion upon which political democracy is based, and hence to the death of our republican system.

The solution, he felt, required the establishment of a framework for industrial relations which would produce a "spirit of partnership in a common enterprise" between the mine operators and the mine workers. Like Frankfurter and Richberg, Stimson sought to put an end to the wasteful chaos of industrial warfare by creating a decentralized institutional framework which would contribute to a growing spirit of cooperation between labor and capital. [38]

Specifically, Stimson recommended the establishment of state industrial commissions equipped with the power to obtain from both labor and management financial data which could be made public. The pressure of informed public opinion, Stimson believed, could be a powerful force in encouraging responsibility in industry. Donald Richberg had similar hopes for those provisions of the Railway Labor Act which likewise called for the publication of the findings of impartial investigative boards. Stimson also advised that the unions and operators work out a mutually agreeable code regarding working conditions in the industry. The great cost to society arising from the disruption of essential coal supplies by occasionally violent labor disputes convinced Stimson that the government ought to be given added powers to guarantee the ongoing functioning of the coal industry in times of emergency. Stimson recommended that the federal government be allowed to insist on the principle of compulsory arbitration in any dispute in which at least one of the parties involved requested it. Compulsory arbitration, in Stimson's view, would not, in such instances, represent an example of political power being used to corrupt the normal operations of private industry. Rather, it was simply a measure of last resort by which the "principles of reason" could be introduced into industrial conflicts which threatened to divide society into warring classes. Finally, Stimson called for the incorporation of unions and an end to the dues check-off system in order to put restraints on labor comparable to those already in existence for capital.[39]

Stimson clearly recognized the desirability of some form of labor organization. Like Richberg and Frankfurter, he thought that labor and management could most effectively work together in a decentralized institutional framework. Looking ahead, however, he believed that it was impossible to predict whether labor relations in the coal industry were going to evolve in the direction of non-union labor, company unions, or independent unions. What he wanted was to "let that form of relations survive which can show itself most consistent with American ideals and of the greatest service to the industry." Unlike Richberg and Frankfurter, Stimson did not oppose company unions on principle. Although the two younger men envisioned the possible development of a harmonious cooperative relationship between labor and capital in the future, for the time being, they remained wary enough of the motives of management to insist on the importance of independent labor organization. In contrast, Stimson had more faith in the good will of industry's present leadership, claiming that "there never was a time when American business stood more firmly upon character" than in the Twenties. Stimson, therefore, was less concerned than either Richberg or Frankfurter with the possibility that company unions would be used simply to control, rather than to represent, labor.[40]

While Stimson did not see company unions as necessarily the most desirable form of labor organization, his willingness to tolerate them was a reflection of a relatively unambiguous corporatist outlook. He viewed labor organization, when rightly conceived, almost excusively as a means toward the corporatist end of harmonious, conflict-free, industrial relations. Unlike

Richberg and Frankfurter, Stimson did not occasionally lapse into a pluralist conception of unions as simply a balance to the power of organized capital. All three men, however, shared the basic assumption that no intractable conflict of interest existed between labor and capital. Moreover, they agreed that the role of government ought to be to encourage the development of voluntaristic mechanisms by which to solve those industrial problems which did exist.

During the 1920s, representatives of American industry effectively appealed to corporatist and voluntarist values as they proclaimed the emergence of a new form of "welfare capitalism." "Industrial relations" became a primary focus of management. Profit-sharing, pension plans, and shop committees were increasingly introduced as means of demonstrating to workers the existence of a community of interest betwen labor and capital. While there had been obvious worker unrest immediately after the First World War, by 1923, a period of relative labor peace began which lasted until the end of the decade. The apparently widespread prosperity of the Twenties seemed a harbinger of a new and better America.[41]

The picture for American workers in the 1920s, however, was not nearly so bright as publicists for American business claimed. The declining power of the nation's railway workers, noted earlier, was characteristic of the experience of the American working class as a whole. Unions remained virtually nonexistent in many of the nation's major industries, most notably steel and automobiles; and union membership actually declined as a percentage of the total non-agricultural labor force, dropping from almost 20 percent in 1920 to about 10 percent in 1930. Richberg and Frankfurter may have sincerely hoped that management would voluntarily recognize the advantages of independent labor organization, but the experience of the 1920s demonstrated that industry was unlikely to accept such a development unless compelled to do so.[42]

The disparity in organizational power between labor and capital in the 1920s, moreover, resulted in an increasingly unequal division of the rewards produced by their joint endeavors. Between 1923 and 1929, the share of national income going to capital rose from 19.6 to 25.5 percent, while the share going to labor declined from 77.9 to 72.9 percent. This shift in the distribution of income, in turn, contributed to a growing concentration of wealth. The share of personal sector wealth held by the top one percent of American adults rose between 1922 and 1929 from 31.6 to 36.3 percent. In fact, in 1929, when inequality in the distribution of wealth may have reached an all-time peak in American history, just one half of one percent of the population owned 32.4 percent of all personal wealth in the United States. Although wages did increase during the decade, in the peak prosperity years of 1923–29, per capita annual disposable income for the average American went down slightly, from $566 in 1923 to $544 in 1929. In contrast, per capita disposable income for the wealthiest one percent of the population increased from $9,641 to $15,721 in this same period. Such figures belied the community of interest between labor and capital which liberals such as Richberg, Frankfurter, and Stimson, as well as more self-interested spokespersons for business, continued to proclaim in the Twenties.[43]

## III

While workers fought a losing battle in the 1920s to maintain the strength of their unions, businessmen were reaping the benefits of organization as never before. The accumulation of huge undistributed surpluses during the First World War helped make possible a new surge of business consolidations which compared in scope to the massive merger movement of the turn of the century. In contrast to the previous wave of mergers, which consisted for the most part of many single-function firms consolidating to form unified companies, the combinations of the Twenties often involved the acquisition of one large integrated enterprise by another large integrated firm. Vertical integration and diversification thus became increasingly characteristic of capital's attempts both to extend its control over a thoroughly coordinated process of production and distribution and to guarantee a steady flow of profits. The strength of large-scale business organization was demonstrated not only by capital's increasing share of national income, but also by the growing concentration of wealth and power within the business community. The largest five percent of American corporations raised their share of total corporate income between 1918 and 1929 from 79.6 to 84.3 percent. By the end of the 1920s, the nation's biggest 200 corporations controlled 38 percent of all business wealth in America. Increasing concentration was also characteristic of the nation's banking industry. In 1929, 250 banks, just one percent of the total, controlled more than 46 percent of the country's banking resources.[44]

Mergers were only one way by which capital sought to concentrate its control and rationalize business activity. In the Twenties, another form of business organization also arose as a powerful force shaping the nation's industrial economy. In many industries where consolidation remained either impossible or still to be achieved, the development of trade associations enabled businessmen to emulate the attempts of oligopolists to create more stable and profitable business conditions. Trade associations, of an informal nature, had first appeared just afer the Civil War. It was not until the twentieth century, however, that they began to play any meaningful role in the nation's economic life. The First World War, as we have seen, served as a great spur to the growth of trade associations. In the post-war decade, these business organizations became increasingly important, contributing not only to the development of more efficient and standardized industrial techniques, but also to the stabilization of market conditions, even to the point of price-fixing.[45]

No man in America did more to encourage the growth of trade associations in the 1920s than Secretary of Commerce Herbert Hoover; but it was Bernard Baruch who had played a crucial role, during and immediately after the First World War, in first bringing to public attention the reputed benefits to society to be gained from this form of voluntary organization. When the final War Industries Board report was published in 1921, Baruch made clear his belief that the nation would benefit from the continued existence of the type of business organization whose development he had helped to foster. Reviewing the "consequences" of the war ten years after the Armistice, Baruch concluded that the "most important" effect of the war on the "nation's general economic pattern" had been the impetus given

to "various industries" to form "into powerful and highly integrated groups." These organizations made possible the "effective pooling of information and energy and the elimination of
waste," and, ultimately, the development of a "more efficient"
system of "production and distribution." The public, he observed, had been not only prompt "to recognize the beneficial
effect of this increased efficiency, but also to question whether
earlier and stricter readings of the anti-trust laws were not sub-
versive of the public interest."[46]

Felix Frankfurter also found much to praise in the trade association movement of the 1920s. He, too, questioned the advisability of allowing too strict an interpretation of the Sherman
Anti-Trust Act to hamper the development of trade associations.
In 1923, he observed:

Broadly speaking, independent units in the various industries seek to
pool their knowledge, or the means for securing knowledge, to make
of business a profession instead of a gamble. The steady growth and
unrestricted dissemination of knowledge is at the core of trade association activities and indispensable to a rational industrial society. The
necessity of "continuous intelligent inquiry," as the basis of knowledge finds no obstacle in the Sherman Law so long as knowledge is
scientifically acquired and publicly communicated.

Frankfurter, however, went on to warn that when trade associations moved from the communication of information to "cooperative action," the "dubious ghost of the Sherman Law"
could then make its "appearance at the business banquet."
Frankfurter seemed to believe that the Sherman Law had little
practical relevance to the demands of modern industrial life, but
he did not rule out the necessity of the government occasionally
using the law as one means of maintaining a check on the potential abuses of trade associations and large concentrations of
capital.[47]

Neither Frankfurter nor Baruch was personally involved with
the trade association movement which spread through American industry in the 1920s. Henry Stimson, on the other hand,
did become directly associated with two such organizations. He
had undertaken his study of the coal industry in the capacity of
counsel to the coal operators' national trade association. At the

time, Stimson praised the efforts of his clients to establish a "united viewpoint" before the United States Coal Commission, and he also came to respect the association's attempts to make the entire industry more efficient through a widespread exchange of information. Even before taking on the coal industry assignment, Stimson had been hired by the Cement Manufacturers' Protective Association, a regional organization of Eastern producers, to represent that group in a law suit brought against it by the federal government for alleged violations of the antitrust laws. Stimson's participation in this suit allowed him to examine the issue of trade associations in depth. It also involved him in a case which was of great importance in the evolution of a legal definition of the acceptable scope of trade association activities.[48]

Ironically, while Hoover took office as Secretary of Commerce intent on encouraging the growth of trade associations and other forms of voluntary cooperation in industry, Warren Harding's Attorney-General, Harry Daugherty, responded to public concern and political pressures about the problem of monopoly by initiating a campaign in 1921 to limit the scope of trade association activities. The suit against the cement producers was the first step in this campaign. Central to the case was the issue of "open pricing." In a number of industries, the exchange of statistical information relating to pricing between supposedly competing firms had become a means of virtual price-fixing. In defending the Cement Manufacturers' Protective Association, Stimson refused to admit that his clients had actually engaged in price-fixing. He argued that the producers had made no attempt to establish definite pooling arrangements based on fixed prices, and that all their activities had been carried on publicly and on a voluntary basis. The trade association's activities thus bore no resemblance, in Stimson's opinion, to the predatory type of destructive competition and restraint of trade practiced by the trusts of an earlier day. Stimson's defense of the cement manufacturers clearly reflected his own belief that the trade association movement, rather than deserving condemnation, merited praise for its contribution to the development of more rational decision-making processes in industry. The cement case itself had a tortured history and failed to become the first major court test to define the legal limits of trade association activities. In another case, though, the Supreme Court upheld the logic of Stimson's argument.[49]

Stimson believed that the growth of trade associations would further the development of a more orderly and efficient economy in much the same way that the organization of labor would contribute to the same end. The voluntary organization of businessmen, like the voluntary organization of workers, would allow for the introduction of a more scientific basis for industrial life, since it would make possible a greater degree of coordination and cooperation between the various sectors of the economy. The trade association movement thus offered a means of rationalizing economic activity without any additional government intervention in the nation's industrial life. Looking back on the developments of the post-war years, Stimson declared in 1929 that:

. . . modern life is a life of organization and that the man, the business organization, or the country, which wishes to make progress today must learn the art of organization. Particularly is that true in the case of trade organizations. It has been my experience in the United States to come in contact with the recent growth of trade organization which has been one of the features of the last twenty-five years in the United States. . . . And no one can do that without feeling how important it is for every business to organize and how helpless the business man is who has not the benefit of membership in a great business or trade organization.

In all areas of life, according to Stimson, "the organization of private citizens in the different ways in which they are interested" was conducive to the development of a healthy society. Such organizations could also "bring home to the Government" the criticisms and the information which were at different times needed to insure "good government."[50]

The increasing emphasis on organization, coordination, and cooperation which can be seen in the thinking of the men considered here reflected a continuing evolution in their conception of the function of the marketplace in a liberal society. Richberg expressed this changing perspective when he observed in 1922 that it had become necessary to admit that the law of supply and demand had "been amended or annulled by modern industrial organization." Stimson welcomed the movement toward more standardized and coordinated industrial practices because he believed it would help eliminate the kind of erratic price competition which had formerly been a source of instability for the American economy. Baruch echoed this theme when he noted that, in the case of the steel industry, the nation's interests were better served by allowing U.S. Steel to act as a "stabilizer" than by insisting on a return to "uneconomic competition." "Our whole system of modern business," Baruch proclaimed, had come to be based on the assumption that "noncompetitive selling will get me a fairer price than competitive selling." Baruch even went so far as to call for the establishment of a "high court of commerce" to serve as a "properly constituted arbitral authority" before which "business men would come with such questions as whether in time of over-production and low prices they could cut down production and fix a price."[51]

Neither Baruch, nor any of the other men discussed in this study, however, were prepared to abandon completely their faith in the ultimate desirability of a market economy. Jordan Schwarz accurately describes Baruch as being "ambivalent" about the question of whether corporate decision-making could, or ought to, supplant the "organic market forces of supply and demand." At almost the same time he suggested the possibility of creating a "court of commerce," Baruch acknowledged that industrial planning of the sort attempted during the First World War remained both impractical and undesirable.

The thought naturally arises, why if regulation of prices and distribution of production can be done in war time, they cannot be done in peace time. The answer is that this cannot be done. In war there is the urge of common danger and common sacrifice and a spirit of service which, in my opinion, cannot be brought about in peace time. We have not yet found during time of peace anybody wise enough to say what individuals shall do, nor have we found a substitute for personal initiative. Even during the war, when regulations were put into effect, the endeavor was always made to leave as untrammeled as possible personal initiative and opportunity to gain from it so far as it did not affect the general interest.[52]

To understand the modified role assigned to the market by the liberals examined here, it is necessary to distinguish between their conception of the function of cooperative activity within a given industry and their view of the function of market forces in the economy as a whole. Although liberals were increasingly willing to see the "visible hand of management" replace the "invisible hand of market forces" as the coordinator of the production process, they still relied on the market to determine the overall demand for goods and services. Administrative expertise might be used to speed the flow of goods through industry and to try to even out the swings of the business cycle, but the market would, at least in the long run, determine both what products would be produced and the value of those products. As Baruch put it, consolidations would have to continue in order to insure "quantity production and quantity distribution," but within an increasingly stable and ordered framework "competition in price and service" would have to be "preserved between the larger units" which remained.[53]

Liberals such as Baruch and Stimson realized that cooperative activity and vertical integration in industry entailed possible dangers, as well as potential benefits. Trade associations could be used as a means of manipulating market conditions to the detriment of the consumer. Baruch's proposal for a "court of commerce" clearly reflected his realization of the need to have a public body "clothed with the power and charged with the responsibility of standing watch against and preventing [the] abuses" which cooperative activity made possible. Far more important than the court's negative watchdog function, however, would be its role in putting the imprimatur of government sanction on decisions made by voluntary organizations in the private sector. Yet it is important to keep in mind that Baruch's proposed commerce court was intended essentially as a court of last resort to be utilized in times of economic stress. Baruch did not envision a centralized agency of economic planning responsible for either creating or approving master plans for the entire economy. Baruch, as well as the other men discussed here, still doubted that any individual or group of individuals could possess the wisdom or character needed to justify comprehensive economic planning.[54]

In groping toward a new conception of a more highly organized and rationalized market economy, Stimson and Baruch, in particular, both saw great promise in the development of what would later be called "managerial capitalism." Extensive government oversight or control of an increasingly concentrated private sector would remain unnecessary because, in the words of Stimson, a trend toward "popular ownership" of industry had contributed to the evolution of a new type of business leader who showed a "much more enlightened respect for the rights and interests of the public" than had the robber barons of an earlier era. Stimson and Baruch both believed that as more and more people purchased stock in the nation's great corporations, the gulf separating producers from consumers would narrow. Buyers and sellers, according to Stimson, were already coming to realize their "unity of interest" in much the same way that organized labor and management were coming to appreciate their common interests. Baruch claimed that "perhaps no single circumstance in post-war development" had "done more to increase and secure the solidarity of our economic and social structure" than the spread of stock ownership to a larger proportion of the population.[55]

Donald Richberg, in contrast, dissented from the view that the "new proprietorship" might "transform the conflicting interests of seller and purchaser . . . into the common interest of genuine cooperators." He continued to believe that so long as the "competitive instinct" remained a fundamental part of human nature, and "competition" remained "the life of trade," buyers and sellers of goods would continue to have divergent interests. These divergent interests, it should be noted, were, in Richberg's view, the healthy and natural product of a market economy, not a potential source of socially divisive class conflict between labor and capital. In fact, while Richberg discounted the possibility that stock dispersion might alter the relation between consumers and producers, he was hopeful that stock purchases by employees in the companies for which they worked might help eliminate much of the unhealthy "competition between employer and employee" which was a threat to social stability and industrial efficiency. Richberg thus saw employee stock purchases as a constructive way of reinforcing labor and capital's common identity as producers involved in a collaborative enterprise.[56]

Implicit in Stimson and Baruch's enthusiasm for the growth

of "popular ownership" was the assumption that this trend was accelerating the development of a more professional, as well as more socially responsible, industrial leadership consisting of career managers devoted to the ideal of efficiency, rather than capitalist entrepreneurs intent on the maximization of profits regardless of social cost. Some social scientists would subsequently claim that the growing separation between ownership and the actual control of industry occurring in the 1920s marked the arrival of a "managerial revolution" which permanently changed the nature of American capitalism. The dispersion of stock ownership required by the immense capital demands of modern corporations, and the increasing importance of bureaucratic, as opposed to entrepreneurial, skills, combined to make the professional manager the key decision-making figure in modern business enterprise. Both Baruch and Stimson in the 1920s, and many writers since, have thus held out the hope that the "managerial revolution" would bring with it the development of a more rational and less exploitative form of capitalism.[57]

Such a view, however, had little basis in reality. To begin with, stock ownership in the 1920s (and since) remained the prerogative of just a tiny minority of the American people. In 1929 only about one percent of the population, one and a half million people, had individual stock holdings. Within that group, 51,000 individuals received half the value of all the cash dividends given out to individual shareowners. Ownership of industry may have become indirectly dispersed through stock purchased by financial and savings institutions, but very few Americans had any sense of themselves as "owners" of American industry.[58]

Moreover, while the route to power in industry may have changed, the professional managers whose climb up the bureaucratic ladder brought them into positions of leadership differed only in style and tactics, not ultimate objectives, from their entrepreneurial predecessors. Although the managers who came to direct American industry may not have had controlling ownership interests in the companies they operated, they still often had sizable stock holdings in their own firms. Because of their interest in maximizing the scope of their administrative control and guaranteeing the full use of the bureaucratic hierarchies which they headed, managers may often have put the goals of expansion and diversification above short-term profits. However, in the long run, according to one leading student of modern management, "the profit orientation of executives in management-controlled firms is about as strong as it is for executives in owner-controlled companies." The new professionals who increasingly began to take over direction of American industry in the 1920s were neither democratically selected nor did they define their professional task as serving the public interest. Rather, they gained their power simply because their special training made them highly effective servants of the long-term interest of capital.[59]

**IV**

Jordan Schwarz observes that the plight of the nation's farmers in the 1920s provided an especially "stern test of the efficacy" of the voluntaristic philosophy advocated by liberals such as Bernard Baruch and Herbert Hoover. While Baruch had done so much to encourage the growth of trade associations in industry during the First World War, in the Twenties he became personally preoccupied with the efforts of American farmers to use similar techniques of voluntary organization and cooperation to stem the oncoming tide of agricultural depression. Baruch's activities in the field of agriculture, in effect, closely paralleled the efforts of Richberg, Frankfurter, and Stimson to assist the self-organization of workers and businessmen.[60]

American farmers experienced unprecedented prosperity during the First World War as the United States became the world's major supplier of food. After the war, however, farm prices collapsed and farm mortgage foreclosures increased dramatically, remaining at high levels throughout the Twenties. Although the disposable income of farmers began to increase steadily after 1921, it still lagged far behind that of other groups in the economy. America farmers, consequently, ruefully compared their situation in the 1920s to the halcyon days of war and looked for some means of gaining a greater share in the prosperity which other Americans were apparently enjoying in the period.[61]

Prior to the Twenties, Baruch had had little experience with, or interest in, the problems of farmers. His new found concern for the plight of the farmer, therefore, deserves some comment. The immediate cause of Baruch's interest was an invitation in 1920 from the Kansas State Board of Agriculture to participate in a conference dealing with the problems of farmers. Baruch was only one of a number of prominent businessmen and public figures who were invited, but for him the invitation was to take on special importance. Soon, he was publicly speaking out and privately lobbying in Congress in behalf of the farmer's cause. He also began financially backing farmers' organizations throughout the country.[62]

In his autobiography, Baruch claims that childhood memories of life in rural South Carolina and his father's interest in agricultural experimentation predisposed him to respond sympathetically to the plight of the nation's farmers. More to the point, Baruch's attempt to aid the country's farmers undoubtedly provided him with an opportunity to reinforce, both in his own mind, and in the view of others, the Southern identity which he fostered as a counter to his image as a Wall Street Jew. In addition, showing concern for the impoverished farmer allowed him to maintain his war-time image as an unselfish public benefactor. Baruch himself observed that the war:

. . . had taken me out of Wall Street, often described as a narrow alley with a graveyard at one end and a river at the other, and plunged me deeply into the broad stream of national and international affairs.

Since Wall Street now "appeared dull" to Baruch, the farmer's plight offered a new cause with which to become involved.[63]

The field of agriculture held out a special challenge for Baruch. It was one sector of the economy which was "a glaring example of the evils of unbridled competition," evils which could be "as bad, if not worse, than those of monopoly." Baruch realized that millions of farmers throughout the country remained "highly independent and individualistic while all the commercial world around them was forming itself into efficient organizations and integrations, corporate or otherwise." Farmers had to sell their product in a buyer's market because they were "blindly competing with one another" and, at the same time, buy goods in "a more or less orderly market" because other groups in society enjoyed the advantages of organization. Proclaiming that "the people who are organized are the only ones who ever get anything," Baruch saw his task as encouraging and assisting farmers to develop their own forms of voluntary organization so that they, too, would be able to reap the benefits of cooperation and planning.[64]

Cooperative marketing became the cornerstone of the plan Baruch presented to Kansas farmers in 1920. Over the next several years, he frequently spoke out in favor of this principle and used his influence in Congress to help spur passage of the Capper-Volstead Act which exempted agricultural marketing cooperatives from the anti-trust laws. Baruch's financial contributions made possible the creation of a number of cooperatives in various regions of the country. More efficient organization, he argued, also required establishing a more reliable basis for farm credit. He proposed to accomplish this objective by encouraging farmers to build modern crop storage facilities and to adopt adequate grading and inspection procedures, which together would make possible the development of a sound commodity-based credit system. He hoped that farmers themselves would create such a system by using their own capital, but in the event that proved impractical, Baruch supported state, though not federal, funding by means of bond issues which would be paid off by the farmers who were to benefit from them.[65]

The agricultural program which Baruch advocated in the early Twenties was founded on the assumption that while the nation's economy was no longer based on a free market model of competition among individuals, the voluntary organization of various economic interests was creating an "orderly market" system based upon group competition. Such a system could accurately be called pluralistic and would, in Baruch's view, enable the American economy to capitalize on the potential advantages of cooperation and coordination without having to bear the unacceptable costs entailed in the development of extensive political controls over the nation's economic life.

Baruch acknowledged, however, that farm prices would be

determined not only by what farmers did for themselves, but also by world market conditions beyond their control. American agriculture would remain in a relatively depressed state so long as American farmers were unable to sell their products in Europe. Baruch argued that Republican tariff policy in the 1920s, by excluding many European goods from the American market, not only made it difficult for Europeans to earn the dollars needed to pay for imports of American farm products, but also encouraged Europeans to enact tariff walls closing off their markets to American farm products. Baruch thus came to admit that because of the international economic situation, his proposals alone would not be sufficient to bring prosperity to America's farmers. By 1922 Baruch had concluded, therefore, that "in the light of all the circumstances," an approach which would be "less ideal" than the voluntarist one he advocated might prove "more practicable" until such time as the markets of Europe would again offer a profitable outlet for American agricultural exports. When George Peek, one of "Baruch's boys" on the War Industries Board, came up with a plan to involve the government directly in an effort to guarantee the "parity" of farm prices, Baruch became one of the plan's most important backers.[66]

Peek's plan for "equality in agriculture" was incorporated into the McNary-Haugen bills which were introduced in Congress during the 1920s. It represented a significant departure from the traditional liberal conception of the relationship between the government and the economy, since it called for the establishment, by statute, of a "parity price" for major farm commodities based on the average price level for the ten year period preceding the First World War. The exportable surplus would be purchased at the parity price and then resold abroad, at a loss if necessary, by a government-created marketing corporation. By this means, domestic demand and supply were to be brought into a balance more favorable to the nation's farmers, so that domestic prices would be kept from falling to the lower levels set by the world market. Although the government was thus to become heavily involved in agriculture, one of the most "attractive" features of Peek's scheme, in Baruch's view, was that it was "predicated on the principle of self-help," since the farmers themselves would bear all the cost of the program through the payment of an "equalization fee" on the crops they harvested. Given world conditions, and the immense difficulty of creating an effective nation-wide farmers' organization without calling upon the assistance of the government, Baruch found the plan incorporated into the McNary-Haugen bills the most "pragmatic" solution available for the farm problem. His influence helped win enough Democratic support to get the program passed by Congress on two separate occasions. Each time, however, Presidential vetoes prevented the bills from becoming law.[67]

While Baruch backed what he considered a less than "ideal" plan to have the government interfere to an unprecedented extent with the normal operation of the law of supply and demand, his support was couched in limited terms. Testifying before the House Agriculture Committee in 1923, Baruch insisted that he was "not one of those who look upon government as a great mother to whom we can go and lay all our troubles." Under normal conditions, he claimed, he would never have favored any attempt to supplant the results of market decisions with political determinations of what was socially desirable. However, as he later explained, so long as the Republicans were unwilling to:

. . . knock down the old artificiality of the industrial tariff, which interfered with the normal working of supply and demand, we had to build up a new artificiality to offset it. This usually happens when we interpose man-made laws against natural law. We have to interpose another innovation to save us from the effect of the first.

Baruch thus still believed that once tariff barriers were removed and the domestic market for agricultural products was properly organized into larger units, market forces operating on a broad scale would produce socially beneficial results.[68]

Baruch's analysis of the farm problem did not go to the heart of the matter. Even taken together, cooperative marketing and an end to tariff barriers would not have brought prosperity to the nation's farms. It was not so much tariff barriers, but rather the return of European farms to full production after the First World War and the development of agriculture in other areas of the world which resulted in intense international competition and low world prices for farm products. Lowered farm prices then combined with heavy indebtedness to drive many American farmers off the land. In order to expand production during tne war, American farmers had mortgaged their farms on the basis of the inflated values of the time, only to find that the post-war decline in farm prices made those mortgages too heavy a burden to bear. Finally, Baruch never seriously considered the way in which a highly unequal distribution of wealth and the persistence of poverty in the United States limited the domestic demand for agricultural products. Baruch's approach to the farm problem revealed his ambivalence about the viability of a pure market economy. However, in seeking to encourage farmers to adopt the organizational methods of industry, Baruch continued to assume that production for profit was the only feasible economic goal and that the overall distribution of wealth was not a proper concern of government.[69]

It is ironic that the farm issue at one time elicited from Donald Richberg an uncharacteristically forthright statement concerning the existence of class conflict in America. Writing to railway union leader D. B. Robertson in 1926, Richberg observed:

Of all groups of American citizens the farmers have suffered the most at the hands of their self-appointed friends. There are farm journals of wide circulation controlled by, and run for the benefit of, grain speculators who profit by the farmers' losses. There are farm organizations supported by, and maintained in the interest of, public utilities and other private enterprises that exploit the farmers with shameless greed. And the farmers will continue to be poorly paid and heavily burdened workers until such time as they recognize that their problems are the same as those of industrial workers; and that their opponents are the same groups that exploit industrial workers; and that in order to relieve themelves of the same oppression against which the industrial workers have organized and won victories, the farmers must form and control their own organizations . . . [and learn] the simple truth that all men who live by their own labor have common interests in opposition to all those who live by exploiting the labor of other men.[70]

Richberg's use in this instance of what would seem to be the language of class analysis needs some explanation. Richberg was, in fact, venting his anger at the Kansas *Farm Journal* for its editorial opposition to the Railway Labor Act. In calling upon farmers to recognize their common interests with labor, he was actually complaining about a farm journal's failure to support a law which he himself held up as evidence of the possible harmony of interest between labor and capital. Rather than being a statement advocating class struggle, Richberg's remarks ought to be interpreted primarily as an indication of his belief in the importance of voluntary self-organization by all interest groups in society.


## V


The farm problem tested the limits of Baruch's faith in the efficacy of a more "orderly market" system. During the 1920s the question of public utilities provided a similar test for all the men examined in this study. While the focus on voluntary organization was the key to liberal hopes in this period, an examination of the positions the five men discussed here took on the problem of public utilities reveals the inner contradictions and tensions which characterizes their commitment to the liberal tradition.

Public utilities had long posed certain special considerations for liberals, since natural monopolies, such as water and power systems, or public transportation and communication facilities, functioned almost wholly outside the sphere of market conditions. Liberals had generally been concerned not with trying to maintain a nonexistent free market in such cases, but rather with deciding whether government regulation or government ownership provided the best means of safeguarding the interests of the community in the operation of these industries. In the Twenties, policy debates on the public utilities issue gained in significance because of both the tremendous growth and the increasing concentration of control in the electric power industry. Huge holding companies, whose empires extended across many state borders, became the dominant form of organization in the electric power industry. This was not so much because holding companies insured better coordination or greater efficiency, but rather because they could often be used as devices for evading the control of state or local public utilities commissions, defrauding investors through the pyramiding of one corporation on top of another, and draining funds out of their operating companies by making excessive charges for services and goods supplied by the parent firm.[71]

Henry Stimson and Bernard Baruch's positions in the public utility debate of the 1920s demonstrated their willingness to accept government regulation of industries which had a practical monopoly on services essential to society. More importantly, however, their views on this issue also revealed the depth of their ideological opposition to public operation of even the most critical public service industries. As Secretary of War under Taft, Stimson had helped to establish the principle of federal regulation of private industry's right to exploit the hydro-electric power potential of the nation's rivers. Stimson, as well as Baruch, however, felt that government was itself ill-equipped to run the day-to-day operations of any business. Government, Stimson argued, could only be relied upon to engage in "business operations" which followed "standardized and well understood channels," since "initiative" and the capacity to plan efficiently were rarely found in the public sector. The unique conditions of the public utilities industry justified a degree of government regulation greater than that required for other aspects of the economy. Stimson believed, however, that public operation, as opposed to government regulation, of the nation's electric power industry would result in the appointment of a government manager who "would be a far more powerful and irresponsible autocrat than anything this country has ever seen." Economic decisions in the private sector, he believed, were at least ultimately subject to the constraints of market forces and had to be made under the watchful eye of government. In the event of public operation of utilities, though, economic decisions would be turned into potentially arbitrary political choices not subject to any outside controls. Regulated private operation based on the incentive of reasonable profits was, therefore, not only more efficient than public operation based on a politically determined view of the public interest. It was also, in Stimson's view, more conducive to the maintenance of a free society.[72]

While Stimson and Baruch were especially opposed to federal control of the utilities industry, they also rejected the more limited idea of municipal ownership. Both men were concerned that public operation of city services such as water and power, or transportation, had, in Stimson's words, an "inevitable tendency" to "drift into paternalism." By this, he meant that the inefficiency of government operation tended to build up deficits which an irresponsible management would then make up by increases in the burdens of general taxation. To Stimson and Baruch, this represented a form of class government in that it forced the substantial property-owning citizens of a city to subsidize the operation of services which might disproportionately benefit the poorer elements of the community. Stimson and Baruch thus went further in their application of the test of class government than the other men examined in this study, but their argument was based upon a generally shared ideological assumption that government ought to engage only in activities designed to have an equal impact on all citizens.[73]

The public utilities issue was viewed in a different light by Donald Richberg and Felix Frankfurter. For them, it proved to be a much more severe test of their faith in the private sector's ability to fulfill public needs. Richberg first became personally involved with this problem in 1915, when he was hired by the city of Chicago to represent it in an attempt to force Samuel Insull's Peoples Gas Company to lower its rates and to return to the city's residents money previously collected as a result of excessive charges. Richberg's work on this case lasted well into the Twenties. It helped to convince him that those who controlled a community's public utilities had "a power practically of life and death . . . a power greater than that of any government in modern times." He concluded, moreover, that:

History has shown that human beings cannot be safely entrusted with such power which would destroy democratic government and put an end to individual liberty. That is why we have public regulation of public utilities.[74]

Clearly Richberg was as fearful of the private control of essential social services as Stimson was of their political control. Throughout the 1920s, however, Richberg, like Stimson and

Baruch, supported government regulation, rather than public ownership, of utilities as the most hopeful means of safeguarding the interests of consumers. In particular, he concentrated on the problem of revamping the system of rate regulation. He fought to establish the principle that "the earning power of a public utility should be allowed to equal but not exceed, the cost of service," including a fair return on the capital actually invested. Richberg thus focused primarily on the problem of insuring reasonable rates by curtailing the excessive charges which resulted from private capital's attempts to maximize profits. He still apparently agreed with Stimson and Baruch that government operation was either undesirable or impractical. He thus failed to consider the potential benefits to be gained from planning based on community needs rather than on the quest for profit.[75]

Richberg, however, did become increasingly disenchanted, during the 1920s, with the effectiveness of government rate regulation. He claimed that regulatory commissions were too frequently staffed by individuals tied to the industries they were supposedly policing, and that judges too often interfered with, and, in effect, undermined, the operation of existing regulatory agencies. He warned that if public regulation could not be made more effective, the alternative of public ownership would become more appealing. Richberg acknowledged that "our political machinery is poorly adapted to the selection of the best men to operate public services." He noted that after "reading government ownership literature for years," he had still "not become convinced that this is a cure all." However, by the end of the decade, the continuing irresponsibility of utility industry leaders like Insull, and the growing importance to the community of the services which were at issue, caused Richberg to question the advisability of continued private ownership of utilities. He expressed his ambivalence about the reliability of the private sector when he observed:

I would point out that the industrial machinery, although fairly well adapted to the selection of the best men to operate private business for private profit, is very poorly adapted to the selection of the best public servants to handle public business.[76]

Felix Frankfurter was reaching similar conclusions about the public utilities industry in this period. Frankfurter's first contact with the problem of utility regulation came during his years as an aide to Stimson in the War Department. He stayed on in the Department for a year under Stimson's successor principally to help work on the proposals which ultimately led to the creation of the Federal Power Commission in 1920. Subsequently, Frankfurter taught a course on the subject of utility regulation throughout his career at Harvard.[77]

Frankfurter, like Richberg, argued against excessive judicial intervention in the regulatory process. He also favored a revision of the rate-making basis for utilities to reflect real investment, rather than the replacement value of industry equipment. Frankfurter recognized that there was no "identity of interest between the utilities and the community which the utility serves." He was confident, though, that in most cases government regulation, rather than ownership, would serve to "reconcile" the "conflicting interests" of industry and community on the basis of the "theory of Anglo-Saxon law," that is, by achieving "a balanced representation of those interests." Although Frankfurter was thus optimistic about the potential effectiveness of regulation, he was willing to support public development in the field of hydro-electric power in order to insure that "the greatest natural resource owned by the State can be used predominantly for the public welfare and not for profit." When Franklin Roosevelt was elected Governor of New York in 1928, Frankfurter became an important adviser to the future President on the issue of utility regulation and in Roosevelt's campaign for public development of the hydro-electric power of the St. Lawrence River.[78]

The public utility issue revealed the ambivalence that both Frankfurter and Richberg felt about relying on private enterprise and the profit motive for the promotion of the public welfare. Both men, however, failed to generalize the concern they had in the public utilities field into a broader critique of the operating principles of the nation's capitalist economy. If it was necessary for government to regulate the price of power, then it should have been equally necessary for it to regulate the price of such other economic essentials as coal or steel. Even more importantly, if government development and operation of the hydro-electric power which lay stored up in the nation's rivers was necessary to insure that the welfare of the public became the guiding principle in the decisions taken in this field, then why was it not also imperative to make democratically determined goals, rather than private profit, the guiding principle in the operation of all essential industries? The public utility issue tested the logic of Richberg and Frankfurter's commitment to the liberal tradition. It demonstrated that in spite of their recognition of certain inherent weaknesses in that tradition, they were unwilling or unable to transcend its limits when they considered the political economy as a whole.

Josephus Daniels' career during the 1920s was marked by relative obscurity, but his response in this period to the problem of how best to operate public utilities and develop the nation's natural resources is quite revealing. Back home in North Carolina, Daniels continued to be a strong advocate of strict government regulation of public utilities. Like Richberg and Frankfurter, he favored tying utility rates to the actual money invested so that consumers would not have to pay excessive charges based either on watered stock or on inflated replacement costs for existing capital equipment. Daniels' approach to the problem of government regulation of utilities was, for the most part, an expression of a liberalism which was fairly conventional for the Twenties. However, on the issue of government ownership and development of certain natural resources, Daniels seems to have stretched his liberal faith more than any of the other men examined in this study.[79]

One public controversy, the Teapot Dome scandal, did temporarily bring Daniels back into the national spotlight in the 1920s. As Secretary of the Navy, Daniels had led the fight in the Wilson administration to prevent the naval oil reserves at Teapot Dome, and elsewhere, from being leased to private developers, arguing that their "sacred setting aside" ought not be reversed simply for the benefit of a few profit-hungry oil companies. Daniels was unable to convince Congress that government oil lands ought not to be leased under any circumstances, but he did succeed, in 1920, in winning a compromise victory in which Congress decided to give to the Secretary of the Navy the power to decide how best to utilize and develop government oil reserves. Soon after Harding took office, however, a new executive order transferred control over the reserves to the Interior Department. Secretary of the Interior Al-

bert Fall then leased Teapot Dome to oilman Edward Doheny—
after Doheny extended Fall a personal "loan" of $100,000.[80]

When news of a possible scandal surfaced in 1922, Daniels
eagerly assisted Robert La Follette's first Congressional probe
into the matter. In the next two years, Daniels was further drawn
into the growing controversy when Republican partisans tried to
link him to the scandal by pointing to his role in having supported the legislation which affirmed the government's right to
lease areas in the public domain to private developers. Daniels,
of course, had favored such legislation only because it enabled
him, as Secretary of the Navy, to reject offers of private development, and he ultimately emerged from the scandal as one of
the country's most effective advocates of reserving the resources of the public domain for public purposes.[81]

Initially, Daniels supported the protection of oil reserves as
a measure of "national preparedness." Having been a war-time
Secretary of the Navy, he realized the military importance of
guaranteeing adequate and reasonably priced supplies of oil in
time of war. For similar reasons, Daniels had favored government development, during and after the war, of the nitrate
sources located at Muscle Shoals. In the latter case, moreover,
he observed that the government's completion of the project
begun during the war at Muscle Shoals (later to become the
heart of the Tennessee Valley Authority) would also have the
benefit of insuring the "conservation of water power for all the
people" of the area.[82]

Daniels soon came to believe that the issue of Teapot Dome
ought to be considered within the broader context of the need
to protect all of the country's natural resources from unnecessary exploitation by private developers. In 1924, Daniels suggested that the Democratic campaign platform deal with the
scandal in a comprehensive plank entitled "Thou Shalt Not
Steal," and he once again expressed sympathy with an idea
which he had first raised publicly in 1916, public development
of certain natural resources. Discussing the proposd Democratic
platform for 1924, his Raleigh *News & Observer* editorialized:

The call for government control of the anthracite mining and other
corporations controlling the necessities of life where public welfare
has been subordinated to private interests will meet a responsive echo
in many minds. The coal mining interests have been robbing the peo-

ple time out of mind. The time has come for drastic action. Long ago coal, oil and water power ought to have been nationalized.[83]

Daniels thus seriously questioned the assumption that private enterprise based on the incentive of profit was necessarily the most efficient and desirable means of developing the country's resources. Public development, he recognized, offered a feasible and perhaps essential alternative, at least in certain natural resource industries affecting the "necessities of life." There is no indication, however, that Daniels' interest in nationalization extended beyond a few special cases. Daniels' social background and ideological upbringing prepared him to be ever watchful of the rich and the powerful, but it also caused him to see acts of economic exploitation as evidence of individual wrongdoing, rather than as the inevitable products of a capitalist system. In situations where a long history of wrongdoing prevailed, or in which vital resources still remained in the public domain, public development might be called for as a means of providing for the general welfare and of punishing those who had abused the power of private ownership. Public development, however, was not seen by Daniels as part of a general restructuring of the economic system. Nationalization was not to be extended to more than a handful of industries involving natural resources, and public planning was not to replace, or even significantly supplement, the force of market decisions in the operation of the economy as a whole. Still, Daniels' call for the nationalization of the coal, oil, and water power resources of the country indicates the inner tensions which existed within his liberal ideology. His commitment to the ideals of equality and democracy was, in this instance, coming into open conflict with his faith in capitalism.

## VI

Until fairly recently, most historians regarded the Twenties as a period of ideological conservatism and political retrenchment reminiscent of the Gilded Age. While there is no denying that the popular political climate of the post-war decade differed significantly from that of the pre-war era of reform, the present study confirms the view emerging from recent scholarship that the Twenties marked an important period in the continuing evolution of a "new liberalism" engaged in the "search for a modern order." During these years, the men discussed here participated in a broad ongoing movement which sought to adapt America's liberal inheritance to the demands of life in an increasingly bureaucraticized industrial society.[84]

In the Twenties, the liberals considered in this study continued to move away from an unqualified belief in the virtues of a pure market economy. They also recognized more clearly than ever before that an ideology based on the unbridled individualism of the past would be an anarchronism in the highly complex and interdependent society of the twentieth century. For at least four of these five men, increased voluntary organization and the further utilization of professional administrative expertise in the private sector seemed to offer the best hope for bringing about both greater economic efficiency and greater social justice. The Twenties were thus a key transition period in the continuing "organizational revolution" in American life, as liberals such as those discussed here increasingly came to see the group and the organization, rather than the individual, as the basic units of social and economic life.

In favoring voluntary organization as a means of creating a more stable and more orderly market economy, the men considered here were not, however, always clear or consistent as to whether the political economy they envisioned for the future would be essentially corporatist or pluralist in character. A number of historians have noted the growth in the 1920s of both corporatist and pluralist thinking, the former assuming a harmony of interest between labor and capital which would make possible the establishment of self-regulating corporate communities governed by a sense of common goals, the latter based on the notion that competition between interest groups of roughly equal power would produce a stable and equitable social balance in which no one group would be able seriously to exploit any other. Most historians, however, have not fully realized the extent to which these two seemingly contradictory sets of ideas could be simultaneously entertained by the same people. Yet these liberals at times found both conceptions of voluntary organization appealing.

During the Twenties, these men were still grasping for a way to adapt their liberal inheritance to the world which they saw changing around them. They recognized the importance of ever more extensive organization and planning in economic life, but they continued to resist the idea that the state itself should be the ultimate arbiter in the overall allocation of resources and wealth. In their view, the profit motive continued to be the most effective incentive for productive activity, and government coercion remained the greatest threat to liberty. While they acknowledged the growing importance of group identities and group organization in modern life, they still believed that American capitalism had not created and need not necessarily create in the future any fundamental conflicts or divisions along class lines. Corporatism and pluralism both had an appeal for liberals in the 1920s because both conceptions of political economy reaffirmed not only the essentially anti-statist bias of liberals, but also their fear of the possible development of class consciousness in American society. At the same time, both corporatism and pluralism justified a greater degree of economic coordination and rationalization than had been possible so long as a more purely individualistic version of free market capitalism held sway. None of the men discussed here had yet definitely opted for either a thoroughly corporatist or a thoroughly pluralist conception of liberalism in the Twenties. While it may be clear in hindsight that the two sets of ideas are in many ways contradictory, this incompatibility was not so apparent to those living in the 1920s when corporatist and pluralist ideas were still in an early stage of development. Thus, during the Twenties liberals such as those studied here could simultaneously entertain both conceptions as possible alternatives to both the laissez-faire individualism of the past, which they viewed as anachronistic, and the socialist collectivism which they saw looming dangerously in the future if liberalism was not successfully adapted to modern needs.

The men discussed here looked with optimism in the 1920s to the continuing development of a prosperous and just society built on liberal principles. Certainly there was much to be optimistic about with regard to the performance of the American economy between 1919 and 1929. Manufacturing output in these years increased by 64 percent, and the total GNP, in constant prices, rose by 40 percent. These liberals refused, however, fully to come to terms with certain basic inequities which continued to characterize the American political economy.[85]

Control of income-producing assets remained in the hands of a numerically small social class, and this elite became the principal beneficiary of the economic boom which took place in the Twenties. Between 1919 and 1929, the top five percent of the population increased its share of national income from 24.3 to 33.5 percent. While the overwhelming majority of the American people had only a slight increase of about six percent in their disposable income over the course of the entire decade, the top one percent of the non-farm population enjoyed nearly a doubling of their disposable income. With the increasing disparity in the distribution of income came an increasing disparity in the distribution of wealth. By 1929, just half of one percent of the population owned about one third of all personal wealth in the United States.[86]

American capitalism in the 1920s continued to produce not only inequality, but also significant levels of poverty. One recent study estimates that 43 percent of the American people enjoyed less than a minimally adequate standard of living in 1929. A Brookings Institution report for that year arrived at even more shocking conclusions. According to the Brookings Institution study, a family in 1929 needed $2,000 per year to pay for the cost of "basic necessities." Yet nearly 60 percent of American families had incomes of less than $2,000 in 1929. Given the growing complexity and the interdependent nature of modern life, and given the increasing separation of ownership from actual managerial control of the nation's huge corporate empires, America's maldistribution of wealth and its extensive poverty could hardly be justified as the just product of a system allocating rewards on the basis of each individual's productive contribution to society.[87]

Finally, while economic growth was obviously taking place in the 1920s, it was occurring either in haphazard fashion according to the fluctuating demands of the market or in the interest of private planners seeking to maximize the profit going to a small part of the population. Except in the field of public power, the liberals examined here remained generally unwilling to consider the possible benefits to be gained from planning economic growth on the basis of publicly determined goals. Fear of state coercion convinced them of the necessity of leaving power over the nation's economy either to the supposedly invisible hand of the market or to the grasping hand of private enterprise.

The stock market crash of 1929 and the Great Depression which followed would soon reveal the glaring weaknesses and inequities of the American political economy. As a result, the voluntaristic liberalism of the Twenties would be severely tested, and these men would be compelled to clarify their thinking about the relative merits of corporatist as opposed to pluralist solutions for America's social and economic problems.

# CHAPTER VII

# The Great Depression and the Crisis of Liberalism 1929-1933

As the decade of the Twenties was coming to an end, many Americans shared the exultant optimism of Herbert Hoover, who claimed during his campaign for the Presidency in 1928 that the country "was nearer to the final triumph over poverty than ever before in the history of any land." Among the men discussed here, Bernard Baruch also felt confident, in the Summer of 1929, that the "economic condition of the world" seemed to be "on the verge of a great forward movement." Donald Richberg, in contrast, declared at about the same time that "no man of any political intelligence or economic wisdom has been able to defend the existing economic order since the World War laid bare its utter inadequacy and its insane consequences." Yet neither Richberg nor Baruch, nor any of the other men considered in this study, anticipated, or were prepared for, the economic catastrophe which soon enveloped the nation. The Great Depression which began following the stock market crash of 1929 and then lasted throughout the next decade not only demonstrated the inadequacy of the voluntarist philosophy of the 1920s, but also provided the severest test the men examined here ever faced of their abiding faith in the basic principles of the American liberal tradition.[1]

The crisis conditions of the Thirties, however, offered these men a great opportunity, as well as a disturbing challenge. For the shock to the nation's political economy brought on by the depression created the chance for ideas and proposals which had previously been practically unthinkable to gain a serious hearing. The 1930s thus seemed to offer the most propitious opportunity of the twentieth century for efforts designed at reshaping the American social and economic order. The men studied here did, in fact, come to accept the need to expand further the role of the state so that the government could do more to bring about both economic recovery and the establishment of a more equitable economic system. In so doing, they attempted to apply the lessons they had learned during their previous thirty years of reform activity. During the first few years of the depression, they groped to find a way of building upon the reform methods of the past. They hoped that it would be possible to end the crisis brought on by the depression by utilizing some combination of the policing, planning, pluralist, and corporatist approaches to reform which had come out of the Progressive era, the First World War, and the 1920s.

An analysis of the reactions of these men to the depression, and of their roles in the shaping of public policy to combat it, reveals that the Thirties marked the culmination of a decades-long process of evolution in their thinking. Nevertheless, while they in some ways broadened their conception of liberalism during this period, they still remained bound within the basic ideological framework of America's long standing liberal consensus. The tragic consequences for the nation of the continuing dominance of this consensus become clearer during the crisis of the 1930s than at any other time in the lives of the men considered here. For the inability of these men, and of their fellow liberals, to acknowledge the essential inadequacies of the American liberal tradition contributed not only to the nation's failure to achieve a satisfactory level of economic recovery prior to the outbreak of war, but also to the nation's squandering of an unparalleled opportunity for substantially altering the fundamentally unequal distribution of wealth and power which characterized American society. The nation's experience in the depression thus provides the most telling demonstration of the limits of liberalism.

I

When Herbert Hoover left the White House in March of 1933, the nation's economy had reached the nadir of the worst depression in American history. In less than four years following the stock market crash of 1929, the combined value of stocks listed on the New York Stock Exchange plummeted from 87 to 19 billion dollars. More than five thousand banks throughout the country collapsed in this period, destroying, in the process, the life savings of thousands of Americans. Farmers, whose income had already lagged behind that of other groups in the economy during the Twenties, were particularly hard hit. Their combined income, which stood at 12 billion dollars in 1929, dropped to only 5 billion dollars in 1932. Industry fared little better than finance or agriculture. In less than four years, the physical volume of industrial production was cut nearly in half. By the end of 1932, the United States was utilizing only 42 percent of its plant capacity. Well over twelve million Americans, or one out of every four workers in the country, were unemployed.[2]

While reformist efforts at countering the depression and redressing the imbalances in the American economy did not reach a culmination until Franklin Roosevelt initiated the New Deal, the Hoover years of the depression proved to be a critical gestation period for the birth of modern American liberalism. In seeking to understand the reasons for the economic collapse which occurred in the years after the stock market crash of 1929, American liberals were forced to consider carefully the basic strengths and weaknesses of the nation's political economy. Moreover, although Herbert Hoover has often been depicted as a do-nothing President who failed to respond in any meaningful way to the development of the worst economic crisis in American history, his administration, in fact, sought to reverse the disastrous downturn in business activity by pushing the philosophy of voluntarism to its limits. The policies and programs of the Hoover administration, many historians now realize, actually provided an important bridge between the liberalism of the New Era and the liberalism of the New Deal. Hoover's efforts to combat the depression, and the reaction these efforts elicited from liberals such as those discussed in this study, were thus crucial in setting the stage for the later development of Roosevelt's brand of welfare-state liberalism.[3]

Only one of the five men considered here held an important position of government authority while Hoover was President. However, as Secretary of State, Henry Stimson focused almost all of his attention on foreign affairs. In the shaping of domestic policies to combat the depression, he remained essentially a loyal observer. Between 1929 and 1933, Josephus Daniels continued in the highly partisan role of editor and publisher of the Raleigh *News & Observer*. During this period, Donald Richberg still served as chief counsel for the nation's railway brotherhoods, and Felix Frankfurter remained a member of the Harvard Law School faculty. These three men were certainly active politically, but they had little influence on the course of government policy while Hoover was in office. Bernard Baruch, in contrast, though a private citizen in these years, was, in the view of Jordan Schwarz, "the most powerful Democrat in Hoover's Washington." His influence in Congress, particularly in the Senate, made him a key figure in the legislative debates over domestic policy which took place in the early years of the depression.[4]

During the ever worsening economic crisis which unfolded between the stock market crash of 1929 and Roosevelt's inauguration as President in 1933, the men examined here all developed their own views of the causes of the depression and of how the government could best help the nation's economy recover. It is necessary to examine these views in order to understand the ways in which these men subsequently contributed and responded to the emergence of the New Deal.

Generational differences in ideological outlook influenced the ways in which these five men analyzed the causes of the depression which engulfed the United States after 1929. Daniels, Stimson, and Baruch had been raised with and retained such a powerful and unquestioning faith in the merits of capitalism that even the terrible events of the 1930s could not shake their confidence in the essential soundness of capitalist principles. However, while Stimson and Baruch consequently attributed America's economic troubles to temporary natural forces of maladjustment or to forces operating beyond America's borders, Daniels, who had always been readier than his two contemporaries to acknowledge the existence of a disparity between the ideal of competitive capitalism and the reality of American economic life, blamed the depression on America's departure from what he considered to be the true principles of capitalism. Frankfurter and Richberg, on the other hand, had learned at the outset of their careers to question the inevitability of America's capitalist order and to challenge some of the assumptions upon which that order was based. With the coming of the depression, they would experience even more doubts about the viability of American capitalism. In contrast to Stimson, Baruch, and Daniels, their analyses of the causes of the economic crisis of the 1930s not only focused more clearly on certain long-standing structural defects in the American economy, but even touched upon the problems inherent in a capitalist system.

Henry Stimson was, by his own admission, "never an expert in economics." In seeking to understand the causes of the depression which gripped the nation in the early 1930s, he depended upon the advice of those whom he did consider to be experts in the field. Confident that the American economy was fundamentally sound, Stimson came to accept the reasoning of Hoover and the leading figures in the Treasury Department, Andrew Mellon and Ogden Mills, that America's continuing economic problems resulted primarily from dislocations in the international economy over which the United States had little control. The root causes of the depression, he believed could be traced back to the impact of the First World War. In the Fall of 1931, Stimson recorded in his diary a conversation with Mellon in which they apparently agreed that the war's ultimate effect had been to disrupt the normal patterns of production and trade.

We were organized to a high rate of mass production and had geared everything up on the belief that the period following the war was normal. Instead of that it was a very abnormal time when the rest of the world's markets were left open to our use on account of their industries being crippled by the Great War. Now they were beginning to take those markets back again and to raise tariff barriers against us, and that I did not see but what we would have to readjust very seriously.[5]

As the American economy continued its downward plunge at the end of 1931, Stimson still believed that the United States remained in a far "better condition for ultimate recovery" than most other nations. America's recovery, he thought, was being retarded largely because of the collapse of the international system of trade and finance brought on by the war's unfortunate legacy of unpaid debts and reparations, and by the failure of other nations to remain on the gold standard. Ironically, the United States was suffering, in Stimson's view, because its economy had become so productive that its health had become inextricably linked to the health of a world economy which was now disintegrating.[6]

Bernard Baruch's analysis of the causes of the depression was, in many ways, similar to Stimson's. Testifying before a Senate committee in February 1933, Baruch contended that "our troubles" stemmed from "four effects" of the First World War: "inflation, debt and taxes, national self-containment, and excess productive capacity." Like Stimson, he believed that because of high tariffs, unpaid foreign debts, and the weakness of the economies of Europe culminating in the collapse of the international gold standard, the development of a vast productive capacity in America had become a burden rather than a blessing.[7]

While Baruch shared Stimson's confidence in the underlying strength of the American economic system, he gave much more thought than the Secretary of State to some of the purely internal problems made apparent by the onset of the depression. The First World War, he argued, had significantly accelerated the development of America's productive capacity, but the long-term trend toward greater "combination and coordination in industry" which had made the American economy "so efficient" that in recent years production had increased "three times as fast as population," sooner or later, would have posed the problem of "over-production." The depression, consequently, was a dramatic indication of the nation's failure to develop adequate means "to regulate production to consumption or at least restrain it when it races so wildly." Thus, although Baruch contended that prosperity could not be restored until the international economic situation was stabilized, he believed that the United States would also have to find ways to deal domestically with the problem of over-production.[8]

Josephus Daniels was no more sophisticated an economic

thinker than Henry Stimson. His view of the depression was not the product of any thorough study of economic conditions, but rather a reflection of his long held Jeffersonian conception of economic problems. Instead of looking to external factors beyond the control of the United States to explain the hard times of the early 1930s, Daniels quickly came to focus on the continuing post-war erosion of the principle of "equal rights to all and special privileges to none." Daniels recognized that the loss of foreign markets had contributed to the depression in America, but he blamed this loss on the Republican party's foreign policy, and especially on its support for high tariffs. Daniels, moreover, saw the Republican policy on the tariff as but one aspect of a more general "governmental system of favoritism" toward big business and the wealthy which had ultimately led to the stock market crash and the ensuing economic crisis. He claimed that, before 1929, Republican policy had included not only an excessively high protective tariff, but also "tax favoritism," and the "encouragement of the investment of money in stock gambling." The Republicans had also permitted the Sherman Anti-Trust law to be trodden under foot for 'private interests.' " In Daniels' view, the rapid growth of "monopolistic mergers" in the Twenties had led inevitably to the widespread unemployment of the early Thirties.[9]

By the Fall of 1931, Daniels was proclaiming that capitalism in America had been largely supplanted by an iniquitous system of "Feudalism" in which a "score of directorates, some of them interlocking," ruled "American business and American government as completely as their predecessors, the Feudal Lords, ruled Britain when Feudalism was in flower." It was the development of "feudalism" which was responsible, according to Daniels, "for most of the depression and unemployment" that afflicted the country. The increasing power of monpolies in America had not only closed off the possibility of new entrepreneurs entering the field of industry in order to establish effective competition, but it had also left in control of the economy a group of men "having no heart and charged with no duty" to put the interests of the mass of Americans above the interests of the few. Daniels did not blame American capitalism for the depression. Rather, he believed that it was the subversion of true capitalist principles made possible by the government's irresponsible policy of allowing "monopoly" to ascend the "throne" in the United States which had brought on the twin evils of "Feudalism" and depression.[10]

Writing in early 1933, Felix Frankfurter also refused to accept the argument that the depression had arisen as a consequence of factors operating outside the confines of America's domestic economy. He insisted that the depression had resulted from the nation's failure to respond adequately to a number of long term social and economic trends which had brought about "basic changes" in American society. The problems of the Thirties, he claimed, stemmed from the fact that "we were using ideas and institutions" and "habits" which were "no longer adapted to our needs" or to "the problems of our day." America had failed to develop the "moral" and "social" controls which were necessary to "cope with the extraordinary material" developments which had taken place in economic life. Frankfurter acknowledged that the heightened competition for foreign markets and the burden of international debts which had grown out of the war were factors in the crisis of the early 1930s, but he explicitly rejected the view that the depression could be explained as primarily an after-effect of the First World War.[11]

Like Baruch, Frankfurter argued that a growing imbalance between production and consumption was a crucial factor in the depression. Unlike Baruch, however, Frankfurter thought that this had arisen not so much because of the tremendous efficiency of American industry and the artificial stimulus of the First World War, but rather because of the highly unequal distribution of wealth and income which acted as a drag on the growth of mass purchasing power. Frankfurter observed that, given the maldistribution of wealth, the boom of the Twenties had only been possible because of the large increase in indebtedness among the middle and lower classes and the sale of large quantities of luxury goods to the rich. The seeming prosperity of the 1920s had thus been built on a very weak domestic foundation.[12]

The great "disparities in wealth" which characterized the economy of the Twenties were, in Frankfurter's view, not only a key factor in the economic breakdown of the Thirties, but they were also "inconsistent" with the continuing existence of "a democracy like ours." Such inequality, Frankfurter argued in 1931, constituted the "core problem of American society." While Frankfurter did not himself believe that the depression was an inevitable product of American capitalism, he realized that many other Americans were beginning to doubt the viability of capitalism and that this very fact had become an important aspect of the nation's economic crisis.[13]

Donald Richberg's analysis of the causes of the depression was similar to Frankfurter's in its emphasis on the relationship between inequality and the lack of mass purchasing power. Richberg, moreover, was at times as stinging in his criticisms of the irresponsibility of American business leaders as Daniels. In fact, of the men discussed here, Richberg developed perhaps the most comprehensive and radical critique of the state of the American economic system. He was even more explicit than Frankfurter in his avowal of what came to be known as the underconsumptionist theory of the depression. "The nation-wide depression of today," he wrote in 1931, "has been caused by low wages, by the excessive profits of the few and the underpayment of the many, whose purchasing power would not absorb the flood of goods that industry produced." It was foolish, therefore, to view the depression as an unfortunate result of too much production or too efficient an industrial economy when the great mass of America's underpaid workers remained an as yet incompletely tapped pool of potential consumers.[14]

Testifying before a Senate committee in the Winter of 1933, Richberg went on to blame the "greedy and ignorant" leaders of American industry for the economic crisis then gripping the nation. The "selfish pursuit of power and wealth" by these men had resulted in a "misuse of money power" and a dangerous gambling with "the natural and human resources of the Nation." The lack of purchasing power among the country's workers, Richberg contended, was the direct outgrowth of the undemocratic organization of American industry, in which a few corporate heads exercised irresponsible powers over both their workers and the nation at large. "No sane man," Richberg wrote in 1932:

. . . can approve of a mad program of organizing for mass production without organizing for mass consumption; or of socializing industry under monopolistic controls in order to preserve individual freedom and the competitive incentives; or of enthroning a class control of government in order to avoid a class struggle and to preserve democracy; or of promoting public service and advancing the general welfare by inciting selfish greed and encouraging the hope of extortionate private profits.[15]

## II

Even today, economists and economic historians cannot agree about the causes of the Great Depression of the 1930s. However, while there is little question that events abroad, especially the collapse of the international monetary system in 1931, contributed to the length and severity of the depression in the United States, few experts would now support Herbert Hoover's claim that developments taking place beyond America's borders were primarily responsible for transforming what would have been a normal downturn in business activity in the United States into an economic catastrophe of unprecedented proportions. In the first place, it was a decline in the American economy which set off the world-wide depression. Subsequently, the situation abroad steadily deteriorated principally as a product of what Milton Friedman and Anna Schwartz describe as a "feedback effect," that is, largely in "response to the prior severe economic and monetary decline in the United States." One must examine the American economy, not the international system of trade and finance, in order to understand the origins of the depression. The American economy itself was, in the words of John Kenneth Galbraith, "fundamentally unsound" in 1929.[16]

One area of weakness was the nation's banking system. By the eve of the stock market crash, America's financial structure had come to resemble a house of cards which was highly susceptible to the destabilizing forces set in motion by the collapse of stock prices in 1929. The stock market boom of the late 1920s had largely been made possible by the leverage created by the reckless extension of credit in the form of margin trading and by the expansion of financially unsound investment trusts and pyramidded holding companies. Once stock prices broke in 1929, the effects of leverage were reversed, so that a powerful deflationary force was exerted throughout the nation's banking system. Moreover, Federal Reserve Board policies, which had acted to encourage speculation before the crash, then made matters worse by choking off credit after the break in stock prices had already dealt a major deflationary blow to the economy. Consequently, the gradual collapse of what was essentially a chaotic and unregulated banking system played an important role in the development of the depression.[17]

While some economists, most notably Friedman and Schwartz, have claimed that monetary forces were the crucial factor in causing the distressed conditions of the 1930s, most analysts of the depression have accepted what Peter Temin has labeled "the spending hypothesis," namely, that a sharp and prolonged decline in expenditures, in the form of both consumption and, even more importantly, investment, was the principal causative factor in the economic debacle of the Thirties. Perhaps the most revealing statistic concerning the Great Depression is the decline in gross investment from 16.2 billion dollars in 1929 to only .3 billion dollars in 1933. The apparent drying up of investment opportunities in the late 1920s, particularly in what had been the great growth industries of the New Era, construction and automobiles, is frequently cited as the key to the business downturn which rapidly accelerated after the stock market crash. In fact, one influential economist, Alvin Hansen, claimed that the American economy by 1929 had reached a state of "maturity" in which opportunities for new investment had permanently declined because of the passing of the frontier, the decrease in the rate of population growth, and the improbability of future technological innovations having an expansionary impact comparable to that exerted previously by the development of railroads, electricity, and automobiles.[18]

While a decline in investment may thus be viewed as the key factor in the development of the depression, it is impossible to grasp the full significance of this problem without considering the way in which investment decisions were determined in the American economy. The "exhaustion" of investment opportunities in the early 1930s was more a consequence of the workings of an economic system built on the pursuit of private profit and dominated by oligopolies than it was the result of a lack of potentially useful and socially beneficial investment outlets. Throughout the depression, the American people could still have benefitted from investments in such areas as health and education. Such investments were not considered sufficiently attractive, however, because, by their very nature, they held no promise of a profitable return to the relatively few Americans who controlled the nation's supply of capital. Private profit, not social need, remained the basis upon which decisions about the allocation of capital were made in the American economy. Even in an industry such as construction, which many economists cite as an area of "overinvestment" in the late 1920s, a myriad of opportunities still existed for investment. The country's need for public facilities, schools, hospitals, museums, community centers, parks, was hardly sated in 1929. Given the maldistribution of wealth, the effective demand for housing may have been exhausted in the late 1920s, but the need for more and better housing was still apparent in a society in which more than half of all Americans did not own their own homes and in which urban slums were a persistent blight.[19]

The oligopolistic nature of the American economy at the end of the 1920s further exacerbated the problem of finding adequate investment outlets for the nation's growing surplus of capital. Because of the decline of effective price competition, firms in oligopolistic industries were able to pursue a strategy of maintaining high profits by keeping prices relatively stable, even if such prices served to discourage the growth of consumer demand for the firm's products. The relative inflexibility of prices thus led to a situation in which it was normal for industry to underutilize its full productive capacity. Even before the crash of 1929, America was utilizing only 83 percent of its manufacturing capacity. This underutilization of capacity, in turn, acted as a depressant on the incentive of American firms to re-invest their profits in order to expand further their productive capability. In addition, oligopolies had a lesser incentive to re-invest profits as quickly as possible to take advantage of new technologies. Not fearing the full rigors of competition, these firms might choose to allow their existing capital equipment to wear out before deciding to re-invest in new, more efficient, machinery.[20]

Although economists today generally focus on the role of

investment, rather than consumption, as the primary determinant of the business cycle, Frankfurter and Richberg were not wrong in the early 1930s when they argued that inequality in the distribution of income, and the restriction in the growth of mass purchasing power which resulted, contributed to the development of the Great Depression. In their stress on underconsumption, Franfurter and Richberg were far closer to an accurate analysis of the causes of the depression than were Stimson and Baruch, who both conceived of the problem as one of over-production.

The disparity in power between labor and capital in the 1920s not only resulted in profits advancing three times more rapidly than wages, but also caused the United States, according to Irving Bernstein, to lag "behind every other industrial nation in the world" in reducing the length of the work week and in developing a response to the rising problem of technological unemployment. These developments all contributed to the increasingly skewed distribution of income in America. As a consequence, the growth of consumption was slower than it might have been, and this weakness in demand, in turn, served as a restraint on investment. As Galbraith has observed, no evidence exists to prove that the desire of the American people "for automobiles, clothing, travel, recreation, or even food was sated" during the 1920s. On the contrary, "all subsequent evidence," according to Galbraith, has demonstrated that there still existed in 1929 a tremendous potential for a large further increase in consumption, if only the American people had received additional income to spend. "A depression," concludes Galbraith, "was not needed so that people's wants could catch up with their capacity to produce." [21]

In addition, the growing dependence of consumption on credit buying made necessary in the 1920s by the failure of wage increases to match increases in productivity, meant that consumer spending was likely to decline significantly if credit became tight and consumers became pessimistic about the future of the economy. The uneven distribution of income had also made the economy more dependent on the kind of luxury buying by the rich which was unlikely to continue in a period of economic uncertainty. Thus, in the event of a decline in investment, there was little chance that an increase in consumer spending might temporarily take up the slack and prevent the economy from falling into a depression. In fact as Temin notes, the decline in consumption in 1930 was "unusually large" and proved to be more striking than the decline in investment in the early stages of the depression.[22]

Once the downturn in business activity began, moreover, the structure of American industry caused the decline to accelerate by contributing to a further reduction of purchasing power which made any new investment even less attractive. Given the power of many sectors of American industry to "administer" relatively fixed prices, the nation's corporate leaders responded to decreases in demand in the wake of the stock market crash by cutting production rather than prices, even though this resulted in increasing unemployment and thus further reduced the demand for goods and services. In most competitive sectors of the economy, prices fell drastically in the early years of the depression, while production remained fairly constant. For instance, farm prices dropped 63 percent between 1929 and 1933, although production fell by only 6 percent. In contrast, in those areas dominated by a few firms, production was slashed in order to maintain artificially high prices. The auto industry, as one example, witnessed an 80 percent decline in production between 1929 and 1933, though prices went down by only 16 percent. Similarly, iron and steel output dropped 83 percent in three years, while prices fell just 20 percent. Although even oligopolistic firms had difficulty making money during the heart of the depression, corporations with net assets of $50 million or more still managed, as a group, to show a profit in 1931 and 1932. In contrast, all smaller-size categories suffered net losses as a group. America's corporate giants were thus able to protect their own interests during the crisis of the early 1930s. In the process, however, they threw millions of Americans out of work and contributed to a vicious downward cycle in which the American economy threatened to become mired in a permanent state of depression.[23]

Although the Great Depression was clearly a product of a fatally flawed economic system, even two of the severest critics of American capitalism, Paul Baran and Paul Sweezy, acknowledge that "there was nothing 'inevitable' about the steepness of the descent after 1929." The operation of the profit motive in a private enterprise system, the concentration of control in industry, and the highly unequal distribution of wealth in American society, together, all made the economy particularly vulnerable to prolonged periods of stagnation, but certainly purely fortuitous, rather than systemic, factors also played a role in transforming the economic decline of the early 1930s into a depression of catastrophic proportions. The ineptitude of the Federal Reserve Board, both before and after the stock market crash, the mushrooming of unsound and even fraudulent corporate structures in the late 1920s, and the weakness of the international system of finance and trade were not necessarily inherent features of a capitalist economy. Yet, the depression still revealed, in stark form, the problems inherent in an economy which, while lacking institutions for planning in the interest of society as a whole, came under the domination of a relatively small number of giant corporate firms whose purpose was production for private profit rather than social needs.[24]

Henry Stimson and Bernard Baruch thus ignored or almost totally misunderstood the underlying structural problems which brought on the Great Depression. Josephus Daniels, Felix Frankfurter, and Donald Richberg, in contrast, recognized that the growing concentration of power in industry and the increasing maldistribution of wealth in society had been key factors in the economic crisis of the Thirties. However, they continued to view these problems essentially as aberrations of American capitalism, and not as logical products of an industrial system based on the pursuit of profit by privately controlled corporate organizations. While Richberg, for one, at times questioned the viability of the profit motive, neither he nor any of the other men considered here fully came to grips with the problems posed by the nature of the investment process in a capitalist economy. For all five of these men, the coming of the depression demonstrated only the need to revitalize liberalism and reform American capitalism, not the necessity of transcending the liberal tradition and moving toward a socialized economy.

## III

All five men considered in this study agreed that the growing economic crisis of the early Thirties necessitated an unprecedented governmental response to help halt the nation's downward slide into depression. The remedies each man supported to cure the nation's economic ills, though, were quite naturally a reflection of each man's limited understanding of the underlying causes of the breakdown of the economy. Moreover, in trying to come up with the right formula for stemming the tide of the depression, all five looked primarily to their own past experiences in public life. Thus, the solutions they advocated were essentially evolutionary, rather than revolutionary, in nature, in that they were generally based on the approaches to reform which American liberals had been developing during the previous thirty years. By the time Herbert Hoover left office in 1933, however, the strictly voluntarist approach for which Hoover had become the nation's most prominent spokesman had clearly been tried and found wanting.

While Henry Stimson and Herbert Hoover had significant differences of opinion regarding the conduct of American foreign policy, there is no evidence to indicate that Stimson significantly disagreed with Hoover's handling of domestic policy in response to the depression. Although Stimson claimed that "the causes of the present depression [were] far beyond the control of governmental action," he recognized that as a matter of "pure expediency" it was necessary "to interfere with the laws of economics . . . upon a transitory basis" in order "to preserve our humanitarian standard." Stimson praised Hoover as the first President ever to respond affirmatively and decisively with executive leadership at the onset of a depression. In the Fall of 1930, Stimson contended that the measures taken by the Hoover administration had "thus far served to greatly palliate what might otherwise have been a most disastrous situation."[25]

The program which won Stimson's praise and which Hoover relied upon for the first two years of the depression was not totally unprecedented, but it did represent a more concerted effort than had ever previously been made by an American President in similar circumstances. Hoover's policies also reflected the Great Engineer's modern faith in the ability of rational business managers to cooperate voluntarily with an enlightened government in an attempt to control the business cycle. Hoover's initial program consisted of two main parts. First, the President actively encouraged the country's key economic interest groups to use the techniques of voluntary organization and co-operation to stabilize their own sectors of the economy. Hoover especially urged businessmen to refrain from drastic wage cuts in the early stages of the depression in order to avoid setting off an uncontrollable deflationary spiral through the destruction of mass purchasing power. The White House, consequently, was the scene of numerous high level conferences among businessmen, bankers, farmers, and labor leaders which were designed to encourage those in positions of power to take a broad, public spirited, view of the nation's economic situation. Second, the President authorized a speeding up of planned public works projects as a means of combating unemployment and countering the downward drift in economic activity. In addition, because Hoover believed the depression to be largely a problem of business confidence, rather than a product of structural weaknesses in the economy, he orchestrated a vigorous public relations campaign, in which Stimson and other members of the administration participated, in an attempt to counter growing pessimism about the economy's future performance.[26]

After two years of an ever worsening depression, however, the inadequacies of a voluntarist approach, which should have already been apparent during the superficial prosperity of the Twenties, had become obvious even to Hoover and Stimson, as they sought to find means of preventing the economy from deteriorating further. While both men increasingly spoke of the importance of restoring a sound basis for the international system of finance and trade in order to reverse the course of the economic decline in the United States—with Stimson, in particular, becoming a key figure in the movement to cancel war debts and establish a more reasonable tariff policy—they both realized that the power of the federal government would have to be used more directly to try to prevent the collapse of the American economy at home.[27]

Stimson consequently, supported a significant shift in government policy at the end of 1931. At that time, Hoover began to develop a new program which centered on an attempt to bolster the nation's credit system with the power and resources of the federal government. Central to this effort was Hoover's backing of legislation to create the Reconstruction Finance Corporation to permit the refinancing of many of the nation's mortgages, and to prevent the financial collapse of the country's major railroads. In the view of one student of the subject, the RFC, in particular, "played a critical role in the transition from voluntary efforts to end the depression to federal management of the economy."[28]

The Hoover administration's attempts to manage the economy through governmental action, however, remained quite circumscribed. Still convinced that the American economic system needed no fundamental alteration, both Hoover and Stimson grudgingly came to accept the federal government's responsibility to provide more active leadership to the effort to counteract the disastrous effects of the business cycle. Ultimately, Hoover, as well as Stimson, was willing to see the government intervene to the extent of using its power and resources to try to shore up the major pillars of the nation's financial system. Both men viewed such action, though, simply as an expedient means of helping the key financial institutions of the economy weather a storm which had its origins beyond the country's borders. Neither Hoover nor Stimson wished to see the government assume any real control or direction over the nation's economy. In addition, both Hoover and Stimson remained so wedded to the economic orthodoxy of a balanced budget as a key to business confidence and sound credit that they supported the enactment of a national sales tax in 1932 which not only would have been highly regressive, but which also would have further undermined aggregate demand and made recovery less likely if it had been adopted.[29]

Moreover, neither Hoover nor Stimson was willing to see the federal government assume direct responsibility for the welfare of the nation's citizens, although, in 1932, Hoover did reluctantly accept the need for the RFC to grant loans to state governments to be used for relief. In recalling his support for the evolving program of the Hoover administration, Stimson observed in his autobiography that all of the actions taken by Hoover had properly been based on the conviction that the powers of the "Federal Government must be used to reinforce, and not to undermine the functions of state and local government." While few liberals before 1933 put forth programs for recovery which were much more comprehensive than those offered by the Hoover administration, much of the liberal community would eventually focus its hostility to the incumbent President on the administration's failure to accept the federal government's responsibility for direct relief in the face of unprecedented individual suffering.[30]

Like Stimson and Hoover, Bernard Baruch thought that the American economy remained basically sound in spite of the unfolding depression and that it was dangerous to allow "too much government in . . . business," since "we cannot oppose legislation to natural law." In the early months of the depression, consequently, Baruch advocated a governmental response to the nation's developing economic problems which was quite similar to that actually adopted by the Hoover administration. He called for a speeding up of public works projects already envisioned for the future and also believed that optimistic statements by prominent Americans about the prospects for a quick recovery were important as a means of bolstering business confidence.[31]

Subsequently, as the depression worsened, Baruch supported Hoover's shift to a more interventionist policy in late 1931. In fact, he played an important role in developing the plan for the establishment of the RFC, though he turned down a chance to act as a director of the new agency. By 1932, Baruch, like Hoover, also came to support an expanded program of self-liquidating public works projects. These projects would be financed by bonds and would begin paying for themselves upon completion. Such a program, both men believed, would be a financially responsible way of relieving the growing problem of unemployment in the country. Baruch envisioned building bridges, tunnels, and "above all the destruction of the slum districts in the great industrial centers." While some liberals in Congress favored a less conservatively financed and far larger program of public works than that advocated by Baruch and

Hoover, a plan very similar to Baruch's was ultimately adopted in 1932.[32]

Because of his experience with the WIB years earlier, Baruch continued to feel an ambivalent attraction to the possibility of using the power of government to interfere in the marketplace for socially beneficial results. Before long, Baruch's conception of what the government could do to "aid and hasten and guide" the "curative" effects of "natural processes" in a time of depression began to diverge from Stimson's and Hoover's. To begin with, Baruch concluded that, in the face of increasing unemployment and hardship, the "first and foremost" requirement of government policy ought to be to "make adequate provision against human suffering," even if that meant involving the federal government directly in relief efforts for the nation's citizens.[33]

Baruch's most important difference with the Hoover administration centered around his increasing doubts that a purely voluntarist approach could succeed in resolving the crucial problem of over-production. As the economy slid downward, Baruch reached the conclusion that the government would have to play a more assertive role in the effort to reduce the industrial and agricultural surpluses which, in his view, were acting as the main drag on the economy. Baruch looked back on his experience with the War Industries Board and saw in it both a precedent and a guide for a coordinated attempt to bring a greater degree of planning to the economy.

In May of 1930, Baruch resurrected the plan for establishing a "supreme court of business" which he had first tentatively proposed in the early 1920s. This body would provide a "common forum" in which businessmen could come together under government supervision specifically for the purpose of enacting production restrictions in industries where such restrictions were necessary for the good of the entire economy. Restrictions on production would be allowed only when accompanied by some regulation of prices and by the establishment of guidelines as to how the restricted output would be distributed.[34]

In the first years of the depression, Baruch still doubted that it would be possible or desirable to create an institution as powerful as the WIB had once been. The WIB, he observed, had required a war crisis to generate the national consensus which had made its widespread acceptance possible. Baruch, therefore, stressed the fact that his proposed "supreme court of business" would not exercise power over the entire economy but rather would be restricted to issuing or approving production controls only in those industries which voluntarily sought such regulation. In addition, Baruch explained that the new agency he had in mind would possess "no power to repress or coerce," but would instead rely on its ability to "convoke conference, to suggest and to sanction or license such common-sense cooperation among industrial units as will prevent our economic blessings from becoming unbearable burdens." Baruch continued during the next three years to call for the creation of a body organized along these lines. By February, 1933, moreover, he supported such a call by arguing that the depression had indeed become even "worse than war," so that it demanded whatever "sacrifice" was necessary to defeat an enemy which was "everywhere, even within us." [35]

Baruch had been concerned with overproduction in agriculture even before the onset of the depression. While he still hoped to find a way of subsidizing farm exports so that domestic prices would be kept from falling to the world market level, by February of 1933 he testified before Congress that it was imperative to establish a government program for curtailing farm surpluses. He favored giving the Secretary of Agriculture the authority to pay farmers to take marginal land out of production. Such a program, he argued, could be financed by a tax on processors and offered the only means of attacking the heart of the farm problem, overproduction. [36]

By early 1933, Baruch had thus come up with his own comprehensive plan for dealing with the depression, but while it held out the hope of stabilizing business profits, it was, in effect, a prescription for planned scarcity and continuing unemployment. Baruch's failure to understand the sources of the nation's economic difficulties led him to propose a one-sided recovery plan which would have exacerbated the very problems which had helped cause the depression: a maldistribution of income, insufficient aggregate demand, and an excessive concentration of power in industry.

While Baruch's proposed program differed from the policies of the Hoover administration insofar as it was more explicit in its focus on the goal of reducing production, and in its acceptance of a more direct role for the government in lending its official seal of approval to the cooperative efforts of industry, the two approaches still had a great deal in common. Baruch may have been more forthright in calling for a suspension of the anti-trust laws, but like Hoover and Stimson, he sought to avoid the development of mandatory or coercive government controls on the economy. Even in February 1933, Baruch continued to warn against the dangers of government intervention in behalf of either the rich or the poor:

The predatory strong are apt to go to government to exploit it—the weak go to get the government to do for them the things which our forefathers ordained that, under our system, they should do for themselves . . . . Concessions to the powerful require regulatory bureaus for protection. Concessions to the weak result in dispensing bureaus. Both create a maze of restricting administrative law.

Although, in the field of agriculture, both Baruch and the Hoover administration recognized the need for more extensive government intervention than in the field of industry, both would have been horrified at the thought of the government either assuming control over the nation's faltering investment process or taking over the powers exercised by private management.[37]

Neither did Baruch or the Hoover administration propose to make any basic alteration in the distribution of wealth in America. In fact, Baruch, like Hoover and Stimson, remained so strongly committed to the idea that "a balanced budget is the first and greatest requisite of reconstruction" that he became, in the words of Jordan Schwarz, "perhaps the most influential man" behind the campaign to win Congressional approval of a national sales tax in 1932. Not only did he support a regressive tax which would have further compounded the negative effects of his program of planned scarcity, but he also called for a one third reduction in government expenditures which would have had an additional deflationary impact on the economy.[38]

Although Baruch was willing to go beyond what Hoover

found acceptable in terms of using the power of government to compel cooperative efforts to end the depression, he still shared Hoover and Stimson's basic aim of using government power primarily to assist the private sector's own efforts to make the adjustments necessary to restore the health of the economy. Ironically, Baruch's ideas would not gain a full hearing until Hoover had left the White House and Franklin Roosevelt had initiated his experiments with the National Recovery and Agricultural Adjustment Administrations.

Since neither Stimson nor Baruch considered the irresponsible and inequitable practices of big business to be major causes of the economic crisis of the early Thirties, neither felt that an attack on the power of business was necessary to bring the country out of the depression. Josephus Daniels' contrasting analysis of the causes of the depression, on the other hand, led him to make such an attack a cornerstone of the policy he advocated for curing the country's economic ills. Daniels' approach to the problem of curtailing the power of business and of fostering recovery, however, was largely negative. The dominant theme in both Daniels' reaction to the policies of the Hoover administration and in his own policy proposals before 1933, was that a return to the simple principle of "equal rights to all and special privileges to none" was the "only hope" the great majority of Americans had for achieving renewed prosperity.[39]

In the weeks immediately following the stock market crash, Daniels' Raleigh *News & Observer* praised Hoover's attempts to convince employers of the importance of maintaining existing wage scales. As the situation in the country worsened, though, Daniels' differences with the Hoover administration quickly became apparent. Unlike Hoover, Daniels came to recognize the necessity of having the federal government assume a direct role in the relief of distress. He thus accepted an important, though limited, expansion of the basic functions of the federal government. Daniels' strongest criticism of Hoover's handling of the depression, however, focused on what the Democratic editor called the "Republican policy of percolation." The Hoover administration, Daniels argued in the Fall of 1930, believed:

. . . in extending favors to the organized few, and telling the many that their prosperity will come because the beneficiaries of government will be able to give them employment and higher wages.

Such a policy, in Daniels' view, was an "undemocratic and un-American . . . plan for the survival of feudalism."[40]

Thus well before Hoover had developed the policy of "percolation" into the more clearly defined program of 1932, Daniels had completely rejected such an approach as an appropriate means of counteracting the effects of the depression. Not only did Daniels claim that the "percolator does not percolate" since "the benefits are not passed down," but he also contended that any attempt to utilize the government to extend "favors, subsidies, immunities," or "special privileges" to the great mass of Americans would result in the whole machinery of government breaking down in "failure and confusion."[41]

In other words, Daniels called for the government to contract, rather than expand, its efforts to interfere with the operations of the economy. While favoring a new role for government in the relief of individual suffering, he seemed to believe that the development of new government mechanisms to regulate the economy was less important than simply reversing, or putting an end to, the Republican policies of the past. In three areas though, Daniels did call for a positive assertion of government power. First, as noted previously, he accepted the need for emergency relief measures by the federal government. Second, although Daniels, like Stimson and Baruch, was totally committed to the concept of a balanced budget, he favored achieving this goal not by the imposition of a regressive sales tax, but rather by creating a more equitable tax system based on the ability to pay. Third, Daniels naturally supported a greatly reinvigorated policy of enforcing the anti-trust laws already on the books. Although Daniels had himself proclaimed in 1932 that "we must not be afraid to be radical in applying new methods to the ills and evils which caused the debacle" of the depression, his own plan for stimulating recovery by reducing the power of "feudalism" in America was based essentially on the policy which Woodrow Wilson twenty years earlier had described as the New Freedom.[42]

Felix Frankfurter agreed with Daniels that the irresponsible exercise of almost unlimited power by huge private corporations would have to be ended if the economy was again to become healthy. In commenting on a successful anti-trust prosecution against the meat packing industry in 1932, however, Frankfurter observed that to expect "adequate regulation of such a basic industry through intermittent lawsuits is to ask of courts what they cannot give." Frankfurter's greater appreciation of the complexity of the economy, and his fuller understanding of the causes of the depression, made it impossible for him to believe that a program such as that offered by Daniels, with its emphasis on government action to restore competition, would be sufficient to bring about economic recovery.[43]

However, as Frankfurter grappled with the problem of what needed to be done to get the economy moving again, he found himself confronted by what seemed to him a practically unresolvable dilemma. He believed that the unequal distribution of wealth in America was a major factor in the development of the depression. He also voiced his "distrust of the capacity for disinterested insight and courageous thinking on the part of those who" had enjoyed "the dominant direction of affairs" during the Twenties. Still, Frankfurter could not bring himself to repudiate the existing economic order or to reject the liberal ideology which continued to justify that order. In April of 1932, Frankfurter explained his dilemma to Walter Lippmann:

Mine being a pragmatic temperament, all my scepticism and discontent with the present order and tendencies have not carried me over to a new, comprehensive scheme of society, whether socialism or communism. Or perhaps, ten years in government, and as many more of intensive study of its problems, have made me also sceptical of any full-blown new scheme and left me most conscious of the extraordinary difficulties of the problems of the Great Society. Not that I do not wonder sometimes whether the thorough-going integrity of an artist like Edmund Wilson, with all his innocence or perhaps because of it, does not go to the root of things more trenchantly and more fearlessly than I do. At all events, I do not embrace, and indeed distrust, a full-blown, "rational" counter-system.[44]

While Frankfurter thus rejected the idea that there was a single "royal road to governmental effectiveness, except trial and error," in conjunction with Supreme Court Justice Louis Brandeis, at this time his most intimate associate in political affairs, Frankfurter developed a concrete program designed to foster recovery by increasing mass purchasing power and curbing the unchecked powers of concentrated wealth. At one time, as Nelson Dawson points out, most historians rather simplistically focused on Brandeis' opposition to bigness, and Frankfurter's supposedly unqualified agreement with the Justice's outlook, when describing the anti-depression plan formulated by these two men before FDR took office in 1933. Yet, scholars who have recently studied Frankfurter's career have correctly concluded that Frankfurter neither fully shared Brandeis' animus against bigness, nor did he, or Brandeis, for that matter, put much faith in the anti-trust laws as an effective instrument of reform or recovery.[45]

By the beginning of 1933, the first priority in Frankfurter's agenda for recovery was the establishment of a public works program significantly larger than the one enacted by Congress in 1932. Frankfurter believed that such a program, whose purpose would be not only to provide emergency work relief, but also to stimulate general economic recovery, should be financed by progressive estate and personal and corporate income taxes, not through a regressive and counter-productive sales tax. Although Frankfurter had not yet abandoned the idea that a balanced budget was desirable, he felt certain that trying to balance the budget through regressive taxes or by cuts in government social services would be "suicidal." Frankfurter, therefore, supported direct government relief for those facing destitution, as well as an expanded public works program, even if it meant an unbalanced budget.[46]

Frankfurter also favored the adoption, at least on the state level, of unemployment insurance, workmen's compensation, minimum wage, and maximum hours laws in order to improve the situation of workers and thereby boost their potential purchasing power. In addition, Frankfurter remained a strong supporter of labor organization as a means of establishing a balance to the power of management. In 1932, he finally saw the enactment by Congress of the Norris-LaGuardia Anti-Injunction Act which he and Richberg had helped to write.[47]

Frankfurter and Brandeis did hope to use the government's

powers of taxation as a weapon against concentrated economic power, as well as a means of financing an expanded program of public works and relief. Moreover, the coming of the depression confirmed their belief in the necessity of stricter government regulation for two sectors of the economy, banking and public utilities, whose practices had been especially irresponsible in the past and whose excesses had helped bring on the economic crisis of the Thirties. In particular, Frankfurter publicly supported the separation of investment and commercial banking. In advocating increased government regulation, Frankfurter argued that the depression had proven the necessity of establishing in the United States a far more highly trained and professionalized civil service to guarantee the "efficiency" of government. In his view, only the more extensive use of impartial scientific expertise could save the country from the crisis into which it had fallen.[48]

While Frankfurter was highly critical of the limited steps taken by Hoover to fight the depression, the recovery program which he proposed was not really a radical departure from the approach adopted by the Hoover administration because it entailed no systematic attempt to change the structure and guiding principles of the nation's political economy. Even at the depth of the depression, Frankfurter remained fearful of too great or too rapid an expansion of government power and warned against the dangers of drifting toward the "regimented life" of either fascism or communism. Writing to Walter Lippmann in 1932, Frankfurter contended that it still was not "the time to propose comprehensive reform." He then observed, in words which are striking for their similarity to criticisms made later by others of the New Deal:

I have felt nothing but a feverish temper of mind on the part of our leaders for these many months. And I submit that the physicians that deal with the fever ought not to deal with it feverishly. One measure after another has been concocted and hurriedly concocted as though it were an injection that would save life, and indeed one by one they have been advertised as saviors of life. I distrust this attitude, and on the whole it obstructs clear thinking about government, especially in times of great stress, to think about it in figures of speech. As each of

the Washington remedies have been concocted they have been de-
nominated emergency efforts, and any plea for deliberation, for detailed discussion, for exploration of alternatives, has been regarded as
obstructive or doctrinaire or both.

As the depression approached its crisis point, Frankfurter felt torn
between his understanding of the need for significant reform and
his fear of any government action which would be either too
radical or too hastily conceived.[49]

In his analysis of the depression, Donald Richberg, like
Daniels and Frankfurter, focused on the disastrous consequences of entrusting a few "gamblers," "profiteers," and
"money-mad megalomaniacs" with control over almost all of
America's essential industries. Unlike Daniels, however, Richberg felt that a government policy based primarily on an attempt
to break up the country's large concentrations of capital would
prove futile. The central problem of government policy posed
by the depression, in his view, was how to create a system in
which those who exercised control over the economy could
also be made to recognize their social responsibility. Only ten
days after Bernard Baruch presented Congress with plans for a
coordinated program for reducing production, Richberg came
before the same Senate committee to offer his own comprehensive plan for dealing with the depression.[50]

To counter the immediate effects of the depression, Richberg proposed a three-pronged legislative program. First, he
called for the quick passage of the five hundred million dollar
appropriation for direct relief which was then pending in Congress. Second, he advocated a "courageous program to create
an immediate mass purchasing power" through credit exten-
sions by the government and through a coordinated effort to
raise farm prices. Richberg did not propose a conscious policy
of deficit spending, but he was willing to see the federal government incur deficits as an unavoidable consequence of taking
the emergency actions necessary to keep Americans from starv-
ing. Unlike Hoover, Richberg argued that the power and resources of the federal government should be used not just to
prop up major financial institutions, but to assist citizens on an
individual basis as well. In rejecting the percolator theory of
government aid, Richberg went even further than Daniels by ac-

cepting not only humanitarian relief measures by the government, but also direct government intervention in the economy in the form of financial assistance to the lower strata of society for the purpose of stimulating recovery by increasing mass purchasing power.

The heart of Richberg's proposed program, however, was a far-reaching plan for the enactment of legislation which would make it possible to "reorganize our political economic system." For years, Richberg had been considering possible ways of restructuring or reforming American industry so that power and responsibility would be made to go hand in hand. As the nation plumbed the depths of the depression, it seemed that Richberg might finally have the opportunity to get a serious hearing for his ideas.

In explaining his program, Richberg claimed that "throughout the era of capitalism" the object of industry had been viewed "upside down." Instead of placing the highest priority on profits, that is, on "compensation for the use of money and property," henceforth, he declared, "our institutions must be operated for the primary purpose of employing as many workers as possible at the highest possible wages." Richberg further argued:

If the welfare of those employed were the supreme object of the management of every enterprise, the highest possible wages would be paid and the purchasing power of the masses, upon which all large enterprises depend, would be maintained. We should not have sudden collapses of purchasing power under such conditions. Markets would be maintained. Consumption and production would be naturally related. If we had planned production, excessive production followed by excessive unemployment would not periodically wipe out capital accumulations. Therefore, money could be more safely invested; and investors, feeling more secure, would be satisfied with lower rates of interest and their purchasing power would be more constant.

Richberg then went on to describe how such a transformation of industry could be brought about. The key element of his plan was the establishment of "industrial councils" for each of the nation's essential industries. Such councils would be "composed of representatives of managers, investors, and workers." In order to achieve fair representation on these councils, as well as a full commitment to the new ethic of social responsibility,

Richberg recommended two steps. First, it was necessary to eliminate from positions of great power those who had, in the past, clearly demonstrated an irresponsible and selfish individualism in their conduct of industry. This Richberg proposed to accomplish by having Congress establish a "legal limitation upon profit-making in the essential industries." With such a law on the books, the reckless profiteers who sought personal profit regardless of social cost would be relegated to non-essential and newly developing industries. Second, it would be necessary to guarantee the right of industrial workers to be "adequately organized." Worker representation on the industrial councils was a crucial element of Richberg's vision in that he saw workers representing not only their own interests as wage earners, but also the interests of the nation's consumers. Richberg also wanted to see the federal government create a "national council" composed of representatives from each of the individual industrial councils. At the national level, "all purchasing and consuming interests would be so represented that one group could hardly obtain sanction for a policy clearly contrary to the public welfare."[51]

While Richberg had long been critical of the profit motive, the depression had moved him to attack this fundamental tenet of capitalism more directly than ever before. Only a little more than a year prior to his Senate appearance, Richberg had still been sceptical about any attempt to eliminate the profit motive in essential industries. Writing to David Lilienthal, he observed that although he felt that humanity was being "drawn or evoluted" in the direction of a non-profit oriented system, it was necessary to remember that "we can only apply any principle of abstract virtue where tradition, custom, or superstition permit." Far from voicing any faith in radical solutions, Richberg confessed to Lilienthal that "we can no more make over the world than we can make over our own weak characters." All we could hope to accomplish, he concluded at that time, was to "improve things a little."[52]

Had Richberg abandoned this scepticism by the time he presented his plan to Congress in early 1933? He seemed poised at the brink of making a fundamental break with the liberal tradition when he called for a basic restructuring of American industry. Richberg's proposal, however, left a number of key questions unanswered. The one phrase he used to sum up his program was "self-government in industry." Ironically, Bernard Baruch, on occasion, used the same phrase in explaining the intent of his proposed "supreme court of business." In calling for the government to encourage industry to adopt his council plan, Richberg never made clear whether he wanted the government to force business to go along; nor did he describe in detail the type of labor organization he envisioned as part of his program. In defending his proposal, Richberg claimed that its goal was to enable America to remain true to its liberal traditions by avoiding the alternatives of socialism or fascism which loomed dangerously on the horizon. He described his plan as the program of a "reconstructed individualist" and argued that in the face of the existing crisis it represented the best means of actually keeping the government out of the operation of industry.[53]

In a memo prepared on the subject of national economic planning before his Senate appearance, Richberg acknowledged that the "American people have not shown a favorable disposition" to such schemes because of a fear of monopoly and the danger of class interests gaining control of the planning process. This was especially true because of the lack of effective representation in industry for interests other than capital. While calling for "government sponsorship" of any attempt at planning, Richberg observed that the government's role generally ought to be restricted to providing statistical information and acting as a mediator between conflicting interests. He envisioned only a voluntary and cooperative form of planning, in other words, in which the government would not use its power to coerce industry. In the New Deal years which were to come, Richberg's uncertainty about the role to be played by government in compelling the reorganization of industry would take on great practical importance, and his underlying scepticism about the possibility for radical change would again reassert itself.[54]

As Herbert Hoover's four year term in office neared its end, American liberalism appeared to be at a crossroads. By 1933, the nation was facing an economic catastrophe of unprecedented proportions which demonstrated that the conception of liberalism held by men such as Hoover and Stimson was woefully inadequate to the tremendous challenges of the day. But while American liberalism was obviously in crisis, many liberals outside the Hoover administration, including Baruch, Daniels, Frankfurter, and Richberg, stood ready with a variety of proposals to put the country back on its feet again. These men still believed that the right combination of reforms based on the lessons of the past could put an end to the depression. Thus, they looked forward with guarded optimism to the institution of a new deal which would more effectively utilize the government's power to police the economy, increase coordination and planning in industry, and encourage the growth of voluntary organizations throughout society. Such a program, they felt, could still succeed in vindicating the American liberal tradition.

# CHAPTER VIII

# The New Deal and the Culmination of Liberalism 1933–1939

THE inauguration of Franklin Roosevelt as President in 1933 marked an important turning point in the efforts of liberals to use the power of the federal government to combat the depression. While Hoover had by no means refrained from government action in the face of the mounting crisis of the early 1930s, the New Deal initiated by FDR entailed a far more significant departure from the philosophy of voluntarism than did Hoover's anti-depression program. The experimental and eclectic nature of the New Deal gave liberals of various persuasions an unprecedented opportunity to test in actual practice the efficacy of the approaches to reform which they had been developing during the previous thirty years.

Of the five men discussed here, three played prominent roles in the New Deal. Arthur Schlesinger notes that Richberg, Baruch, and Frankfurter were each, at various times in the Thirties, viewed by the press as FDR's most influential adviser. Donald Richberg entered the government under Roosevelt as General Counsel of the National Recovery Administration, later became that agency's chief executive officer, and continued to serve as a speech writer and adviser to FDR until the end of the 1930s. Bernard Baruch never held an official position in the New Deal, but he was the largest contributor to the Democratic campaign in 1932 and, by Roosevelt's own estimation, "owned"

sixty Congressmen. Consequently, the new President felt compelled, especially in the early days of his administration, to lis-
ten carefully to the advice of one of the Democratic party's most
powerful figures. Moreover, the two men who were named to
head the crucial National Recovery and Agricultural Adjustment
Administrations in 1933, Hugh Johnson and George Peek, were
regarded as "Baruch men" because of their long associations
with Baruch dating back to the War Industries Board. Until being
named by Roosevelt to the Supreme Court in 1939, Felix Frankfurter held no office in the New Deal, turning down an offer in
1933 to become Solicitor-General because he believed that he
could be more influential in shaping overall policy if he remained free of routine, everyday responsibilities. Throughout the
New Deal, however, Frankfurter not only served the President
as a close political advisor and legislative draftsman, but also
became noted as Washington's most important "one-man employment agency," helping to place many of his former students
and friends in influential positions throughout the Roosevelt administration.[1]

In contrast to Richberg, Baruch, and Frankfurter, Josephus
Daniels and Henry Stimson remained on the periphery of the
New Deal, though Daniels, Roosevelt's one-time superior in the
Navy Department, was appointed Ambassador to Mexico, a position he held from 1933 to 1940. While Daniels was thus far
removed from the center of power, he kept up a steady personal correspondence with FDR, as well as with other public
figures across the country, in which he made known his views
concerning the issues confronting the New Deal at home. Henry
Stimson left office in 1933 as one of the few high officials in the
Hoover administration to maintain relatively good relations with
the incoming President. Stimson, subsequently, remained a private citizen, practicing law on a part-time basis, until Roosevelt
called on him in 1940 to serve as Secretary of War. In the intervening years, Stimson had no power to affect government policy, but his criticisms of the New Deal shed light on the reactions of a significant group of old-line Republican liberals to the
developments of the Thirties.[2]

By the time the outbreak of war abroad diverted the nation's attention from domestic problems, the New Deal had per-

manently expanded the federal government's power to regulate business, encourage and even sponsor interest group organization, and influence the overall level of activity in the economy. In creating the foundation of the modern "welfare" and "broker" state, the New Deal represented the culmination of a decades-long process of evolution in the American liberal tradition. An examination of both the accomplishments and the failings of the New Deal thus reveals, in clearest form, the limits of liberalism.


I


As the Presidential campaign of 1932 approached, all of the men considered in this study, with the exception of Stimson, believed that a change in leadership was critical if the American economy was to be revived and the nation's faith in its liberal tradition maintained. Daniels was the first of these men to perceive Franklin Roosevelt as the best hope for such leadership. He had, in fact, supported FDR for the Presidency as early as 1928. Frankfurter had first met Roosevelt while the two men were both students at Harvard, and he served as an adviser to Roosevelt after FDR had been elected Governor of New York in 1928. Although Frankfurter initially preferred Al Smith for the Presidency in 1932, Smith's increasing conservatism and Roosevelt's growing attractiveness as a potential vote-getter convinced Frankfurter to throw his support to FDR. Baruch has been described by one historian as the "acknowledged leader of the stop-Roosevelt coalition" at the Democratic convention, favoring instead either Albert Ritchie or Newton Baker. However, after Roosevelt won the convention's nomination, Baruch closed ranks, contributing between fifty and two hundred thousand dollars to FDR's campaign and, along with Frankfurter, helping to persuade Al Smith to support the nominee of the Democratic party. Richberg had not personally met Roosevelt before 1932, but the two men became acquainted during the campaign. Richberg subsequently did some speech writing for the Democratic candidate and, together with Frankfurter, served on the National

Progressive League, a pro-Roosevelt organization of Republican and former Bull Moose progressives.[3]

By March 1933, when Roosevelt took office, the American economy seemed on the verge of total collapse. FDR himself noted in his inaugural address that the nation asked "for action, and action now" by the government to relieve widespread suffering and to get the country on the road to recovery. During the next six years, Roosevelt would introduce a New Deal consisting of a variety of new programs and policies designed to bring relief, recovery, and reform to the American people. Most historians would agree with the conclusion of John Braeman that neither "Roosevelt personally" nor the "New Deal generally" ever had "any master plan for reshaping the American economy and social order." No single conception of reform ever defined the New Deal as a whole. Even in the formulation and implementation of individual New Deal programs, contrasting or contradictory motives and intentions were frequently at work. Yet the various approaches utilized by FDR in an effort to bring about recovery and reform were all foreshadowed before Roosevelt became President by the anti-depression programs outlined by the five men considered here.[4]

The National Industrial Recovery Act (NIRA) was the centerpiece of the Roosevelt administration's initial attempt to bring about both economic recovery and a reconstruction of the nation's industrial system. The NIRA signed into law by FDR at the end of the First Hundred Days was, as Ellis Hawley correctly observes, a compromise measure which "appealed to the hopes of a number of conflicting pressure groups" by incorporating most of the "conflicting theories of economic recovery" being put forward at the time. One section of the law responded to the proposals of liberals such as Frankfurter, Brandeis, and Senator Robert Wagner by authorizing an expenditure of 3.3 billion dollars for an expanded program of public works to provide work relief and boost mass purchasing power. Government spending would prove to be a crucial aspect of the New Deal and will be discussed later in this chapter. In 1933, however, the other provisions of the NIRA gained even greater attention.[5]

The remainder of the act represented a peace-time experiment in government coordinated economic planning harkening back to the WIB of the First World War and entailing an unstable amalgam of both the corporatist and pluralist conceptions of interest group organization which had developed side by side in the Twenties. The NIRA partially suspended the anti-trust laws and gave to each of the nation's industries the power to draw up, under government supervision, standards to eliminate cutthroat competition and stabilize business conditions. The law also established labor's right to collective bargaining in those industries which sought to utilize the code-making authority provided in the act. In the course of the National Recovery Administration's (NRA) two year existence, the latent differences between corporatist and pluralist thinking would begin to emerge more clearly. By the end of the decade, a more strictly pluralist conception of political economy would become the dominant liberal ideal, and corporatism would take its place alongside Hoover-style voluntarism as a minor tributary current in the mainstream of American liberalism.[6]

Baruch, Frankfurter, and Richberg all played important roles in the history of the NRA. Baruch, in fact, was considered by Hugh Johnson to be the "intellectual father" of the recovery program. Baruch's speech to the Boston Chamber of Commerce in 1930, and his subsequent calls for a revision of the anti-trust laws and the development of government sponsored planning similar to that undertaken by the WIB, presaged the actual provisions of the NIRA. Baruch, of course, was not alone in advocating such an approach to combating the depression, but he did prove instrumental in the selection of Johnson by Raymond Moley, head of Roosevelt's Brains Trust, to help draft the recovery proposal FDR sent to Congress. It was hardly coincidental that only three days after the recovery act was submitted to Congress, Baruch was explaining, in a speech delivered at the Brookings Institution, how the proposed recovery plan could be effectively implemented. Shortly before the NRA began operations, Baruch personally called together a number of prominent business and labor leaders, including John L. Lewis, William Green, Sidney Hillman, Alex Legge, and Gerard Swope, to meet with certain key individuals involved with the NRA, Johnson, Richberg, Frankfurter, and himself, to discuss the prospects for the recovery administration. Roosevelt's choice of Johnson to

head the newly established NRA was, in part, an act of deference to Baruch, though Baruch neither advocated Johnson's selection nor controlled the General's actions once the NRA went
into action.[7]

Frankfurter never played a direct role in the formulation or
administration of the NIRA, but he was indirectly responsible for
Richberg's inclusion in the inner circle which wrote and then
administered the law. While the recovery legislation was being
drafted, Frankfurter, who wished to see the law used to foster
labor organization and improve working conditions and wages,
suggested to Moley that Richberg be called in to represent the
interests of labor. Moley passed the suggestion on to Johnson
who then invited Richberg to write the labor provisions of the
NIRA. Johnson subsequently asked Frankfurter to become General Counsel of the NRA, the number two post in the agency,
but Frankfurter declined the offer for the same reasons he turned
down Roosevelt's offer to become Solicitor-General. Frankfurter, however, advised Johnson to retain Richberg as the NRA's
chief lawyer. Richberg, as a result, became a pivotal figure in
the development of NRA policy.[8]

Two broad areas of policy became the subject of heated
debate within the NRA and throughout the country. From the
start, there was disagreement both as to how the proposed codes
should be written and enforced, and over what economic priorities should be established in them. A recurring question developed as to what role the government was to play at each stage
of the code-making process. In addition to the problems raised
by the planning provisions of the NIRA, there was also a second
major area of controversy surrounding the implementation of
labor's right to collective bargaining under Section 7a of the recovery act. Out of these two controversies evolved the eventual
triumph of a clearly pluralist conception of interest group organization and a general disillusionment with cooperative economic planning based on corporatist assumptions.

The government's role in writing and enforcing codes of
fair competition for industry had been left vague in the NIRA.
Under the law, the President was granted the power of licensing
businesses and of imposing codes upon industries which either
refused, or were unable, to set adequate standards on their own.

No one directly involved in the drafting of the law, or in its subsequent administration, however, ever seriously considered using these powers to turn the NRA into an experiment in comprehensive government-dictated economic planning. The licensing section of the NIRA was a dead letter from the moment it was incorporated into the law. As Richberg himself noted, "the draftsmen" of the recovery act "themselves agreed that it was too drastic for successful use, that its validity might be seriously questioned and that it probably never would be or should be employed."[9]

Richberg, moreover, made clear in his first public address as General Counsel of the NRA that the administration had no intention of "trying to establish public management of private business." Over nation-wide radio, Richberg reassured the country, and especially the country's business community, that there would be no attempt "to fix prices or wages by governmental orders." Explaining the official policy of the newly constituted NRA, Richberg, in words which closely resembled those used earlier that year by Baruch, declared that the "Administration cannot and should not undertake to prepare codes" for individual industries, since it was not the "function of government" to be "a dictator or controller of industrial policies," nor even to be an "arbitrator between parties in conflict." The "purpose of the Administration," Richberg asserted, was simply to "aid" and "coordinate" the efforts of the nation's industries to "put people back to work at decent wages and reasonable hours," and to watch over "the use of those cooperative powers" authorized by the recovery act in order to "make sure" that they were utilized only in a "manner consistent with the public interest."[10]

Richberg, however, cautioned American businessmen that the "chance" being offered to the country's "industrial leadership" was "perhaps the last" it would have to end the depression without more drastic government action. While he strongly denied that anyone connected with the NRA sought the "political socialization of industry," he warned:

. . . unless industry is sufficiently socialized by its private owners and managers so that great essential industries are operated under public obligations appropriate to the public interest in them, the advance of political control over private industry is inevitable.[11]

Both Daniels and Frankfurter responded enthusiastically to Richberg's initial statement of NRA policy. Writing from Mexico City, Daniels informed Richberg that he considered the address "the best speech I have read coming out of Washington recently." Daniels added that he had advised his son Jonathan, who was then editing the Raleigh News & Observer in his father's absence, "to read every line of it and regard it as a chart." In spite of his own previous emphasis on a vigorous enforcement of the anti-trust laws, Daniels had special praise for Richberg's observation that there was "no choice presented to American business men between intelligently planned and controlled industrial operations and a return to the gold-plated anarchy that masqueraded as 'rugged individualism.' " Frankfurter, too, wrote to Richberg immediately after the boradcast of the speech and lauded the NRA General Counsel for saying "just what needed to be said."[12]

The establishment of the NRA, by directly involving the government as a sponsor of the code-making process in industry, and by vesting in Washington the ultimate authority to approve and enforce the codes which industry was to devise, marked a significant movement beyond the voluntarism of the Twenties. However, the widespread initial support for the NRA, coming from liberals as diverse as Daniels, Baruch, Richberg, and Frankfurter, was a clear indication that the recovery program was not generally perceived as an attempt to have the government itself assume responsibility for the direction of American industry. The use of government coercion to enforce comprehensive mandatory controls on business was still viewed with fear by the men discussed here. Baruch and Richberg, in particular, saw the NRA as an instrument for cooperative economic planning based on the assumption that under the aegis of government sponsorship true concerts of interest could be created in most, if not all, of the nation's major industries. The combined actions of these concerts of interest would, they believed, be able to lift the country out of the depression.

In applauding Richberg's initial statement of NRA objectives, Frankfurter focused more on the new agency's power to insure decent wages and working conditions than on its potential as a sponsor for the development of some form of corporative commonwealth. Frankfurter, in fact, read into Richberg's speech an "unmistakable warning . . . to the irreconcilable gentry" that:

. . . if within a reasonable time no codes are forthcoming from the chief labor-absorbing industries, the General and you would evolve codes for promulgation by the President at least on the two crucial features for recovery: appropriate limitations of hours at appropriate minimum wages. If these standards indispensable for re-absorption of labor are enforced by the government, the gentry can take their own sweet time about the other subjects appropriately to be dealt with by a code.[13]

The creation of decent wage and hour standards did become a focus of the NRA's early activities. In pursuing these objectives, though, the recovery administration never renounced the philosophy of industrial self-government initially set forth by Richberg. No attempt was ever made by the NRA to impose unilaterally on industry mandatory labor standards. However, soon after the NRA was established, it became obvious that if wages were to be quickly improved, or at least stabilized, and hours reduced, then it would not be possible to wait until each industry drew up its own code. For at the time Richberg delivered his inaugural address in early July, only the cotton textile industry had succeeded in drafting a code of fair competition which Richberg could praise as a product of the "uncoerced desire" of an industry "to govern itself wisely and in the public interest." The nation's other major industries, however, suffered from too much internal disorganization and conflict, as well as from a fear of the possible consequences of recognizing labor's right to collective bargaining under Section 7a, to come up quickly with acceptable codes.[14]

Confronted with the possibility of a serious delay in getting the NRA experiment off the ground, Johnson devised a plan which he thought would not only meet the need of rapidly establishing a floor under labor standards, but which would also spur industry to faster action in drawing up its own codes. The

Blue Eagle campaign which Johnson launched in mid-July was remarkably similar to a proposal which Baruch had first made public in his May speech to the Brookings Institution. Baruch, like the other men discussed here, appreciated the need for a quick stabilization of wages and hours and suggested, in May, that once the NRA was established, a blanket rule on wages and hours be devised by a conference of leaders from industry and labor. Baruch argued that this blanket rule ought not to be made compulsory, but rather that it ought to be submitted to each of the country's trade associations "for their voluntary acceptance or requests for modification," with "exceptional cases" then being sent to the government's recovery administration for approval. The key element in Baruch's proposal was the subsequent method of enforcement:

It is just here that the mobilization of public opinion becomes important. If it is commonly understood that those who are cooperating are soldiers against the common enemy within, and those who omit to act are on the other side, there will be little hanging back. The insignia of governmental approval on doorways, letterheads and invoices will become a necessity in business. This was the method used with success in 1918. It is a short cut to action and to public support without which no such plan can succeed.[15]

Johnson's plan centered on the promulgation of a President's Reemployment Agreement (PRA). The PRA was a simple document with provisions banning child labor, setting a minimum wage of twelve dollars a week and a maximum work week of forty hours, and granting labor the right to collective bargaining as provided for in Section 7a of the original NIRA. However, the labor standards created by the PRA were neither to be imposed on industry as Frankfurter had hoped, nor offered to the country's trade associations for prior approval as Baruch had suggested. Instead, Johnson embarked on a massive public relations compaign to convince business firms, large and small, to sign up voluntarily, on an individual basis, in return for the right to display the NRA's Blue Eagle emblem. There was almost unanimous opposition to Johnson's plan within the NRA because it seemed both too ambituous and too difficult to enforce. Richberg, though, while not as enthusiastic about the Blue Eagle as Johnson, still called the idea a "stroke of genius." He warned, however, that "any failure to get a universal response" might discredit the whole NRA program.[16]

The Summer of 1933 witnessed a tremendous drive to get employers throughout the country to sign the PRA. This campaign may not have had a direct impact on the economy, but it did produce several important results. First, it proved effective in hastening the code-making process in essential industries, since they came under great public pressure to cooperate with the NRA. Rather than accepting only the labor standards entailed in the PRA, these industries preferred to earn the right to display the Blue Eagle by working out comprehensive codes of fair competition designed specifically for their own needs. By September, almost every major industry had developed a code approved by the NRA.

The Blue Eagle campaign, though, also raised certain problems. Baruch complained to Johnson at the beginning of November that the NRA had become so carried away with the drive to bring every business under the Blue Eagle emblem that it had gotten away from the original design of the program. Instead of involving only those industries which voluntarily sought to utilize the government-sanctioned code procedure, Baruch claimed that "the whole field of industry" was "being forced into codes which are really impositions by the Government itself." Public demand for strict enforcement of the PRA and of the various industry codes also rapidly increased, and, in the opinion of both Richberg and Baruch, produced an atmosphere of coercion and pressure for government intervention in the economy which violated the original spirit of the NIRA.[17]

While the spectre of extensive government coercion may have been raised by Johnson's handling of the Blue Eagle campaign, in fact, the various industry codes which were drawn up were, as Baruch originally suggested, largely written and enforced by the leadership of the nation's existing trade associations. The continuing reluctance of both Johnson and Richberg to order business to adopt government-imposed policies, as well as the rapidity with which the NRA's activities and responsibilities expanded under the weight of the Blue Eagle crusade, meant that the NRA lacked not only the will, but also the resources to direct or strictly supervise either the writing or the administration of the codes which were established. Most of the individual code administrators representing the government were themselves either businessmen or military officers.[18]

Richberg, for one, had originally envisioned "self-government in industry" as being a cooperative effort not only among the various firms involved in the same economic activity, but also between labor and capital. However, the drafting and enforcement of NRA codes were as much, if not more, dominated by corporate business leaders, to the exclusion of representatives of labor, then the WIB had been fifteen years earlier. Of the more than five hundred code authorities established under the NRA, less than ten percent actually had labor representatives. Not even one percent of these code authorities had members designated as representatives of consumer interests.[19]

The economic priorities established in the NRA codes reflected the dominance of businessmen who shared Baruch's view of the causes of the depression. While Baruch and others concerned with the problem of overproduction admitted the need to increase mass purchasing power, they were still anxious to see the NRA code-making process used primarily as a means of increasing profits by reducing production. Henry Stimson observed as late as November of 1933 that he believed that it was "an economic mistake to try to raise wages before a revival of business" occurred. Frankfurter, on the other hand, sent a comprehensive five-page memo to Richberg, Senator Robert Wagner, and Secretary of Labor Frances Perkins shortly after the NIRA was introduced in Congress, arguing that an attempt to use the proposed NRA to restrict production might result in a stabilization of profits, but that it would do so at the probable cost of forcing America to "become habituated to the standards of living of India or Peru."[20]

By allowing the dominant trade associations in each industry to write and enforce their own codes, the recovery administration headed by Johnson and Richberg permitted the NRA to be used largely as a means of planning for scarcity in a nation which already suffered from a shortage of goods and services. Even as Baruch and members of the business community began to complain in the Fall of 1933 about excessive government regulation, the code authorities of the major industries were generally implementing the kind of restrictionist policies which Baruch and Stimson had incorrectly argued were necessary to bring about recovery. In some instances, the code authorities also engaged in price-fixing whereby the government, in effect, sanctioned the disastrous administered price policies developed by American businessmen in the 1920s. Although both Johnson and Richberg had lavish praise for the NRA's economic achievements during its first months of existence, it is clear that the NRA had embarked on a course which had little chance of getting the country out of the depression. Frankfurter had been correct when he warned that a stabilization of profits would not necessarily lead to a general economic recovery.

Long before the Supreme Court declared the NIRA unconstitutional in 1935, liberals of all persuasions had become disillusioned with the NRA's experiment in economic planning. Frankfurter and Daniels, who had reluctantly accepted the idea of industrial self-government as an emergency measure, had quickly become unhappy with the way the code-making process had been used largely to protect profits. Henry Stimson may have been initially more favorable to the concept of industrial cooperation embodied in the NRA, but he, too, noted his displeasure with the "absence of clear landmarks in the course of the administration" of the recovery agency and observed that the NRA had come to represent an attempt to "combine reform with recovery to the disadvantage of the latter."[21]

Advocates of planning as diverse as Baruch and Richberg had also developed doubts as to the efficacy of the NRA. Even though the two men had begun with different conceptions of the objectives to be pursued through planning, both agreed that the government ought to lend only a guiding, and not a controlling, hand in the planning process. By 1934, both men found reasons for believing that the NRA had failed to live up to their initial expectations. Baruch complained that the government was trying to force politically influenced standards upon business and recommended to FDR that the NRA be abandoned and replaced by a program in which industry would be "self-regulating," but in which a "High Court of Commerce" would be available as an ultimate arbiter of seemingly unresolvable disputes. Richberg, on the other hand, became concerned that the power of the government was being used to enforce decisions made by and for the economy's dominant interests. Although Richberg had once hoped that the NRA would culminate in the development of a national planning council, after only one year's experience with the recovery administration, he had reached the conclusion that too much had already been attempted in the code-making process, opposing, in particular, the use of NRA authority to restrict production and fix prices.[22]

Richberg had become especially disenchanted, for both personal and philosophical reasons, with Johnson's flamboyant performance as head of the NRA. The General was, in fact, forced out of his job in the Summer of 1934, and Richberg eventually became chairman of a newly constituted National Industrial Recovery Board. On various occasions in 1934, Richberg contended that the only way to salvage the NRA would be to lower the agency's public profile and simplify greatly the codes already in operation. Except in the case of certain particularly distressed industries, Richberg contended that the NRA codes should henceforth cease to regulate such matters as production and prices, and that they should concentrate, instead, only on basic standards of fair competition with regard to labor practices.[23]

The Schechter decision handed down by the Supreme Court in May of 1935 tolled the death knell for the NRA. None of the men discussed here subsequently called for any attempt to revive the emergency program in its original form. Neither Frankfurter nor Daniels were especially unhappy to witness the death of a program which had suspended the anti-trust laws and given great powers to business. Frankfurter, however, quickly reiterated his belief in the importance of establishing effective labor standards and recommended to FDR that the positive aspects of the NRA could be continued by attaching fair labor clauses to all government, or government-financed, contracts. In addition, he advised the President to state publicly that voluntary labor codes would not be considered by the administration to be in violation of the anti-trust laws. He also called on Roosevelt to urge Congress to pass legislation which would have enforced the right of individual states to keep out goods produced under conditions not meeting their own fair labor standards.[24]

Henry Stimson wrote to FDR soon after the death of the NRA and informed the President that he believed that "most rightminded men" were in "hearty sympathy" with the "general objectives" of the recovery administration, namely to:

. . . preserve the essentials of real competition while curbing the evils of cutthroat competition;—to secure the stabilization of modern industry, the prevention of unfair practices, and the prohibition of the exploitation of labor.

Stimson, however, agreed with the Supreme Court's judgment that the NRA had exceeded the constitutional limits on government intervention in the economy. He apparently wished to see a return to the more purely voluntaristic methods of the Twenties and an expansion of the role of the individual states in attempting to establish fair standards for business.[25]

Although neither Baruch nor Richberg gave up on the idea of industrial self-government following the Schechter decision, both men had become disillusioned with the NRA experiment. For a variety of reasons, the NRA experience undermined the appeal that corporatist solutions would subsequently have for American liberals. Baruch believed that the country's economic problems could be solved if the nation's corporate leaders were provided with a proper forum for cooperative planning. He realized, however, that the Great Depression had demonstrated the impossibility of relying strictly on the initiative of American business leaders themselves to establish mechanisms which would be effective in stabilizing the economy at a high level of productivity. Government had to play an active role not only in sponsoring the growth of industrial self-government, but also in serving as an authority of last resort in cases where industry leaders could not themselves reach a consensus as to the proper course of action. Baruch thus acknowledged that the successful development of a corporatist concert of interests in industry was not likely to take place on a purely voluntarist basis.

In rejecting a purely voluntarist philosophy of industrial self-government, however, Baruch continued to fear the dangers of

moving toward a statist version of corporatism in which the government might use its powers of coercion to compel industry to
submit to an externally imposed conception of the common interest. Baruch clearly exaggerated the threat of government
coercion actually posed by the NRA. Yet he was by no means
alone among American businessmen in perceiving the NRA, as
it developed under Johnson, as a potential first step toward a
regimented and bureaucratized economic system operating under government control. The ideological bias against state power
was so strong in American liberalism that it could distort the
perceptions even of those corporate leaders who in reality exercised control over NRA policies and stood to benefit the most
from the codes which were actually drawn up. Baruch thus concluded that it was extremely difficult, in practice, to steer a precise course between an ineffective and discredited voluntarist
conception of corporatism and an equally unattractive statist
version of corporatism based on coercion. Baruch remained
committed to the idea that cooperative planning was essential
for the health of the economy, but he found himself in a quan-
dary as to how such planning could be fostered by the government without moving the country in the direction of either socialism or fascism.

Richberg officially left the Roosevelt administration after the
NRA's demise, but he remained an adviser to FDR and, according to Hawley, acted as "the chief spokesman" for those inside
and outside the administration who still wanted "a government-
sponsored program of business cooperation." Richberg had invested much of his own personal reputation in the NRA's effort
to develop a cooperative approach to economic planning predicated on the hope that industrial self-government could be established on the basis of a concert of interests. As his biographer
observes, Richberg continued to believe in "government-business cooperation as firmly when he left the administration as
when he entered it, despite the evidence of the intervening two
years that his faith was not completely justified."[26]

Yet, in 1934, Richberg himself had publicly acknowledged
the failure of many industrial leaders to take a broad disinterested view of what needed to be done to get the country out
of the depression. At that time, he openly questioned the wis-

dom of vesting private bodies with extensive, quasi-public, authority, noting that those involved in the NRA "found few trade associations truly representative of an entire trade or industry and even in the best of them the capacity for self-government was pretty weak." The ideal of "industrial republics" characterized by business-government cooperation remained attractive to Richberg, but the NRA experience, like the WIB experience before it, demonstrated the difficulty of advancing the interests of society as a whole by relying on the public spiritedness of those groups and institutions which were already in a dominant position in the economy.[27]

The NRA, however, did not ignore labor's claim to play a more significant role in the nation's industrial life. While Baruch and Richberg both tended to see the NRA as an instrument for achieving a corporatist harmony of interests in which management would play the main leadership role in the process of industrial code-making, the NRA's commitment to the organization of labor also had the potential for fostering the growth of a pluralistic balance of interests between opposing forces of labor and capital.

## II

The adoption of Section 7a of the NIRA represented a landmark in the history of the American labor movement. For the first time, government gave effective support to the organization of the nation's workers into unions. Richberg and others may have envisioned such a government policy as contributing ultimately to the development of harmonious and cooperative relationships in industry between representatives of organized labor and organized capital. At the time of the NIRA's enactment, however, Section 7a was more commonly understood as a means of strengthening labor's bargaining position so that it might develop into a more effective countervailing force to the power of capital.

Long before the depression, the liberals discussed in this study had come to support the organization of labor as a matter of economic efficiency and social justice. During the Twenties, they had all come to the conclusion that the development of voluntary organizations among workers and other groups in society would help make unnecessary the growth of a coercive centralized government, but they had not always been clear or consistent in their own minds whether the organization of workers would contribute to the emergence of a corporatist or a pluralist society. By the time New Deal labor policy culminated in the adoption of the National Labor Relations Act, a pluralist conception of labor organization had become clearly dominant in American liberalism.

Richberg himself expressed such a conception in his book *The Rainbow*, a personal account of the history of the NRA published in 1936. He claimed that the growth of unions would play an important part in establishing "a balance of power" in the economy and "a system of checks and balances that [would] prevent any class control . . . and compel every separate economic interest to accept responsibility to all others." Such a development would make "the regimentation of people under state control of industry" unnecessary. Unions, when properly integrated into a well balanced economic order, would thus inhibit the rise of both dangerous class conflicts and a divisive sense of class consciousness by making it impossible for any "one class" to become a "ruling class."[28]

At the outset of the New Deal, there was general agreement among the various ideological factions supporting a comprehensive recovery program that such a program would have to lend some form of legitimization to labor organization to balance the proposed legitimization of industry trade association activities. Labor organization had an additional appeal to liberals such as Richberg and Frankfurter who considered the depression a product of insufficient mass purchasing power. They believed that an expanded and strengthened union movement would increase wages and thereby speed recovery by boosting the purchasing power of workers. While it was widely expected that Roosevelt's recovery program might include some protection for labor's right to collective bargaining, there was controversy from the start over the nature of such a provision. Even after Section 7a was written into law, controversy continued to surround its interpretation and enforcement during the NRA's two years of existence.

When Donald Richberg was given the primary responsibility for drafting the section of the NIRA which was to establish and protect labor's right to collective bargaining, his selection was widely regarded as a political concession by the administration to the American Federation of Labor. During the next few years, Richberg became a central figure in the debate within the Roosevelt administration over the formulation of labor policy. Schlesinger, in fact, describes him as the "most influential labor adviser at the White House" during the period.[29]

As originally written by Richberg, Section 7a of the recovery act that FDR sent to Congress in May of 1933 included two key clauses relating to labor organization. Any code adopted by industry under the terms of the proposed recovery bill had to incorporate language providing:

1) that employees shall have the right to organize and bargain collectively through representatives of their own choosing 2) that no employee and no one seeking employment shall be required as a condition of employment to join any organization or to refrain from joining a labor organization of his own choosing.[30]

Organized labor was gratified by the inclusion of Section 7a in Roosevelt's proposed program, but the AFL's leadership was not entirely satisfied with the language which Richberg had used to protect labor's rights. During the Congressional debate over the final wording of Section 7a, a breach began to develop between Richberg and the American labor movement which was eventually to widen into a seemingly unbridgeable gulf. Not only did Richberg fail to agree to support AFL-backed proposals for strengthening the wording of Section 7a, but he even later testified in favor of industry-inspired amendments which would have clearly made company unions permissible, and which might have been interpreted as generally weakening the law's protection for labor's right to bargain collectively.

The Congress, however, adopted the revised wording of Section 7a recommended by organized labor. As a result, the first clause in the section was strengthened by the addition of language taken directly from the Norris-La Guardia Anti-Injunction Act which both Richberg and Frankfurter helped to write. Employees were thus given the added protection of being:

. . . free from the interference, restraint, or coercion of employers of labor, or their agents, in the designation of such representatives or in self-organization or in other concerted activities for the purpose of collective bargaining or other mutual aid or protection.

The second clause of Section 7a was also amended under AFL pressure to prohibit "as a condition of employment," not, as in Richberg's original draft, the joining of "any organization," but rather, the joining of "any company union." [31]

The impact of Section 7a of the NIRA signed into law by Roosevelt in June of 1933 was both immediate and dramatic. Irving Bernstein describes the enactment of the labor provisions of the NIRA as "the spark that rekindled the spirit of unionism within the American labor movement." Under the aegis of the legal protections afforded by the law, far-sighted labor leaders such as John L. Lewis, Sidney Hillman, and David Dubinsky completed organizing campaigns which succeeded, in little more than a year, in making up the tremendous losses in union membership which had taken place over the previous decade. [32]

The NRA's task of implementing Section 7a, however, proved to be difficult and controversial. The victory of organized labor in the fight over the wording of the labor provisions of the NIRA was by no means complete. Just as the significance of the planning provisions of the law ultimately depended on the way in which they were interpreted and administered by Johnson and Richberg, so, too, did the recovery act's protections for labor's right to collective bargaining ultimately depend on the way in which the NRA administration chose to enforce them.

The enactment of Section 7a immediately gave rise to a large number of labor disputes. As a result, within less than two months of the establishment of the NRA, Roosevelt approved the creation of a National Labor Board to serve as a mediator between labor and management in disputes arising out of the implementation of Section 7a. Although the NLB originally had neither a legislative mandate nor any specifically defined executive authority, under the leadership of its chairman, Senator Robert Wagner, it began to build up a body of quasi-judicial interpretations of the meaning of the labor provisions of the NIRA. The President subsequently issued several executive orders during the NLB's first year of existence to give the board's actions a firmer legal foundation. The NLB, nevertheless, remained essentially dependent on the NRA for the enforcement of its decisions, since an NRA order withdrawing the right to display the Blue Eagle became the principal means available to the NLB for punishing those it found in violation of the provisions of Section 7a.

Although Richberg and Johnson had approved the creation of the NLB, serious disagreements soon developed between them and the labor board over the proper interpretation of Section 7a. The most important issues over which Richberg and Johnson clashed with Wagner and the NLB were the legitimacy of company unions, the principle of majority rule in the determination of a single agent for the purpose of collective bargaining, and the enforceability of closed shop agreements. On all of these issues, Richberg, as chief legal officer of the NRA, opposed the positions of the NLB and his one-time friends and associates in the labor movement. In so doing, he helped to weaken the impact of the NLB's generally pro-labor interpretations of Section 7a.[33]

The problem of company unionism plagued the recovery program in spite of the apparent resolution of the issue in the Congressional debate over the NIRA. The failure of Section 7a to include an outright ban on company unions was quickly exploited by industry. Soon after the recovery act was adopted, many employers rushed to establish company unions in an attempt to satisfy the requirements of the law for collective bargaining while still avoiding any recognition of independent unions. Although the passage of the NIRA led to a rapid increase in the number of workers belonging to independent unions, the proportion of all union members in the country belonging to company unions actually increased from 40 percent in 1932 to 60 percent in 1935. Richberg himself acknowledged that the establishment of company unions became the "favorite method of obstruction" employed by management to frustrate "genuine collective bargaining." The strong protests of labor over this issue, including a rash of strikes in the first months of the NRA's existence, contributed significantly to the creation of the NLB. Richberg and the NRA, however, refused to adopt a strong enforcement policy to assist the NLB in its attempt to halt the spread of illegitimate company-dominated unions.[34]

Another source of controversy growing out of the implementation of Section 7a involved the question of whether a union chosen by a majority of employees had to be recognized by a company as the exclusive bargaining agent for all the workers in its plant. Soon after the NLB was set up, it decreed that "majority rule" was the "keystone of any sound, workable system of industrial relationship by collective bargaining." Richberg and Johnson agreed that labor-management relations could most rationally be conducted if there were only one bargaining agent on each side. However, they denied the authority of the NRA to compel industry to accept the majority rule principle, and, in early 1934, they practically repudiated the NLB's position on the issue by publicly affirming the right of minorities and individuals to bargain separately with an employer.[35]

Richberg also incurred the wrath of organized labor by his stand on the question of the closed shop. The language of Section 7a made it impossible for the NLB to establish the closed shop as a compulsory standard, but, at least in two specific cases, the NLB handed down decisions in which it moved toward sanctioning the closed shop in instances where such a condition had been incorporated into a contract voluntarily agreed to by labor and management. Again, though, Richberg and Johnson lessened the pro-labor impact of the NLB's interpretation of Section 7a by refusing to involve the NRA in the enforcement of any agreement requiring a worker to join a union as a condition of employment.[36]

Thus Richberg, along with Johnson, was responsible for the NRA adopting a labor policy which undermined both the effectiveness of the NLB and the strength of the supposed protections of labor's rights written into Section 7a. By the end of 1934, both Josephus Daniels and Felix Frankfurter, who had greeted Richberg's inaugural statement of NRA objectives with enthusiasm, had become deeply disturbed with the NRA labor policies which Richberg had helped to establish. Commenting on the "confusion" created by the conflict between the NRA and the NLB over the question of majority rule, Daniels warned FDR that the failure effectively to enforce the labor board's position on the matter endangered the government's entire effort "to achieve industrial peace with justice." Frankfurter was especially upset at the actions of the man whom he had originally recommended for the number two post in the NRA. He confided to Harold Ickes that he could not "understand" what had "happened inside of Richberg" to make him take up a position which represented "exactly the opposite point of view from that which was supposed to be the one of the Administration."[37]

Less than one year after working with Wagner to insure the inclusion in the NIRA of a government guarantee of labor's right to collective bargaining, Richberg had become one of the leading opponents within the Roosevelt administration of Wagner's efforts to give substance to that guarantee. Yet, in spite of his seemingly anti-labor stands as General Counsel of the NRA, Richberg remained a firm believer in the essential role of labor unions in a liberal society. What, then, caused Richberg to oppose Wagner's attempts to insure that Section 7a would be interpreted and enforced in such a way as to give maximum protection to the right of workers to form independent unions?

Richberg's position in the various disputes surrounding Section 7a reflected both his continuing fears of the dangers of government coercion and his ambivalent hopes for the possible development of a harmony of interest between labor and capital. By the time the NIRA was being formulated, Richberg, as well as Frankfurter, Wagner, and the other liberals discussed here, agreed that it was both necessary and proper for the government to encourage and protect the development of unions among workers. The enactment of Section 7a of the recovery bill thus marked a turning point as government policy moved beyond the more purely voluntaristic approach which characterized liberal efforts in the 1920s. The coming of the depression had clearly altered the political climate in the country so that it became possible for men such as Richberg, Frankfurter, and Wagner to push successfully for a more active role for government in fostering labor organization.

Richberg, however, insisted that in entrusting the government with the power to protect the right of workers to form their own independent unions, it was necessary to avoid giving the state the power to compel either labor or management to accept a single pre-determined form of organization. Throughout the debate over the wording, and then the interpretation, of Section 7a, Richberg consistently maintained that the government's powers of coercion ought to be used only to prevent employers from interfering with their workers' essential right to self-organization. Any attempt to have the government compel workers either to join unions against their will or to abandon company unions which they had voluntarily entered into, Richberg argued, would have represented a violation of the right to "freedom of association." [38]

While serving in the NRA, Richberg continued to insist that he was no supporter of "tame cat organization," and that he retained his commitment to "independent, courageous, vigorous labor organization." He also reaffirmed his belief that "if the fundamental principle of Section 7(a) were adhered to, many employers might wisely make contracts agreeing to employ only men belonging to the labor organization with which they had a contract." However, at the same time, he refused to call for any outright ban on company unions and opposed any attempt to use the authority of an employer or of the government "as the means of coercing men to join" a particular union. Explaining his position to printers' union president George Berry, Richberg observed:

I don't think a labor organization which isn't a voluntary association of men working together because they want to work together for their common interest is of much service, either to labor or to the general welfare. [39]

Richberg's stand on majority rule in the determination of collective bargaining agents stemmed from similar ideological considerations. He acknowledged that there could "be little question of the benefit to both employer and employees of having only one agent for collective bargaining." Nevertheless, he argued that Section 7a had not given the NRA the power to force majority rule on industry, and, moreover, that it would have been unwise to have given the government such power. Any effort to create a compulsory requirement of majority rule, Richberg contended, conflicted not only with "the express grant of a right to all employees to organize and bargain collectively free from the 'restraint' of employers," but also with the "constitutional" right to "liberty of contract" which had been established by the Supreme Court.[40]

While a deep-seated fear of the dangers inherent in the growth of a coercive state played a critical role in Richberg's increasingly cautious stand on NRA labor policy so, too, did the corporatist conception of labor organization which seemed so attractive to Richberg in the 1930s. Although Richberg continued, at times, to conceive of unions as a counterforce to the power of capital that would make possible the development of a balance of interests in industry, his policy decisions with the NRA demonstrated that he found a vision of a harmony of interests between an organized labor force and a public-spirited management even more compelling. Because he wanted to see the government succeed in fostering a cooperative, rather than an adversarial, relationship between labor and capital, he was reluctant to antagonize unduly the nation's businessmen at the outset of the New Deal by supporting a policy based on the assumption that company unions were universally the product of management's bad faith. It was not possible simply to rely on the good will of the nation's business community, but it was necessary, in Richberg's view, for government, through "mediation and conciliation," to begin establishing a foundation of mutual trust and respect upon which a true harmony of interests in industry could be built.[41]

Richberg's view of the proper scope of labor organization was also shaped by his continuing commitment to the principle of decentralization. Power had to be decentralized in the private, as well as in the public, sector. Although he had long fought against company unions in the railroad industry, Richberg sympathized with the argument made by a number of businessmen that the destruction of all company unions, and their replacement by unions nation-wide in scope, would lead to an undesirable concentration of power and to a possible increase in divisive class consciousness. He noted that not all employers favored company unions for cynical reasons:

The fear of an uncontrollable, unreasonable formulation of policies on a national scale, that may endanger the integrity, even the solvency, of an individual enterprise, is very real in the minds of most managers of large properties. A local strike for local reasons is within the control area of a manager. But a sectional or industrial strike may destroy all his plans without giving him any chance to keep his business out of trouble. The antagonism of an employer to "outside dictation" is not wholly a product of a desire to have the advantage of dealing only with those dependent on him for a livelihood. Much of it rises out of the fear of being involved in a quarrel not of his making and beyond his *individual power* of adjustment.[42]

Richberg had long doubted the desirability of "the universal association of workers in one type of organization or . . . of a centralized control of all associations." Either of these developments posed the "grave danger" of creating a labor organization with "too great a power and responsibility for successful administration." While Richberg viewed the organization of workers on a decentralized basis as a healthy development, he warned that the creation of a monolithic and centralized labor movement would lead:

. . . to a steady rise of hostility in all other groups, such as farmers, businessmen and professionals, which would produce a class struggle for political power, which would seriously menace our institutions of self-government.

The harmony of interests that Richberg envisioned, in other words, could not emerge if American society became divided into just a few nationally organized interest group.[43]

Certain more personal concerns also affected Richberg's actions as a member of the NRA. Richberg seems to have perceived his first entry into government service as an important personal test of the validity of his ideal of disinterested public service. When he was brought into the group charged with the task of drafting a comprehensive recovery bill, Richberg was seen by other administration advisers, such as Frankfurter, Moley, and Johnson, as a self-conscious advocate of labor's special interests. Richberg, however, saw himself quite differently. In spite of his relationship to the nation's railway brotherhoods, he viewed himself as an independent-minded public servant. From the outset of his involvement in the New Deal, Richberg seems to have been particularly concerned with dispelling the notion that he was little more than a special pleader for the intersts of organized labor. As a result, he went out of his way to demonstrate to the nation's business community that his commitment to the success of the administration's overall recovery program took precedence over his concern for the particular interests of labor. It was as if he wanted to prove by his own example that harmonious and cooperative relations between representatives of industry, labor, and government were possible, even if it meant, in his own case, bending over backwards to conciliate the business community.

Vanity, and personal ambition, as well as idealism, may have also influenced Richberg's increasingly sympathetic attitude toward industry. As his attempts to appease America's business interests began to alienate him from his former friends and associates in progressive and labor circles, Richberg found himself more and more being welcomed into the company of the nation's leading businessmen. After he left the Roosevelt administration in 1935, Richberg opened what soon became a lucrative law practice in Washington catering to a wealthy and powerful clientele. Ever since finishing law school, Richberg had always worried about the state of his personal finances and had even considered turning down FDR's offer to enter government service because of his concern about the difficulty of discharging his financial responsibilities on a government employee's salary. Having been politically and socially rejected by many of his former friends, Richberg had a number of reasons by the mid-1930s for trying to maintain good relations with his new found associates in the business community.[44]

Richberg still shared many common assumptions with liberals such as Frankfurter and Daniels about the need for labor organization and the dangers of excessive government coercion, but he increasingly diverged from the mainstream of liberal thought regarding the precise limits of government intervention in the field of labor relations and the role of labor unions in the ultimate development of a pluralistic society. By 1935 most liberals were willing to follow the lead of Robert Wagner who argued not only that Congress needed to clarify and strengthen the legal guarantees of labor's right to collective bargaining, but that legislation was also required to establish a new and independent NLB possessing a clear mandate to enforce its own decisions. Writing to FDR in January of 1935, Josephus Daniels voiced a widely shared opinion that the actions of many of the nation's largest firms during the previous two years under the NRA had proven that they would "continue their ancient feudalistic practices unless Government 'hauds the wretch in order.'" Daniels contended that Section 7a:

. . . ought to be changed or defined, or some other way found to prevent those big industries defying the power of the Government to achieve industrial peace with justice. Next spring will probably see more strikes and more trouble unless Uncle Sam has the power and exercises it to require obedience to his rulings.[45]

Six months after Daniels sent his letter to Roosevelt, the President signed into law the National Labor Relations Act (NLRA). The Wagner Act, as it is more commonly known, essentially wrote into law the rulings handed down by the original NLB on such issues as majority rule, company unions, and the closed shop. It also banned a list of specifically defined unfair labor practices by management and gave a newly constituted National Labor Relations Board effective enforcement powers to prevent these unfair practices and to safeguard the right of labor to genuine collective bargaining.[46]

Felix Frankfurter was both a strong supporter of the National Labor Relations Act and a close adviser to Wagner while the New York Senator steered his bill through Congress. Frankfurter acknowledged that the Wagner Act entailed an extension of the government's power to coerce industry, but he argued that "all our recent experience" demonstrated that "employers as a class" could not "be relied upon, voluntarily and out of the goodness of their hearts, to give a square deal to unorganized labor." The degree of government intervention called for in the Wagner Act was necessary to guarantee that workers would be able to achieve a bargaining position roughly comparable to that already enjoyed by management.[47]

Frankfurter, in fact, defended the NLRA in explicitly pluralistic, rather than corporatist, terms. He claimed that "sound labor relations" could not be founded simply on "mutual understanding and good will between capital and labor" because the American economic system was built upon "an economic struggle or competition between employer and employee as to the share of division between them of the joint product of labor and capital." So long as this competition took place under the ground rules established by the Wagner Act, no life and death struggle between labor and capital was likely to arise which might destroy the underlying "community of interest in the prosperity of the industry upon which both wages and dividends depend." The Wagner Act thus represented the culmination of an evolving liberal belief in the necessity of establishing a pluralistic balance of interests in society. It was the cornerstone in the creation of a "broker state" which, in the words of Hawley, encouraged the growth of "counter organizations" among various "economic power blocs" so that those blocs would ultimately be able to "look out for themselves."[48]

The ideal of pluralism upon which the labor policy of the New Deal came to be based entailed neither an acceptance of the inevitability of fundamental class conflict, nor an acknowledgement of the government's right to intervene in economic affairs to advance the interests of one class above the interests of all other classes in society. The liberals considered in this study all agreed that the attempt by the government to foster independent labor organization was appropriate as a means of channeling competition between labor and capital into healthy and essentially non-destructive forms. The Wagner Act was, according to the NLRB's first chairman, Lloyd Garrison, a "safety measure" which worked against the spread of radicalism in several ways. It strengthened a labor movement overwhelmingly committed to a form of unionism predicated on the continued existence of capitalism, and it also seemingly demonstrated that the government, rather than being strictly an instrument of capital, was capable to taking action to foster an equal balance of power between the various economic blocs in society.[49]

Bernard Baruch recognized the potentially constructive impact the Wagner Act could have on American labor relations. In 1938 he advised General Motors President Alfred Sloan that it was neither "realistic" nor "sensible" for business to advocate the repeal of the act and that, moreover, "it would be unfortunate" if the law were removed from the books. Baruch complained to Sloan that industry had "fallen down . . . in the managerial side as regards" the new laws relating to labor by foolishly "fighting a losing, rear-guard action" to retard the development of genuine collective bargaining and fair labor standards. Baruch thought that it would be wise for American industry to declare openly its approval of both collective bargaining and the principles embodied in the Wagner Act in order to "win back" the support and cooperation of "the general public and labor." By resisting what was a natural development in labor-management relations, American businessmen, in Baruch's opinion, had contributed to the rise of a widespread feeling that the interests of labor and capital were inevitably in conflict. Baruch believed that, in the long run, the danger involved in the spread of such a feeling was to be feared more than the difficulties raised by dealing with strong but responsible unions.[50]

Baruch's support for the Wagner Act, however, was not unqualified. In its original form, the law banned certain "unfair" labor practices by management but imposed no comparable restrictions on the activities of unions. Baruch believed that the law could have been improved and made more equitable by amendments making it "bilateral" in its application to both management and labor. Even Daniels, who assumed that still more extensive organization of labor was necessary to insure in the future "a fairer division between labor and capital than in the past," privately voiced his concern in 1938 that "as the pendulum swings and labor gets more power it will dominate just as" capital had dominated in years gone by. "Under the skin," Daniels observed, "there is no difference between a selfish capitalist and a selfish labor leader."[51]

Like Baruch, Henry Stimson also favored modifying the NLRA. Speaking out against Wagner's re-election to the Senate in 1938, Stimson acknowledged that the "country at large recognizes that labor must secure fair conditions for collective bargaining," but he insisted that the enforcement of such a right had to be "coupled with corresponding fairness towards the employer, the consumer, the public and all others involved." Stimson did not call for the outright repeal of the Wagner Act.

However, he did argue that the law, as originally written, was too one-sided by virtue of its failure to require that employees, as well as employers, refrain from unfair practices. In addition to supporting changes in the law to allow management to file complaints against labor, Stimson called for a separation between the judicial and investigative functions of the NLRB in order to make it possible for the labor board to render more impartial judgments.[52]

Donald Richberg not only disagreed with Wagner's initial interpretations of Section 7a, but he also subsequently sought to block the Senator's efforts in 1934 and 1935 to get legislation passed to create a new and more powerful NLRB. Richberg did not oppose, in principle, the establishment of a permanent labor board, but he continued to argue that such a board should not be entrusted with the power of coercing labor and management into accepting a single model for labor relations. Moreover, Richberg shared Baruch and Stimson's concern that the Wagner Act failed to set a standard of proper behavior for labor, as well as for management. He contended that organized labor's growing power meant that it, too, ought to be required to "accept and fulfill corresponding responsibilities and legal obligations to the public welfare."[53]

Richberg's differences over labor policy with liberals such as Frankfurter and Daniels, of course, had great practical significance. Yet, even while warning against the dangers of government favoritism toward either labor or management, Richberg, in his review of the history of the NRA, essentially summed up the pluralist philosophy which was becoming a crucial component of modern liberalism.

When . . . government is brought in to assist this coordination and conciliation of conflicting interests, a desire will always be aroused among the contending parties to use the compulsory powers of lawmaking and enforcement to advance the plans and interests of organized groups. . . . The truth is that the public interest is a composite of all private interests and is advanced by an intelligent compromise of them, which is best assured when there is a balance of economic powers. But the use of political power to reestablish or to maintain this balance is fraught with the constant danger of increasing unduly the power of one group to advance its special interests.

There was a real and justified fear that, if the Recovery Act opened the way for the cooperation of managers, relieved of anti-trust restrictions, the interests of workers and consumers would suffer. To meet this fear and to maintain an economic balance of power it was necessary, first, to encourage a more adequate and independent organization of labor, and, second, to establish governmental supervision for the protection of all other interests.[54]

Writing in 1936, Richberg claimed that "one permanent gain" resulting from the first years of the New Deal could "surely be recorded," the enormous speeding up of "the organization of the various interests of owners, managers, and workers for collective planning and cooperative action." Richberg's assessment was in large part correct. While most liberals, to Richberg's dismay, had become disillusioned with the NRA's experiment in government-sponsored cooperative planning, the recovery program did have a lasting impact on labor relations in the United States. It proved to be a crucial impetus toward the ultimate triumph of a pluralistic conception of labor organization; for it paved the way for the adoption of the Wagner Act and the fuller integration of organized labor into the American economic order. Largely as a result of New Deal labor policy, union membership rose dramatically from 2.8 million in 1933 to 8.8 million in 1939.[55]

William Leuchtenburg has called the Wagner Act "one of the most drastic legislative innovations of the decade." Certainly it is still hard to explain how Congress passed a law which "compelled employers to accede peacefully to the unionization of their plants" without imposing "reciprocal obligations of any kind on workers." Yet the radicalism of both the philosophy underlying the Wagner Act and the impact which the law actually had on American society ought not to be exaggerated. In 1939, more than seven out of ten non-agricultural workers in the United States remained unorganized. While unionization finally came to most basic industries, those workers who had traditionally been the most poorly paid and the least privileged in America remained unorganized and, therefore, virtually powerless to affect the economic decisions which directly shaped their lives.[56]

In addition, even as unions finally gained wide acceptance

as a necessary counterpart to consolidated capital, their role in the economic order continued to be viewed in narrow terms. Donald Richberg may have at one time envisioned organized labor participating, along with management, in the overall determination of basic economic decisions. By the time New Deal labor policy came to fruition, however, Richberg, as well as the other men discussed here, seemed to have almost completely given up any commitment to the goal of guaranteeing organized labor a major voice in determining the general direction of economic affairs. Instead, Richberg and the other liberals considered in the study had come to focus on the role to be played by unions as organizations concerned almost solely with the defense and furtherance of the immediate interests of workers in matters such as wages and hours which were easily subject to the traditional process of collective bargaining. The balance of power envisaged in the liberal conception of pluralism thus amounted to little more than a system of checks on the worst abuses of capital. With government-directed economic planning never even seriously considered by most liberals, and with government-sponsored corporatist planning largely discredited, the limited degree of conscious control over basic economic decisions that was possible in the American political economy continued to be exercised by the tiny elite which managed the small number of dominant corporations in the private sector.[57]

## III

The New Deal's efforts to bring about recovery and reform were not restricted to corporatist-inspired attempts at industrial self-government or pluralist designs for the establishment of a balance of interests in the economy. The New Deal also included a number of other policies and programs which have frequently been labelled as "Brandeisian" attempts to deal with the problem of achieving prosperity and social justice. Some historians, most notably Arthur Schlesinger, have argued that the New Deal can be understood as having gone through a two stage process of development, with each stage being defined by a clearly discernible ideological focus. According to Schlesinger, the "First

New Deal" lasted from 1933 to 1935 and was dominated by policy makers who wished to develop some form of "central planning." The "Second New Deal" emerged between 1935 and 1938 and was shaped by disciples of Louis Brandeis who repudiated planning in favor of an "assault on the concentration of wealth and economic power" in the United States. In Schlesinger's view, Richberg, Johnson, and the members of FDR's Brains Trust, Raymond Moley, Rexford Tugwell, and Adolph Berle, were the "key figures" in the first New Deal; while Frankfurter and his protégés, Thomas Corcoran and Benjamin Cohen, were the leading advocates of the "Brandeis version of the progressive creed" which dominated the Second New Deal.[58]

It is true that by mid-1935 FDR had largely abandoned the planning approach embodied in the NRA. However, the two New Deal interpretation not only exaggerates the ideological purity and consistency of purpose of the New Deal in both its early and late stages, but also overstates the extent to which Roosevelt's closest advisers can easily be divided into two distinct and ideologically antagonistic groups. The NRA itself, as we have seen, was not simply an experiment in planning. It incorporated several different approaches to recovery. Even while the NRA was in existence, FDR also sought to expand the government's regulatory powers over banking and finance and to use the government's spending power in order to prevent destitution and encourage recovery. Moreover, important legislation of the so-called Second New Deal, such as the Wagner Act, Social Security, and the Labor Standards Act, had its origins in the first two years of the Roosevelt administration. The chronological division of the New Deal into two clear-cut stages thus distorts the complex pattern of evolution which actually occurred in government policy during the 1930s.[59]

Although Rexford Tugwell, in his memoirs of the New Deal, has reaffirmed Schlesinger's argument that a wide ideological gulf separated the Brains Trust from the Frankfurter-Brandeis group of advisers, Frankfurter and Moley themselves subsequently denied that such a clear-cut dichotomy existed. Writing privately to Schlesinger in 1963, Frankfurter protested:

I must reject your assumption that there was a real clash of views between Moley-Tugwell and F.F.-Brandeis. This assumes that the respective parties had coherent and systematic views on some of the problems that are involved in Roosevelt's policies.

While Frankfurter is frequently portrayed as an obstinate foe of the "collectivist" policies of the early New Deal, he was, in fact, willing to give at least tentative support to such government experiments in planning as the NRA and the AAA. As he explained at the time: "I am not for a planned society *en gros* [but] I am prepared to get these [results] by *ad hoc* treatment of specific problems."[60]

The New Deal may well have changed in emphasis, personnel, and political rhetoric after 1935, but the various approaches to recovery and reform which FDR adopted both before and after the demise of the NRA were all based on certain common underlying liberal assumptions. This becomes apparent when one examines those programs most directly associated with the Frankfurter-Brandeis school of thought and then compares the assumptions underlying these programs to the assumptions underlying the corporatist and pluralist policies which have already been discussed.

One recent student of Frankfurter's career expresses the widely held view that "the ideological core of Brandeisian liberalism was its emphasis on smallness" and that "trust busting" was the "key program" put forward in the Thirties by the Brandeisians in their attempt "to restore the simple and decentralized market economy of the nineteenth century." Josephus Daniels was certainly one Brandeisian who argued both before and after 1933 that a concerted campaign to enforce the anti-trust laws ought to have been made a key element of government policy to fight the depression. Daniels, nevertheless, gave his support to FDR in 1933 when the President called for the NRA's partial suspension of the anti-trust laws. Well before the Supreme Court ruled the NIRA unconstitutional, however, Daniels began to urge Roosevelt "to restore the effectiveness of the anti-trust laws." Throughout the remainder of the decade, Daniels continued to warn the President that "we must destroy monopoly or monopoly will destroy the benefits of the New Deal."

Yet the notion that liberals such as Daniels or Frankfurter wanted to return to the atomized political economy of the nineteenth century by having the government adopt a vigorous anti-trust policy is highly simplistic and misleading.[61]

Daniels acknowledged in 1935 that in the forty-five years since the passage of the original Sherman Act, no Presidential administration had found it feasible to make a "consistent and persistent" effort to enforce the anti-trust laws. Frankfurter, in a letter written to FDR several months after the Schechter decision, expressed his long held belief that anti-trust prosecutions, even if forcefully pursued, could have little real impact on the economy.

Under the present interpretation of the Sherman Law, businessmen can do practically everything by way of cooperation which fair-minded businessmen feel that trade associations could be allowed to do. . . . (Brandeis has been the great leader of a philosophy of permitting businessmen to undertake anything decently fair through trade associations as a counter-balance to the necessity of avoiding Sherman Law restrictions by actual mergers and monopoly.) The fact is that big business wanted to get out from under the Sherman Law, not knowing how light the burden of the Sherman Law really was.[62]

The initiation in late 1937 of what Hawley describes as "the most intensive anti-trust campaign in American history" elicited fears from Stimson and Richberg that FDR had given his approval to the "fanatic trust busters" in the administration to conduct a "rampage" against business. Their fears were, in fact, unwarranted. Frankfurter and Brandeis themselves realized at the time that the campaign launched by Thurman Arnold, the newly appointed head of the Justice Department's Anti-trust Division, was primarily a symbolic gesture designed more for its political appeal than for its actual economic impact. Trust busting, even under Arnold's vigorous direction, never became a central focus of the New Deal and, in the view of a leading historian of the period, produced "few substantive gains."[63]

The approach of Frankfurter, the New Deal's leading Brandeisian, to the problem of recovery and reform consisted of far more than a simple program of trust busting by traditional means. Frankfurter clearly feared the consequences stemming from the concentration of wealth and economic power, but he was no more intent on trying to reestablish the economic conditions of the nineteenth century than were liberals such as Baruch or Richberg. As noted already, Frankfurter was an influential advocate of a pluralistic conception of labor organization based on the assumption that the purely individualistic ethic of the past had become an anachronism in twentieth-century America. Frankfurter did call for government more effectively to curb the power of concentrated wealth, but his support for new measures of government regulation, taxation, and spending were not simply the product of an implacable hostility to bigness. They were also the logical result of Frankfurter's analysis of the causes of the depression.

Ever since the Progressive era, there had been a clear consensus among liberals that the federal government had the right, and even the obligation, to establish certain standards of reasonable behavior for those individuals and firms doing business in the open marketplace. In the years after the Progressive era, however, liberals had generally placed less emphasis on a negative conception of government regulation of business than they had on other approaches to the problem of how to create a just and prosperous political economy. During the New Deal, Brandeisians again turned to government regulation as a means of making business more socially responsible, but their efforts in this regard focused primarily on the limited field of finance and were much less important than their attempts to use other forms of government action to reform the American economy.

Back in 1913, Louis Brandeis had first warned about the dangers arising from the increasing concentration of control over "other people's money" which characterized the development of the American system of finance. Two decades later, Frankfurter and Danels both argued that the irresponsibility and ignorance of the country's banking and financial leaders had significantly contributed to the nation's terrible depression. Frankfurter, in 1933, noted that "Brandeis saw it all with a seer's discernment more than twenty years ago, and everything that he prophesied since has been vindicated with an almost tragic uncanniness." Daniels, at about the same time, claimed that the Morgan and Mellon interests were the "two influences in America that were doing the most harm." At the outset of the New

Deal, Brandeisians such as Frankfurter and Daniels therefore supported some form of government action to reform the nation's financial system.[64]

Frankfurter, along with two of his former students, James Landis and Benjamin Cohen, became the principal draftsmen of the legislation which Roosevelt signed into law in May 1933 as the first step in extending the government's regulatory powers over Wall Street. The Securities Act of 1933 required that all new issues of stock and securities be accompanied by a thorough statement of relevant financial information by the company involved. Such a statement was to be filed with the Federal Trade Commission. Company directors were made both criminally and civilly liable in the event of misrepresentation.[65]

The following year, Cohen teamed with another disciple of Frankfurter, Thomas Corcoran, to draft the legislation which was to complete the Roosevelt administration's effort to bring Wall Street under federal regulation. Although Frankfurter was out of the country at the time of the drafting of the second securities bill, he wrote FDR soon after the act was introduced in Congress to express his pride in his protégés' "astonishingly careful and acute piece of draftsmanship."[66]

The Securities Exchange Act of 1934 brought all important national securities exchanges under federal supervision. The act banned such manipulative devices as planted tips by brokers and short selling by officers and major shareholders of their own companies' stock which had previously been used by market insiders at the expense of the average investor. It also extended the publicity requirements of the Securities Act of 1933 to all, rather than just newly issued, securities traded on the open market. In addition, the Federal Reserve Board was given the power to establish margin requirements as a means of making unlikely the recurrence of the kind of excessive speculation which had helped to bring on the crash of 1929. Finally, the law created a new Securities and Exchange Commission to administer the provisions of the act, as well as those of the Securities Act of 1933.[67]

While Frankfurter had virtually nothing to do with the major banking legislation enacted in 1933 and 1935, he did play a key role in the drafting of the final version of the Public Utilities

Holding Company Act of 1935. This highly controversial bill not only gave the Federal Power Commission responsibility for the regulation of certain utility rates, but also strengthened the newly established SEC's ability to oversee the financial organization of the nation's public utilities. As originally presented to the Congress by FDR, the bill included a "death sentence" which would have abolished all holding companies in the utility industry within five years. Although Josephus Daniels strongly supported the death sentence clause as an important spur to competition, Frankfurter himself was never enthusiastic about the idea and, in fact, was responsible for drafting a substitute provision which watered down the principle so that the bill would be acceptable to the Congress. In its final form, the Holding Company Act abolished only those holding companies which had been pyramided to more than three tiers and those whose existence could in no way be justified in terms of economic efficiency.[68]

Schlesinger observes that the New Deal's Brandeisian measures to regulate finance were based on an attitude toward business "quite different from that involved in NRA." Frankfurter and his associates, in Schlesinger's view, saw "business not as a power to be propitiated or, at the very least, as a partner to be cajoled, but as an erratic and irresponsible force requiring strict social discipline." At the time of the enactment of the Securities Act of 1933, Henry Stimson expressed his concern to both Frankfurter and Roosevelt that the new legislation seemed dangerously anti-business in spirit. While sympathizing with the aims of the Securities Act, Stimson feared that the legislation placed too great a burden of disclosure on companies and established overly harsh criminal penalties which had little chance of actually being invoked by juries against individual underwriters or company directors. Stimson worried, moreover, that the law was likely to retard recovery by discouraging many companies from attempting to raise needed capital through the securities market. Writing to Frankfurter, Stimson concluded: "I still feel that in this matter you are a little over-influenced by what I should call, without the slightest desire to give you offense, an excess of crusader's zeal."[69]

Frankfurter was certainly less solicitous of businessmen's

concerns and more suspicious of their motives than Stimson. He proudly asserted that the New Deal's securities legislation had succeeded in establishing:

. . . the principle that when a corporation seeks funds from the public it becomes in every true sense a public corporation. Its affairs cease to be the private perquisite of its bankers and managers; its bankers and managers themselves become public functionaries.

Yet, the leading students of the subject all agree with Vincent Carosso's assessment that, "considering the conditions at the time and the mood of the public," the system of government controls over Wall Street created by the New Deal was "a conservative response to a widespread demand for reform" and that it did not alter "radically the substance of the investment banking function" in American capitalism.[70]

The social obligations imposed on those involved in issuing and trading securities by the regulatory legislation of 1933 and 1934 entailed no more than the requirement that such "public functionaries" refrain from engaging in fraud or other patently deceitful tactics in the exercise of their still formidable powers. Frankfurter himself acknowledged that the 1933 law which he had helped to write was little more than "a belated and conservative attempt to curb the recurrence of old abuses which, through failure of adequate legislation, had attained disastrous proportions."[71]

Although Frankfurter was obviously concerned about the dangers arising from the excessive concentration of control in the nation's financial system, he apparently feared even more the possible consequences of entrusting the state with the responsibility of directing the allocation of the country's capital resources. Neither Frankfurter, nor any of his Brandeisian associates, seems ever to have considered socializing the nation's system of finance so that basic investment decisions could be made in accordance with a democratically determined conception of the public interest. Nor, in spite of their fear of centralization, did they ever seriously contemplate a thoroughgoing effort to dissolve the huge investment houses of Wall Street.

Given their commitment to the American liberal tradition and to a capitalist economic system, the Brandeisians attempted only to impose upon the leaders of the financial community an enforceable code of good conduct. Unwilling to seek fundamental change in the economic system, the Brandeisians had to be content with establishing certain basic rules of fair play to protect the average investor and the public from the most obvious forms of exploitation. Hawley sums up the philosophy underlying the Brandeisian approach to regulation by stating that "the thesis implied in such laws" as the securities bills:

. . . was that the exchanges had failed to provide a free market, and the remedy was not state capitalism or even government control of investment decisions. It was the revival of free and fair competition, the restoration of a system where savers and businessmen could bargain on the basis of all the known facts and arrive at the fair market value of any offered security.[72]

Such an approach did not necessarily require the atomization of the nation's financial system. Even the Holding Company Act, which is frequently cited as the New Deal's most concerted effort to strike against the "curse of bigness," was designed more as a means of ridding the economy of the kind of clearly unstable and economically unjustifiable corporate structures which had proven susceptible to collapse during the depression, than as a means of attacking bigness per se. In fact, while most historians focus on the Brandeisians' hostility to bigness, Frankfurter himself maintained that he was more influenced by Brandeis' insistence that "effective and generous opportunity" be given "for the pursuit of reason." In reviewing a re-issue in 1935 of Brandeis' book, *The Curse of Bigness*, Frankfurter hardly mentioned the jurists' hostility to large corporate enterprises, emphasizing, instead, Brandeis' belief in the necessity of making political and economic decisions on the basis of a thorough knowledge of all the relevant facts. In practice, this meant that Frankfurter always stressed the importance of creating flexible administrative mechanisms by which the broad policy goals established through legislation could be implemented. Thus, Frankfurter remarked to FDR shortly before the President signed the first securities act in 1933: "No one knows better than you that in the last analysis legislation means predominantly administration."[73]

Although the idea of establishing a Securities and Exchange Commission separate from the existing Federal Trade Commission did not originate with Frankfurter or his protégés, the general concept of regulation by administrative commission was a crucial aspect of Frankfurter's approach to reform. He had long emphasized the importance of having government utilize scientific expertise in its handling of social problems, and during the Thirties he found himself in a unique position to place "well-trained, disciplined, imaginative, modest, and devoted administrators" throughout the Roosevelt administration. Frankfurter argued that since the nation's economic and social problems had become "so deeply enmeshed in intricate and technical facts," scientifically trained public servants had to be entrusted with a large degree of discretionary power if the government was effectively to protect the public interest. Josephus Daniels was also a strong supporter of extending government's regulatory powers, but he had less faith than Frankfurter in regulation by commission. At one time, he advised FDR that he liked "the idea of abolishing Commissions and having a single commissioner" in most cases in order to fix responsibility more clearly.[74]

The regulatory legislation of the New Deal may have succeeded in eliminating some of Wall Street's most glaring excesses, but it failed to address the most basic problems posed by the continuation of an investment process guided by the pursuit of private profit rather than a concern for the public welfare. The Brandeisians' willingness to accept the existing institutional framework in the field of finance and to limit their efforts to the establishment of a larger oversight role for the government ultimately worked, by Frankfurter's own admission, to strengthen, rather than weaken, the position of the major investment houses in the nation's capitalist economy. In spite of their initial opposition to the regulatory legislation of the early New Deal, Wall Street and the American business community, in general, soon came to appreciate the validity of Frankfurter's argument that such legislation, by destroying only "those business practices which should never have been born," would "fortify [popular] confidence in the proper activities of investment banking."[75]

Before the decade of the Thirties had come to an end, America's financial and industrial leaders had learned that the approach to regulation embodied in the New Deal's securities legislation actually worked to their advantage by creating a more stable and responsible stock market in which fly-by-night operators were largely eliminated. Moreover, because the regulatory approach of the Brandeisians was based on the assumption that the field of investment banking would continue to be dominated by private firms, the SEC subsequently allowed influential financiers and businessmen to play a major role in shaping the regulatory process itself. Thus, a familiar pattern in the history of twentieth-century American reform was repeated. Reforms initiated by liberals seeking to bring about a more just and democratic society were ultimately coopted by the very interests these reforms were intended to control. This occurred because the well-intentioned sponsors of reform failed to transcend the assumptions of the liberal tradition.[76]

The inadequacy of the Brandeisians' approach to the problem of reforming the nation's investment mechanism is most clearly demonstrated by the continuing failure of private investment to return, during the Thirties, to levels sufficient to bring full recovery. As late as 1937, private investment remained one-third below the level it had achieved in 1929. Of course, businessmen at the time blamed the New Deal's "anti-business" policies for the continuing reluctance of American capitalists to invest in the economy. However, the central problem of the depression was still not the lack of socially useful investment possibilities, but rather the lack of social control over the nation's capital resources. The government had become able to prevent companies from fraudulently attempting to raise capital in the securities markets, but it had not gained the power to compel private investment houses and financial institutions to put the capital at their disposal to productive uses. So long as private interests were not guaranteed a high enough rate of return to attract the capital under their control, investment would remain at low levels. As a consequence, the economy would function well below its potential capacity, and the public interest would suffer.[77]

## IV

While Frankfurter thought regulation by government commission was likely to be a more effective instrument of reform than anti-trust prosecutions under the Sherman Act, as the New Deal unfolded he increasingly came to focus his attention on another method of limiting the power of concentrated wealth. The government's power to tax remained, in Frankfurter's view, an as yet largely unused instrument for reforming the American social order. Tax policy could be used to accomplish a wide variety of goals, but most importantly, it could be used to break up unjustified concentrations of economic power and to redistribute wealth more equally among the American people.

Well before FDR became President, both Frankfurter and Daniels had criticized the Republican tax policies of the Twenties for being socially unjust and economically counterproductive. Both men had argued that the tax system needed to be changed so that the burden of taxation would be placed more fully on those best able to bear it. A regressive tax system was not only undemocratic; it was also a drag on the development of the mass purchasing power which was required to get the country out of the depression. With the coming of the New Deal, Frankfurter, in particular, began to push for more progressive taxes on personal and corporate incomes as a means of both financing federal relief and public works programs and decentralizing the power attendant upon concentrated wealth.

Roosevelt remained unwilling to pursue the highly controversial issue of tax reform during the first two years of his administration. The President chose, instead, to use his political influence with Congress in behalf of other legislative priorities. By the Summer of 1935, however, the political situation in the country had changed, in large part because of Huey Long's increasingly popular Share Our Wealth campaign. Consequently, FDR began to see the political advantages to be gained by presenting Congress with a new and comprehensive tax reform program. Between 1935 and 1938, Roosevelt annually asked Congress to adopt major changes in the tax codes, with Frankfurter playing a key role in the formulation of policy on the subject. Even before FDR first publicly revealed his proposals for tax reform in 1935, Frankfurter informed the President that his decision to press for changes in the tax codes had made "Brandeis's face light up . . . with warm satisfaction." [78]

Specifically, during these years, Frankfurter advised the

President to call not only for the establishment of a federal inheritance tax supplemented by a tax on gifts, but also for new taxes on undistributed corporate surpluses, inter-corporate dividends, and capital gains. In addition, Frankfurter voiced the Brandeisians' support for higher taxes on incomes of over one million dollars and for the replacement of the existing fixed rate tax on corporate incomes by a progressive graduated tax.[79]

Frankfurter contended that the "undue concentration of economic power over other people's fortunes, other people's businesses, and other people's lives" in America represented a great danger to "freedom." It was, therefore, necessary to use the government's taxing power for the purpose of "breaking down" such "socially and economically unwarranted power" in order to "promote our traditional system of private property." Still, Frankfurter did not look nostalgically back to the simpler days of the nation's pre-industrial past. He was too modern a thinker to believe that it was either possible or desirable to tax out of existence all large corporations. He did, however, think that "government tax policy ought to encourage the simplest form of corporate structure." A tax on undistributed corporate profits, Frankfurter argued, would prevent corporations from accumulating "surpluses far beyond their economic needs," surpluses which in the past had often been used by large corporations to finance the acquisition of other firms rather than to expand production or increase productivity. The absence of a tax on undistributed profits, according to Frankfurter, had thus in effect contributed to "the growth of giant holding companies controlling an ever greater proportion of business enterprise."[80]

While Frankfurter did not fully share Brandeis' hope that "by taxation bigness can be destroyed," he did believe that the revisions in the corporate tax code which he recommended would have the effect of encouraging the survival of "small enterprises" without which "our competitive economic society would cease." Frankfurter argued that such small businesses suffered a "disproportionate strain" in times of depression because of their meager reserves, even though they still played an indispensable role in assuring a "fairly distributed national prosperity." A tax on undistributed corporate profits would help equalize the contest between large and small firms by forcing corporate surpluses onto the open financial markets where all prospective business borrowers would have access to them. The establishment of a graduated corporate income tax would also help new and moderate-sized firms and would, in addition, be an important step toward greater equity in the tax system. Since, in Frankfurter's view, "the advantages and protections conferred upon corporations by government increase in value as the size of the corporation increase," it was only fair that the rate at which a corporation be taxed increase along with its size. Josephus Daniels also believed that it was proper that those who "received most of the benefits of government and who are most able to pay should pay the bulk of the expenses of government." [81]

The tax proposals advocated by Frankfurter and his fellow Brandeisians were also based on an explicit recognition of the injustice and economic irrationality of America's widely skewed distribution of wealth. According to Frankfurter:

Wealth in the modern world does not come merely from individual effort; it results from a combination of individual effort and of the manifold uses to which the community puts that effort. The individual does not create the product of his industry with his own hands; he utilizes the many processes and forces of mass production to meet the demands of a national and international market. Therefore, in spite of the great importance in our national life of the efforts and ingenuity of individuals, the people in the mass have inevitably helped to make large fortunes possible.

Frankfurter contended, therefore, that steep inheritance and gift taxes were justified because the inheritance of tremendous "economic power is as inconsistent with the ideals of this generation as inherited political power was inconsistent with the ideals of the generation which established our government." [82]

A more progressive tax system was necessary, in Frankfurter's opinion, as a matter of both equity and efficiency. He believed that a redistribution of wealth through taxation was required not only because the "social unrest" and "deepening sense of unfairness" growing out of the existing maldistribution constituted "dangers to our national life," but also because the system of excessively regressive taxation then in effect impeded the growth of consumer purchasing power needed for lasting prosperity. As a general principle, Frankfurter declared that "modern industrial society must increasingly rely upon progressive taxation" while avoiding "regressive taxation which curtails the purchasing power of the great mass of consumers." Frankfurter also defended increased taxes on the wealthy as a means of guarding against "oversaving" by "higher income groups," i.e., the tendency of the rich, especially in times of low profits, to hold onto part of their income as liquid reserves rather than to use it for employment-generating investment or consumption expenditures.[83]

Perhaps on no other issue of public policy during the 1930s was there a greater difference of opinion between Frankfurter and Daniels, on the one hand, and Baruch, Stimson, and Richberg, on the other, than on the question of taxation. Jordan Schwarz notes that "taxation became Baruch's central point of contention with the New Deal." Given his own vast wealth, Baruch, of course, had a great deal to lose personally if a significantly more progressive tax system had been instituted. Baruch's opposition to Roosevelt's tax proposals, however, was based more on principle than on self-interest. He feared that the tax policies advocated by Frankfurter and Daniels would endanger the functioning of the profit motive and undermine business confidence in America, and thereby discourage the private investment needed to get the country out of the depression.[84]

Baruch wrote privately to Daniels in 1936 to express his concern that the nation's industrial and financial leaders were being put into a "position where they do not want to try any more" because they were being "made to feel that success in their lives is unsocial." Testifying about taxation before a Senate committee in 1938, Baruch proclaimed:

There is an idea abroad that this is a way to share our wealth, but I say it is sharing our poverty, because it removes the steam from our engine of production—the hope of gain. When we have done that, there will be less effort and hence less output. There will be less to go round. The poor will be poorer and the rich less rich. I believe our whole system will collapse in political revolution and economic ruin, because we shall have destroyed its dynamo through failure to recognize the economic and human laws that govern it.[85]

Baruch did not oppose "an increase in taxation for the purpose of doing just and fair things," but he warned against trying to use the taxing power "to punish or to equalize that which neither Nature nor God intended should be equal." In Baruch's opinion, it was no more possible to "make people equal in the results of their efforts" than it was "to make them equals as athletes, hunters, lawyers, singers, or what not." To adopt a tax system which, in effect, stigmatized success would be "a very bad thing because we must have able direction, otherwise the ignorant or incompetent cannot be taken care of."[86]

Henry Stimson fully shared Baruch's attitudes about taxation. Stimson acknowledged that he "was well aware of the fact that a majority of wealth is held by a minority of all our people," but he believed that any attempt to bring about anything "like an even distribution of all the wealth would put a stop at once to that smooth running business adjustment upon which the comfort of us all, rich and poor alike, primarily depends." Stimson attempted to counter the arguments of those who voiced concern about the failure of the rich to spend as large a proportion of their income as did the poor by claiming that the ability of the wealthy to save and thereby accumulate capital was "one of the basic reasons for the great benefits which have come to the world during the industrial revolution." The willingness of the rich to refrain from spending and to invest their capital in "new business operations" had made it possible for "all the world" to have been "kept so comfortable and the poor employed."[87]

Stimson also warned against government itself trying to invest the funds that might be raised through confiscatory taxation of the rich.

. . . if instead of distributing the wealth equally between rich and poor, you should give the surplus now held by the rich to the government, you would then be in equally bad shape; because you would substitute the wasteful inefficiency of government management and operation for the more efficient and greater initiative of private operation. The machine would run down . . . And the final result would be that the poor would be the ones to suffer.

Yet Stimson revealed his lack of sophistication in the field of economics by attributing his own views on the benefits of an unequal distribution of wealth to John Maynard Keynes. Stimson apparently failed to understand the distinction which economists such as Keynes were beginning to make between savings which actually flowed into investment and "oversavings" which did not. Oversaving, as Frankfurter correctly argued, was a key factor in the depression.[88]

Donald Richberg, too, had become so concerned by 1938 with the importance of maintaining a government policy which would both give encouragement to the nation's "system of free enterprise" and reinforce business confidence, that he also argued against any measures of "punitive taxation or other devices to destroy initiative, efficiency, and economy in business."[89]

From 1935 until the coming of the Second World War, Roosevelt's tax proposals became perhaps the most hotly debated aspect of the New Deal. Critics such as Baruch, Stimson, and Richberg contended that the tax reforms which FDR managed to get through Congress in these years were anti-business, soak-the-rich schemes which helped prevent the country from fully recovering from the depression. However, while New Deal tax legislation did, in the words of James Patterson, represent "a definite step away from Republican tax policies of the 1920s," the impact of the legislation adopted between 1935 and 1938 was actually more symbolic than substantive. Tax rates on individual incomes and estates were made somewhat more progressive, and corporate incomes were also made subject to a slightly graduated tax, as were capital gains. The Revenue Act of 1936 did impose a tax on undistributed corporate surpluses. However, even some of these reforms were short lived. In 1938, with Baruch exercising significant influence on the decision, Congress voted to repeal the tax on corporate surpluses and to eliminate the principle of progressive tax rates on capital gains. By the end of the Thirties, the federal government still took in less revenue from progressive estate and individual and corporate income taxes than it did from regressive excise and employment taxes. Taken as a whole, the tax reforms actually written into law during the course of the New Deal did very little either to affect the structure of American industry or to redistribute wealth.[90]

Of all the issues raised by the New Deal, tax reform stands out in some ways as being unique. The Brandeisian-supported plans for restructuring the nation's tax system may well have represented the New Deal's most important effort at redressing some of the basic inequities in American society. This was true not because the Brandeisians' proposals sought to restore the small-scale entrepreneurial economy of the nineteenth century, but rather because they constituted the New Deal's most significant attempt to respond to the problem of inequality in a modern capitalist society. The potential effectiveness of the tax reforms advocated by FDR was, however, never really tested. In contrast to his success in gaining Congressional approval for the substance of most of his other reform proposals, Roosevelt met stiff resistance in Congress on the issue of tax reform and was able to get enacted only a pale shadow of the program initially advocated by Frankfurter and Brandeis. Thus, tax policy is perhaps the only important field in which the impact of New Deal efforts at economic reform were restricted more by the political obstacle of a recalcitrant Congress than by the ideological limitations of the New Deal reformers themselves.[91]

The debate over tax policy certainly revealed important differences in outlook between some of the men being discussed here. Baruch and Stimson had always tended to conceive of the liberal ideal of equality almost purely in terms of equality of opportunity. Consequently, they opposed the idea that taxation ought to become an instrument for reversing what they perceived as the outcomes of a fairly conducted competition for monetary rewards. While Frankfurter and Daniels also placed great store in the ideal of competitive equality, in contrast to Baruch and Stimson, they did not virtually ignore the problem of substantive equality. In their view, it was appropriate for government to use its taxing power so that the benefits produced by the country's complex, interdependent, industrial economy would be more widely shared.

Frankfurter and Daniels were obviously more suspicious of bigness and concentrated wealth than Baruch, Stimson, or even Richberg, but, still, it is important not to exaggerate their enmity toward corporate America or their desire to achieve a communitarian ideal of social equality. Frankfurter, in particular, believed that tax rates could be made significantly more progressive without either eliminating the incentive of material rewards for success or destroying individual initiative. Subsequent evidence has shown that Frankfurter was more accurate in this regard than Baruch and Stimson; for a recent study has confirmed the view that "sensitivity to taxes" plays only a minor role in affecting either the work patterns or investment decisions of the wealthy.[92]

Both Frankfurter's emphasis on the substantive aspects of equality and Baruch's conception of equality as primarily a question of opportunity stemmed from their commitments to America's liberal tradition. While the conception of equality held by Baruch and Stimson was undoubtedly the more dominant in that tradition, Frankfurter's concern with substantive social equality was also a reflection of the democratic ethos which was implicit in American liberalism.

Although Daniels and Frankfurter's approach to taxation was based on a greater commitment to substantive economic equality than that felt by Baruch, Stimson, and Richberg, it remains open to question whether their proposals, even if fully implemented, would have succeeded in transforming America into a just society in which prosperity would have been equally shared. Frankfurter may have explicitly acknowledged that wealth in a modern industrial society was the product of a collective enterprise. However, he did not challenge the right of a small elite to continue to lay claim to the ownership and control of the material means by which that wealth was produced. The establishment of a more progressive tax system would certainly not have been inconsequential in its results, but it would still have represented only a reform superimposed on a structure which was fundamentally flawed. In the first place, as the experience of the First World War had demonstrated, and as later experience would confirm, it was very difficult for government, in the actual process of collection, to make progressive tax rates fully effective. Avoiding a serious maldistribution of income before it occurred was likely to be a more effective way of fostering equality than trying to correct the problem after the fact.[93]

Perhaps even more importantly, tax reform along the lines advocated by Frankfurter did not address the problems faced by those Americans whose lack of income-producing assets and inability to find work prevented them from earning enough money to enjoy a decent standard of living. Frankfurter did not actually call for government to set out on a conscious policy of taking from the rich in order to give to the poor and disadvantaged. Rather, he simply insisted that the wealthy ought to bear a larger burden of the costs entailed in the normal functions of government. Finally, although tax codes can be written in such a way as to encourage certain types of economic behavior, taxation remains a very crude instrument by which government can attempt to influence the setting of priorities for the economy as a whole. Tax reform was still based on the assumption that a market economy, even one increasingly subject to private management, was superior to an economy characterized by planning in accordance with democratically determined objectives.

## V

While the New Deal failed to reshape American society through meaningful tax reform, it did lay the foundation for the development of a new approach to the problem of countering the negative effects of the business cycle. However haltingly, the New Deal set in motion what economist Herbert Stein has called "the fiscal revolution," the increasing effort by government to make calculated use of fiscal policy, the manipulation of "the large aggregates in the budget—total expenditures and total receipts and the difference between them," in order to affect "certain overall characteristics of the economy, such as employment and unemployment, price levels, and the total share of government activity in the economy." No legacy of the New Deal has proven to be more important than its introduction of fiscal policy as an instrument of government influence over the general level of economic activity in the country. Although fiscal policy ultimately had a wide appeal among liberals of various persuasions, in the early years of the New Deal, Felix Frankfurter and his fellow Brandeisians were among its most important advocates in Washington.[94]

During the 1930s, John Maynard Keynes developed a comprehensive theoretical explanation of the stimulative effect of government budget deficits on a stagnating economy. Keynes' great contribution to political economy was that he presented a new general theory of business cycles, as well as a comprehensive program for counter-cyclical action by government. Keynes acknowledged that investment decisions by individual businessmen remained the key factor in economic life. However, he claimed that in a time of depression, the highest priority had to be placed on raising the level of aggregate demand as a means of restimulating investment in the private sector. Keynes' major concern during the Thirties, therefore, was the problem of inducing an increase in the level of mass purchasing power. This, he argued, could be most effectively accomplished by government spending financed by borrowing rather than by taxing present income. Keynes specifically recommended public works as the most efficient and desirable outlet for such deficit spending, but he admitted that spending for any purpose, so long as it was financed by borrowing, would have a stimulating effect on a depressed economy.[95]

Keynes argued that it was the size of the deficit itself, not the amount of government spending per se, which determined how effective government fiscal policy would be in stimulating economic activity. Yet, at least through Roosevelt's first term, the New Deal, and most American liberals, approached the problem of government counter-action against the depression primarily in terms of spending for particular emergency programs, rather than in terms of a conscious effort on the part of the government to create budget deficits. Only by the end of the Thirties did the New Deal and Keynesian economics, which, in Stein's words, had been separately "developing along parallel tracks," begin to converge so that true fiscal policy became "established as *the* solution in Washington thinking" to the problem of economic stagnation.[96]

Even before Roosevelt became President, Frankfurter had considered government spending on a massive public works program as the first priority in his recovery plan. Although Frankfurter and his mentor, Louis Brandeis, gave greater emphasis to the importance of large-scale spending on relief and public works than the other men considered in this study, Baruch, Richberg,

Daniels, and Stimson had also concluded by 1933 that increased expenditures for such purposes were necessary not only to relieve suffering, but also as a means of helping to stabilize the level of mass purchasing power. Government stabilization of the economy through a counter-cyclical expansion of public works had, in fact, become a widely accepted idea by the time of the depression. Throughout the 1920s, Herbert Hoover had himself done much to publicize the potential of accelerating already planned public works projects as a means of countering the onset of a recession.[97]

As the depression worsened in the early 1930s, controversy developed not so much over the idea of emergency government spending, but rather over the extent of such spending and the manner by which it ought to be financed. Hoover, with Stimson's support, resisted calls by Frankfurter and others for a public works program of massive proportions because he believed that only a limited number of well thought out projects were ready to be undertaken immediately, and because he feared that rapidly declining federal revenues raised the danger of a huge deficit if spending were increased dramatically. In fact, none of the men discussed here, nor any other prominent figure in American public life in the early Thirties, challenged the conventional wisdom of the day regarding the desirability of a balanced budget.

It was true, however, as Stein points out, that by 1933 the idea of a balanced budget had become an "elastic concept." Even Baruch, who supported the adoption of a national sales tax in 1932 in order to bring the budget into balance, suggested the possibility of a "dual budget" consisting of separate categories for emergency and regular expenditures. In such an accounting system, the budget could be considered "balanced" so long as tax revenues covered the cost of regular expenditures plus the servicing charges on the debt incurred by government borrowing to pay for the extraordinary emergency expenses brought on by the depression. During the budget debate of 1932, Frankfurter and Daniels did not favor a deficit for its own sake, but they sharply disagreed with Baruch and Stimson about the advisability of trying to balance the budget by increasing the tax burden on those least able to afford it. If increased expenditures could not be financed by progressive taxation, then Frankfurter, for one, was willing to accept an unbalanced budget.[98]

With the coming of the New Deal in 1933, Frankfurter was not only hopeful about the possibility for a major expansion of federal spending on public works, but he also came to see the desirability of financing such spending by borrowing rather than by taxes. Frankfurter had first met Keynes at the Versailles Peace Conference and had retained a highly favorable impression of the English economist ever since that time. In July of 1933, Frankfurter informed FDR that "for some years" he had believed that Keynes was "the best economic bet." A few months later, Frankfurter set sail for England where he was to spend the 1933–34 academic year as a visiting scholar at Oxford. Once there, he quickly renewed his friendship with Keynes and became an important channel of communication through which the noted economist and his followers in England were able to transmit their ideas directly to FDR back in the United States. Frankfurter helped orchestrate the New York *Times'* publication of Keynes' famous open letter to President Roosevelt in late 1933 and was subsequently responsible for arranging the personal meeting between Keynes and Roosevelt which took place in the Spring of 1934. In the early stages of the New Deal, Frankfurter thus played a key role in trying to spread the Keynesian gospel that the "prime mover" in any recovery program had to be an "increase of national purchasing power resulting from governmental expenditure which is financed by loans and not by taxing present income."[99]

As a complement to the attempt to raise purchasing power through public works spending, Frankfurter, and especially Brandeis, also favored the enactment of a permanent program of unemployment insurance. With such a program in place, future downturns in economic activity would not cut so deeply into consumer spending and, therefore, would be less likely to turn into lengthy depressions. Brandeis had long been the country's most important advocate of this form of social insurance. There were serious differences within liberal ranks over the best means of administering unemployment insurance, but there is no question that Brandeis' and Frankfurter's efforts were important in guaranteeing the incorporation of the general concept into the

Social Security Act which was adopted in 1935. The other provisions of the Social Security system, old-age pensions and aid
to certain categories of the needy, also had the potential for
sustaining purchasing power in a time of recession, and the program as a whole received the enthusiastic support of both
Frankfurter and Daniels. Baruch, too, recognized that Social Security was a constructive reform, but he questioned the wisdom
of financing the program through payroll taxes out of a fear that
such taxes would lead businessmen to replace workers with
machines.[100]

The method of financing the largest component of Social
Security, old-age pensions, raised another problem as well. The
establishment of an old-age pension system represented a unique
opportunity for stimulating the economy by putting money into
the hands of people who were likely to spend it very quickly.
However, the payroll taxes which were adopted in order to finance the system negated the program's potential for giving a
boost to mass purchasing power. In fact, when the system first
went into operation, it had a clearly deflationary impact on the
economy since taxes were to be collected for several years before disbursements were to begin being made. In spite of the
advice of many well respected economists, Roosevelt's decisions on expenditures during his first term continued, according
to Stein, to be "made in terms of the needs and direct benefits
of particular programs . . . rather than in terms of the indirect
contribution of spending to total employment and prosperity."[101]

The recession of 1937–38 proved to be the crucial turning
point in the New Deal's explicit use of fiscal policy. During the
first four years of Roosevelt's Presidency, the economy slowly
rebounded from the 1933 low point of the Great Depression.
By 1937 the physical volume of industrial production had finally
returned to pre-depression levels, and five million fewer Americans were unemployed. Moreover, the mood of despair which
had gripped the nation in 1933 had been transformed by FDR's
contagious optimism and by the apparent success of many of his
New Deal programs. But the economy was still far from healthy,
and Roosevelt's decision to reduce spending on relief and public works in 1937 helped trigger perhaps the most precipitous

decline in economic activity in the nation's history. In the nine months between the Summer of 1937 and the Fall of 1938, industrial production fell by about one third. At the low point of the "Roosevelt Recession," forty percent of the nation's plant capacity again stood idle. Payrolls dropped by 35 percent, and the overall unemployment rate soared once more to 19 percent. Five years after the New Deal had begun, ten million Americans were jobless.[102]

Confronted with this new crisis, FDR's first response was to try even harder to balance the budget by cutting expenditures in order to restore business confidence. As the recession worsened, however, Roosevelt was finally persuaded of the necessity of adopting a policy of spending "for its own sake," even though he continued to find Keynesian theory incomprehensible. Not all Americans were yet convinced of the wisdom of deficit spending. Baruch still argued in 1938 that continuing budget deficits, rather than being a way to "cure unemployment," were instead largely responsible for its continuation because they had a detrimental effect on business confidence. Writing years later in his autobiography, Baruch observed that Keynes' "contributions to economics have left me singularly unenthusiastic" and that nothing "has done more harm to the economic, and, indeed, spiritual fiber of nations than the policies which have been inspired by Keynes's ideas." Nevertheless, by 1938, government spending in time of recession had become, in Stein's words, an "inevitable policy." For almost half a century, no American President would again attempt to balance the budget by cutting expenditures in the midst of a recession.[103]

Fiscal policy may have emerged by the end of the Thirties as the government's main weapon for fighting downturns in business activity, but the fiscal revolution was still a highly ambiguous development. In order to understand the significance of the fiscal revolution, it is necessary not only to consider why Keynesian policies ultimately had such an appeal to American liberals, but also why, even in 1938, fiscal remedies were applied in such meager doses. Only as a result of American involvement in World War II did the federal government finally incur deficits of sufficient size to bring about a full recovery from the depression.

Stein points to a number of reasons for the triumph of fiscal policy in 1938. To begin with, in spite of Baruch's claims to the contrary, Roosevelt at last realized that "the idea of stimulating business investment by promising to balance the budget was a chimera." Moreover, concern about the size of the federal debt had diminished among most economists and businessmen since the doubling of government indebtedness between 1932 and 1937 had not been accompanied by a rise in interest rates. In fact, interest rates on government bonds had actually declined, thus demonstrating that increased borrowing need not impair the government's credit. Stein notes, as well, that since 1933, not only had the government developed the machinery for implementing a large increase in spending, but there also had arisen "a politically important clientele in the Congress, in the party machinery, in state and local governments, and among direct beneficiaries" which supported government spending for self-interested motives. Finally, in Stein's words, "some of the policy possibilities that had seemed alternatives to spending in 1933 were no longer in the picture" by 1938. Government encouragement of pluralistic interest group organization and increased government regulation of certain sectors of the economy had become widely accepted, but they were essentially reform, rather than recovery, measures and offered little promise of yielding quick results in halting the economy's downward plunge in 1937–38. Only planning had at one time appeared as a potential alternative method for stimulating a rapid recovery, but this option had been eliminated with the collapse of the NRA.[104]

Fiscal policy also proved to be attractive to liberals for another more general reason. It was a measure which could be superimposed on the existing economic structure without having to alter any of the basic principles upon which that structure was built. Frankfurter and Brandeis may have supported a policy of government spending in part because of their enthusiasm about the possibility of enriching the public domain through a program of large-scale public works. However, as Keynes himself noted, government spending (or more properly, the creation of government deficits) could be effective in stimulating the economy no matter what form the spending took. As Keynes put it:

If the Treasury were to fill old bottles with banknotes, bury them at suitable depths in disused coal mines which are then filled up to the surface with town rubbish, and leave it to private enterprise on well-tried principles of *laissez-faire* to dig the notes up again (the right to do so being obtained, of course, by tendering for leases of the note-bearing territory), there need be no more unemployment and, with the help of the repercussions, the real income of the community, and its capital wealth also, would probably become a good deal greater than it actually is.

Fiscal policy was essentially a means of evening out the drastic ups and downs of the business cycle in a capitalist economy. As such, it could be used to stabilize the existing system at the most general macroeconomic level without actually involving government directly in the operation of industry or in the establishment of specific priorities in the basic allocation of resources and rewards.[105]

Still, in spite of criticisms both in the Thirties and since that Roosevelt engaged in profligate deficit spending, New Deal deficits were, in fact, not significantly larger than the one incurred by the Hoover administration in 1932. Government spending between 1932 and 1939 did almost double, but tax receipts in the same period rose more than two and one half times. If one takes into consideration spending and taxation at all levels of government, local, state, and federal, there was not a single year between 1933 and 1939 in which the expansionary impact of fiscal policy equalled that of 1931. Even in 1938, when FDR accepted the need for a deliberate program of spending, he called upon Congress to appropriate only about three billion dollars for emergency expenditures, an amount which was large enough to reverse the downward plunge in economic activity and restore the *status quo ante,* but not to bring about full recovery and true prosperity. There is virtually unanimous agreement among economists with Cary Brown's assessment that "fiscal policy . . . seems to have been an unsuccessful recovery device in the 'thirties—not because it did not work, but because it was not tried."[106]

Thus, by 1939 the American economy was still mired in the Great Depression. Although the GNP of 1939 was greater than it had been in 1929, increases in population and productivity meant that the performance of the economy as a whole remained significantly poorer than it had been ten years earlier. After a full decade of liberal efforts to find a solution to the nation's economic woes, 17 percent of America's workers were unemployed, and 28 percent of the country's plant capacity continued to go unused. The nation clearly faced the prospect of massive unemployment becoming a permanent feature of American life.[107]

If Roosevelt had become convinced of the necessity of spending for its own sake in 1938, why then did he not propose a deficit large enough to bring about full employment? The answer is complex. While spending had become politically very popular by 1938, Roosevelt, the Congress, and most Americans, could not really conceive of the spending levels which would have been required for fiscal policy to have had its full potential impact. In addition, Roosevelt and many other liberals retained a lingering concern, even guilt, about the possibility of deficit spending becoming a permanent policy. Moreover, as Stein argues, Roosevelt personally never felt intellectually committed to Keynesian policies. Like the other liberals discussed here, he continued to believe that other options, planning, structural reform, a redistribution of wealth, might also prove to be useful tools in the government's struggle against economic stagnation.[108]

Two other factors also proved crucial in the New Deal's failure to adopt a full-fledged policy of deficit spending. Both stemmed from the opposition of the nation's dominant economic interests, not so much to spending or deficits per se, but rather to the possible side effects which could arise from deficit spending if the objectives of fiscal policy were not narrowly defined. Many of the nation's leading businessmen by 1938 opposed a policy of large-scale spending primarily because they feared that increased spending would inevitably mean increased taxes. In their view, the more government spent, the greater the likelihood that the kind of progressive tax policies advocated by liberals such as Frankfurter and Brandeis would actually be implemented. Although as Stein correctly observes, "high spending and big deficits did not lead to higher taxes by any logical necessity," it would appear that Baruch and others who shared his outlook concluded that fiscal and tax policy were inextricably linked. While Baruch, in Schwarz's words, "was all for social programs for the masses, provided that the masses paid for them," he feared that a concerted spending effort would lead to the type of taxes which he believed would destroy individual initiative and the incentive to invest.[109]

The country's business community, and liberals such as Stimson and Baruch, were also deeply concerned about the form government spending might take. The New Deal's initial efforts at spending largely took the form of direct relief payments to the needy. However, the "dole" seemed to run counter to the traditional liberal belief in the importance of the work ethic. Consequently, there was widespread support for the shift in focus from direct relief to work relief which soon took place in the New Deal. Work relief, though, presented a number of problems. It frequently entailed either the creation of seemingly unnecessary make-work projects or the construction of substantial public works which threatened to introduce government competition with the private sector. Baruch and Stimson had long been adamant in their opposition to government operation of any business which could be handled by the private sector. Even Frankfurter, however, who favored major public works projects involving the construction of hydroelectric plants, housing, and other socially useful facilities, never attacked directly the notion that private enterprise was inherently superior to public enterprise, nor did he explicitly support the idea of government competition with businesses operating in the private sector. While the leaders of American business may have been willing to accept government deficit spending as a tool for raising the overall level of economic activity, they successfully appealed to liberal values when they blocked any attempt to use fiscal policy as a means of subverting the dominance of private enterprise and the profit motive. Thus, the Works Progress Administration was prevented from engaging in projects which competed with private firms and was required, moreover, to pay wages beneath prevailing rates so as not to deter people from seeking employment in the private sector.[110]

Yet there was one form of government spending which would ultimately find favor with the American business community and which would be done on a sufficiently massive scale finally to bring the country out of the depression. Keynes himself acknowledged in 1933, in his open letter to Roosevelt, that in the past, nations had accepted only one "legitimate excuse" to justify the kind of spending policies which he advocated to fight the depression. War alone had caused politicians, businessmen, and economists to overcome their dogmatic commitment to a balanced budget and to use the power of government to borrow against future generations for the sake of national survival. Not only was such a war-time application of "Keynesian theory" then justified in terms of national survival, but it also had the added advantage of representing a form of government expenditure which did not result in public competition with the private sector. Keynes had hoped that Roosevelt would become a pioneer in the effort to employ "in the interests of peace and prosperity the technique which has hitherto been allowed to serve the purposes of war and destruction." The events of the 1930s, however, proved his hope to be largely unjustified. Only the coming of the Second World War caused the United States government at last to spend at a level sufficient to put an end to the disastrous ten-year-long depression of the 1930s. Whereas the largest deficit incurred by the New Deal in any year between 1933 and 1939 was a little over four billion dollars, during World War II annual deficits soared to well over fifty billion dollars. As Keynes had prophesied, the impact on the economy was dramatic.[111]

In the years after World War II, heavy military spending would, of course, become a permanent feature of the American political economy. However, fiscal policy would also gain increasing favor as it became clear that deficit spending in times of recession or slow economic growth could be achieved by cutting taxes, as well as by increasing spending on social programs or public works. Keynesian economics, as Robert Lekachman observes, may not be "conservative, liberal, or radical," since its "techniques of economic stimulation and stabilization" are capable of being used to distribute "national income either more or less equitably" and to increase or decrease "the importance of the public sector in the economy." Yet, so long as Keynesian policies are applied strictly within the context of

America's liberal consensus, they will continue to function as instruments for buttressing the existing social order rather than as means of transforming America into a more truly humane and democratic society.[112]

<h1 style="text-align:center">VI</h1>

Historians have long disagreed as to whether the New Deal entailed a fundamental departure from past efforts at reform or whether it represented the triumph of the progressive tradition which had been forged around the turn of the twentieth century. Richard Hofstadter and William Leuchtenburg, for example, have both noted what they perceive as a basic difference in spirit between the reforms of the New Deal and the reforms of the Progressive era. Similarly, Otis Graham concludes from his influential study of well over one hundred former progressives that a majority of "old progressives" who lived into the Thirties opposed the New Deal because they saw it as a threat to the values for which they had fought two decades earlier. All three of these historians contrast the progressives' moralistic individualism and opposition to government coercion, class legislation, and centralization with the New Deal's pragmatic collectivism and acceptance of both increased federal power and interest group politics.[113]

The New Deal unquestionably resulted in a significant expansion of the government's role in the nation's economic life. This change can be measured in several ways. Whereas in 1932, the federal government had about 600,000 civilian employees (excluding those engaged in temporary public works projects), just seven years later the number had jumped to over 950,000. Similarly, while government spending before the onset of the depression was usually in the neighborhood of three billion dollars a year, in 1939 the government's expenditures were close to nine billion dollars. With the establishment of Social Security, the government would soon be collecting and disbursing far greater sums of money as it became the agent through which many Americans began to purchase a minimal form of social insurance. In addition, the government's role as a regulator of

business, especially of banking and finance, had expanded, as
had its function in stimulating interest group organization among
workers, farmers, and other groups in society. The philosophy
of strict voluntarism which had been associated with Herbert
Hoover had clearly given way to a widespread acceptance of a
far more direct role for government in the nation's economic
life.[114]

As Graham acknowledges, the reforms of the New Deal
were too varied and multifaceted to win either the "monolithic
approval or rejection" of most old progressives. Certainly the
five men studied here greeted the many programs and policies
which made up the New Deal with varying degrees of enthusiasm. Yet, the resistance of many former progressives to certain
aspects of the New Deal should not obscure the fact that the
continuities between progressivism and the New Deal remain
more significant than the discontinuities. For the various approaches to reform which Roosevelt tried out during the course
of the New Deal had their origins in the liberal reform efforts of
the previous quarter century and were all formulated within the
context of a continuing commitment to the American liberal tradition. Arthur Link is thus correct when he argues that the New
Deal was "the culmination of American Progressivism" because
it "brought to completion the progressive program" which had
been in the process of development since the turn of the century.[115]

Although the five men discussed in this study obviously had
important policy differences during the 1930s, they all continued to share certain common assumptions about the proper limits to government intervention in the economy. These assumptions, moreover, provided the ideological foundation upon
which the New Deal was built. American capitalism, these liberals agreed, needed to be reformed, not rejected. Private enterprise and the pursuit of profit had to be maintained as the
guiding principles of economic life. Government might become
an agency for furthering the special interests of various groups
in society, but only in such a way as to insure the creation of
an overall balance of interests. Liberals remained agreed not only
that the state ought never to become an instrument which could
be used exclusively in behalf of the interests of a single class,

but also that group competition should never be allowed to turn into class warfare. Finally, the men studied here recognized that the power and responsibilities of the state might have to be increased, but they continued to oppose the creation of a highly centralized government wielding extensive coercive powers over the American people. An anti-statist bias still exercised a significant influence over New Deal liberalism.

The New Deal certainly mitigated the suffering and despair created by the Great Depression. In addition, it established certain built-in stabilizing mechanisms and a precedent for the use of fiscal policy which would make far less likely the recurrence in the future of another depression of the magnitude of the one which plagued the nation in the 1930s. The New Deal, however, was hardly the "revolution" which some historians have labelled it. Not only did the New Deal fail to bring about either a full recovery from the depression or any fundamental redistribution of wealth and power in American society, but it also failed to create any lasting mechanisms for comprehensive public planning.[116]

The Great Depression was a much more significant equalizer of incomes and wealth than were the programs of the New Deal. Income did become more equally distributed between 1929 and 1939, with the share of national income being received by the top one percent of the population falling from 14.5 to 11.8 percent. This share, nevertheless, continued almost to equal that received by the forty percent of the American people at the bottom of the income scale. Moreover, almost all the decline in income inequality occurred by 1933, before the New Deal went into effect. It is particularly striking that while the share of personal wealth held by the richest one-half of one percent of the population fell significantly between 1929 and 1933, this economic elite's share of wealth actually rose from 25 to 28 percent between 1933 and 1939. In addition, as Douglass North observes, the redistribution of wealth and income which did occur during the Thirties generally favored "middle-income rather than lowest-income groups."[117]

The persistence of depression, of course, also meant the incidence of high levels of poverty. In the mid-Thirties, roughly half of all Americans lived below the poverty line. While that number declined significantly by 1939, it was still then the case, as it had been throughout the first four decades of the twentieth century, that the average annual earnings of a full-time industrial worker were not sufficient to support a family of four at a minimum level of adequacy.[118]

In spite of the desires of liberals such as Frankfurter and Daniels to curb the power of the nation's corporate giants, the New Deal did virtually nothing to undermine the position of dominance enjoyed by a relative handful of business firms. In fact, the share of total corporate net income received by the largest five percent of the nation's corporations underwent a slight, though uneven, upward trend from the late Twenties through the late Thirties. In 1939, while the smallest 75 percent of American corporations took in only three percent of total corporate income, the largest five percent received over 84 percent of net corporate income.[119]

While wealth and power remained concentrated in the hands of a small number of Americans, widespread disillusionment with the NRA experiment meant that the New Deal ultimately foreswore any significant attempt at coordinated national planning, whether by businessmen espousing a philosophy of corporatism or by representatives of the public looking toward the socialization of industry. In fact, the triumph of a pluralistic approach to interest group organization created a government and a society which, in the words of Otis Graham, were so "thoroughly Balkanized" that "social management on a national scale" became more difficult and less likely to be realized in the future. By accepting and even legitimizing the power exercised by various private interest groups and institutions, the New Deal broker state, according to Graham, caused:

. . . partial planning and broker interventionism [to be] built deep into the structure of American public life. Power sectors had been created that would later on resist any nationalizing or rationalizing integration.[120]

Thus, the New Deal repeated the pattern of previous twentieth-century American reform movements. Because it remained bound by the ideological framework of the American liberal tradition, the New Deal failed fully to come to grips with the root causes of injustice, inequality, and economic stagnation in America. While the New Deal sought to transform America into a more humane and democratic society, its efforts met with only limited success. Once again, those who ultimately gained the most from the New Deal were those who had the most to start with and who initially feared that a popular wave of reform might undermine their privileged positions in American society. In the long run, though, the New Deal's liberal approaches to regulation, interest group organization, and fiscal policy all served to reinforce, rather than revolutionize, the existing social order. As a result, America would continue to suffer from poverty amidst plenty, wide disparities in the distribution of wealth, the dominance of private rather than public decision-making, and the absence of any effective mechanism for establishing rationally planned economic priorities.

# CHAPTER IX

# Liberalism's Ambiguous Legacy

THE evolution of American liberalism did not come to a halt with the end of the New Deal, but by the end of the 1930s, the American political economy had taken the basic shape it would retain for decades to come. Liberals would continue to disagree about the precise limits of the government's role in the nation's economic life, but such debate would take place within the framework established by the New Deal. Thus, the start of the Second World War in 1939 marked a clearly definable end to what Richard Hofstadter has labeled "the age of reform."

While an examination of the post-New Deal careers of Daniels, Stimson, Baruch, Richberg, and Frankfurter remains beyond the scope of the present study, it is possible to give at least some indication of the course of their careers after 1939. After having served as Ambassador to Mexico for eight years, Josephus Daniels returned to North Carolina in 1941 where he again resumed active direction on the Raleigh *News & Observer* until his death in 1948. Henry Stimson, at the age of 72, was called back to government service by Franklin Roosevelt. In large part because of the advice of Felix Frankfurter, FDR named Stimson Secretary of War in 1940, a position which Stimson continued to hold until the end of the Second World War. After five years in retirement, Stimson died in 1950. Bernard Baruch lived until 1965, playing an important role as an advisor and trouble shooter in the nation's mobilization for World War II and acting as U.S. Representative to the newly formed United Nations Atomic Energy Commission in 1946. Well into his eighties, Baruch continued to be an influential voice in Washington. For each of these men, there was a clear continuity of purpose and consistency of ideological outlook between the earlier and later stages of their careers.

Such ongoing consistency of purpose was not so obvious in the careers of Felix Frankfurter and Donald Richberg after 1939. Frankfurter was named by FDR to the Supreme Court in 1939 and remained on the bench until 1962. Three years after leaving the court, Frankfurter died. During his long tenure on the Supreme Court, Frankfurter disappointed many of his former liberal allies and came to be regarded as a one-time "radical" turned "conservative." Yet, his elevation to the Supreme Court did not so much change his ideological commitments as it did the vantage point from which he felt compelled to render judgments on public issues. For him, such issues no longer could be considered strictly in terms of his own policy preferences. Having long been a critic of judges who seemingly usurped the power of legislatures by striking down legislation which did not conform to their own political ideas, Frankfurter himself adopted a philosophy of judicial restraint on the bench. Whereas in the first four decades of the twentieth century such an approach generally meant upholding progressive legislation, in the years after 1940 judicial restraint meant sustaining legislation which seemed antithetical to many liberal values. Especially in the area of civil liberties, which came to dominate the court's deliberations in the 1940s and 1950s, Frankfurter developed a checkered record. However, there is no evidence to indicate that he ever repudiated his faith in the economic reforms of the New Deal.[1]

On the other hand, Richberg with the passage of time did become more and more estranged from his New Deal past. After leaving the Roosevelt administration in 1935, Richberg became a highly successful corporate lawyer in Washington and later taught at the University of Virginia Law School. Before his death in 1960, Richberg became a vehement anti-communist and an ardent critic of the American labor movement, even helping to write an early draft of legislation similar in purpose to the Taft-Hartley Act which was subsequently adopted in 1947. Thus, the man who had at one time been the furthest to the left on the political spectrum among the men discussed here ended up the furthest to the right. However, Richberg himself believed that he had remained consistent throughout his life in his commitment to liberalism and opposition to centralized authority and coercion. Only in the later stages of his life the threats posed by "big government" and "big labor" seemed to him greater objects of concern than the dangers posed by "big business."[2]

During the forty years from the end of the nineteenth century to the beginning of the Second World War, the American liberal tradition underwent a dramatic evolution. In response to the tremendous social and technological developments which transformed American society during this period, liberals such as those examined here were forced to change or relinquish many of the beliefs that they had held at the outset of their careers. In their effort to make the liberal tradition relevant to the needs of a modern industrial society, these men all eventually came to accept, albeit in varying degrees, the necessity of a pluralistic organization of the nation's political economy. In place of the nineteenth-century ideal of a free-market economy characterized by individual competition and a strictly limited role for government, these men had come to acknowledge the inevitability, and even the desirability, of an administered economy characterized not only by managed competition among groups and organizations, but also by a greatly expanded role for government both as a sponsor of interest groups and as an overseer and stabilizer of the economy. Even Josephus Daniels, who remained a committed Jeffersonian to the end of his life, recognized that the simpler world of the late nineteenth century had given way to a world in which experts and large-scale organizations in both the private and public sectors had become indispensable.

While the American liberal tradition experienced a marked evolution during the first forty years of the twentieth century, the continuities within that tradition remained even more striking than the changes. American liberalism continued to be based on the crucial assumption that a capitalist economy provided the necessary foundation for a free society. Moreover, even as liberalism's conceptions of individualism and the market came to be modified, the values which had originally been associated with these conceptions continued to have a lasting impact on the ideological outlook of American liberals.

A fear of class consciousness and class conflict and a denial of the existence of fundamental class distinctions in America remained basic to the American liberal creed. While the liberals discussed in this study eventually came to view American society in pluralistic terms, their acceptance of pluralism was predicated on the assumption that the development of interest group organizations would help to keep America free from the possible growth of class identities. Liberals came to see interest group organizations as the only means by which individuals in the modern world could realize their hopes and ambitions. They believed, however, that the rise of a wide variety of such organizations would make it impossible for any one group to establish its dominance over society as a whole. In theory, the establishment of a multitude of interest groups in society would create a balance of power which would serve to protect individual freedom. Pluralists would subsequently argue that since Americans identified with many different interest groups, they were therefore less likely to think of themselves as members of a monolithic social class. The development of pluralism, in other words, reinforced the liberal conception of America as essentially a classless society.

The liberals considered in this study had all inherited an individualistic fear of coercive power and centralized authority. They had learned early in their lives to conceive of liberty principally as freedom from being controlled or directed by some other identifiable individual or group. Liberal ideology, as it existed at the turn of the century, was based in large part on the fear of allowing an individual to be coerced into doing something against his or her will by another person, especially if that person represented the authority of the state. While liberals came to accept an expanded role for government during the first forty years of the twentieth century, an anti-statist bias and a fear of coercive power and centralized authority remained important features of the American liberal tradition. The persistence of this fear helps to explain why the model of anonymous or impersonal authority embodied in the concept of a free functioning market continued to exert such a powerful sway over American liberals throughout the first half of the twentieth century. In spite of the fact that they acknowledged significant changes in the functioning of the marketplace, they clung to the myth that a modified market system was still a safer and more desirable means of arriving at basic economic decisions than any politically-determined mechanism could ever be.[3]

Each of the men discussed here realized early in his own career that he could not achieve personal satisfaction in life through a single-minded pursuit of material gain. Each, therefore, sincerely dedicated himself to an effort to act in behalf of the public good. None of them, however, were ever convinced that such unselfishness could realistically be expected to inspire the average citizen in his or her daily life. Throughout their careers, each of these men continued to operate on the assumption that a market system based on the individual pursuit of profit and self-interest was the only effective means of motivating the majority of human beings to work diligently and on a sustained basis.

The continuing dominance of a liberal consensus has left America with an ambiguous legacy. On the one hand, liberal ideology, with its commitment to the ideals of individual liberty and equality of opportunity, has inspired many Americans, including the men studied here, to engage in ongoing efforts to make America a better place in which to live. The American liberal tradition has thus been a tradition of reform, as liberals have constantly sought to make America live up to its high ideals. In fact, in the years since the New Deal there has been a significant increase in the standard of living for all Americans and a parallel reduction in the extent of poverty, even when measured in relative terms. In addition, income and wealth have become more equally distributed since the end of the 1930s. Yet, while the persistence of a liberal consensus has continually invigorated the reform impulse in America, it has also ultimately proven to be an obstacle to the development of a more just and humane society.

Even in the post-World-War-II period, when the United States could fairly claim to have become the richest and most powerful nation in the history of the world, America continued to be plagued by serious problems of injustice, inequality, and poverty. Depression and war did contribute to a reduction in economic inequality between 1929 and 1948, but it was still the case in the 1960s that the richest five percent of the population in the United States possessed greater wealth than all of the rest of the population combined. Moreover, since the late 1940s the pattern of wealth and income distribution has remained virtually unchanged. Economic growth in the post-war period did dramatically reduce the extent of poverty, but even in the late 1970s, twenty-five million Americans continued to live below the poverty line. Although liberals consistently refused to think of America as being divided into social classes, American society would continue to be characterized by a high degree of inequality and injustice so long as a relatively small number of Americans were allowed to claim the rights of private ownership over the nation's key wealth-producing assets.[4]

In fact, the years since the Second World War witnessed a slow but steady increase in the concentration of control in industry. By the early 1970s, the one hundred largest manufacturing corporations in the United States owned nearly 48 percent of the nation's manufacturing assets and earned more than 50 percent of all profits from manufacturing. Large-scale corporate enterprise obviously did bring with it many benefits, and it was clear to most liberals, even as early as the Progressive era, that the outright destruction of such organizations would do far more harm than good. Frankfurter, and especially Daniels, continued during the first half of the twentieth century to speak of the advantages of competition and small-scale enterprise, but, for the most part, liberals realized that their task was not to destroy bigness, but rather to bring about some form of accommodation between the power of the new corporate giants and the interests of the public. Here, however, the continuing commitment of American reformers to the basic tenets of the liberal tradition prevented them from successfully making this accomodation; for they failed to see the necessity of transforming private organizations designed for the purpose of amassing private profits into public institutions dedicated to the furtherance of the common good.[5]

What liberals such as those discussed here did succeed in

doing by the end of the 1930s was to create a political economy in which the role of government was greatly expanded, but in which there still existed no mechanisms for coordinated planning in the public interest. In defending the development of the pluralist broker state, liberals essentially created an updated version of the myth of the market as an impartial and efficient arbiter of human affairs. Only, instead of untrammeled competition between individuals producing the desired effect, liberals came to believe that government-sponsored competition among a multitude of organized groups would yield a balance of interests which would theoretically work to the benefit of everyone in society. Yet, what Theodore Lowi has labeled "interest group liberalism" remains flawed both in theory and in practice.[6]

There is no logical reason to believe that a balance of interests in society, even if it were actually achieved, would automatically produce optimally beneficial results. In fact, as Lowi and others have argued, the process of bargaining between special interest groups which has become the essence of pluralism represents almost the antithesis of public planning for common goals. Government itself comes to be seen as an arena for bargaining and competition among fragmented special interests, rather than as a true public realm in which an effort can be made to determine common objectives and priorities for society as a whole. Fearing authority and coercive power, American liberals have continued, in the words of Grant McConnell, "to cherish the illusion that power need not exist."[7]

Yet, in reality, power does exist, and the exercise of private power poses no less a danger to freedom than does the exercise of public power. Although pluralism assumes the existence, or at least the creation, of a balance of power among a number of disparate interest groups in the private sector, such a balance has never actually existed in America. The New Deal did succeed in helping to encourage the organization of certain segments of the American working class which had never before been effectively organized, but power remained very unequally distributed among the different organized groups in American society. The United States has not been ruled by a small and tightly unified capitalist elite. However, it is still the case that those who have owned or controlled the nation's means of production have exerted far more influence on the course of events than have those who have been poor and propertyless. While the development of a pluralist state has made comprehensive public planning impossible, huge corporate firms in the private sector have been able to improve their ability to protect their own interests through the use of a more narrowly conceived approach to planning.[8]

The present study has revealed that throughout the first half of the twentieth century, liberal efforts at reform continuously failed to come to grips with the actual sources and distribution of power in America. As reformers, rather than radicals, liberals continued to accept the basic attributes of the existing system of political economy and refused to repudiate either their liberal faith in private enterprise, the profit motive, and the myth of a classless America, or their fear of coercive state authority. Their approach to social and political change could thus fairly be described as "incrementalist," in that they sought only gradual modifications in the existing order. Yet, such an approach served consistently to frustrate their ability to accomplish their goal of enabling America to realize fully its democratic potential. For incrementalism ultimately allowed the nation's wealthiest and most powerful interests to preserve their positions of privilege in the United States.[9]

In commenting on the legacy of the New Deal, John Braeman observes:

No doubt the New Deal did save American capitalism by remedying its worst abuses, assuring the mass of the nation's citizens a minimum level of well-being, and giving a larger number of Americans than ever before a stake in the system. But the vast majority of the American people in the 1930's appear to have wanted no more. Those—whether Marxists of different hues or "independent liberals" such as John Dewey—who demanded more fundamental changes in the economic and social structure failed to gain a substantial popular following. If one is to bewail the limitations of the New Deal, then one's quarrel lies with the values and aspirations of the American people themselves.[10]

Braeman is correct in asserting that liberals such as those discussed here thought and acted within the context of what was politically acceptable to the American people. More radical change at any time during the first half of the twentieth century may well have been a political impossibility, even if the men here had advocated it. Yet, America would have been better served if those who were intent on making America a more just and democratic society had realized the limits of liberalism and begun the process of education and debate about the need to transcend America's liberal tradition. In looking to the future, as the United States faces growing economic and social problems in the 1980s, an ability to learn from the lessons of the past may well prove crucial to the fate of the American people.

# Notes

## Abbreviations Used in Notes

BB MS      Bernard M. Baruch Papers, Princeton University Library

JD MS      Josephus Daniels Papers, Library of Congress

FF MS      Felix Frankfurter Papers, Library of Congress

DR MS/CHS      Donald R. Richberg Papers, Chicago Historical Society

DR MS/LC      Donald R. Richberg Papers, Library of Congress

HS MS      Henry L. Stimson Papers, Yale University Library

## I. The Significance of a Liberal Consensus

1. For a general overview of the history of the writing of American history in the twentieth century, see Gene Wise, *American Historical Explanations: A Strategy for Grounded Explanations* (Minneapolis, 1980 ed.). The most comprehensive description of the literature by and about consensus historians is Bernard Sternsher, *Consensus, Conflict, and American Historians* (Bloomington, 1975).

2. Daniel J. Boorstin, *The Genius of American Politics* (Chicago, 1958 ed.), p. 1. Boorstin's explanation of the idea of "givenness" is found in pp. 8–35.

3. Louis Hartz, *The Liberal Tradition in America* (New York, 1955). Hartz expands on the ideas found in this book to come up with a general theory about the development of new, transplanted, colonial societies in Louis Hartz, *The Founding of New Societies* (New York, 1964).

4. Robert A. Dahl, *Pluralist Democracy in the United States: Conflict and Consent* (Chicago, 1967), p. 357. See also Daniel Bell, *The End of Ideology: On the Exhaustion of Political Ideas in the Fifties* (New York, 1962 ed.); and Seymour Martin Lipset, *Political Man: The Social Basis of Politics* (Garden City, 1963 ed.), especially pp. 439–456.

5. See, for example, the works of Dahl and Lipset cited in the previous footnote.

6. John Higham, "The Cult of the 'American Consensus': Homogenizing American History," *Commentary* 27 (February 1959): 93–100, offers one of the first major critiques of consensus history.

7. Marian J. Morton presents a highly critical view of the political perspective embodied in consensus history in her book, *The Terrors of Ideological Politics: Liberal*

*Historians in a Conservative Mood* (Cleveland, 1972). See also Sternsher, *Consensus,* for a compendium of criticisms of Boorstin and Hartz. For a critique of certain aspects of pluralist social science, see Michael Paul Rogin, *The Intellectuals and McCarthy: The Radical Specter* (Cambridge, 1969 ed.).

8. Boorstin states at the beginning of his book: "If what I say is true, it has profound consequences both for our understanding of ourselves and for our relation to Europe. It speaks to those who say that what we need in this country is a clearer 'philosophy' of democracy. It speaks to those who think we should try to compete with the Russians in a war of philosophies. This book adds up to a warning that, if we rely on the 'philosophy of American democracy' as a weapon in the worldwide struggle, we are relying on a weapon which may prove a dud." Boorstin, *Genius of American Politics,* p. 4.

Hartz, in contrast, observes that: ". . . the question is not whether our history has given us something to 'export' but whether it has given us the right thing. And this question has to be answered in the negative. If we want to meet the action of Communism on this score, our job, in addition to repeating the Declaration of Independence, the 'American Proposition,' as the *Fortune* editors put it, is to transcend the perspective it contains." Hartz, *Liberal Tradition,* p. 305.

9. Boorstin, *Genius of American Politics,* p. 6; Hartz, *Liberal Tradition,* p. 11.

10. This passage is from the concluding chapter, "Conflict and Consensus in American History," of Richard Hofstadter, *The Progressive Historians: Turner, Beard, Parrington* (New York, 1968), pp. 451–52. In the introduction to *The American Political Tradition: And the Men Who Made It* (New York, 1948), Hofstadter wrote: "The following studies in the ideology of American statesmanship have convinced me of the need for a reinterpretation of our political traditions which emphasizes the common climate of American opinion. The existence of such a climate has been much obscured by the tendency to place political conflict in the foreground of history. . . . The fierceness of the political struggles has often been misleading; for the range of vision embraced by the primary contestants in the major parties has always been bounded by the horizons of property and enterprise. However much at odds on specific issues, the major political traditions have shared a belief in the rights of property, the philosophy of economic individualism, the value of competition; they have accepted the economic virtues of capitalist culture as necessary qualities of man." pp. vii–viii.

11. In 1900, only one percent of all families had central heating; three percent had electricity; five percent had telephones; and less than one percent had automobiles. Stanley Lebergott, *The American Economy: Income, Wealth, and Want* (Princeton, 1976), pp. 8, 334. U.S. Department of Commerce, Bureau of the Census, *Historical Statistics of the United States: Colonial Times to 1957* (Washington, 1960), pp. 14, 74, 91, 95, 97, 98, 462, 480; Simon Kuznets, *National Income: A Summary of Findings* (New York, 1946), p. 41.

12. Lebergott, *American Economy,* p. 321; Edward C. Budd, ed., *Inequality and Poverty* (New York, 1967), p. xiii; Robert J. Lampman, *The Share of Top Wealth-Holders in National Wealth, 1922–1956* (Princeton, 1962), p. 24. The distribution of income and wealth, it is true, has become somewhat more equal in the years since 1940, with the Second World War, in particular, having an equalizing effect. Nevertheless, in 1962 the richest one percent of the American population still owned 33 percent of the nation's wealth. Taxation, on the whole, has not served as a means of redistributing wealth in the United States, since the combined effect of local, state, and federal taxes has fallen as heavily on the poor as on the rich. In 1958, those with an income of less than $2,000 paid 33 percent of their earnings in taxes as compared to only 25 percent for those earning between $10,000 and $15,000. Even the very wealthy whose income was over $15,000 in 1958 paid only 36 percent of their income in taxes. Budd, *Inequality and*

*Poverty,* pp. xxii, xvii. Gabriel Kolko, in *Wealth and Power in America: An Analysis of Social Class and Income Distribution* (New York, 1962) argues that the basic pattern of maldistribution of income and wealth remained virtually unchanged in the twentieth century up through the beginning of the 1960s, but he undoubtedly overstates the case. See also Jeffrey G. Williamson and Peter H. Lindert, *American Inequality* (New York, 1980).

13. Budd, *Inequality and Poverty,* p. xxxii.

14. Oscar Ornati, *Poverty Amid Affluence* (New York, 1966), pp. 147–48, 158. Ornati calculates the percentages of Americans living below a level of "minimum adequacy" for 1929, 1935–36, and 1941. The rough figure of 37 percent for the turn of the century is derived by using Lebergott's income distribution for 1900. He calculates that 37 percent of American families in that year had an income of less than $600. Assuming that the budget required for minimum adequacy in 1900 may have been slightly lower than the $625 required for 1905, the figure of 37 percent serves as a fair estimate for the extent of poverty at the beginning of the century.

Ornati's study also defines "minimum subsistence" and "minimum comfort" budgets for the years between 1905 and 1960. Using a minimum subsistence standard for poverty significantly reduces the percentage of the population defined as living in poverty. For example, in 1941 only 17 percent of American families lived below a minimum subsistence level. On the other hand, using a minimum comfort standard significantly increases one's estimation of the extent of poverty. For 1941, the figure would rise to 48 percent. Throughout this study, I will make use of the minimum adequacy standard as defining the poverty line. The extent of poverty has certainly been reduced since 1941 (to 26 percent in 1960 according to Ornati, and considerably less by the late 1970s, perhaps as low as 11 percent). However, most of the reduction in poverty has been directly related to American involvement in wars. The number of people in poverty went down dramatically during the Second World War, only to rise somewhat between 1945 and 1950, before again going down rapidly during the Korean War. Poverty actually increased throughout most of the years of peacetime in the 1950s and then declined once more with the advent of the war in Vietnam. It would be hard to demonstrate that the lower level of poverty in the United States today is a result of conscious efforts to eradicate this enduring social evil, rather than a by-product of war-dependent economic growth. Ornati, *Poverty,* p. 158; Theodore R. Marmor, ed., *Poverty Policy: A Compendium of Cash Transfer Proposals* (Chicago, 1971), p. 21; James T. Patterson, *America's Struggle Against Poverty 1900–1980* (Cambridge, 1981).

15. Robert L. Heilbroner, *The Economic Transformation of America* (New York, 1977), pp. 112–13; M. A. Adelman, "The Measurement of Industrial Concentration," *Review of Economics and Statistics* 33 (November 1951): 283–84; Merle Fainsod and Lincoln Gordon, *Government and the American Economy* (New York, 1948 ed.), p. 18. For the effects of industrial concentration—a subject which will be discussed at length in the pages to follow—see John M. Blair, *Economic Concentration: Structure, Behavior and Public Policy* (New York, 1972).

16. Solomon Fabricant, *The Trend of Government Activity in the United States Since 1900* (New York, 1952), pp. 19, 196–97; *Historical Statistics,* p. 711. For a useful survey of the development of modern liberalism, written from the point of view of a committed liberal, see Harry K. Girvetz, *The Evolution of Liberalism* (New York, 1963).

17. Popular perceptions of social mobility are clearly related to the question of the lower class commitment to liberalism. One interesting study of the problem of social mobility notes that although the actual rates of social mobility for all Western industrialized nations have been comparable, America has benefited more than other nations from such mobility in terms of social and political stability because most Americans see

social mobility as a defining characteristic of their society. The interaction between the actual possibility for social mobility and the development of a dominating ideological faith in the openness of American society merits a great deal more examination by historians and sociologists. See Seymour Martin Lipset and Reinhard Bendix, *Social Mobility In Industrial Society* (Berkeley, 1964 ed.), especially chapter 3; and Stephan Thernstrom, *The Other Bostonians* (Cambridge, 1973), especially the concluding chapter.

## II. Coming of Age in the Traditions of Nineteenth-Century Liberalism: Josephus Daniels, Henry Stimson, and Bernard Baruch

1. The biographical information about Daniels in this chapter comes from Daniels, *Tar Heel Editor* (Chapel Hill, 1939); and Joseph L. Morrison, *Josephus Daniels: The Small-d Democrat* (Chapel Hill, 1966).

2. Daniels, *Tar Heel*, pp. 104, 118.

3. Winthrop S. Hudson, *American Protestantism* (Chicago, 1961), pp. 100–01; Editorial, Raleigh *News & Observer*, October 18, 1931; Daniels to Jonathan Daniels, October 26, 1931, JD MS.

4. This passage is part of a farewell address delivered by Daniels before he went to Washington to become Secretary of the Navy in 1913, quoted in Jonathan Daniels, *End of Innocence* (Philadelphia, 1954), p. 48.

5. Max Weber, *The Protestant Ethic and the Spirit of Capitalism,* trans. by Talcott Parsons (New York, 1958 ed.). Daniels' outlook also exemplifies what Edmund Morgan has called the "Puritan ethic," a constellation of political values, which in Morgan's view, contributed to the American revolution. See Edmund S. Morgan, "The Puritan Ethic and the Coming of the American Revolution," *William and Mary Quarterly* 24 (January 1967): 3–43.

6. Daniels to Addie Daniels, February 24, 1888, JD MS.

7. Editorial, Raleigh *News & Observer*, March 8, 1896; Daniels, "Building the World's Most Powerful Warships," *Saturday Evening Post* 193 (March 26, 1921): 68; Daniels to Jonathan Daniels, December 7, 1937, JD MS.

8. Daniels, *The Navy and the Nation: War-Time Addresses by Josephus Daniels* (New York, 1919), p. 77; Daniels, Untitled address, Colorado (1913?), JD MS; Editorial, Raleigh *News & Observer,* March 14, 1903. While supporting women's rights, Daniels still believed: "The God who made us implanted the mutual love of man and woman and so long as time lasts woman will prefer marriage to any personal career, if her heart meets its affinity." Address to alumnae of the Peace Institute, North Carolina, May, 1906, JD MS.

9. Daniels, Address at Berry Schools, Mount Berry, Georgia, January 13, 1932, JD MS.

10. Daniels, "Three Repositories of Power," July 21, 1887, JD MS. The seriousness of Daniels' commitment to his calling was well expressed in a letter he wrote to his son Jonathan (who succeeded his father as editor of the *News & Observer* and later served as FDR's press secretary) describing an offer made to him for his paper. Daniels recounted that he told the prospective buyer that the paper "was not for sale—that it was not property, but an institution dedicated to the public service. He insisted on me naming a price. I did so and said: 'the same price I would charge for my wife and four sons.' " Daniels to Jonathan Daniels, March 15, 1922, JD MS.

11. For information on Wilson, see Hugh Talmage Lefler and Albert Ray Newsome,

*North Carolina: The History of a Southern State* (Chapel Hill, 1973 ed.), pp. 419–24, 714; and U.S. Department of Commerce, Bureau of the Census, *Ninth Census of the United States, 1870: Statistics of Population,* pp. 53, 226. Daniels, *Tar Heel,* pp. 113, 136; Editorial, Raleigh *News & Observer,* February 13, 1896.

12. Daniels, *Tar Heel,* pp. 172–73.

13. Daniels, *Tar Heel,* p. 113; Daniels to Mary Daniels, November 1, 1886, quoted in Joseph L. Morrison, *Josephus Daniels Says* (Chapel Hill, 1962), p. 24; Daniels to Raymond Moley, September 26, 1933, JD MS; Merril D. Peterson, *The Jeffersonian Image in the American Mind* (New York, 1962, ed.), pp. 255–56. Peterson cites Daniels as one of the most exemplary exponents of the Jeffersonian tradition in late nineteenth century America.

Daniels once observed: "I had one rule in life, to wit: Not to belong to any organization which was not open to membership to everybody—no secret societies, however good—from which a man could not withdraw without asking anybody's permission. That left open to me only two organizations to my liking—the Methodist Church and the Democratic Party." Daniels, *Tar Heel,* p. 243.

14. Daniels, Address, Elizabethtown, North Carolina, October 13, 1930, in Raleigh *News & Observer,* October 14, 1930; Daniels, Address, Rocky Mount, North Carolina, October 5, 1931, in Raleigh *News & Observer,* October 6, 1931.

15. Daniels occasionally warned that cities fostered a "spirit of exclusiveness" and "snobbery" among the rich and tempted the poor with "whiskey and cocaine and immorality." However, he became a member of North Carolina's Watauga Club, a society devoted to the industrial development of the state. Editorial, Raleigh *News & Observer,* February 13, 1896; Daniels, Address at unnamed Negro industrial college (1909?), JD MS.

Daniels' attitude toward industrial progress, tinged as it was with an agrarian cast, is illustrated by a story he once told regarding his reaction to hearing about an Indian who had entered white society and become highly educated, but who then returned many years later to the primitive life of his ancestors because he had concluded that such a life offered greater happiness. Daniels' account of the Indian's decision is sympathetic, but he ends the story by commenting: "For myself, with all its evils, I believe I prefer electric light and a hot bath, and above all things the safety razor, the greatest invention for the happiness of man in the history of the world." Daniels, *Shirt-Sleeve Diplomat* (Chapel Hill, 1947), p. 305.

16. Daniels to Franklin Roosevelt, August 20, 1937, JD MS; Jon. Daniels, *End of Innocence,* pp. 34–35.

17. Daniels, *Navy and Nation,* pp. 43–44; Editorial, North Carolina State *Chronicle,* March 11, 1886, quoted in Morrison, *Daniels Says;* Address as Ambassador to Mexico, quoted in E. David Cronon, *Josephus Daniels in Mexico* (Madison, 1960), p. 88.

18. Editorial, Raleigh *News & Observer,* January 21, 1896; Daniels, *Navy and Nation,* p. 42.

19. Editorial, Raleigh *News & Observer,* July 3, 1903; Daniels, Diary, October 2, 1937, JD MS; Daniels to Franklin Roosevelt, June 1, 1933, JD MS; Daniels, Address, in Raleigh *News & Observer,* October 14, 1930.

20. Daniels, Address in support of an "industrial awakening," North Carolina (pre-1900?), JD MS.

21. The biographical information about Stimson in this chapter comes from Stimson and McGeorge Bundy, *On Active Service in Peace and War* (New York, 1948); and Elting E. Morison, *Turmoil and Tradition: A Study of the Life and Times of Henry L. Stimson* (New York, 1964 ed.). The quotation is from Morison, p. 345.

22. While in Europe, Lewis Stimson studied with Louis Pasteur for a year. Henry

Clark Stimson, in whose home Henry lived as a boy, had himself retired from the stock market after suffering financial losses in the Panic of 1873.

23. Stimson, *Active Service*, p. xii; Morison, *Turmoil and Tradition*, p. 18. For background on the Presbyterian church and the Genteel Tradition, see two works by Henry F. May, *Protestant Churches and Industrial America* (New York, 1967 ed.), pp. 192–93; and *The End of American Innocence: A Study of the First Years of Our Own Time, 1912–1917* (Chicago, 1964 ed.), pp. 9–31.

Stimson's religious orientation and reluctance to speak in specifically religious terms is clearly expressed in a letter he wrote fairly late in his life: "I sympathize with you in your apprehension as to the great dangers into which the ease and luxury of modern civilization and the consequent materialism and selfishness attendant upon them have led us. I also share your feeling that the remedy must come in a revitalization of personal religion as taught by Christ and I should rather talk with you about this than try to write. It is a subject which for various reasons I have found very difficult even to talk about but with your sympathetic standpoint perhaps I might break through the crust." Stimson to Francis B. Sayre, February 4, 1938, HS MS.

24. Stimson, Diary, July 27, 1942, HS MS; Stimson, Address to National Security League, New York, June 14, 1915, HS MS; Stimson, "The Position of the Republican Party on the Eighteenth Amendment," radio address, June 16, 1932, HS MS; Stimson, *Active Service*, p. 672.

While a law student at Harvard in the late 1880's, Stimson was at first shocked by the sense of religious scepticism which pervaded the campus. At this time, the teachings of John Fiske, who forged a combination of Christianity and evolutionary thought, deeply impressed the young Stimson. Morison, *Turmoil and Tradition*, pp. 38–39; Stimson to James Conant, December 27, 1949, HS MS.

25. Stimson, *Active Service*, pp. xii, 286; Stimson, Founders' Day address at Phillips Academy, October 11, 1913, HS MS.

26. Morison, *Turmoil and Tradition*, p. 22.

27. Stimson to Conant, December 27, 1949; Stimson, Founders' Day address, October 11, 1913; Stimson, Diary, January 7, 1912, HS MS.

28. Stimson, Letter to the editor, New York *Times*, March 7, 1939. In his career as a diplomat, Stimson found "personal conference" and "face to face" discussions to be an "indispensable" factor in developing "mutual understanding" between nations. Stimson, *The Far Eastern Crisis: Reflections and Observations* (New York, 1936), p. 200.

29. Stimson, Address at Andover alumni dinner, 1907, HS MS; Stimson, Address at Phillips Academy commencement, 1908, HS MS. May cites Stimson as an example of the "well-known Eastern political type" who "combined a kind of political progressivism with impeccable conservatism of taste and manners." May, *American Innocence*, p. 52.

30. Stimson, Founders' Day address, October 11, 1913; Stimson, *Active Service*, p. xvi. See also Stimson, *My Vacations* (n.p., 1949), in HS MS.

31. Stimson, "Suffrage Not a Natural Right," May 24, 1915, pamphlet published by the New York State Association Opposed to Woman Suffrage, in HS MS. Richard Current quotes Stimson as arguing against women's suffrage at a preparedness rally before American entry into the First World War in the following words: "Participation in the decision of such questions by woman, who is not wholly ignorant of the methods of force, but whose very nature shrinks from the thought of it, cannot but be a source of peril to the government which permits it." Current, *Secretary Stimson: A Study in Statecraft* (New Brunswick, 1954), p. 25.

32. Stimson, "Bases of American Foreign Policy During the Past Four Years," *For-*

*eign Affairs* 11 (April 1933): 386; Stimson, "First-Hand Impressions of Philippine Problem," *Saturday Evening Post* 199 (March 19, 1927): 7. Examples of Stimson's racial attitudes toward southern Europeans, Malays, and blacks may be found in Stimson, Address, New Haven, Connecticut, February 27, 1917, HS MS; Stimson, "Future Philippine Policy Under the Jones Act," *Foreign Affairs* 5 (April 1927): 459–71; Stimson, Diary, September 27, 1940, HS MS; Stimson to Alfred Stearns, January 30, 1942, HS MS.

33. Stimson, unlike Daniels, thus came to accept, explicitly, the idea of the "white man's burden" on the world scene. He once observed: "Three hundred years of Spain worked a wonderful operation on the Malay race even if it killed a lot of them in doing it." Stimson to Gen. Frank McIntyre, October 27, 1926, HS MS. See also Current, *Secretary Stimson*, p. 120.

34. Stimson, "Public Operation vs. Private Operation of Public Utilities," address given to National Republican Club, January 24, 1925, HS MS.

35. Stimson, "Defend Our Seas with Our Navy: Freedom Cannot Be Saved Without Sacrifice," *Vital Speeches* 7 (May 15, 1941): 450; Stimson, Founders' Day address, October 11, 1913; Stimson to John Lee, March 1, 1934, HS MS.

36. Stimson, "Philippine Policy," pp. 460, 469; Stimson, "Inaugural Address of Henry L. Stimson, Governor-General of the Philippines," *Far Eastern Review* 24 (May 1928): 212–13; Stimson, *American Policy in Nicaragua* (New York, 1927), pp. 122–23; Stimson, *Democracy and Nationalism in Europe* (Princeton, 1934), p. 79.

37. Stimson to Henry A. Stimson, April 17, 1916, HS MS; Stimson to Irving Fisher, October 16, 1922, HS MS; Stimson, *Nicaragua*, p. 11. See also Stimson, "Two Great Political Parties: The Ideal of Self-Government," (1914?), in HS MS.

38. Stimson, Lincoln Day address, Utica, New York, February 12, 1914, HS MS; Morison, *Turmoil and Tradition*, p. 114; Stimson, *Active Service*, p. 22; Stimson, Address at Columbia University, New York, October 12, 1910, HS MS.

39. Stimson, Address in behalf of W. H. Taft's candidacy for President, Buffalo, October 16, 1912, HS MS. Stimson once observed: "The trouble with a republican form of popular government is its inefficiency. We pay a sacrifice in efficiency, ordinarily, to the general contentment that comes from the fact that everybody has a hand in the government,—and that means that republics are very apt to blunder on and blunder on and allow grievances to last which, in a more efficient form of government, would be remedied." Address to political science class at the University of Pennsylvania, May 16, 1912, HS MS.

40. Morison, *Turmoil and Tradition*, pp. 162–63.

41. Morison, *Turmoil and Tradition*, pp. 165–66.

42. Stimson to Richard Templeton, August 5, 1912, HS MS; Stimson to Charles Chamberlain, September 5, 1896, HS MS; Stimson to Daniel Haggerty, October 8, 1896, HS MS; Stimson, *Active Service*, p. 81; Stimson, Address at Hamilton College, June 13, 1938, HS MS.

43. The biographical information in this chapter about Baruch comes from: Baruch, *Baruch: My Own Story* (New York, 1957); Baruch, *Baruch: The Public Years* (New York, 1960); Margaret L. Coit, *Mr. Baruch* (Boston, 1957); Carter Field, *Bernard Baruch: Park Bench Statesman* (New York, 1944); W. L. White, *Bernard Baruch: Portrait of a Citizen* (New York, 1950); Jordan A. Schwarz, *The Speculator: Bernard M. Baruch in Washington, 1917–1965* (Chapel Hill 1981).

44. Baruch, *My Story*, p. 298.

45. Baruch, Address at James Monroe High School, April 28, 1948, BB MS. Schwarz observes that "Baruch's Jewishness was something he never flaunted and never, to his credit, denied." *Speculator*, p. 9. Baruch, I believe, was more uncomfortable with his

own Jewishness than Schwarz's statement would indicate. Schwarz, however, does effectively capsulize Baruch's desire to remain an outsider with the title of his study, *The Speculator.*

46. Coit, *Baruch,* pp. 26–27; Baruch to Hugh Johnson, June 13, 1940, BB MS.

47. Baruch, *My Story,* p. 52. Coit reports that Baruch once told her: "I could have been President of the United States—if I had not been a Jew." Coit, *Baruch,* p. 359.

48. Baruch, "Educating Ourselves for Peace and Freedom: Today, Thinking Has Become a Neglected Art," *Vital Speeches* 19 (June 1, 1953): 510; Baruch, "Regulating One's Behavior: False Gospel of Security by Deficit Spending," *Vital Speeches* 16 (June 15, 1950): 524.

49. Baruch, *My Story,* p. 289.

50. Schwarz, *Speculator,* pp. 8–9.

51. Baruch, *My Story,* pp. 32, 307; Baruch, *Public Years,* pp. 5, 177; Schwarz, *Speculator,* p. 35.

52. Baruch, *Public Years,* p. 5.

53. *My Story,* pp. 55–56. Newcomb was an outspoken defender of the rights of property and a close friend of noted Social Darwinist William Graham Sumner. S. Willis Rudy, *The College of the City of New York: A History, 1847–1947* (New York, 1949), pp. 144–45. The laissez-faire tradition in economic thought which influenced Baruch is well described in Sidney Fine, *Laissez Faire and the General-Welfare State: A Study of Conflict in American Thought, 1865–1901* (Ann Arbor, 1964 ed.); and Thomas C. Cochran and William Miller, *The Age of Enterprise: A Social History of Industrial America* (New York, 1961 ed.), especially pp. 119–28.

54. Baruch, Commencement address at Union College, June 14, 1937, BB MS; Baruch, "Output as Inflation Cure," *United States News* 20 (April 5, 1946): 75; Baruch, *Public Years,* pp. 218–19.

55. Baruch, Statement, Paris, March or April, 1919, BB MS; Baruch, "Regulating One's Behavior," p. 524; Baruch, Commencement address at the University of South Carolina, June 10, 1925, BB MS.

56. Baruch, *My Story,* pp. viii–ix.

57. Baruch, Testimony, in U.S. Congress, Senate, Special Committee to Investigate Unemployment and Relief, *Hearings,* 75th Cong., 3d sess., February 28 and March 1, 1938; Baruch, "This I Believe," *Reader's Digest* 64 (April 1954): 69; Baruch, "The Wilsonian Legacy for Us," New York *Times Magazine* (December 23, 1956): 12; Baruch, "Self-Discipline, the Key to Peace," *Vital Speeches* 17 (June 1, 1951): 487.

58. Baruch, Senate testimony, February 28 and March 1, 1938; Baruch, *Public Years,* pp. 199–200. Baruch once wrote to Josephus Daniels: "I have seen a lot of fiat measures. I don't think any of them will ever work until we pass a fiat changing the law of supply and demand, and the workings of human nature." Baruch to Daniels, July 14, 1933, JD MS.

59. Baruch to Sen. Joe Robinson, June 28, 1935, BB MS; Baruch, *My Story,* p. 52.

60. Baruch to Gov. Albert Ritchie, September 14, 1930, BB MS.

61. Baruch, Address to Federation of Jewish Philanthropists, New York, December 12, 1944, BB MS; Baruch, Commencement address at University of South Carolina, June 10, 1925.

62. Baruch to Mark Sullivan, April 3, 1929, BB MS; Baruch, Address to Boston Chamber of Commerce, May 1, 1930, BB MS.

## III. The Shaping of Two Twentieth-Century Liberals: Donald Richberg and Felix Frankfurter

1. John Richberg moved to Knoxville just before Donald's birth in order to start a mining enterprise; however, the business did not prove successful, and the Richberg family returned to Chicago when Donald was only two years old. The biographical information about Richberg in this chapter comes from Richberg, *My Hero: The Indiscreet Memoirs of an Eventful but Unheroic Life* (New York, 1954); Thomas E. Vadney, *The Wayward Liberal: A Political Biography of Donald Richberg* (Lexington, 1970); and a biographical sketch of Eloise Richberg, in DR MS/CHS.

2. Richberg, *A Man of Purpose* (New York, 1922), p. 289; Richberg, *In the Dark* (Chicago, 1912), typescript copy in DR MS/LC, p. 25. Richberg's first published novel was *The Shadow Men* (Chicago, 1911).

3. Richberg, *Hero*, p. 215; Richberg, *Man of Purpose*, pp. 240–41.

4. The quotations are from a statement entitled "My Faith," attributed to the hero of Richberg's novel, *A Man of Purpose*, p. 239.

5. Richberg, *G. Hovah Explains* (Washington, 1940), p. 3; Richberg, *Hero*, p. 5; Richberg to Paxten Hibben, January 17, 1922, DR MS/CHS.

6. Richberg to Joseph Knapp, January 23, 1914, DR MS/LC; Richberg, *Shadow Men*, p. 309; Richberg, Untitled article, typescript, 1924, later appeared in *Locomotive Engineers' Journal* (March, 1925), in DR MS/CHS.

In the last cited article, Richberg observed: "Undoubtedly a vast majority of the American people have some religious faith, and down in their souls, believe that life is something more than getting and spending, something more than eating and sleeping; and believe that the ultimate satisfactions of life arise from service performed for others and not from service compelled from others, and from the building of character rather than from physical achievements. . . . How can we pretend that the purposes of such a government as ours can be fulfilled unless the government functions primarily for the general welfare, and by that I mean, functions in aid of the spiritual aspirations of the people as well as for their material well being."

7. Richberg's biographer observes: "Although Richberg shunned any loyalty to organized religion, he shared many of its ideals, but saw a more rational approach as the way to realize them. For Richberg, the social sciences would provide the key to improving man's lot, not formal religion. Yet the rational content of his ethical system did not eliminate the moralizing style of thought and action of a man who, after all, was born and raised in the Victorian age. Despite his analytical approach to ethics, Richberg's values were shaped by his background perhaps more than he realized." Vadney, *Wayward Liberal*, p. 9.

8. Morton White, *Social Thought in America: The Revolt Against Formalism* (Boston, 1957 ed.). See also Eric F. Goldman, *Rendezvous with Destiny: A History of Modern American Reform* (New York, 1977 ed.); and Sidney Fine, *Laissez Faire and the General-Welfare State: A Study of Conflict in American Thought, 1865–1901* (Ann Arbor, 1964 ed.) for two broad surveys of the changes in social thought which occurred during this period.

9. Louis Wirth, "The Social Sciences," in *American Scholarship in the Twentieth Century*, ed. by Merle Curti (Cambridge, 1953), p. 42; Fine, *Laissez Faire*, p. 264. See also Richard J. Storr, *Harper's University: The Beginnings* (Chicago, 1966); and Roscoe Pound, "The Law School, 1817–1929," in *The Development of Harvard University: Since the Inauguration of President Eliot, 1869–1929*, ed. by Samuel Eliot Morison (Cambridge, 1930).

Looking back at his experience at the University of Chicago a decade after he had graduated, Richberg complained that his education there had not sufficiently fostered "originality" or "intellectual courage." However, his close association with the university continued after he returned to Chicago from Harvard. Richberg married the sister of poet and novelist Robert Herrick, who was a member of the University of Chicago faculty, and the Richbergs settled near the university campus, so that Richberg became essentially part of the academic community. In spite of his dissatisfaction with his own undergraduate education, his thinking was clearly affected by the new trends in social thought which were so important at the University of Chicago. See Richberg, "A University Consciousness," *The University of Chicago Magazine* 2 (March 1910): 156–61; Richberg, "The Same Door Wherein I Went," *The University of Chicago Magazine* 4 (June 1912): 268–71; Richberg, "Why Not Try Education," (1914?), DR MS/LC.

10. Richberg, "Developing Ethics and Resistant Law," *Yale Law Journal* 32 (December 1922): 109.

11. Richberg, "Developing Ethics," p. 121.

12. Richberg, "Where Are the Progressives Going—and How," supplement 1927, DR MS/CHS; Richberg, "The High Cost of Low Thinking," *New Republic* 32 (October 18, 1922): 194.

13. Richberg, *Tents of the Mighty* (Chicago, 1930), pp. 226–27. Christopher Lasch has perceptively observed of Richberg: "The twentieth century made the virtuous knights and fair ladies of traditional romance obsolete, and science denied the comfort of the absolute . . . Having destroyed those assumptions, science knew neither absolute virtue nor absolute evil; in the world of science, as Richberg had already discovered, there were no clearly discernible and unalterably opposed sets of alternatives from which an individual could at any time choose without hesitation. Choice was never easy for the scientist. Choice became a matter of analysis, deliberation and careful adjustment of conflicting facts and opinions. The scientist, moreover, was always obliged to keep an open mind, to admit the possibility of error and, if one set of ideas led him to err, to abandon those ideas and take up new ones which he would in turn try and test, discarding them when they proved useless." Christopher Lasch, "Donald Richberg and the Idea of a National Interest" (Unpublished M.A. thesis, Columbia University, 1955), pp. 6–7.

14. Richberg, "Planning and Controlling Business Activities," *Vital Speeches* 1 (December 17, 1934): 170; Richberg, "Seeking the Law in Vain," *The Survey* 49 (December 1922): 291.

15. Richberg, *Tents,* pp. 253–57.

16. Richberg, "Seeking the Law," p. 291; Richberg, "Security—Without a Dictator," New York *Times Magazine* (January 28, 1940), p. 23.

17. Richberg to Herbert Hoover, January 21, 1920, DR MS/CHS; Richberg, "The Black-Connery Bill," *Vital Speeches* 3 (July 15, 1937): 586; Richberg, *Government and Business Tomorrow: A Public Relations Program* (New York, 1943), p. 110; Richberg, *Hero,* p. 352.

Testifying before a Senate Committee in 1924, Richberg stated: "It is recognized that the good order of society rests upon contract, that democratic government enforces primarily the voluntary obligations of a man to his fellow man or to the community. The rights of minorities are protected by the agreement of majorities and the will of majorities is enforced through the express or implied agreement of minorities to obey majority rules. Any other theory of government is autocratic or anarchistic. Therefore any compulsion exerted by government in a democracy must be based on contract." Richberg, Testimony before subcommittee of the U.S. Senate Committee on Interstate Commerce, investigating arbitration between carriers and employees, 68th Cong., 1st sess., March, 1924, copy in DR MS/CHS.

18. Richberg, "The Future of Power and the Public," *The Annals of the Academy of Political and Social Science* 159 (January 1932): 155; Richberg, Statement, "Depression Causes and Remedies," in U.S. Congress, Senate, Committee on Finance, *Hearings on Investigation of Economic Problems,* 72d Cong., 2d sess., February 23, 1933, pp. 643–52.

19. Richberg, "The Fair Share in Industry," (1925?), DR MS/LC; Richberg, "Big Government and Little People," address to the Law Club of Chicago, December 16, 1949, DR MS/CHS. Richberg also once criticized any attempt to establish a "class-conscious, paternalistic state," claiming that both socialists and "industrial autocrats" shared a "mental kinship" in their "desire to exercise coercive power over their fellow men." Richberg, "The Key to Knowledge," address to the Law Club of Chicago, February 25, 1921, DR MS/CHS.

20. Alexander Bickel, "Applied Politics and the Science of the Law: Writings of the Harvard Period," in *Felix Frankfurter: A Tribute,* ed. by Wallace Mendelson (New York, 1964), p. 160.

21. The biographical information about Frankfurter in this chapter comes from Liva Baker, *Felix Frankfurter* (New York, 1969); Frankfurter, *Felix Frankfurter Reminisces* (recorded in talks with Dr. Harlan B. Phillips) (New York, 1960); and Michael E. Parrish, *Felix Frankfurter and His Times: The Reform Years* (New York, 1982).

22. Frankfurter, *Reminisces,* p. 289; H. N. Hirsch, *The Enigma of Felix Frankfurter* (New York, 1981), p. 23; Frankfurter, Foreword to *Chaim Weizmann* (1944), reprinted in *Of Law and Men: Papers and Addresses of Felix Frankfurter, 1939–1956,* ed. by Philip Elman (New York, 1956), p. 353.

Frankfurter's interest in Zionism and his active involvement in the cause stemmed from his relationship with Louis Brandeis, the leader of American Zionism before the First World War. Frankfurter attended the Versailles Peace Conference as the official representative of the Zionist Organization of America. Following the break in international Zionism between Brandeis and Weizmann in 1921, however, Frankfurter became less active, though no less interested, in the movement. See Frankfurter, "The Palestine Situation Restated," *Foreign Affairs* 9 (April 1931): 409–34.

23. Frankfurter, "The Worth of Our Past: Civilization Our Business," *Vital Speeches* 7 (July 15, 1941): 603; Frankfurter, "Public Opinion and Democratic Government," *Reference Shelf* 20 (1947): 147; Baker, *Frankfurter,* p. 290. Baker goes on to quote Frankfurter as having stated: "As one who has no ties with any formal religion perhaps the feelings that underlie religious forms for me run into intensification of my feelings about American citizenship. I have known, as you hardly could have known, literally hundreds of men and women of the finest spirit who had to shed old loyalties and take on the loyalty of American citizenship. . . . American citizenship implies entering upon a fellowship which binds people together by devotion to certain feelings and ideas and ideals summarized as a requirement that they be attached to the principles of the Constitution."

Hirsch argues that Frankfurter remained ambivalent about his Jewishness and sought "almost desperately" to become an "insider" through intimate associations with such prominent establishment figures as Oliver Wendell Holmes, Henry Stimson, and Franklin Roosevelt. He goes on to claim that Frankfurter developed a "textbook case of a neurotic personality" and that Frankfurter's unconscious need to vindicate an "overblown" self-image had a crucial effect on his public career. While Hirsch presents useful evidence regarding the importance of the darker side of Frankfurter's personality, he does not adequately analyze the substance of Frankfurter's ideological outlook or the political and economic context in which Frankfurter acted. These, I believe, are more important to an understanding of Frankfurter's public career than personality factors.

24. Frankfurter to Walter Lippmann, May 31, 1932, in *Roosevelt and Frankfurter: Their Correspondence, 1928–1945,* ed. by Max Freedman (Boston, 1967), p. 63; Frankfurter, *Reminisces,* p. 291.

25. At Harvard, Dean James Barr Ames and James Bradley Thayer were the most immediate influences on Frankfurter's thinking. Although Frankfurter did not become personally acquainted with Holmes and Brandeis until several years after his graduation from Harvard, he was well prepared by then to incorporate their contributions to anti-formalist thought into his own conception of the world. While at Harvard, Frankfurter did get to know William James and also shared an apartment with Morris Cohen, a man who went on to become an important twentieth-century philosopher. Frankfurter to Learned Hand, June 27, 1946, FF MS; Frankfurter, *Reminisces,* pp. 20, 299–300. See also S. Willis Rudy, *The College of the City of New York: A History, 1847–1947* (New York, 1949); and Pound, "The Law School."

26. Frankfurter to Marion Denman, May 11, 1914, FF MS; Frankfurter, Rally Day address at Smith College, Springfield (Mass.) *Republican,* February 23, 1933, in FF MS; Frankfurter, "Alfred North Whitehead," originally in New York *Times,* January 8, 1948, reprinted in *Of Law and Men,* p. 289; Frankfurter, "Review of new edition of *Curse of Bigness* by Louis Brandeis," *Atlantic Monthly* 155 (May 1935): 16; Frankfurter to Henry Stimson, May 19, 1913, FF MS; Frankfurter, "Dean James Barr Ames and the Harvard Law School," originally an address to the fiftieth reunion of Frankfurter's law school class, June 13, 1956, reprinted in *Of Law and Life & Other Things that Matter: Papers and Addresses of Felix Frankfurter, 1956–1963,* ed. by Philip B. Kurland (New York, 1965), p. 33.

27. Frankfurter, *Reminisces,* p. 37; Frankfurter, "Mr. Justice Brandeis and the Constituion," originally in *Harvard Law Review* 44 (November, 1931), reprinted in *Law and Politics: Occasional Papers of Felix Frankfurter, 1913–1938,* ed. by Archibald MacLeish and E. F. Prichard, Jr. (Gloucester, 1971), p. 122; Frankfurter, *The Commerce Clause Under Marshall, Taney and Waite* (Chapel Hill, 1937), pp. 7–9; Frankfurter, "The Conditions for, and the Aims and Methods of, Legal Research," originally in *Iowa Law Review* 15 (February, 1930), reprinted in *Law and Politics,* pp. 289, 296; Frankfurter, *Mr. Justice Holmes and the Supreme Court* (Cambridge, 1938), p. 61.

As a scientific student of the law, Frankfurter was not only a follower of Holmes and Brandeis, but also an important innovator in his own right. Together with Roscoe Pound, he was one of the directors, in 1922, of the landmark survey of the criminal justice system of the city of Cleveland. This survey pioneered in the use of statistical analysis to improve the effectiveness of the administration of criminal justice. Frankfurter subsequently called "reliable statistics" the foundation of "all scientific standards in dealing with social problems." In addition, Frankfurter helped establish a new technique of legal scholarship by utilizing statistical analysis to gain a fuller understanding of the actual institutional workings of the federal judiciary. See Roscoe Pound and Felix Frankfurter, eds., *Criminal Justice in Cleveland* (Cleveland, 1922); Frankfurter, "Surveys of Criminal Justice," *Proceedings of the National Conference of Social Work* (Chicago, 1930), p. 64; and Frankfurter and James M. Landis, *The Business of the Supreme Court* (New York, 1927). See also Bickel, "Applied Politics."

28. Frankfurter to Walter Lippmann, October 10, 1929, FF MS.

29. Frankfurter, *The Public & Its Government* (New Haven, 1930), p. 151; Frankfurter to Newton Baker, November 13, 1924, FF MS.

30. Frankfurter, "Review of *The American Leviathan* by Charles A. Beard and Wil-

liam Beard," originally in *Harvard Law Review* 44 (February 1931), reprinted in *Law and Politics,* pp. 17–18; Frankfurter, "Review of *Encyclopedia of the Social Sciences,* vol. 1,*" Harvard Law Review* 43 (May 1930): 1169; Frankfurter, "The Shape of Things to Come," originally in *Survey Graphic* 27 (January, 1938), reprinted in *Law and Politics,* p. 351.

31. Frankfurter, "Mr. Justice Brandeis and the Constitution," in *Mr. Justice Brandeis,* ed. by Frankfurter (New Haven, 1932), p. 115; Frankfurter, Draft proposal for 1936 Democratic party platform, in *Roosevelt and Frankfurter,* p. 350.

32. Frankfurter, *Mr. Justice Holmes,* p. 49.

33. Frankfurter, Draft for 1936 Democratic platform, p. 352; Frankfurter, *Address to Harvard Law Society of Illinois, April 28, 1955* (n.p., 1955); Frankfurter, "The Zeitgeist and the Judiciary," originally in *Survey* (January, 1913), reprinted in *Law and Politics,* p. 6.

34. Frankfurter, "Review of *The American Leviathan,*" p. 18; Frankfurter, *Public & Its Government,* p. 49; Frankfurter, "Review of *Interstate Transmission of Electric Power* by H. L. Elsbree," *Harvard Law Review* 45 (February 1932): 763.

35. Frankfurter, "Review of *Interstate Transmission,*" p. 763; Frankfurter, *Mr. Justice Holmes,* p. 16; Frankfurter, *Public & Its Government,* p. 152.

36. Frankfurter, "What Standard of College Education Is Defensible?" radio address, May 22, 1933, FF MS; Frankfurter, *Public & Its Government,* p. 145; Frankfurter, *Business of the Supreme Court,* pp. 217–18; Frankfurter, "The Young Men Go to Washington," originally in *Fortune* 13 (January, 1936), reprinted in *Law and Politics,* p. 242; Frankfurter, "Memorial to Joseph B. Eastman," originally in New York *Times,* March 17, 1944, reprinted in *Of Law and Men,* p. 300; Frankfurter, "The Interstate Commerce Commission," address, April 5, 1962, reprinted in *Of Law and Men,* p. 241.

Frankfurter's faith in the scientific administration of public affairs was not restricted in its application to the problems of government. He became, for awhile, a supporter of the Taylor movement for "scientific management" in industry and was a close personal friend and admirer of Robert Valentine, a pioneer in the effort to create a new profession of industrial counseling. See Frankfurter, "The Manager, the Workman, and the Social Scientist," *Bulletin of the Taylor Society* 3 (December, 1917); and Frankfurter, "Robert Grosvenor Valentine, '96," *Harvard Alumni Bulletin* (December 14, 1916).

37. Frankfurter, it might be added, finished at the head of his class at Harvard each of his three years at the law school. While Frankfurter was much closer to Richberg than to Stimson in his conception of public service, he was less concerned with the spiritual role to be played by scientifically trained administrators than was Richberg.

38. Frankfurter and Nathan Greene, *The Labor Injunction* (New York, 1930), p. 205; Frankfurter, *Criminal Justice in Cleveland,* p. v.

39. Frankfurter, "The Shape of Things to Come," p. 351; Frankfurter, "The Worth of Our Past," p. 602; Frankfurter, "The Bold Experiment of Freedom," address, Aaronsburg, Penn., October 23, 1949, reprinted in *Of Law and Men,* p. 221; Pennekamp v. Florida, 328 *U.S. Reports* 331 (1946).

40. Frankfurter, "The Shape of Things to Come," p. 351; Frankfurter, *Reminisces,* p. 290; Frankfurter, Rally Day address, February 23, 1933.

41. Frankfurter, "Mr. Justice Brandeis," p. 117; Frankfurter to Walter Lippmann, March 6, 1933, FF MS. Frankfurter considered the *Federalist Papers* to be particularly insightful on the problem of the relation of economic interests to politics, describing it as one of his three favorite books, along with John Morley's *On Compromise* and James Boswell's *Life of Samuel Johnson.* Freedman, *Roosevelt and Frankfurter,* p. 721.

42. Frankfurter, *Address to Harvard Law Society of Illinios,* p. 16; Frankfurter, *Public & Its Government,* p. 36.

43. Frankfurter, "Summation of the Conference," *American Bar Association Journal* 24 (April 1938): 286.

Richard Hofstadter makes the interesting observation that the "distrust of authority" has been a "well established trait in the national character." He writes: "While it has been a familiar observation at least since the time of Tocqueville that the American yields all too readily to the tyranny of public opinion it is important to understand that in this context public opinion is hard to locate rigorously: it is diffuse and decentralized, and it belongs, after all, to the people themselves—or so it seems. But authority that can be clearly located in persons, or in small bodies of persons, is characteristically suspect in America. Historically, individual enterprise has been at a premium. For many tasks that cannot be handled by individuals, Americans have preferred to found voluntary group associations. For the remaining tasks that cannot be handled without the sanction of government and law they have preferred where possible to act through local government, which seems close to them, and then through state government; and only when these resources have failed have they called upon the federal government for action. This distrust of authority has often been turned against government, particularly when government was felt to be growing in strength. . . . But this distrust of authority has on other occasions been turned primarily against business, or at least against some portions of the business community." Richard Hofstadter, *The Age of Reform: From Bryan to F.D.R.* (New York, 1955), pp. 228–29.

## IV. The Rise of Progressivism 1900–1914

1. Baruch, *Baruch: My Own Story* (New York, 1957), p. 307; Baruch to R. W. Austin, October 7, 1916, BB MS.

2. Daniels' first public speech was delivered in 1881 in favor of state-wide prohibition. In 1882 he editorially backed the losing Democratic side in the state elections and, as a result, his mother lost her patronage job as postmistress of Wilson. It was not until 1884 that Daniels cast his first ballot in a Presidential election by voting for Cleveland. Daniels, *Tar Heel Editor* (Chapel Hill, 1939).

3. Daniels to Mary Cleaves Daniels, March 22, 1886, JD MS.

4. Daniels was disappointed with the extent to which the railroads were able to control or nullify the actions of the state's commissions. See Daniels, *Tar Heel*, pp. 388–410, 468–75; Daniels, *Editor in Politics* (Chapel Hill, 1941), p. 327; and C. Vann Woodward, *Origins of the New South, 1877–1913* (Baton Rouge, 1966 ed.), p. 380.

Daniels' support for education led him to favor, as early as 1886, federal aid to the states for this purpose. Other reforms which gained Daniels' support in this period included child labor laws, employer liability legislation, and civil service reform.

5. Elting E. Morison, *Turmoil and Tradition: A Study of the Life and Times of Henry L. Stimson* (New York, 1964 ed.), p. 61.

6. Stimson to Elihu Root, February 16,, 1901, HS MS. For background on New York politics in this period, see Harold F. Gosnell, *Boss Platt and his New York Machine* (Chicago, 1924).

7. While Stimson took pride in the passage of the primary law, Gosnell points out that it applied only to major cities in New York, and, in fact, was more important in hampering independent or non-partisan movements than in curtailing the power of boss rule. A third achievement frequently attributed to the reform Republicans, the nomination and election of Theodore Roosevelt (whom Stimson first met in 1894) to the Governorship, was more directly attributable to the independent decision of Platt than to

the influence of the insurgents. Gosnell, *Boss Platt*, pp. 78–89; Stimson and McGeorge Bundy, *On Active Service in Peace and War* (New York, 1948), pp. xix–xx.

8. Daniels, *Editor in Politics*, pp. 265–70; Daniels, *Tar Heel*, p. 182; Editorial, Raleigh *News & Observer*, April 1, 1898; Stimson, *Active Service*, p. xix; Morison, *Turmoil and Tradition*, pp. 72–73.

9. David P. Thelen, *The New Citizenship: Origins of Progressivism in Wisconsin, 1885–1900* (Columbia, 1972), p. 129. For contrasting views of the relationship between the political activity of the mid-1890s and that of the post-1898 period see: Richard Hofstadter, *The Age of Reform: From Bryan to F.D.R.* (New York, 1955); George E. Mowry, *The Era of Theodore Roosevelt and the Birth of Modern America 1900–1912* (New York, 1962 ed.); and Robert H. Wiebe, *The Search for Order, 1877–1920* (New York, 1967).

10. Editorials, Raleigh *News & Observer*, November 1, 1896; October 20, 1898; Joseph L. Morrison, *Josephus Daniels Says* (Chapel Hill, 1962), pp. 104–07; Daniels, *Editor in Politics*, pp. 283–312, 374. The election law supported by Daniels was modeled after the Grandfather Clause recently adopted in Louisiana. Daniels personally visited that state in order to study the effectiveness of the law and returned to North Carolina with a favorable report.

11. Woodward, *New South*, p. 372; Morrison, *Daniels Says*, p. 86. See also C. Vann Woodward, *Tom Watson: Agrarian Rebel* (New York, 1963 ed.) for further background on the subject.

12. The initial quotation is from an editorial praising Tom Watson for his "ringing denunciation of socialism." Daniels went on to accuse the Northern and Western elements of the Populist movement, rather than its Southern branch, of being especially susceptible to such appeals. Raleigh *News & Observer*, January 21, 1896. The other quotation is from an editorial in the Raleigh *News & Observer*, November 3, 1896. See also Morrison, *Daniels Says*, pp. 40–62, for a full discussion of Daniels' criticisms of the Populist party.

13. Stimson to Charles Chamberlain, September 5, 1896, HS MS; Stimson to Daniel Haggerty, October 8, 1896, HS MS. While Thelen's work on the origins of progressivism in Wisconsin offers many valuable insights on the subject, its failure to consider the role of the Populist party or the impact populism had on future progressives is a significant omission.

14. Alfred D. Chandler, Jr., *The Visible Hand: The Managerial Revolution in American Business* (Cambridge, 1977), pp. 1, 320. For general surveys of the economic history of the period, see also Thomas C. Cochran, *The American Business System* (New York, 1962 ed.); Thomas C. Cochran and William Miller, *The Age of Enterprise* (New York, 1961 ed.); Harold U. Faulkner, *The Decline of Laissez Faire 1897–1917* (New York, 1968 ed.); Ross M. Robertson, *History of the American Economy* (New York, 1964 ed.); and Robert L. Heilbroner, *The Economic Transformation of America* (New York, 1977).

15. Cochran, *American Business*, p. 55; John Whiteclay Chambers II, *The Tyranny of Change: America in the Progressive Era, 1900–1917* (New York, 1980), p. 45. For an interesting study of the impact that the rise of large corporations had on the thinking of certain intellectuals during the period covered by the present study, see James Gilbert, *Designing the Industrial State: The Intellectual Pursuit of Collectivism in America, 1880–1940* (Chicago, 1972).

16. Chandler, *Visible Hand*, p. 286. Doubts as to the importance of economies of scale in production as a factor in the merger movement are presented in George W. Stocking and Myron W. Watkins, *Monopoly and Free Enterprise* (New York, 1951), pp. 497–500; John M. Blair, *Economic Concentration: Structure, Behavior and Public Policy*

(New York, 1972), pp. 257–64; F. M. Scherer, "Economies of Scale and Industrial Concentration," in Harvey J. Goldschmid, H. Michael Mann, and J. Fred Weston, *Industrial Concentration: The New Learning* (Boston, 1974).

17. Heilbroner, *Economic Transformation,* pp. 113–14.

18. Cochran and Miller, *Age of Enterprise,* pp. 188–89. The combined assets of all American financial institutions rose from nine billion dollars in 1899 to twenty-eight billion dollars in 1911. Although the number of savers in the population increased, in 1910 only eight percent of the American people had savings in financial institutions which could be used for investment. Arthur S. Link and William B. Catton, *American Epoch: A History of the United States Since 1900:* Vol I *An Era of Economic Change, Reform and World Wars 1900–1945* (New York, 1980 ed.), p. 34; Vincent P. Carosso, *Investment Banking in America: A History* (Cambridge, 1970), pp. 84–85. See also Morton Keller, *The Life Insurance Enterprise, 1885–1910: A Study in the Limits of Corporate Power* (Cambridge, 1963).

19. Stanley Lebergott, *The American Economy: Income, Wealth, and Want* (Princeton, 1976), p. 90; Chambers, *Tyranny of Change,* p. 58.

20. Blair, *Economic Concentration,* p. 406; Heilbroner, *Economic Transformation,* p. 114; Chambers, *Tyranny of Change,* p. 54. See also Leonard W. Weiss, "The Concentration-Profits Relationship and Antitrust," and William P. Mueller, "Industrial Concentration: An Important Inflationary Force?" both in Goldschmid et al, *Industrial Concentration.*

21. William S. Comanor and Robert H. Smiley, "Monopoly and the Distribution of Wealth," *Quarterly Jounral of Economics* 89 (May 1975): 177–94. Jeffrey G. Williamson, "American Prices and Urban Inequality Since 1820," *Journal of Economic History* 36 (June 1976): 319–20; C. L. Merwin, "American Studies of the Distribution of Wealth and Income by Size," *Studies in Income and Wealth,* Vol. III (New York, 1939), pp. 3–84; Lebergott, *American Economy,* p. 321.

22. Chandler, *Visible Hand,* pp. 1, 11.

23. Daniels to Mary Cleaves Daniels, March 22, 1886; Daniels, *Tar Heel,* pp. 182–83, 468–75; Editorial, Raleigh *News & Observer,* March 27, 1896.

24. Morrison, *Daniels Says,* p. 45; Daniels, *Editor in Politics,* p. 356; Editorials, Raleigh *News & Observer,* especially September 13 and November 9, 1904.

25. Editorials, Raleigh *News & Observer,* May 5, 1906; April 11, 1903; March 19, 1904; Daniels, *Editor in Politics,* pp. 515, 559–60, 601.

26. On Daniels' support for state regulation of business, see editorials in the Raleigh *News & Observer,* February 20 and March 8, 1903. The quotation on municipal ownership is from an editorial which, coincidentally, was inspired by the fight for municipalization in Chicago in which Donald Richberg was gaining his introduction to politics. Raleigh *News & Observer,* April 23, 1905, cited in Morrison, *Daniels Says,* p. 178.

27. Editorials, Raleigh *News & Observer,* May 8 and May 15, 1906.

28. Editorials, Raleigh *News & Observer,* January 11, 1903 and November 1, 1908.

29. Editorial, Raleigh *News & Observer,* September 18, 1908. See also Morrison, *Daniels Says,* pp. 155–57; Daniels, *Editor in Politics,* pp. 395, 482, 588–89; Editorials, Raleigh *News & Observer,* March 11, 1903 and September 13, 1908.

30. Morison, *Turmoil and Tradition,* pp. 82–84.

31. Stimson, Notes for lecture to be delivered at Harvard, May 5–6, 1910, HS MS; Stimson to Judge Emory Speer, December 2, 1910, HS MS.

32. Stimson's proposals are most clearly spelled out in a speech to the Republican Club of New York, December 15, 1911, HS MS. Stimson recalls in his diary his attempts to get Taft to endorse such a policy, and Taft's unwillingness to do so without qualifi-

cation. Taft, in fact, held up approval of Stimson's major address on trust policy until he had himself made public his own more equivocal approach to the problem in a speech to Congress. Stimson, Diary, March, 1913, HS MS; Stimson, *Active Service*, pp. 44–48; Frankfurter, *From the Diaries of Felix Frankfurter, with a Biographical Essay and Notes by Joseph P. Lash* (New York, 1975), pp. 104–23.

33. Stimson, *Active Service*, pp. 60–62; Stimson to James Callanan, March 15, 1912, HS MS. As Secretary of War, Stimson sought to apply sound business principles to his administration of the War Department. This resulted in his attempting to assure "maximum effectiveness" and "maximum efficiency" at minimum cost, while at the same time, pursuing a policy which put military considerations above partisan politics. See Stimson, "The Needs of Our Army," *Harper's Weekly* 56 (August 31, 1912): 12; Morison, *Turmoil and Tradition* pp. 130–36.

34. Stimson, Campaign address, Shortsville Wheel Works, Octoberr, 1910, HS MS; Leon Stein, *The Triangle Fire* (Philadelphia, 1962), p. 207. Stimson gave up his position as head of the Citizen's Committee when he was named Secretary of War soon after the committee's work had begun.

35. Liva Baker, *Felix Frankfurter* (New York, 1969), pp. 13–32.

36. Frankfurter, *Diaries*, pp. 104–23; Frankfurter to Learned Hand, September 23, 1912, FF MS.

37. Frankfurter, "The Zeitgeist and the Judiciary," originally an address to twenty-fifth anniversary dinner of the *Harvard Law Review*, 1912, reprinted in *Law and Politics: Occasional Papers of Felix Frankfurter, 1913–1938*, ed. by Archibald MacLeish and E. F. Prichard, Jr. (Gloucester, 1971 ed.), pp. 4–6 See also Baker, *Frankfurter*, pp. 50–58.

38. Thomas E. Vadney, *The Wayward Liberal: A Political Biography of Donald Richberg* (Lexington, 1970), pp. 10–18; and Richberg, *My Hero: The Indiscreet Memoirs of an Eventful but Unheroic Life* (New York, 1954), pp. 26–27. Harold Ickes, Richberg's one-time law partner, describes the political struggles in Chicago over municipal reform in some detail in *The Autobiography of a Curmudgeon* (Chicago, 1969 ed.), pp. 101–07.

39. Richberg, "Why Should Not Corporations Be Imprisoned," reprint from Chicago *Daily Tribune*, March 26, 1906, in DR MS/LC; Richberg, "The Imprisonment of Criminal Corporations," copy of statement given to U.S. Senate Interstate Commerce Committee considering possible changes in the antitrust laws, 62d Cong., 2d sess., December, 1911, in DR MS/LC. See also Richberg, *Hero*, pp. 33–35.

40. The plot of the novel deals with a man who becomes innocently involved in the shady operations of a firm for which he is an employee. He ultimately goes to prison, taking the punishment which rightfully should have been suffered by those higher up in the organization. After he gets out of prison, this man experiences the same cycle of events, only this time he escapes prison because a jury is convinced that business morality is essentially a social problem and that putting one man, a flunkey at that, in prison is no solution. Richberg, *The Shadow Men* (Chicago, 1911).

41. Chambers, *Tyranny of Change*, p. 108.

42. Baruch, *My Story*, p. 233.

43. Baruch, *My Story*, p. 233; Baruch, *Public Years*, p. 5.

44. Baruch, *Public Years*, p. 8; Margaret L. Coit, *Mr. Baruch* (Boston, 1957), pp. 43–44, 50.

45. Baruch, *My Story*, pp. 177–78.

46. Baruch, *My Story*, p. 192.

47. Baruch, *My Story*, p. 233. See also Carter Field, *Bernard Baruch: Park Bench Statesman* (New York, 1944), pp. 70–73.

48. Baruch, *My Story,* pp. 225–26, 235; Field, *Baruch,* pp. 71–75.

49. Coit, *Baruch,* p. 140. See also Field, *Baruch,* pp. 26, 95; and Baruch *Public Years,* pp. 8–10.

50. Morison, *Turmoil and Tradition,* pp. 16–18, 33–49.

51. Stimson, *Active Service,* p. 17.

52. Richberg, *Hero,* p. 209; Richberg, "Why Not Try Education," (1914?), DR MS/LC.

53. Richberg to William Harper, October 20, 1904, DR MS/LC; S. J. Woolf, "Richberg: The President's No. 1 Man," *Literary Digest* 118 (December 1, 1934): 5.

54. Richberg, *Shadow Men,* p. 309; Richberg to Joseph Knapp, January 23, 1914, DR MS/LC.

55. Frankfurter, *Felix Frankfurter Reminisces* (recorded in talks with Dr. Harlan B. Phillips) (New York, 1960), p. 34.

56. Frankfurter to Stimson, April 8, 1914, FF MS.

57. Frankfurter *Reminisces,* p. 47.

58. Daniels, "The Three Repositories of Power," July 21, 1887, JD MS; Daniels to Mary Cleaves Daniels, March 22, 1886.

59. Hofstadter, *Age of Reform,* pp. 135–37; Wiebe, *Search for Order,* pp. 111–32, 165–66. Mowry also sees progressivism as primarily a movement of the old middle class. See *Era of Theodore Roosevelt,* pp. 85–88.

60. Hofstadter actually cites Stimson as a prime example of a progressive. *Age of Reform,* pp. 162–63. George M. Frederickson observes that "Hofstadter's theory of the "status revolution' . . . needs modification [because] the men of the 'mugwump' type, whom Hofstadter describes as losing status to the new businessmen, were themselves often men of great power in the business community. It would seem in fact that the 'mugwumps' acted as spokesmen for a large segment of that community, articulating the prevailing attitude of businessmen toward government, education, philanthropy, etc." In the specific case of Oliver Wendell Holmes, Frederickson argues that the famed jurist may have suffered from "the 'status revolution' described by Richard Hofstadter, but more likely he was concerned with the fact that so many of his fellow Brahmins had retained their status at the price of joining the Gilded Age as successful businessmen, thereby denying themselves the possibility of being a noncommercial aristocracy." *The Inner Civil War* (New York, 1968 ed.), pp. 221, 266.

Josephus Daniels is described by one historian as having "many of the traits" of Hofstadter's "typical progressive," since he was "young, middle-class, of old stock," and fought "the good fight both for clean government and against the trusts." However, Daniels does not easily fit into either Hofstadter or Wiebe's description of a typical progressive. Neither was his family financially secure or well established, nor did he identify with the newly rising class of professionals and bureaucrats. Daniels' commitment to the progressive cause reflected his desire to win recognition for the rights not of the comfortable old middle class, nor of an ascending new middle class, but rather of the lower middle class yeomen, small entrepreneurs, and workers who had never enjoyed power or prestige in America. See Melvin I. Urofsky, "Josephus Daniels and the Armor Trust," *North Carolina Historical Review* 45 (July 1968): 239.

Ironically, Bernard Baruch suffered indirectly as a result of the decline in power experienced by the nation's old elite, since this "Protestant establishment" reacted to its decline by creating a number of new social barriers, including anti-semitism, by which to exclude the nouveau riche from social, if not economic, prominence. See E. Digby Baltzell, *The Protestant Establishment: Aristocracy & Caste in America* (New York, 1966 ed.).

61. Frankfurter to Stimson, June 26, 1913, FF MS; Frankfurter, *Reminisces,* p. 9.

62. H. N. Hirsch describes Frankfurter's relationship with Stimson as "probably his

most significant . . . at this time in his life." Frankfurter, according to Hirsch, adopted Stimson as his "mentor" and in the process internalized the older man's essential "value system." H. N. Hirsch, *The Enigma of Felix Frankfurter* (New York, 1981), p. 27.

63. John D. Buenker, *Urban Liberalism and Progressive Reform* (New York, 1973), p. 221; Thelen, *New Citizenship.* For a similar view of progressivism as composed of "shifting coalitions of self-interested groups uniting temporarily over different issues and behind different political leaders," see Chambers, *Tyranny of Change,* p. 110.

64. As previously noted, Baruch admired Roosevelt and voted for him in 1904. Baruch, *Public Years,* p. 5.

65. Daniels, *The Wilson Era: Years of Peace, 1910–1917* (Chapel Hill, 1944), pp. 3–20, 31–35, 69; Editorials, Raleigh *News & Observer,* July 6, April 24, and May 30, 1912.

66. Richberg, *Hero,* p. 44; Vadney, *Wayward Liberal,* pp. 17–21.

67. Baker, *Frankfurter,* p. 33; Frankfurter to Hand, September 23, 1912, FF MS.

68. Stimson, ironically, had entered the Cabinet with the approval of Roosevelt in a move which seemed intended to quiet rumors of a final split between Taft and TR. Stimson, *Active Service,* pp. 48–55; Morison, *Turmoil and Tradition,* pp. 111–17.

69. Stimson to Theodore Roosevelt, September 2, 1910, cited in Stimson, *Active Service,* p. 22.

70. Frankfurter to Stimson, September 9, 1911, FF MS. Lewis Gould insightfully argues that an attack on political partisanship was an essential part of the progressive movement's support for expanded government regulation. He attributes this decline in partisanship both to a growing disenchantment with the "anarchronistic and constricting" political practices of the Gilded Age and to the ending of the two party equilibrium which characterized American politics from 1876 to 1896. "As the two parties became less competitive across the nation, the emphasis shifted to intraparty strife in the selection of candidates. The rise of the direct primary probably owed as much to the enhanced significance of party nominations in determining who held office as to a desire to involve citizens generally in the nominating process. Voter turnout declined dramatically from Gilded Age highs as the electorate withdrew its interest from partisan affairs. . . . In a period usually assumed to have fostered the expansion of popular participation in political life, the exact opposite seems to have occurred." Lewis L. Gould, *Reform and Regulation: American Politics, 1900–1916* (New York, 1978), pp. v, 7.

71. Baruch states in his autobiography: "Although Woodrow Wilson's election pleased me greatly, it did not alter my life in any way. I played no part, contrary to what some have written, in the introduction of those measures which Wilson called the New Freedom, although I fully supported the administration in what it sought to achieve." *Public Years,* p. 10.

72. Daniels, *Years of Peace,* p. 273. For a detailed, though not very analytical, review of Daniels' first three years as head of the Navy Department, see Innis L. Jenkins, "Josephus Daniels and the Navy, 1913–1916: A Study in Military Administration," (Unpublished doctoral dissertation, University of Maryland, 1960). See also Daniels, *Years of Peace,* pp. 253–79; Morrison, *Josephus Daniels,* pp. 50–77.

73. On Daniels' dealings with trusts, see Urofsky, "Daniels and the Armor Trust." Urofsky criticizes Daniels' seemingly single-minded concern for creating conditions of competition in the bidding on armor-plate contracts. He argues that Daniels failed to take into consideration the fact that since the government was the only customer for armor-plate, Navy purchases from only the single lowest bidder would have, in effect, driven the other two steel companies out of armor-plate production. Then, if an emergency arose, it would have been very difficult rapidly to expand industry-wide production of needed armor-plate. See also Daniels, *Years of Peace,* pp. 351–56.

74. Daniels fought with the Rockefeller interests over oil and with the Du Ponts over smokeless powder while he was in office. A smokeless powder plant was built by the government, and an armor-plate factory was approved by Congress, but never completed. Daniels, Testimony, in U.S. Congress, House, Committee on Naval Affairs, *Hearings on Estimates Submitted by the Secretary of the Navy*, 64th Cong., 1st sess., April 3, 1916; Daniels, *Years of Peace*, pp. 344, 355–63; Morrison, *Josephus Daniels*, pp. 55–56.

75. Daniels, House testimony, April 3, 1916; Daniels, Testimony, in U.S. Congress, Senate, Committee on Public Lands, *Hearings on Leasing of Oil Lands*, 64th Cong., 1st sess., February 6, 1916.

76. Morison, *Turmoil and Tradition*, pp. 173–79. See also Philip C. Jessup, *Elihu Root*, Vol. II: 1905–1937 (New York, 1938), pp. 289–308, for a discussion of the convention and Stimson's relation to Root.

77. Stimson, "Responsible State Government: A Republican Constitution Program," *Independent* 79 (July 6, 1914): 15.

78. Stimson, "Responsible State Government," p. 14.

79. Stimson, *Active Service*, p. 79; Stimson to Walter Arndt, October 15, 1914, HS MS; Stimson, "The Secret Center of Our Government: A Remedy for Inefficient Legislation," *Harper's Weekly* 57 (June 21, 1913): 15–22.

Although Stimson and Root succeeded in getting the convention to adopt most of the reforms they favored, the proposed constitutional revisions, which were offered to the electorate as a single package, were turned down in the state election. See Finla G. Crawford, "Constitutional Developments, 1867–1915," in *History of the State of New York: Modern Party Battles*, ed. by Alexander C. Flick (New York, 1935), pp. 199–239.

80. Baker, *Frankfurter*, pp. 34, 41–45; Stimson to Frankfurter, June 28, 1913, FF MS. Frankfurter also consulted with Theodore Roosevelt, Herbert Croly, Oliver Wendell Holmes, and Louis Brandeis. Only Brandeis advised him to accept the offer from Harvard.

81. Frankfurter, *Reminisces*, pp. 80–84.

82. When Brandeis went onto the Supreme Court, Frankfurter took his place as counsel fot the National Consumers' League and argued the Bunting v. Oregon and Stettler v. O'Hara cases before the Supreme Court. These cases involved a state ten-hour law for men and a minimum-wage law, both of which were upheld by the court. Frankfurter, *Reminisces*, pp. 96–104; Baker, *Frankfurter*, pp. 47–57.

83. Richberg, *Hero*, pp. 50–59; Vadney, *Wayward Liberal*, pp. 22–26.

84. Vadney, *Wayward Liberal*, p. 22; Richberg, "Legislative Reference Bureaus for Political Parties," *Proceedings of the American Political Science Association at its Tenth Annual Meeting, Supplement to the American Political Science Review* 8 (February 1914): 222–23.

85. Arthur S. Link, *Wilson: The Road to the White House* (Princeton, 1974), p. 489; Link, *Wilson: The New Freedom* (Princeton, 1956), p. 11.

86. Baker, *Frankfurter*, pp. 17, 35; Samuel Haber, *Efficiency and Uplift: Scientific Management in the Progressive Era, 1890–1920* (Chicago, 1964), pp. 51–55. The Eastern Rate case involved an attempt to get the ICC to refuse to allow a railroad rate increase on the grounds that the elimination of waste would by itself raise profits significantly.

87. Frankfurter to Hand, September 23, 1912; Frankfurter, "Mr. Justice Brandeis and the Constitution," in *Mr. Justice Brandeis*, ed. by Frankfurter (New Haven, 1932); Daniels, *Years of Peace*, p. 542.

88. Haber, *Efficiency and Uplift*, pp. 75–82.

89. Gould, *Reform and Regulation*, p. 155; Link, *New Freedom*, p. 238.

90. Carosso, *Investment Banking*, pp. 110–92; Gabriel Kolko, *The Triumph of Con-*

*servatism: A Reinterpretation of American History, 1900–1916* (Chicago, 1967 ed.), pp. 139–58, 217–54.

91. Baruch, *Public Years*, p. 10; Carosso, *Investment Banking*, p. 190; Lawrence E. Clark, *Central Banking Under the Federal Reserve System* (New York, 1935), pp. 19–26, 346–70; Daniels, *Years of Peace*, p. 230.

92. Link, *New Freedom*, p. 95. Brandeis' biographer agrees that Brandeis' support for the FTC was wholly consistent with his previous position on the trust issue, though he notes that Wilson did, in fact, change his stand on the question. Alpheus Thomas Mason, *Brandeis: A Free Man's Life* (New York, 1946), pp. 399–404.

93. Daniels, *Years of Peace*, p. 236; Daniels, "According to Plan: A Review of Woodrow Wilson's First Year in the White House," *Harper's Weekly* 58 (March 7, 1914): 8; Stimson, Diary, March, 1913, HS MS; Stimson, Address to the New York Republican Club, December 15, 1911.

94. Richberg, *Hero*, pp. 53–56; Richberg, "Five Brothers to Trust Triplets: A Vital Issue Between Democrats and Progressives," *The Outlook* 106 (March 21, 1914): 638–39.

95. Richberg, "Five Brothers," pp. 638–39; Richberg, *Hero*, p. 80. It should be recalled that Josephus Daniels had earlier criticized TR for allowing the regulatory power established by the Hepburn Act to be weakened by being made subject to court review.

96. Baruch, *Public Years*, pp. 10–11.

97. On the effects of the antitrust laws, see Blair, *Economic Concentration*, pp. 560–65; Chandler, *Visible Hand*, pp. 567–68; Merle Fainsod and Lincoln Gordon, *Government and the American Economy* (New York, 1948 ed.), pp. 452–73; Donald J. Dewey, "The New Learning: One Man's View," in Goldschmid, *Industrial Concentration*, pp. 1–14.

98. On the impact of the FTC, see Susan Wagner, *The Federal Trade Commission* (New York, 1971); Kolko, *Triumph of Conservatism*, pp. 270–78; Robert H. Wiebe, *Businessmen and Reform: A Study of the Progressive Movement* (Chicago, 1968 ed.), pp. 147–48; Chambers, *Tyranny of Change*, pp. 242–44.

While there is little disagreement among historians as to the pro-business tendencies of the FTC in its early years of existence, there is a heated debate concerning the role of the ICC in the Progressive era. Gabriel Kolko argues that the ICC was an instrument of "political capitalism" which the railroads themselves used in an attempt both to escape more radical state regulation and to rationalize what was an uncomfortably competitive industry. Albro Martin, in contrast, claims that the ICC's shortsightedness and anti-railroad bias caused it to block management requested rate hikes which were required as a means of financing needed expansion. Martin, in fact, attributes the long-term distintegration of the nation's railroad service to the constricting impact of the ICC's inept handling of the rate issue before World War I. Undoubtedly, for at least a brief period in the Progressive era, the ICC tried to act as an overseer, rather than as an advocate, of the railroad industry. However, it never saw its role as initiating any comprehensive planning in behalf of a consciously defined public interest, nor did it ever see its role as in any way defending the interests of the workers in the industry it was regulating. Ultimately, its purpose became one of upholding the status quo in the industry. See Gabriel Kolko, *Railroads and Regulation, 1877–1916* (New York, 1970 ed.); Albro Martin, *Enterprise Denied: Origins of the Decline of American Railroads, 1897–1917* (New York, 1971); Ari and Olive Hoogenboom, *A History of the ICC: From Panacea to Palliative* (New York, 1976); and David M. Chalmers, *Neither Socialism nor Monopoly: Theodore Roosevelt and the Decision to Regulate the Railroads* (Philadelphia, 1976).

99. Jeffrey G. Williamson and Peter H. Lindert, *American Inequality: A Macroeco-*

*nomic History* (New York, 1980), pp. 131–32, 316, 50. Williamson and Lindert cite three possible peaks for American inequality: 1860, 1914, or 1929.

100. Williamson, *American Inequality,* p. 132; Oscar Ornati, *Poverty Amid Affluence* (New York, 1966), p. 147; U.S. Department of Commerce, Bureau of the Census, *Historical Statistics of the United States: Colonial Times to 1957* (Washington, 1960), p. 91. The absolute standard cited in Williamson was derived from Bureau of Labor Statistics calculations for 1908. This standard of poverty was then revised only to reflect changes in prices for the years both before and after 1908.

101. David P. Thelen, *Robert M. La Follette and the Insurgent Spirit* (Boston, 1976). See also Chambers, *Tyranny of Change,* pp. 136–39; and Glenn C. Altschuler, *Race, Ethnicity, and Class in American Social Thought, 1865–1919* (Arlington Heights, 1982), pp. 111–13.

102. Kolko, *Triumph of Conservatism,* pp. 2–5.

103. Wiebe, *Businessmen and Reform,* p. 217. See also James Weinstein, *The Corporate Ideal in the Liberal State, 1900–1918* (Boston, 1969 ed.). Weinstein points out many of the important developments which took place in liberal ideology during the Progressive era, but I believe that he exaggerates the statist element in progressive thought.

## V. The Impact of War 1914–1920

1. Murray N. Rothbard, "War Collectivism in World War I," in *A New History of Leviathan,* ed. by Ronald Radosh and Murray N. Rothbard (New York, 1972), p. 66.

2. Frankfurter, *Felix Frankfurter Reminisces* (recorded in talks with Dr. Harlan B. Phillips) (New York, 1960), p. 107; Richberg, *My Hero: The Indiscreet Memoirs of an Eventful but Unheroic Life* (New York, 1954), p. 79.

3. Stimson's remark is from a letter to Frankfurter, May 16, 1917, in FF MS, in which Stimson responded negatively to a suggestion from his younger friend that he accept a position in the Food Administration under Herbert Hoover.

4. While this study is confined to an examination of questions relating to domestic policy, at least a few words should be said about the attitudes of these men toward the war in Europe and America's relation to it. During the period of American neutrality, all five men were more sympathetic to England and France than to Germany and Austria-Hungary, because they identified with what Frankfurter described as the English and French "traditions of freedom." Most of them believed that Germany was the military aggressor in the war. All five men, however, agreed that the United States should do what it could to stay out of the fighting. This was a position which each of them maintained, at least publicly, until early 1917, when Germany resumed unrestricted submarine warfare against American shipping. Among the five, Stimson was by far the most forceful advocate of military preparedness, though Baruch, Richberg, and Frankfurter were also sympathetic to the need for increased military readiness. When Wilson finally called for a declaration of war in April, 1917, he had the support of all five of the men discussed here. Frankfurter to Marion Denman, April 1, 1917, FF MS; Frankfurter, *Reminisces,* pp. 113–14; Stimson to Elihu Root, May 9, 1916, HS MS; Stimson and McGeorge Bundy, *On Active Service in Peace and War* (New York, 1948), pp. 83–89; Joseph L. Morrison, *Josephus Daniels: The Small-d Democrat* (Chapel Hill, 1966), pp. 67–82; Richberg, *Hero,* pp. 78–80, 92; Baruch, *Baruch: The Public Years* (New York, 1960), pp. 19, 33; Charles Forcey, *The Crossroads of Liberalism: Croly, Weyl, Lippmann and the Progressive Era, 1900–1925* (New York, 1967 ed.), p. 260.

As Secretary of the Navy, Daniels actually bore the brunt of much of the criticism directed at the Wilson administration by preparedness advocates in the early part of the war. After the Summer of 1915, however, when Wilson himself changed his position on the subject, Daniels proceeded to direct a massive naval expansion program to make the U.S. Navy "second to none." Stimson and Baruch were among those who were critical of Daniels, Baruch once describing Daniels as "a good, honest, simple-minded jackass who is trying to do well, but who is not able to circumvent the people surrounding him who are using him for their personal ends." Stimson later called Daniels one of the two "most conspicuously unfit members" of the Cabinet. Once Baruch began to work directly with Daniels, his opinion of the Navy Secretary improved significantly, and the two men developed a lasting friendship. Copy of E.M. House diary entry, May 14, 1916, BB MS; Stimson, Diary, March 5, 1919, HS MS; Jordan A. Schwarz, *The Speculator: Bernard M. Baruch in Washington, 1917–1965* (Chapel Hill, 1981), pp. 45, 70. For a review of the preparedness controversy, see Arthur S. Link, *Woodrow Wilson and the Progressive Era, 1910–1917* (New York, 1963 ed.), pp. 174–96.

5. Ellis W. Hawley observes: "If the progressive era laid the basis for modern America, the war experience of 1917 and 1918 catalyzed the process of organizational change and set the pattern for future economic and social management." *The Great War and the Search for a Modern Order: A History of the American People and Their Institutions, 1917–1933* (New York, 1979), p. 20.

6. Daniels, *The Wilson Era: Years of Peace, 1910–1917* (Chapel Hill, 1944), pp. 490–93; Grosvenor B. Clarkson, *Industrial America in the World War* (Boston, 1923), pp. 11–22; Paul A.C. Koistinen, "The Industrial-Military Complex in Historical Perspective: World War I," *Business History Review* 41 (Winter 1967): 378–403; and David F. Noble, *America by Design: Science, Technology, and the Rise of Corporate Capitalism* (New York, 1977), pp. 148–50. Noble's book is particularly insightful on the capitalist framework within which modern-day engineers operate.

7. See the previous chapter for Daniels' encounters with Navy suppliers. Melvin I. Urofsky, *Big Steel and the Wilson Administration* (Columbus, 1969), pp. 108, 222–23; Melvin I. Urofsky, "Josephus Daniels and the Armor Trust," *North Carolina Historical Review* 45 (July 1968): 237–63; Daniels, Testimony, in U.S. Congress, House, Committee on Naval Affairs, *Hearings on Estimates Submitted by the Secretary of the Navy*, 64th. Cong., 1st sess., March 31 and April 3, 1916.

8. Daniels to William McAdoo, June 15, 1917, cited in Urofsky, *Big Steel*, p. 161. See also Daniels to Baruch, June 1, 1917, JD MS.

9. Daniels, *The Cabinet Diaries of Josephus Daniels, 1913–1921*, ed. by E. David Cronon (Lincoln, 1963), p. 114 (March 15, 1917).

10. Daniels, *Cabinet Diaries*, pp. 156, 167 (May 23, June 21, 1917); Urofsky, *Big Steel*, pp. 176–77, 239–40; Schwarz, *Speculator*, pp. 70–77.

11. Urofsky, *Big Steel*, pp. 176–77, 239–40. See also Robert D. Cuff and Melvin I. Urofsky, "The Steel Industry and Price-Fixing During World War I," *Business History Review* 45 (Autumn 1970): 291–306.

12. Daniels to Baruch, September 24, 1918, JD MS; Daniels, *Cabinet Diaries*, pp. 338–39 (October 1 and October 9, 1918).

13. Baruch, *Public Years*, pp. 22–25; Baruch to E.M. House, October 26, 1915, BB MS; Robert D. Cuff, *The War Industries Board: Business-Government Relations During World War I* (Baltimore, 1973), p. 32. Elsewhere, Cuff notes that Baruch was "acutely sensitive to the way in which defense planning could be used to win greater sympathy for the Administration among business groups." He cites a letter from Baruch to Wilson, dated August 17, 1916, in which Baruch comments: "When our tariff board and mobilization committee are appointed, the business men will see more clearly." Robert D. Cuff, "Woodrow Wilson and Business-Government Relations During World War I," *Review of Politics* 31 (July 1969): 387. See also Noble, *America by Design*, pp. 148–50.

Upon announcing the appointment of the Council of National Defense and its seven-man Advisory Committee, Wilson stated: "The organization of the Council likewise opens up a new and direct channel of communication and cooperation between business and scientific men and all departments of the Government, and it is hoped that it will, in addition, become a rallying point for civic bodies working for the national defense. . . . The personnel of the Council's advisory members, appointed without regard to party, marks the entrance of the non-partisan engineer and professional man into American governmental affairs on a wider scale than ever before. It is responsive to the increased demand for and need of business organization in public matters and for the presence there of the best specialists in their respective fields. In the present instance, the time of some of the members of the Advisory Board could not be purchased. They serve the Government without remuneration, efficiency being their sole object and Americanism their only motive." The members of the seven-man Advisory Commission, in addition to Baruch, were: Daniel Willard, President of the Baltimore & Ohio Railroad; Howard Coffin, Vice-President of the Hudson Motor Co.; Julius Rosenwald, President of Sears, Roebuck & Co.; Dr. Hollis Godfrey, President of the Drexel Institute; Samuel Gompers, President of the American Federation of Labor; and Dr. Franklin Martin, Secretary-General of the American College of Surgeons. Grosvenor Clarkson was the Secretary of the commission. Clarkson, *Industrial America*, pp. 21–33.

14. Baruch, *American Inudstry in the War: A Report of the War Industries Board* (*March, 1921*), ed. by Richard H. Hippelheuser (New York, 1941), p. 74; Baruch, *Public Years*, pp. 53–54.

15. Baruch himself notes in his final WIB report that by late September, 1917, the steel industry had come to support government regulation as a necessary stabilizing force. Baruch, *American Industry*, pp. 20, 120–21. See also Cuff, *War Industries Board*, p. 60; Clarkson, *Industrial America*, pp. 299–304; and Schwarz, *Speculator*, pp. 70–77.

16. Baruch, *American Industry*, p. 20.

17. Schwarz, *Speculator*, p. 48; Robert D. Cuff, "Bernard Baruch: Symbol and Myth in Industrial Mobilization," *Business History Review* 43 (Summer 1969): 115–33. Herbert Hoover, in his work on the Food Administration, was at the same time developing a similar approach to the problem of mobilizing the nation for war. For a description and analysis of Hoover's voluntaristic efforts, see Gary Dean Best, *The Politics of American Individualism: Herbert Hoover in Transition, 1918–1921* (Westport, 1975), pp. 8–11; Joan Hoff Wilson, *Herbert Hoover: Forgotten Progressive* (Boston, 1975), pp. 54–62; and Robert D. Cuff, "Herbert Hoover, the Ideology of Voluntarism and War Organization during the Great War," *Journal of American History* 64 (September 1977): 358–72.

18. Baruch, *American Industry*, p. 20. See also Cuff, *War Industries Board*, pp. 104–09.

19. Cuff, *War Industries Board*, pp. 154–56.

20. Clarkson, *Industrial America*, p. 303; Cuff, *War Industries Board*, p. 147. Daniels actively supported Baruch's appointment to head the WIB (or a comparable agency) as early as April, 1917. Daniels, *Cabinet Diaries*, p. 131 (April 9, 1917); Daniels, *The Wilson Era: Years of War and After, 1917–1923* (Chapel Hill, 1946), p. 217.

21. Baruch, "Priorities—The Synchronizing Force," in Baruch, *American Industry*, pp. 465–77; Clarkson, *Industrial America*, pp. 20, 140–41, 150–59, 480–81; Cuff, *War Industries Board*, pp. 193–204.

22. At no time did WIB personnel exceed 1500 in number. During the course of the war, the WIB and the Council of National Defense, together, were responsible for only $771,200 worth of expenditures, $200,000 going to the construction of an office building. Clarkson, *Industrial America*, pp. 180, 254n.

23. Baruch to Daniels, June 14, 1917, BB MS. See also Baruch to Woodrow Wilson, June 4, 1917, BB MS.

24. Clarkson, *Industrial America*, pp. 160–80; Baruch, *American Industry*, p. 122.

25. Frankfurter had formerly worked with Baker when the latter was President of the National Consumers' League while Frankfurter acted as the League's counsel. When labor conditions began to deteriorate in the Massachusetts textile industry under the impact of heavy war orders, Frankfurter urged Baker to set up a committee to look into the situation. Baker then asked Frankfurter to take on the job. Michael E. Parrish, *Felix Frankfurter and His Times: The Reform Years* (New York, 1982), pp. 84–85; Baker, *Frankfurter*, pp. 60–83.

26. Baker, *Frankfurter*, pp. 52–58; Frankfurter, "Hours of Labor and Realism in Constitutional Law," originally in *Harvard Law Review* 29 (1916), reprinted in *Felix Frankfurter on the Supreme Court: Extrajudicial Essays on the Court and the Constitution*, ed. by Phillip B. Kurland (Cambridge, 1970), pp. 8–21; Frankfurter, "Robert Grosvenor Valentine, '96," *Harvard Alumni Bulletin* (December 14, 1916); Frankfurter, "The Manager, the Workman, and the Social Scientist," *Bulletin of the Taylor Society* 3 (December 1917).

27. Among the other cases investigated by Frankfurter was the trial and conviction of Thomas Mooney for the San Francisco Preparedness Day bombing. For background on the President's Mediation Commission, see John Lombardi, *Labor's Voice in the Cabinet: A History of the Department of Labor From Its Origins to 1921* (New York, 1942), pp. 210–27. See also Parrish, *Frankfurter*, pp. 81–101; Baker, *Frankfurter*, pp. 71–74; Frankfurter, *Reminisces*, pp. 115–44.

28. Frankfurter to Marion Denman, October 9 and October 17, 1917, FF MS; Frankfurter to Louis Brandeis, October 20, 1917, FF MS.

29. Lombardi, *Labor's Voice*, p. 216; Parrish, *Frankfurter*, pp. 87–97.

30. The recommendations of the Mediation Commission are cited in Baruch, *American Industry*, pp. 341–43.

31. Lombardi, *Labor's Voice*, pp. 266–67. See also Clarkson, *Industrial America*, pp. 286–87.

32. For Baruch's favorable evaluation of Frankfurter's work on the War Labor Policies Board, and his recommendation that Frankfurter be placed on the Priorities Board, see Baruch to Woodrow Wilson, August 1, 1918, BB MS. See also Clarkson, *Industrial America*, pp. 289–92.

33. Frankfurter to V.A. Olander, September 9, 1918, cited in Baker, *Frankfurter*, p. 81.

34. Urofsky, *Big Steel*, pp. 275–78; Frankfurter, *Reminisces*, p. 141. For Frankfurter's activities as head of the WLPB, see also Parrish, *Frankfurter*, pp. 102–17, 35.

35. Bulletin of the War Labor Policies Board, July 25, 1918, cited in Baruch, *American Industry*, pp. 92–93. See also Baker, *Frankfurter*, p. 82; Lombardi, *Labor's Voice*, pp. 270–71.

36. Frankfurter, *Reminisces*, pp. 122–23.

37. Robert D. Cuff, "The Cooperative Impulse and War: The Origins of the Council of National Defense and Advisory Commission," in *Building the Organizational Society: Essays on Associational Activities in Modern America*, ed. by Jerry Israel (New York, 1972), p. 246.

38. For Daniels' support for government control and operation of transportation and communication facilities during the war, see Daniels, *Cabinet Diaries*, pp. 227, 243, 255, 316 (October 27, November 27, December 24, 1917; July 2, 1918). For Daniels' occasional threats to commandeer uncooperative industries, see Daniels *Cabinet Diaries*, pp. 308, 325, (May 29 and July 31, 1918).

39. Daniels, Address to the American Bankers' Association, Chicago, September 27, 1918, in Daniels, *The Navy and the Nation* (New York, 1919), pp. 250, 253.

40. Stimson, "The Basis for National Military Training," *Scribner's Magazine* 61 (April 1917): 408–12; Stimson, Address to the New York State Bar Association, January 15, 1916, HS MS. See also Stimson, "Why I Shall Vote for Mr. Hughes," *New Republic* 8 (October 28, 1916): 317–19; and Stimson to C.E. Hughes, October 26, 1916, HS MS.

41. Daniels, Address to the Cotton Manufacturers' Association, New York, May 2, 1918, in Daniels, *The Navy and Nation: War-Time Addresses by Josephus Daniels* (New York, 1919), p. 160.

Charles Forcey argues that for such leading progressive thinkers as Herbert Croly, Walter Lippmann, and Walter Weyl, the development of a nationalistic spirit represented the only viable alternative to the dangers of a politics based on class consciousness. Stimson, in particular, is certainly a good example of this type of nationalist. Christopher Lasch, moreover, argues that Richberg was also an exponent of the Herbert Croly conception of an all-encompassing "national interest." While an almost mystical faith in nationalism was an element in liberal thinking during the war, the men discussed here, as we shall see in subsequent chapters, ultimately came to rely on the development of pluralistic interest groups, rather than on an all-encompassing spirit of nationalism, as the most effective way of warding off the possible development of dangerous class conflict. Forcey, *Crossroads of Liberalism;* Lasch, "Donald Richberg and the Idea of a National Interest," (Unpublished M.A. thesis, Columbia University, 1955), especially pp. 118–24.

42. Cuff, *War Industries Board,* p. 42; George Soule, *Prosperity Decade: From War to Depression, 1917–1929* (New York, 1968 ed.), pp. 7–8.

43. Noble, *America by Design,* pp. 323–24.

44. Clarkson, *Industrial America,* pp. 92, 276–77; Lombardi, *Labor's Voice,* pp. 280–87; Daniels, *Years of Peace,* pp. 237–39.

45. Paul A. Baran and Paul M. Sweezy, *Monopoly Capital: An Essay on the American Economic and Social Order* (New York, 1968 ed.), pp. 228–34; Douglas F. Dowd, *The Twisted Dream: Capitalist Development in the United States Since 1776* (Cambridge, 1974), pp. 87–89.

46. Soule, *Prosperity Decade,* pp. 7–8; Harold Underwood Faulkner, *American Economic History* (New York, 1949 ed.), pp. 591–95.

47. A developing shortage of skilled labor may have contributed to the decline in overall production, but, as the nation's experience in the Second World War demonstrated, production could have increased even with the shifting of parts of the work force into the military. Soule, *Prosperity Decade,* pp. 56–58; Clarkson, *Industrial America,* pp. 315–31; Urofsky, *Big Steel,* pp. 186–90.

48. Schwarz, *Speculator,* p. 76; Soule, *Prosperity Decade,* pp. 56–57.

49. Schwarz, *Speculator,* p. 76; Soule, *Prosperity Decade,* pp. 56–57; Clarkson, *Industrial America,* p. 160. See also Baruch, *Public Years,* p. 63.

50. Soule, *Prosperity Decade,* pp. 71–77, 187–88; Faulkner, *American Economic History,* pp. 602–04.

51. Jeffrey G. Williamson and Peter H. Lindert, *American Inequality: A Macroeconomic History* (New York, 1980), pp. 77, 81, 109–12, 316; Soule, *Prosperity Decade,* pp. 74–76. See also Jeffrey G. Williamson, "American Prices and Urban Inequality since 1820," *Journal of Economic History* 36 (June 1976): 303–333.

52. Soule, *Prosperity Decade,* pp. 49, 20, 78–80; Urofsky, *Big Steel,* p. 233.

53. Urofsky, *Big Steel,* pp. 229–34; Soule, *Prosperity Decade,* pp. 78–80. See also Thomas C. Cochran and William Miller, *The Age of Enterprise: A Social History of Industrial America* (New York, 1961 ed.), pp. 302–03.

54. Williamson, *American Inequality*, p. 77. The post-war economic developments cited in this and in the following paragraph will be explored in detail in the chapters to follow.

55. Robert F. Himmelberg, "The War Industries Board and the Antitrust Question in November 1918," *Journal of American History* 52 (June 1965): 59–74; Baruch to Woodrow Wilson, November 27, 1918, BB MS; Cuff, *War Industries Board*, pp. 241–50; Urofsky, *Big Steel*, pp. 296–306; Schwarz, *Speculator*, pp. 98–108.

56. Baruch, *Public Years*, p. 74; Cuff, *War Industries Board*, pp. 262–64. Baruch's desire to see his own reputation enhanced is indicated by the fact that he was later instrumental in financing Clarkson's laudatory history of the WIB. Baruch also later told Daniels that he thought not "enough attention" was being "paid to & not enough credit given to" the WIB. Daniels, *Cabinet Diaries*, p. 564 (November 9, 1920).

57. Baruch, *American Industry*, p. 105.

58. Baruch, *American Industry*, pp. 105–06. One of Baruch's WIB associates, George Peek, was instrumental in the creation of an Industrial Conference Board within the Department of Commerce in 1919. This board was intended to carry on some of the coordinating functions of the WIB, but its existence was short-lived. Robert F. Himmelberg, "Business Antitrust Policy and the Industrial Board of the Department of Commerce, 1919," *Business History Review* 42 (Spring 1968): 1–23.

59. Lombardi, *Labor's Voice*, pp. 302–03; Cuff, *War Industries Board*, pp. 242–44; Frankfurter, "The Conservation of the New Federal Standards," *Survey* 41 (December 7, 1918): 292.

60. Frankfurter, "Industrial Relations: Some Noteworthy Recent Developments," *Bulletin of the Taylor Society* 4 (December 1919): 12–16; "War in the Clothing Industry," *New Republic* 25 (December 15, 1920): 59–61, unsigned article by Frankfurter, copy in FF MS.

61. Daniels, *Our Navy at War* (New York, 1922), pp. 350–51.

62. Daniels, Labor Day address, Indianapolis, September 2, 1918, in Daniels, *Navy and Nation*, pp. 225–28. See also Daniels, *Years of War*, p. 106.

63. Daniels, Address at the University of California, Berkeley, September 3, 1919, JD MS.

64. Soule, *Prosperity Decade*, pp. 81–91, 190–96; U.S. Department of Commerce, Bureau of the Census, *Historical Statistics of the United States: Colonial Times to 1957* (Washington, 1960), pp. 126, 70; Williamson, *American Inequality*, p. 320. Burl Noggle argues that Wilson's "indifference or opposition to reconstruction planning" directly "contributed to [labor's] decline" after 1918. *Into the Twenties: The United States from Armistice to Normalcy* (Urbana, 1974), pp. 49, 67.

65. Richberg, "Democratization of Industry," *New Republic* 11 (May 12, 1917): 49–51.

66. Richberg, *Hero*, p. 93; Richberg to J. Ogden Armour, December 3, 1917, DR MS/LC.

67. Richberg, *Tents of the Mighty* (Chicago, 1930), pp. 81–82; part of the text of Richberg's letters to Armour is quoted in Noggle, *Into the Twenties*, pp. 32–33.

68. Richberg to Herbert Hoover, January 21, 1920, DR MS/CHS.

69. Ibid.

70. Ibid.

71. Ibid.

72. Stimson, "A National Budget System—II," *World's Work* 38 (September 1919): 536; Daniels, "Above All—Patriotism! A Seven-Point Remedy for Our Hectic After-War Fever," *Forum* 63 (March 1920): 301.

73. Stimson to Gifford Pinchot, December 11, 1919, HS MS.

74. Stimson, Letter to editor of unspecified journal, August 6, 1919, HS MS.

75. Stimson, "The Leitch Plan," letter to *The Survey*, December 20, 1919, HS MS.

76. Frankfurter, "Conservation of Standards," p. 292; Frankfurter, "Social Unrest," *Current Affairs* 10 (January 5, 1920): 11.

77. Frankfurter, "Conservation of Standards," p. 292; Frankfurter, "Law and Order," originally in *Yale Review* 9 (Winter 1920), reprinted in *Law and Politics: Occasional Papers of Felix Frankfurter, 1913–1938*, ed. by Archibald MacLeish and E.F. Prichard, Jr. (Gloucester, 1971), p. 215.

78. N.Y. *Times*, June 23, 1919, cited in Schwarz, *Speculator*, p. 165.

79. For information on the National Industrial Conference, see Lombardi, *Labor's Voice*, pp. 330–35; and Urofsky, *Big Steel*, pp. 331–33. For background on the steel strike of 1919, see David Brody, *Steelworkers in America: The Nonunion Era* (New York, 1960).

80. Baruch, *Public Years*, p. 151; Coit, *Baruch*, pp. 305–09; Urofsky, *Big Steel*, p. 291. Wilson convened a Second Industrial Conference in December 1919 to which he invited only individuals designated as representatives of the public at large, rather than of specific interest groups. At this conference, Baruch's war-time rival for public prestige, Herbert Hoover, was the dominant figure. The conference report recommended the widespread introduction in industry of employee representation plans, but the Second Industrial Conference was no more successful than the First in building a solid foundation for industrial peace. See Best, *Politics of American Individualism*, pp. 38–51.

81. Baruch to William Jennings Bryan, November 21, 1919, BB MS.

82. Ibid.

83. Daniels, *Cabinet Diaries*, p. 449 (October 14, 1919).

84. Daniels, "Above All—Patriotism," pp. 302–04. In spite of Daniels' defense of Americanism and his anti-radical sentiments, he was an opponent, within the Wilson Cabinet, of Attorney-General Mitchell Palmer's Red Scare campaign. Richberg and Frankfurter also opposed the Red Scare as a serious violation of civil liberties, Frankfurter becoming a signer of an influential report condemning Palmer's illegal tactics. Stimson, too, spoke out against the expulsion of the socialists who had been elected to the New York State Assembly because he saw the action as a denial of democratic rights. Richberg, Untitled petitions and manuscript articles on the problem of free speech (1919?), DR MS/LC; National Popular Government League, *To The American People: Report Upon the Illegal Practices of the United States Department of Justice* (Washington, 1920); Morison, *Turmoil and Tradition*, p. 205.

85. Best specifically notes Stimson and Richberg's approval of employee representation and observes: "Employee representation could appeal to progressives for a variety of reasons—because of its emphasis, for example, on cooperation rather than conflict between employer and employee, and because it sought to bridle the autocratic power of business by democratizing it, rather than by erecting a countervailing power in the form of a strong labor union movement." *Politics of American Individualism*, p. 46.

86. *Historical Statistics*, pp. 70, 97; Oscar Ornati, *Poverty Amid Affluence* (New York, 1966), p. 147.

## VI. The Growth of Voluntarism 1920–1929

1. Ellis W. Hawley, *The Great War and the Search for a Modern Order: A History of the American People and Their Institutions, 1917–1933* (New York, 1979), p. 58. See also Perri Ethan Arnold, "Herbert Hoover and the Continuity of American Public Pol-

icy," *Public Policy* 20 (Fall 1972): 525–44; Ellis W. Hawley, ed., *Herbert Hoover as Secretary of Commerce: Studies in New Era Thought and Practice* (Iowa City, 1981); Ellis W. Hawley, "Herbert Hoover, the Commerce Secretariat, and the Vision of an 'Associative State,' 1921–1928," *Journal of American History* 61 (June 1974): 116–40; Robert K. Murray, *The Politics of Normalcy: Governmental Theory and Practice in the Harding-Coolidge Era* (New York, 1973); Murray N. Rothbard, "Herbert Hoover and the Myth of Laissez-Faire," in *A New History of Leviathan*, ed. by Ronald Radosh and Murray N. Rothbard (New York, 1972); Joan Hoff Wilson, *Herbert Hoover: Forgotten Progressive* (Boston, 1975); and David Burner, *Herbert Hoover: A Public Life* (New York, 1979).

For two older studies of the continuing legacy of progressive reform in the 1920s, see Arthur S. Link, "What Happened to the Progressive Movement in the 1920's?" *American Historical Review* 64 (July 1959): 833–51; and Clarke A. Chambers, *Seedtime of Reform: American Social Service and Social Action, 1918–1933* (Ann Arbor, 1967 ed.).

2. Frankfurter, "Law and Order," originally in *Yale Review* 9 (Winter 1920), reprinted in *Law and Politics: Occasional Papers of Felix Frankfurter, 1913–1938*, ed. by Archibald MacLeish and E. F. Pritchard, Jr. (Gloucester, 1971), p. 215; Stimson, Address to Philippines Businessmen's Convention, Manilla, February 6, 1929, HS MS; Theodore M. Knappen, "Looking at the Farmers' Side: An Interview with Bernard M. Baruch," *World's Work* 43 (March 1922): 475.

3. In 1922 Richberg published a loosely autobiographical novel entitled *A Man of Purpose*. Richberg would have preferred to make a living as a writer rather than as a lawyer, but as the protagonist of his novel, also a labor lawyer, explained: "I am going back to Chicago [after the war], intent on making money, determined to attain a strong material position in a materialistic world. I don't intend to join the plunderers but I intend to establish myself in the class of those who will not be their victims." Richberg, *A Man of Purpose: A Novel* (New York, 1922), p. 265. See also Richberg to Thomas Y. Crowell Co., January 25, 1922, DR MS/CHS.

4. Joseph L. Morrison, *Josephus Daniels: The Small-d Democrat* (Chapel Hill, 1966), p. 141.

5. Hawley, *Great War*, p. 60; Stimson and McGeorge Bundy, *On Active Service in Peace and War* (New York, 1948), p. 111.

6. Margaret L. Coit, *Mr. Baruch* (Boston, 1957), p. 371; Baruch, *Baruch: The Public Years* (New York, 1960), pp. 177–78; Morrison, *Josephus Daniels*, p. 152. As Southerners and drys, Daniels and Baruch were especially sympathetic to McAdoo, but at the same time they both strongly opposed the KKK whose role at the Democratic convention contributed to the tearing apart of the party. Baruch claimed in the Fall of 1922 that he would have sought the chairmanship of the Democratic National Committee "in order to give the party a thorough reorganization and prepare it for the fight in 1924" if it were "not for the religious question." Baruch to William McAdoo, September 30, 1922, BB MS. See also Jordan A. Schwarz, *The Speculator: Bernard M. Baruch in Washington, 1917–1965* (Chapel Hill, 1981), pp. 174–75 for a discussion of Baruch's sensitivity to anti-semitism in this period.

7. Richberg, *My Hero: The Indiscreet Memoirs of an Eventful but Unheroic Life* (New York, 1954), pp. 136–40.

8. Frankfurter to Learned Hand, October 3, 1924, FF MS; Richberg, "Future of the Progressive Movement," (1924 or 1925), DR MS/CHS. For a brief discussion of the Progressive party platform, see John D. Hicks, *Republican Ascendancy, 1921–1933* (New York, 1963 ed.), pp. 98–99.

Frankfurter's views on the election of 1924 can be traced in a series of articles, mainly unsigned, he wrote for the *New Republic*. See "Why Mr. Davis Shouldn't Run," *New Republic* 38 (April 16, 1924): 193–95; "John W. Davis," *New Republic* 39 (July 23, 1924): 224–26; "Abstemious Liberalism," *New Republic* 39 (August 6, 1924): 285–87; all unsigned articles by Frankfurter, copies in FF MS; and Frankfurter, "Why I Shall Vote for La Follette," *New Republic* 40 (October 22, 1924), reprinted in *Law and Politics*, pp. 314–19.

9. Richberg, *Tents of the Mighty* (Chicago, 1930), p. 263; Richberg, "Where Are the Progressives Going—and How," (supplement, 1927?), DR MS/CHS.

10. Frankfurter, "Letter: A Difference in Figures," *Independent* 113 (November 1, 1924): 352; Frankfurter, "Vote for La Follette," p. 318; Richberg, "The High Cost of Low Thinking," *New Republic* 32 (October 18, 1922): 195.

11. Daniels, Address at the University of California, Berkeley, September 3, 1919, JD MS; Baruch, "The Consequences of the War to Industry," *Current History* 29 (November 1928): 194. See also Baruch, *American Industry in the War : A Report of the War Industries Board (March, 1921)*, ed. by Richard H. Hippelheuser (New York, 1941). Herbert Hoover, as Secretary of Commerce, not only shared Baruch's belief in the importance of government as a collector and disseminator of industrial statistics, but also was in a position to put that belief into practice. See sources cited in footnote 1.

12. Frankfurter, "Rationalization in Industry and the Labor Problem," *Proceedings of the Academy of Political Science* 13 (June 1928): 172; Richberg, *Tents*, p. 182; Richberg, "Why Is a Radical," November, 1923, DR MS/CHS; Richberg, *Tents*, p. 223; Frankfurter, Preface to *Criminal Justice in Cleveland*, ed. by Roscoe Pound and Frankfurter (Cleveland, 1922), p. v; Frankfurter, "Surveys of Criminal Justice," in *Proceedings of the National Conference of Social Work* (Chicago, 1930), p. 64; Frankfurter, "Social Unrest," *Current Affairs* 10 (January 5, 1920): 6.

Frankfurter set a new precedent for analyzing the work of the Supreme Court when he employed statistical techniques to examine the significance of the court's changing case load. See Frankfurter and James M. Landis, *The Business of the Supreme Court* (New York, 1927); and Alexander Bickel, "Applied Politics and the Science of Law: Writings of the Harvard Period," in *Felix Frankfurter: A Tribute*, ed. by Wallace Mendelson (New York, 1964), pp. 164–98.

13. Frankfurter, "Social Unrest," p. 6; Richberg, *Tents*, p. 185; Frankfurter to Walter Lippmann, October 10, 1929, FF MS; Frankfurter, *The Public & Its Government* (New Haven, 1930), p. 160. See also the discussion about Louis Brandeis and his approach to dealing with social problems in a scientific manner in the previous chapter.

14. Richberg and Plumb first worked together in 1915 when the city of Chicago hired them as special counsels in litigation involving Samuel Insull's Peoples Gas Company. The "Plumb Plan" which became well known after the war called for the establishment of a tripartite system of management for the nation's railroads, with equal representation for the existing owners, as well as workers and the government. Thomas E. Vadney, *The Wayward Liberal: A Political Biography of Donald Richberg*, (Lexington, 1970), pp. 33, 40–41; Richberg, *Hero*, pp. 113–14.

15. Irving Bernstein, *The Lean Years: A History of the American Worker, 1933–1941* (Baltimore, 1966 ed.), pp. 211–12, 217; Wilson, *Hoover*, pp. 94–95; Burner, *Hoover*, pp. 177–78; Richberg, "Confidential Report on Railway Labor Act and Board of Mediation," December 22, 1928, DR MS/CHS.

16. Bernstein, *Lean Years*, pp. 216–20.

17. Richberg, "The Fair Share in Industry," (1925?), DR MS/CHS.

18. Richberg, Address to Brotherhood of Railroad Signalmen of America, New York, October, 1926, DR MS/CHS; Richberg, *Tents*, pp. 201, 203.

19. Richberg, Untitled manuscript on the Railway Labor Act, 1929, DR MS/CHS;

Richberg to Russell Weisman (editor of the Cleveland *Plain Dealer*), February 25, 1927, DR MS/CHS; Richberg, "The Key to Knowledge," Address to Law Club of Chicago, February 25, 1921, DR MS/CHS.

Vadney observes of Richberg: "As the decade of the 1920's opened, his speeches and writings continued to emphasize coercion as the main internal contradiction within the American democratic system—especially economic coercion. . . . Political or economic democracy could work only where compulsion was absent, and where each party had the right and—equally important—the ability to carry out its role in the system. Richberg's battles for railway labor were not directed so much at forcing capital to do something for labor, as simply at procuring and safeguarding the right of labor to do things for itself—mainly to organize unions independent of employer influence and to bargain over wages and working conditions with management." Vadney, *Wayward Liberal*, p. 42. Coercion was a central issue for Richberg, but, as noted in the text, political, rather than economic, coercion was ultimately a greater danger in his mind.

Michael Rogin points out that the American Federation of Labor, in opposing the Social Darwinism of the late nineteenth century, originally adopted a philosophy of voluntarism as a means of asserting the possibility of social change. By the 1920s, however, voluntarism had become "an organizational ideology protecting the craft union officials of the AFL." Voluntarism came to signify a denial of the necessity of coercion by creating the myth that interest groups could adequately represent and defend the individuals of which they were composed. Thus, after the First World War, voluntarism increasingly took on an anti-state emphasis, and "by ignoring the problem of power in the name of an abstract defense of freedom, legitimized the existing power distribution and attacked the legitimacy of attempts ot change it." Michael Paul Rogin, "Voluntarism: the Political Functions of an Antipolitical Doctrine," *Industrial and Labor Relations Review* 15 (July 1962): 521–35.

20. Richberg, *Tents*, pp. 203, 198; Richberg to Henry J. Allen (Governor of Kansas), June 15, 1922, DR MS/CHS; Richberg, *Man of Purpose*, pp. 217–18.

21. Vadney, *Wayward Liberal*, p. 67; Richberg, Address to Signalmen, October, 1926.

22. Richberg, "Memo for Railway Labor Executives' Association," August 16, 1926, DR MS/CHS; Richberg, Address to Signalmen, October, 1926; Richberg, "Mutualism," *Academy of Political Science Proceedings* 13 (June 1928): 193.

23. Bernstein, *Lean Years*, pp. 219–20. See also Richberg, "Report of Conference with Board of Mediation, concerning Adjustment Boards, held in Washington, June 1, 1928," DR MS/CHS, for a confidential discussion of some of the actual problems faced by the unions in implementing the Railway Labor Act.

24. Bernstein, *Lean Years*, pp. 219–20.

25. When Frankfurter agreed to defend the clothing workers' union, he refused to accept a retainer, telling Hillman that he went "into this matter not for the sake of the Amalgamated, but because public issues are involved." Frankfurter, *Felix Frankfurter Reminisces* (recorded in talks with Dr. Harlan B. Phillips) (New York, 1960), pp. 171–73. See also "War in the Clothing Industry," *New Republic* 25 (December 15, 1920): 59–61, unsigned article by Frankfurter, copy in FF MS; Richberg, *Hero*, p. 126.

26. Berstein, *Lean Years*, pp. 195, 211–12; Vadney, *Wayward Liberal*, pp. 85–93; Liva Baker, *Felix Frankfurter* (New York, 1969), pp. 134–35. See also the file on the origins of the Norris-La Guardia Act in FF MS; and Frankfurter and Nathan Greene, *The Labor Injunction* (New York, 1930). The other two men involved in drafting the anti-injunction act were Herman Oliphant and Edwin Witte.

27. Frankfurter, *Labor Injunction*, pp. 203–05; Raleigh *News & Oberver*, August 9 and 12, September 5 and 25, 1922.

28. "Exit the Kansas Court," *New Republic* 35 (June 27, 1923), unsigned article by Frankfurter, reprinted in *Felix Frankfurter on the Supreme Court: Extrajudicial Essays on the Court and the Constitution,* ed. by Philip B. Kurland (Cambridge, 1970), pp. 140–42; Frankfurter, *Labor Injunction,* p. 205.

29. Bernstein, *Lean Years,* p. 227.

30. Bernstein, *Lean Years,* p. 227; Baker, *Frankfurter,* pp. 112–14; Frankfurter, "The Question of a Minimum Wage Law for American Industry," (excerpts from Frankfurter's argument in the Adkins case of 1923) *Congressional Digest* 15 (November 1936): 271–73.

31. Baker, *Frankfurter,* p. 115; Frankfurter, "Child Labor and the Court," *New Republic* 31 (July 26, 1922): 248–50. In this instance, Frankfurter's belief in decentralized authority and local responsibility was greater than Daniels' since the North Carolina editor favored the adoption of the Child Labor Amendment. Morrison, *Josephus Daniels,* p. 155.

32. Frankfurter, *Labor Injunction,* pp. 203–04.

33. Frankfurter, "Reply to Protest from Clothing Manufacturers' Association," *New Republic* 25 (January 12, 1921): 202; Frankfurter, *Labor Injunction,* p. 205; Frankfurter to Stimson, January 10, 1923, FF MS.

34. Elting E. Morison, *Turmoil and Tradition: A Study of the Life and Times of Henry L. Stimson* (New York, 1964 ed.), pp. 214–15. For background on the coal strike, see Bernstein, *Lean Years,* pp. 125–32; and Hicks, *Republican Ascendancy,* pp. 69–71.

35. Stimson, "No Time for National Complacency," *World's Work* 41 (April 1921): 546; Stimson to Frankfurter, January 8, 1923, FF MS.

36. In explaining to Frankfurter why he favored both the continued legal option of labor injunctions and the right of management to hire armed guards, Stimson noted that it was "contrary to our Anglo-Saxon history to expect classes to improve in self-restraint upon . . . a regimen of uncontrolled power." Frankfurter responded by saying that he supported the Coronado decision which held that unions, even without being incorporated, were legal entities financially accountable to judgments by juries. He was, however, clearly upset by Stimson's reference to Anglo-Saxon tradition, writing: "Not so long ago, you were good enough to say, and in print, that you thought one of the conspicuous things about me was my Americanism. In England, as you know, the private guard is unknown, and the injunction in labor cases was abandoned after a very brief use. England has its own worries. But has England ceased to be 'Anglo-Saxon in tradition and temperament' because it does not resort to private guards and injunctions, as we do?" Stimson to Frankfurter, January 18, 1923; Frankfurter to Stimson, January 19, 1923, FF MS.

Stimson quickly wrote back, saying: "I am writing now . . . simply to express my regret for having unintentionally hurt your feelings by my remark about Anglo-Saxonism. I have just re-read my letter. What I had in mind was the Anglo-Saxon traditions of law and legal individualistic attitudes which you and I have so often discussed as being the spirit of our English common-law. I am more sorry than I can say that the clumsy way in which I must have put it gave to you a different impression. But you surely must know that now as at all times in the past the intention of insulting you by any other meaning would be the thing most absolutely remote from my mind." Stimson to Frankfurter, January 23, 1923, FF MS. Nothing could better demonstrate the closeness of the relationship between the two men or the contrast in attitude between them toward members of the working class.

37. Morison, *Turmoil and Tradition,* p. 215; Stimson to Attorney-General Harlan B. Stone, November 26, 1924, HS MS; Stimson, *Active Service,* p. 109; Stimson to Frankfurter, August 16, 1923, FF MS.

38. Stimson to Gifford Pinchot, August 27, 1923, copy in FF MS, Morison, *Turmoil and Tradition*, p. 216; Stimson, "The Leitch Plan," letter to *The Survey*, December 20, 1919, HS MS.

39. Morison, *Turmoil and Tradition*, pp. 215–18; Stimson to Pinchot, August 27, 1923.

40. Morison, *Turmoil and Tradition*, p. 217; Stimson, Address to the American Chamber of Commerce, Manila, August 15, 1928, HS MS.

41. For the development of "welfare capitalism" and the growing appeal of a harmony of interests doctrine among both American businessmen and the leadership of the AFL, see Bernstein, *Lean Years*, pp. 156–69; Rogin, "Voluntarism;" and Ronald Radosh, "The Corporate Ideology of American Labor Leaders from Gompers to Hillman," in *For A New America: Essays in History and Politics from 'Studies on the Left,' 1959–1967*, ed. by James Weinstein and David W. Eakins (New York, 1970). In addition, for an insightful analysis of the development of "industrial relations" expertise, see David F. Noble, *America by Design: Science, Technology, and the Rise of Corporate Capitalism* (New York, 1977), pp. 286–302.

42. Bernstein, *Lean Years*, p. 84.

43. Robert Keller, "Factor Income Distribution in the United States During the 1920's: A Reexamination of Fact and Theory," *Journal of Economic History* 33 (March 1973): 258; Robert J. Lampman, *The Share of Top Wealth-Holders in National Wealth, 1922–1956* (Princeton, 1962), p. 24; Charles F. Holt, "Who Benefited from the Prosperity of the Twenties," *Explorations in Economic History* 14 (1977): 277–89.

44. Alfred D. Chandler, Jr., *The Visible Hand: The Managerial Revolution in American Business* (Cambridge, 1977), pp. 371, 473–76; George Soule, *Prosperity Decade: From War to Depression, 1917–1929* (New York, 1968 ed.), pp. 142–43; U.S. Department of Commerce, Bureau of the Census, *Historical Statistics of the United States: Colonial Times to 1957* (Washington, 1960), p. 573; Arthur S. Link and William B. Catton, *American Epoch: A History of the United States Since 1900* Vol. I: *An Era of Economic Change, Reform, and World Wars 1900–1945* (New York, 1980 ed.), pp. 259–61.

45. For background on the trade association movement, see Louis Galambos, *Competition & Cooperation: The Emergence of a National Trade Association* (Baltimore, 1966).

46. Baruch, *American Industry;* Baruch, "Consequences of War," p. 193.

47. Frankfurter, "Review of *Trade Association Activities and the Law* by F. D. Jones," *Columbia Law Review* 23 (June 1923): 601–602.

48. Stimson, Address to the National Coal Association, Atlantic City, N.J., June 20, 1923, HS MS; Morison, *Turmoil and Tradition*, pp. 208–10; Stimson, *Active Service*, p. 109.

49. The government's legal action against the cement manufacturers actually involved two suits, one civil and one criminal. In the criminal suit, Stimson was able in 1923 to get a hung jury; though in the civil suit which came later, a judgment was rendered against his clients. It was not until 1924 that the Supreme Court upheld the right of trade associations to engage in the exchange of statistical information, so long as price-fixing could not be clearly demonstrated to result from that activity. Morison, *Turmoil and Tradition*, pp. 208–10; Robert F. Himmelberg, *The Origins of the National Recovery Administration: Business, Government and the Trade Association Issue, 1921–1933* (New York, 1976), pp. 12–21, 34–47.

50. Stimson, Address to Philippine Businessmen's Convention, Manila, February 6, 1929.

51. Richberg, "Seeking the Law in Vain," *The Survey* 49 (December 1, 1922): 291; Morison, *Turmoil and Tradition*, pp. 209–10; Baruch to Mark Sullivan, March 24, 1925,

BB MS; Baruch, WIB Reunion Address, November 11, 1924, BB MS. See also Schwarz, *Speculator,* pp. 212–19.

52. Schwarz, *Speculator,* p. 221; Baruch, Paper prepared for the School of Social Research, April, 1924, BB MS.

53. Baruch, Untitled memo, 1924, BB MS. The language quoted in the text concerning the functions of the "visible hand" is that of Alfred Chandler, but the men discussed in this study would have found Chandler's analysis both accurate as description and laudable as prescription as to how the economy ought to operate. Chandler, *Visible Hand,* p. 1.

54. Baruch, WIB Reunion Address, November 11, 1924.

55. Stimson, "Public Operation vs. Private Operation of Public Utilities," address to the National Republican Club, January 24, 1925, HS MS; Stimson, "The Effects of Popular Ownership on Public Opinion," *Academy of Political Science: Proceedings* 11 (April 1925): 488–90; Baruch, "Consequences of War," pp. 193–94.

56. Richberg, "Cooperating with Competitors," *Academy of Political Science: Proceedings* 11 (April 1925): 501–08.

57. The first important discussion of the implications of the separation of ownership from control appeared in Adolph A. Berle, Jr., and Gardiner C. Means, *The Modern Corporation and Private Property* (New York, 1932). For a recent analysis of the origins and development of the managerial revolution in American industry, see Chandler, *Visible Hand.*

58. John Kenneth Galbraith, *The Great Crash, 1929* (Boston, 1961 ed.), p. 83; Gabriel Kolko, *Wealth and Power in America: An Analysis of Social Class and Income Distribution* (New York, 1962), p. 50.

59. Robert J. Larner, *Management Control and the Large Corporation* (New York, 1970), p. 63. See also Shorey Peterson "Corporate Control and Capitalism," *Quarterly Journal of Economics* 79 (February 1965): 1–24. David Noble argues quite persuasively that the engineer-managers who rose to positions of power in American industry by the 1920s were guided more by the logic of capitalism than by some "objective" standard of efficiency. Noble, *America by Design.*

60. Schwarz, *Speculator,* p. 228.

61. Farm mortgage foreclosures which stood at under 4 per 1000 farms in 1920 rose to over 16 per 1000 farms in the mid-1920s. Per capita disposable income for farmers in 1929 was only $295 compared to $825 for the non-farm population. Thomas Johnson, "Postwar Optimism and the Rural Financial Crisis of the 1920's," *Explorations in Economic History* 11 (Winter 1973/74): 176; Holt, "Who Benefited from the Prosperity of the Twenties." For general background on the conditions in agriculture during the 1920s, see Soule, *Prosperity Decade,* pp. 103–09, 232–47.

62. Schwarz, *Speculator,* pp. 227–41; Baruch, *Public Years,* pp. 152–70.

63. Discussing his response to the Kansas farmers, Baruch claimed: "None of my activities will be political in any sense." Baruch to William Jennings Bryan, August 24, 1920, BB MS. Baruch, *Public Years,* p. 149.

64. Baruch, *Public Years,* p. 156; Knappen, "Looking at the Farmers' Side," p. 475; Baruch to William McAdoo, September 30, 1922.

65. On the Capper-Volstead Act, see Baruch to Sen. Arthur Capper, May 29, 1922, BB MS; and Hicks, *Republican Ascendancy,* pp. 194–95. Baruch tried unsuccessfully to arrange for the purchase by farmers' organizations of the Armour Grain Company, one of the largest grain marketing firms in the country. By the end of the Twenties, the cooperative movement had still only reached about one-third of the nation's farmers. Baruch, *Public Years,* pp. 159–61; Soule, *Prosperity Decade,* pp. 244–46. See also Knap-

pen, "Looking at the Farmers' Side;" and Baruch, Untitled article intended for the *Country Gentlemen*, 1922, BB MS, for statements of Baruch's agricultural program.

66. Baruch, *Public Years*, pp. 164–65; Gilbert C. Fite, *George N. Peek and the Fight for Farm Parity* (Norman, 1954), especially pp. 32, 44, 56, 67–68, and 148, for Baruch's role.

67. Baruch, *Public Years*, pp. 164–67. On McNary-Haugenism, see Hicks, *Republican Ascendancy*, pp. 197–200; and Grant McConnell, *The Decline of Agrarian Democracy* (New York, 1969 ed.), pp. 61–65.

68. Baruch, Testimony, House Agriculture Committee, January 25, 1923, copy in BB MS; Baruch, *Public Years*, p. 166. Schwarz accurately characterizes Baruch's support for McNary-Haugenism as "ambiguous." *Speculator*, p. 236.

69. Soule, *Prosperity Decade*, pp. 103–04, 232–47; Susan Previant Lee and Peter Passell, *A New Economic View of American History* (New York, 1979), pp. 364–65; Galbraith, *Great Crash*, p. 180.

70. Richberg to D. B. Robertson, with enclosed copy of letter to Kansas *Farm Journal*, July 12, 1926, DR MS/CHS.

71. For background on the rise of holding companies in the 1920s, see Harold Underwood Faulkner, *American Economic History* (New York, 1949 ed.), pp. 613–17; and Hicks, *Republican Ascendancy*, pp. 120–27.

72. On Stimson's role in the development of federal regulation of navigable streams, see Morison, *Turmoil and Tradition*, pp. 140–41; and Frankfurter, *Reminisces*, pp. 73–75. Stimson, "Public Operation vs. Private Operation."

73. Stimson, "Public Operation vs. Private Operation;" Baruch, Untitled memo on municipal ownership, 1927, BB MS; Baruch to William McAdoo, April 10, 1923, BB MS. Baruch was even willing to support Henry Ford's attempt to develop Muscle Shoals as a source of nitrates as a preferable alternative to government development, at a time when Ford was engaging in an anti-semitic campaign which included direct attacks on Baruch. Baruch to Charles MacDowell, February 2, 1923, BB MS; Coit, *Baruch*, pp. 359–62.

74. Richberg was ultimately unsuccessful in his attempt to force the Peoples Gas Company to return its excess charges, though his efforts did result in a somewhat lower rate base than Insull had wanted. The litigation did not finally conclude until 1925. Vadney, *Wayward Liberal*, pp. 32–35; Richberg, "Regulation of Public Utilities," radio address, May 28, 1928, DR MS/CHS.

75. Richberg, "A Permanent Basis for Rate Regulation," *Yale Law Journal* 31 (January 1922): 277. Richberg's most important activity in the field of rate regulation involved his work for the National Conference on Valuation of American Railroads. The railway unions, working tgether with Robert La Follette, created this organization to push for a lowering of railroad rates through a change in the valuation procedures of the ICC. Richberg was successful in convincing the ICC, in the O'Fallon case, to establish the principle that the carriers' profits should be based on the original, rather than the replacement, cost of the railroads. Richberg calculated that this would have saved railroad users over half a billion dollars a year. The case was taken to the Supreme Court where Richberg was allowed to argue the ICC's position only after a special Senate resolution was passed urging the court to hear Richberg, even though he was not the legal representative of the ICC. The Supreme Court, however, reversed the ICC's ruling. Vadney, *Wayward Liberal*, pp. 67–73; Hugh Russell Fraser, "One Man Beats 150," *Outlook* 147 (October 5, 1927): 149–52.

76. Richberg, Summary of Address to Conference on Living Costs, National League of Women Voters, Chicago, April 23, 1928, DR MS/CHS; Richberg, "Regulation of Pub-

lic Utilities," address to Convention of Michigan League of Women Voters, Flint, November 13, 1929, DR MS/CHS.

77. Frankfurter, *Reminisces,* pp. 73–75; Baker, *Frankfurter,* pp. 88, 175.

78. Frankfurter, "The Utilities Bureau," *Annals of the American Adademy of Political and Social Science* 57 (January 1915), pp. 293–94; Frankfurter to Franklin Roosevelt, January 17, 1930, in *Roosevelt and Frankfurter: Their Correspondence, 1928–1945,* ed. by Max Freedman (Boston, 1967), p. 44. See also Frankfurter, *Public & Its Government,* pp. 81–122.

79. Morrison, *Josephus Daniels,* p. 146.

80. Daniels, *The Wilson Era: Years of War and After, 1917–1923* (Chapel Hill, 1946), p. 247; Burl Noggle, *Teapot Dome: Oil and Politics in the 1920's* (Baton Rouge, 1961), pp. 17–19.

81. Morrison, *Josephus Daniels,* pp. 147–50; Noggle, *Teapot Dome,* pp. 34–35, 94.

82. Daniels, *Years of War,* pp. 246–48; Daniels, "Democracy and Conservation," address before the Democratic Women's Club of Philadelphia, February 25, 1924, JD MS.

83. Noggle, *Teapot Dome,* pp. 156–57; Raleigh *News & Observer,* June 29, 1924.

84. See Hawley, *Great War,* for an excellent synthesis of much of the newer scholarship on the Twenties.

85. Link, *American Epoch,* v. 1, p. 249; *Historical Statistics,* p. 139.

86. The figures on the share of national income received by the top five percent of the population reflect income after taxes and including capital gains. The six-percent rise in disposable income is for the 93 percent of the population at the bottom of the income distribution. Lee, *New Economic View,* p. 339; Holt, "Who Benefited from the Prosperity of the Twenties;" Lampman, *Share of Top Wealth-Holders,* p. 24.

87. Oscar Ornati, *Poverty Amid Affluence* (New York, 1966), pp. 148, 158; the Brookings study is cited in Robert L. Heilbroner, *the Economic Transformation of America* (New York, 1977), p. 177. Ornati's estimate of the budget required for a "minimum adequacy" standard of living for a family of four in 1929 is $1,562.

## VII. The Great Depression and the Crisis of Liberalism 1929–1933

1. Joan Hoff Wilson, *Herbert Hoover: Forgotten Progressive* (Boston, 1975), p. 127; Bruce Barton, "Bernard M. Baruch Discusses the Future of American Business," *American Magazine* 107 (June 1929): 137; Richberg, *Tents of the Mighty* (Chicago, 1930), p. 82 (originally published in serial form in *The Survey* during 1929).

Baruch, it should be noted, was cautious enough to transfer his own investments to safe bonds well before the stock market crash, thereby following his own maxim of selling before the market peaked. Baruch, *Baruch: The Public Years* (New York, 1960), pp. 220–25; Jordan A. Schwarz, *The Speculator: Bernard M. Baruch in Washington, 1917–1965* (Chapel Hill, 1981), p. 252.

2. Carl N. Degler, *Out of Our Past: The Forces That Shaped Modern America* (New York, 1970 ed.), p. 379; Samuel Eliot Morison, Henry Steele Commager and William E. Leuchtenburg, *The Growth of the American Republic,* Vol. II (New York, 1969 ed.), p. 471; William E. Leuchtenburg, *The Perils of Prosperity, 1914–1932* (Chicago, 1958), p. 248; Broadus Mitchell, *Depression Decade: From New Era through New Deal* (New York, 1947), pp. 446, 448, 451; Paul A. Baran and Paul M. Sweezy, *Monopoly Capital: An Essay on the American Economic and Social Order* (New York, 1968 ed.), p. 242.

3. For accounts pointing out the role of the Hoover Presidency as preparing the way for the New Deal, see Wilson, *Hoover;* David Burner, *Herbert Hoover: A Public Life* (New York, 1979); Martin L. Fausold and George T. Mazuzan, eds., *The Hoover Presidency: A Reappraisal* (Albany, 1974); Ellis W. Hawley, *The Great War and The Search for a Modern Order: A History of the American People and Their Institutions, 1917–1933* (New York, 1979); J. Joseph Huthmacher and Warren I. Susman, eds., *Herbert Hoover and the Crisis of American Capitalism* (Cambridge, 1973); Albert U. Romasco, *The Poverty of Abundance: Hoover, the Nation, the Depression* (New York, 1968 ed.); Jordan A. Schwarz, *The Interregnum of Despair: Hoover, Congress, and the Depression* (Urbana, 1970); and Harris Gaylord Warren, *Herbert Hoover and the Great Depression* (New York, 1967 ed.). For a recent account with a dissenting view emphasizing the discontinuities between the Hoover and Roosevelt administrations, see Elliot A. Rosen, *Hoover, Roosevelt, and the Brains Trust: From Depression to New Deal* (New York, 1977).

4. Schwarz, *Speculator,* p. 255.

5. Stimson and McGeorge Bundy, *On Active Service in Peace and War* (New York, 1948), p. 201; Stimson, Diary, September 8, 1931, HS MS.

6. Stimson, Diary, November 28, 1931 and November 30, 1932, HS MS.

7. Baruch, Testimony, in U.S. Congress, Senate, Committee on Finance, *Hearings on Investigation of Economic Problems,* 72nd Cong., 2d sess., February 13, 1933.

8. Baruch, Address to the Boston Chamber of Commerce, May 1, 1930, BB MS.

9. Editorial, Raleigh *News & Observer,* October 7, 1930; Daniels, Address at Winston-Salem, N.C., in Raleigh *News & Observer,* November 4, 1930.

10. Daniels, Address at Rocky Mount, N.C., in Raleigh *News & Observer,* October 6, 1931.

11. Frankfurter, Address at Smith College, in Springfield (Mass.) *Republican,* February 23, 1933, copy in FF MS.

12. Frankfurter, Address at Smith College, February 23, 1933; Frankfurter, "What We Confront in American Life," address to annual meeting of Survey Associates, 1933, reprinted in *Law and Politics: Occasional Papers of Felix Frankfurter, 1913–1938,* ed. by Archibald MacLeish and E. F. Prichard, Jr., (Gloucester, 1971), pp. 334–44.

13. Frankfurter to Walter Lippmann, October 23, 1931, FF MS.

14. Richberg, Untitled memo regarding railroad proposals to raise rates, June, 1931, DR MS/CHS.

15. Richberg, Testimony, in U.S. Congress, Senate, Committee on Finance, *Hearings on Investigation of Economic Problems,* 72nd Cong., 2d sess., February 23, 1933; Richberg, "The Future of Power and the Public," *The Annals of the Academy of Political and Social Science* 159 (January 1932): 152.

16. Milton Friedman and Anna Jacobson Schwartz, *The Great Contraction 1929–1933* (Princeton, 1965), p. 18; John Kenneth Galbraith, *The Great Crash, 1929* (Boston, 1961 ed.) p. 182. See also Derek H. Aldcroft, *From Versailles to Wall Street 1919–1929* (London, 1977), p. 281; and Peter Temin, *Did Monetary Forces Cause the Great Depression?* (New York, 1976), p. 13n.

17. See especially Galbraith, *Great Crash,* on the effect of the stock market crash and Friedman and Schwartz, *Great Contraction,* on the importance of monetary forces, in general.

18. Temin, *Monetary Forces,* p. 4; Robert A. Gordon, *Business Fluctuations* (New York, 1961 ed.), pp. 445–46; Alvin H. Hansen, *Full Recovery or Stagnation* (New York, 1938).

19. The figure on home ownership comes from Stanley Lebergott, *The American Economy: Income, Wealth, and Want* (Princeton, 1976), p. 259.

20. Richard Edwards, Michael Reich, and Thomas E. Weisskopf, *The Capitalist System: A Radical Analysis of American Society* (Englewood Cliffs, 1978 ed.), p. 146; Baran and Sweezy, *Monopoly Capital,* pp. 234–44.

21. Gilbert Burck and Charles E. Silberman, "What Caused the Great Depression," *Fortune* 51 (February 1955): 206; Irving Bernstein, *A History of the American Worker, 1933–1941: Turbulent Years* (Boston, 1970), p. 24; Galbraith, *Great Crash,* p. 178. In his recent study of the origins of the world-wide depression, Derek Aldcroft observes: "Theories of under-consumption have never attracted widespread support in explaining cyclical turning-points partly because the more volatile swings in investment, the other major component of national income, have usually been regarded as of greater significance. Yet in so far as investment magnitudes are determined by changes in levels of consumption or income, fluctuations in consumption, though much less dramatic than those in investment, may be crucial at the turning points of the cycle. . . . In a sense, of course, under-consumption or a deficiency of demand in Keynesian terms prevailed throughout the 1920s, which gave rise to an equilibrium, albeit unstable, below the full employment level." Aldcroft argues not only that "the skewed distribution of income gains" in the 1920s "inevitably checked the rate at which consumption expanded," but also that a decline in the rate of growth of consumption between 1928 and 1929 contributed to the apparent drying up of investment opportunities. *From Versailles to Wall Street,* pp. 279–80.

22. Galbraith, *Great Crash,* pp. 180–81; Temin, *Monetary Forces,* p. 172.

23. Gardiner C. Means, *The Corporate Revolution in America: Economic Reality vs. Economic Theory* (New York, 1962), p. 88; Merle Fainsod and Lincoln Gordon, *Government and the American Economy* (New York, 1948 ed.), pp. 13–19; John M. Blair, *Economic Concentration: Structure, Behavior and Public Policy* (New York, 1972), p. 528; Lester V. Chandler, *America's Greatest Depression, 1929–1941* (New York, 1970), p. 28. On the development of administered prices, see also Arthur Robert Burns, *The Decline of Competition* (New York, 1936); and National Resources Planning Board, *The Structure of the American Economy,* Part II (Washington, 1940).

One of John Maynard Keynes great contributions to economic theory was his demonstration that an economy could establish an equilibrium point at less than full employment and then remain functioning at that level indefinitely. See Robert Lekachman, *The Age of Keynes* (New York, 1975 ed.). The relevance of Keynesian theory to public policy in the Thirties will be discussed in the next chapter.

24. Baran, *Monopoly Capital,* p. 240.

25. Stimson, Speech to Republican State Convention, Albany, New York, September 25, 1930, HS MS; Stimson, Diary, April 7, 1931, HS MS. On the differences between Hoover and Stimson over foreign policy, see Robert H. Ferrell, *American Diplomacy in the Great Depression* (New York, 1970 ed.); and Christopher Thorne, *The Limits of Foreign Policy: The West, the League and the Far Eastern Crisis of 1931–1933* (New York, 1973 ed.).

26. For Hoover's actions in this period, see the sources cited in footnote 3. Romasco points out that Theodore Roosevelt in 1907, Woodrow Wilson in 1914, and Warren Harding in 1921 all had used executive authority in an effort to counter serious declines in business activity, so that Hoover's efforts were not totally unprecedented. Albert U. Romasco, "Herbert Hoover's Policies for Dealing with the Great Depression: The End of the Old Order or the Beginning of the New?" in Fausold, *Hoover Presidency.*

27. On Stimson's position on the debts problem, see Elting E. Morison, *Turmoil and Tradition: A Study of the Life and Times of Henry L. Stimson* (New York, 1964 ed.), pp. 278–302; and Ferrell, *American Diplomacy,* pp. 106–19. See also Stimson, Diary,

November 28, 1931 and November 30, 1932, HS MS, regarding Stimson's emphasis on the importance of restoring the world gold standard.

28. James Stuart Olson, *Herbert Hoover and the Reconstruction Finance Corporation, 1931–1933* (Ames, 1977), pp. x–xi.

29. On Stimson's support for a sales tax, see Stimson, Diary, May 24, 1932, HS MS.

30. Stimson, *Active Service*, p. 283.

31. Baruch, Address to Boston Chamber of Commerce, May 1, 1930; Baruch, Senate Testimony, February 13, 1933; Margaret L. Coit, *Mr. Baruch* (Boston, 1957), p. 399; Baruch to Albert Ritchie, September 14, 1930, BB MS; Schwarz, *Speculator*, p. 259.

32. Schwarz, *Speculator*, p. 264; Baruch, *Public Years*, p. 234; Schwarz, *Interregnum of Despair*, pp. 142–78; Baruch, Memo for Senator Joseph Robinson, May, 1932, BB MS.

33. Baruch, Senate Testimony, February 13, 1933; Schwarz, *Speculator*, p. 260.

34. Baruch, Address to Boston Chamber of Commerce, May 1, 1930. See also Baruch to Senator Thomas Walsh, December 2, 1930. BB MS.

35. Baruch, Address to Boston Chamber of Commerce, May 1, 1930; Baruch, Senate Testimony, February 13, 1933; Baruch, Address to 9th annual reunion of the War Industries Board, November 11, 1931, BB MS. In this last speech, he referred to the new agency as the "High Court of Commerce."

For an interesting discussion of the way in which the analogy of war, and the experience of the government's role in the mobilization of the First World War, in particular, was used by those who sought support for extraordinary measures to combat the depression, see William E. Leuchtenburg, "The New Deal and the Analogue of War," in *Change and Continuity in Twentieth-Century America*, ed. by John Braeman, Robert Bremner, and Everett Walters (Columbus, 1964).

36. Baruch, Senate Testimony, February 13, 1933. See also Baruch to Franklin Roosevelt, May 28, 1932, BB MS, in which Baruch sent the future President a memo on the farm problem. Baruch's former WIB associate, Gen. Hugh Johnson, helped in the preparation of Baruch's Senate testimony on the farm problem and was at his side during the hearings.

37. Baruch, "Leaning on Government," address at Johns Hopkins University, February 22, 1933, BB MS. Hoover's administration actually enforced the anti-trust laws more strictly than did the preceding Coolidge administration. In suggesting the establishment of a "supreme court of commerce," Baruch explicitly called for a revision of the nation's anti-trust laws. Robert F. Himmelberg, *The Origins of the National Recovery Administration: Business, Government, and the Trade Association Issue, 1921–1933* (New York, 1976), pp. 92–110; Baruch, Address to Boston Chamber of Commerce, May 1, 1930.

38. Schwarz, *Interregnum of Despair*, pp. 114–15; Baruch, "Federal Taxes Can Be Cut a Billion," from *Nation's Business* (September 1932), copy in BB MS. See also Baruch, Senate Testimony, February 13, 1933; and Baruch, Memo for Sen. Robinson, May, 1932.

39. Daniels, Address at Elizabethtown, N.C., in Raleigh *News & Observer*, October 24, 1930.

40. Editorial, Raleigh *News & Observer*, November 23, 1929; Daniels to Jonathan Daniels, September 28, 1931, JD MS; Daniels, Address in Raleigh *News & Observer*, October 14, 1930.

41. Daniels, Address, in Raleigh *News & Observer*, October 14, 1930.

42. Editorial, Raleigh *News & Observer*, October 3, 1931; Daniels, Address, in Raleigh *News & Observer*, October 20, 1932; Daniels to Baruch, March 29, 1932, BB MS; Daniels to Jon. Daniels, September 28, 1931; Daniels, Address at Berry Schools, Geor-

gia, January 13, 1932, JD MS: Daniels, Address, in Raleigh *News & Observer*, October 6, 1931.

43. "The Packers v. the Government," *New Republic* 71 (May 25, 1932), unsigned article by Frankfurter, reprinted in *Law ad Politics*, p. 275.

44. Frankfurter to Walter Lippmann, April 27, 1932, in *Roosevelt and Frankfurter: Their Correspondence, 1928–1945*, ed. by Max. Freedman (Boston, 1967), p. 71.

45. Frankfurter, "Review of *Interstate Transmission of Electric Power* by H. L. Elsbree," *Harvard Law Review* 45 (February 1932): 763; Nelson Lloyd Dawson, *Louis D. Brandeis, Felix Frankfurter, and the New Deal* (Camden, 1980), especially pp. 173–76. For a discussion of Frankfurter's recovery program, see also Bruce Allen Murphy, *The Brandeis/Frankfurter Connection: The Secret Political Activities of Two Supreme Court Justices* (New York, 1982), pp. 101–05; Michael E. Parrish, *Felix Frankfurter and His Times: The Reform Years* (New York, 1982), pp. 200–12.

46. Frankfurter, "What We Confront," pp. 342–44; Frankfurter, Address at Smith College, February 23, 1933; Frankfurter to Walter Lippmann, March 29 and April 7, 1932, FF MS; Frankfurter to Lippmann, April 12, 1932, in *Roosevelt and Frankfurter*, pp. 66–67; Frankfurter to Franklin D. Roosevelt, February 23, 1933, in *Roosevelt and Frankfurter*, pp. 108–09.

47. In early 1933, Frankfurter helped Governor Herbert Lehman draft labor legislation along the lines referred to in the text for submission to the New York legislature. See copies of messages by Lehman appearing in the New York *Herald Tribune*, February 28, 1933 and in the New York *Times*, April 6, 1933, in FF MS.

48. Murphy, *Brandeis/Frankfurter*, p. 105; Frankfurter to New York *Herald Tribune*, October 19, 1931, in *Roosevelt and Frankfurter*, p. 59; Frankfurter, Address at Smith College, February 23, 1933.

49. Frankfurter, Address at Smith College, February 23, 1933; Frankfurter to Lippmann, April 12, 1932.

50. Richberg, Senate Testimony, February 23, 1933.

51. In addition to his Senate testimony (from which all the quotations in the text come), Richberg made three important statements in 1932 concerning his general views on the need for major reform of the nation's industrial system. See Richberg, "The Future of Power;" Richberg, "Industrial Civilization," *American Federationist* 39 (March 1932): 265–74; and Richberg, "Laborism in This Changing World," address to Brotherhood of Locomotive Firemen and Enginemen, August 28, 1932, copy of reprint from *Brotherhood of Locomotive Firemen and Enginemen Magazine* (November 1932), DR MS/LC.

52. Richberg to David Lilienthal, October 9, 1931, DR MS/CHS.

53. Richberg, Senate testimony, February 23, 1933.

54. Richberg, Memo on national planning for D. B. Robertson (head of Brotherhood of Locomotive Firemen and Engineers) (1931?), DR MS/CHS.

# VIII. The New Deal and the Culmination of Liberalism 1933–1939

1. Arthur M. Schlesinger, Jr., *The Age of Roosevelt*, Vol. II: *The Coming of the New Deal* (Boston, 1958), pp. 546–47. On Baruch, see Schlesinger, *The Age of Roosevelt*, Vol. I: *The Crisis of the Old Order* (Boston, 1957), p. 421; Rexford G. Tugwell, *The Democratic Roosevelt* (Baltimore, 1969, ed.), p. 327; and R. G. Tugwell, *The Brains*

*Trust* (New York, 1969 ed.), p. xxviii. Johnson and Peek are referred to as "Baruch men" by both Tugwell and Ellis W. Hawley, *The New Deal and the Problem of Monopoly: A Study in Economic Ambivalence* (Princeton, 1966), p. 284. On Frankfurter's decision not to become Solicitor General, see Frankfurter, Memo, March 15, 1933, in *Roosevelt and Frankfurter: Their Correspondence, 1929–1945,* ed. by Max Freedman (Boston, 1967), pp. 110–14. For a comprehensive description of Frankfurter's role as a placement bureau in the New Deal, see Bruce Allen Murphy, *The Brandeis/Frankfurter Connection: The Secret Political Activities of Two Supreme Court Justices* (New York, 1982), pp. 113–19; and Michael E. Parrish, *Felix Frankfurter and His Times: The Reform Years* (New York, 1982), pp. 222–30.

2. Daniels was disappointed that Roosevelt did not name him to his former position of Secretary of the Navy, but after turning down a chance to become head of either the Shipping Board or a newly proposed Transportation Agency, he indicated his preference for Mexico among all diplomatic posts. Joseph L. Morrison, *Josephus Daniels: The Small-d Democrat* (Chapel Hill, 1966), p. 170; E. David Cronon, *Josephus Daniels in Mexico* (Madison, 1960), pp. 6–9.

Frankfurter was instrumental in arranging for a personal meeting after the election between FDR and Stimson which kept relations between the two men much more friendly than those between the President-elect and Hoover. Elting E. Morison, *Turmoil and Tradition: A Study of the Life and Times of Henry L. Stimson,* (New York, 1964, ed.), pp. 362–65; Parrish, *Frankfurter,* pp. 217–18.

3. Daniels to Franklin Roosevelt, June 28, 1928, JD MS; Parrish, *Frankfurter,* pp. 200, 203; Liva Baker, *Felix Frankfurter* (New York, 1969), pp. 146–48; Elliot A. Rosen, *Hoover, Roosevelt, and the Brains Trust: From Depression to New Deal* (New York, 1977), p. 306; Jordan A. Schwarz, *The Speculator: Bernard M. Baruch in Washington, 1917–1965* (Chapel Hill, 1981), pp. 266–70; Baruch, *Baruch: The Public Years* (New York, 1960), pp. 245–47; Richberg, *My Hero: The Indiscreet Memoirs of an Eventful but Unheroic Life* (New York, 1954), p. 156; Thomas E. Vadney, *The Wayward Liberal: A Political Biography of Donald Richberg* (Lexington, 1970), pp. 106–07.

4. Ben D. Zevin, *Nothing to Fear: The Selected Addresses to Franklin D. Roosevelt 1932–1945* (New York, 1961, ed.), p. 28; John Braeman, "The New Deal and the 'Broker State:' A Review of the Recent Scholarly Literature," *Business History Review* 46 (Winter 1972): 409.

5. Hawley, *New Deal,* p. 33.

6. On the relevance of the WIB experience to New Deal experiments in planning, see Gerald D. Nash, "Experiments in Industrial Planning: WIB & NRA," *Mid-America* 45 (July 1963): 157–74; William E. Leuchtenburg, "The New Deal and the Analogue of War, in *Change and Continuity in Twentieth-Century America,* ed. by John Braeman, Robert Bremner, and Everett Walters (Columbus, 1964).

7. Schwarz, *Speculator,* p. 289; Bernard Bellush, *The Failure of the NRA* (New York, 1975), p. 9; Baruch, Address to the Brookings Institution, May 20, 1933, BB MS; Hugh Johnson, *The Blue Eagle from Egg to Earth* (Garden City, 1935), pp. 154–57, 201; Frankfurter to Alfred E. Cohn, October 30, 1935, in *Roosevelt and Frankfurter,* pp. 288–91. Baruch, in fact, thought Johnson's appointment was unwise, telling Secretary of Labor Frances Perkins that the General made "a good number-three man, maybe a number-two man, but . . . not a number-one man." Frances Perkins, *The Roosevelt I Knew* (New York, 1964 ed.), p. 200.

8. Irving Bernstein, *A History of the American Worker, 1933–1941: Turbulent Years* (Boston, 1970), pp. 28–29; Frankfurter to Cohn, October 30, 1935.

9. Richberg, *The Rainbow* (Garden City, 1936), pp. 116–17.

10. Richberg, Address to Merchants Association of New York, July 6, 1933, in Richberg, *Rainbow*, pp. 287–95. See also Baruch, Address to Brookings Institution, May 20, 1933.

11. Richberg, *Rainbow*, pp. 287–95.

12. Daniels to Richberg, July 14, 1933, DR MS/LC; Frankfurter to Richberg, July 7, 1933, DR MS/LC.

13. Frankfurter to Richberg, July 7, 1933.

14. Richberg, *Rainbow*, 287–95. The cotton textile industry was so quick to establish a code because its trade association, the Cotton Textile Institute, had already pioneered in the development of cartel-like regulation of prices and production while attempting to combat the depressed conditions which had beset the industry even before the crash of 1929. In February, 1933, Baruch had met with the head of the CTI to discuss the possibility of an NRA-type program. Louis Galambos, *Competition & Cooperation: The Emergence of a National Trade Association* (Baltimore, 1966), pp. 190–230.

15. Baruch, Address to Brookings Institution, May 20, 1933.

16. Richberg, *Rainbow*, pp. 159–61.

17. Baruch to Hugh Johnson, November 1 and 4, 1933, BB MS. See also Richberg, *Rainbow*, pp. 159–78.

18. Hawley, *New Deal*, pp. 56–61; Bellush, *NRA*, pp. 45–46; Galambos, *Competition & Cooperation*, pp. 227–36.

19. Hawley, *New Deal*, p. 61.

20. Stimson to James Grafton Rogers, November 1, 1933, HS MS; Frankfurter, "The National Industrial Recovery Bill and Wage Standards," memo sent to Richberg, May 29, 1933, FF MS.

21. Stimson to Rogers, November 1, 1933.

22. Baruch to Franklin Roosevelt, June 18, 1934, BB MS; Richberg, "Planning and Controlling Business Activities," *Vital Speeches* 1 (Dcember 17, 1934): 171; Richberg, "N.R.A." *Congressional Digest* 14 (January 1935): 14–15; Richberg, "The National Emergency Council," *Vital Speeches* 1 (October 22, 1934): 54–60.

23. Richberg, Address to Conference of Code Authorities and Trade Association Code Committees, March 5, 1934; and Address to Indianapolis Chamber of Commerce, October 15, 1934; both in Richberg, *Rainbow*, pp. 296–319; Richberg, "The National Emergency Council," pp. 54–60; Richberg, "N.R.A.," pp. 14–15.

24. Frankfurter to Franklin Roosevelt, May 30, 1935, in *Roosevelt and Frankfurter*, pp. 273–75. Richberg had, from an early date, pushed for a test case of the NRA's constitutionality and argued the government's side before the Supreme Court. Frankfurter, on the other hand, had tried to delay such a test case, and, in particular, one based on Schecter, in order to avoid a probable political setback for the New Deal. He succeeded in April in convincing FDR to delay action, but by that time Attorney-General Homer Cummings had already set in motion the decision which led to the NRA's demise. Frankfurter subsequently criticized the Supreme Court's Schecter decision for not striking down the emergency act on the narrowest grounds possible and not waving judgment, in the first place, since the NIRA was about to expire anyway. Vadney, *Wayward Liberal*, pp. 162–65; Richberg, *Hero*, p. 195; Baker, *Frankfurter*, pp. 192–93; Freedman, ed., *Roosevelt and Frankfurter*, pp. 259–60; Frankfurter and Henry M. Hart, Jr., "The Business of the Supreme Court at October Term, 1934," *Harvard Law Review* 49 (November 1935): 100–03.

25. Stimson to Franklin Roosevelt, June 4, 1935, copy sent to Frankfurter, November 8, 1935, FF MS.

26. Hawley, *New Deal*, p. 164; Vadney, *Wayward Liberal*, p. 169.

27. Richberg, "Planning and Controlling Business," p. 171.

28. Richberg, *Rainbow,* pp. 47–48, 278.

29. Schlesinger, *Coming of New Deal,* p. 401.

30. Irving Bernstein, *The New Deal Collective Bargaining Policy* (Berkeley, 1950), p. 33.

31. Bernstein, *Collective Bargaining,* pp. 33–37.

32. Bernstein, *Turbulent Years,* p. 37; Milton Derber, "Growth and Expansion," in *Labor and the New Deal,* ed. by Milton Derber and Edwin Young (Madison, 1961), p. 8.

33. Ironically, Johnson had himself suggested the idea of a labor board and insisted to Secretary of Labor Frances Perkins that Senator Wagner be named to head such a board. Frances Perkins, *Roosevelt I Knew,* p. 237. The most complete treatment of the administrative history of Section 7a is found in Bernstein, *Collective Bargaining.*

34. Richard C. Wilcock, "Industrial Management's Policies Toward Unionism," in *Labor and the New Deal,* p. 288; Richberg, *Rainbow,* p. 145.

35. Bernstein, *Collective Bargaining,* pp. 59–62, 86.

36. Bernstein, *Collective Bargaining,* pp. 62–63.

37. Daniels to Franklin Roosevelt, January 7, 1935, JD MS; Harold L. Ickes, *The Secret Diary of Harold L. Ickes: The First Thousand Days, 1933–1936* (New York, 1954), entry for December 17, 1934, pp. 247–48.

38. Richberg, *Rainbow,* pp. 55–56.

39. Richberg, "N.R.A.," p. 15; Richberg to George L. Berry, January 9, 1935, DR MS/LC.

40. Richberg, *Rainbow,* pp. 55–56.

41. Richberg, *Rainbow,* p. 156. Christopher Lasch offers an insightful analysis of the contrast between Richberg's commitment to the "idea of a national interest" and the belief of other New Dealers, such as Harry Hopkins, Harold Ickes, William Douglas, and Robert Jackson, that government ought to be "the agency to which . . . conflicting interests turned for aid in promoting their own ends." Lasch, however, fails to appreciate the degree to which Richberg wavered between a pluralist and a corporatist conception of society, and he also exaggerates the extent to which the pluralism of an Ickes or a Hopkins was based on a nostalgia for the competitive world of an older small town America. Christopher Lasch, "Donald Richberg and the idea of a National Interest," (Unpublished M.A. Thesis, Columbia University, 1955), pp. 99–124.

42. Richberg, *Rainbow,* p. 148.

43. Richberg, *Rainbow,* pp. 54–55.

44. Vadney convincingly makes this argument about the personal factors involved in Richberg's increasingly pro-business attitudes in the *Wayward Liberal,* pp. 120–23.

45. Daniels to Roosevelt, January 7, 1935. For Wagner's role in the formulation of labor policy in the 1930s, see J. Joseph Huthmacher, *Senator Robert F. Wagner and the Rise of Urban Liberalism* (New York, 1971 ed.).

46. The Wagner Act was probably the most important piece of legislation to be enacted during the New Deal which did not originate in the executive branch and which did not receive FDR's backing until its passage in Congress was virtually assured. Bernstein, *Collective Bargaining,* pp. 62–64, 81–87, 131; Bernstein, *Turbulent Years,* pp. 635–81.

47. In the wake of the Schecter decision, Frankfurter advised FDR that the Wagner Act "should be vigorously pushed to passage" since it "has become the effective symbol [of] labor's interests." Frankfurter to Franklin Roosevelt, May 30, 1935, in *Roosevelt and Frankfurter,* p. 274. The quotation in the text is from a memo Frankfurter wrote for FDR in early 1935, also appearing in *Roosevelt and Frankfurter,* pp. 603–05.

48. Frankfurter, 1935 Memo, in *Roosevelt and Frankfurter*, pp. 603–05; Hawley, *New Deal*, pp. 187–88.

49. Garrison is quoted in Bernstein, *Turbulent Years*, p. 788. See also R. W. Fleming, "The Significance of the Wagner Act," in *Labor and the New Deal*.

50. Baruch to Alfred Sloan, May 25 and June 17, 1938, BB MS.

51. Baruch to Sloan, June 17, 1938; Daniels to Jonathan Daniels, November 15, 1938, JD MS.

52. Stimson, Letters to New York *Times*, October 21 and November 3, 1938, copies in HS MS. While Stimson opposed Wagner's reelection to the Senate, Daniels recommended to FDR that Wagner be appointed to the Supreme Court, claiming that the New York Senator stood "before the country today like Brandeis did when Wilson named him for the bench." Daniels to Franklin Roosevelt, July 21, 1938, JD MS.

53. Richberg, "Constitutional Aspects of the New Deal," *Annals of the American Academy of Political and Social Science* 178 (March 1935): 30; Richberg, *Hero*, pp. 299–301.

54. Richberg, *Rainbow*, pp. 176–77.

55. Richberg, *Rainbow*, p. 81; U.S. Department of Commerce, Bureau of the Census, *Historical Statistics of the United States: Colonial Times to 1957* (Washington, 1960), p. 98. See also Sidney Fine, *The Automobile Under the Blue Eagle: Labor, Management, and the Automobile Manufacturing Code* (Ann Arbor, 1963) on the long-term impact of the NRA on labor relations.

56. William E. Leuchtenburg, *Franklin D. Roosevelt and the New Deal, 1932–1940* (New York, 1963), p. 151.

57. For an insightful discussion of the triumph during the New Deal of a privately controlled, piecemeal approach to planning, rather than a comprehensive, publicly controlled approach based on the pursuit of national objectives, see Otis L. Graham, Jr., *Toward a Planned Society: From Roosevelt to Nixon* (New York, 1977 ed.).

58. Arthur M. Schlesinger, Jr., *The Age of Roosevelt*, Vol. III: *The Politics of Upheaval* (Boston, 1966 ed.), pp. 235–36, 386–92; Schlesinger, *Crisis of Old Order*, p. 418.

59. Leuchtenburg, in his highly influential study, recognizes that a shift did take place in the New Deal in 1935, but he warns against exaggerating the extent of the ideological shift which then occurred. Basil Rauch, who originated the First and Second New Deal terminology in his 1944 study of the Roosevelt era, later acknowledged that with the benefit of greater hindsight he had become inclined "to underline the unity of the New Deal more than its shift from early to later policies." Leuchtenburg, *FDR and the New Deal*, p. 163; Basil Rauch, *The History of the New Deal 1933–1938* (New York, 1963 ed.), p. vii. For a particularly vehement criticism of the two New Deal thesis, see Rosen, *Hoover, Roosevelt*, pp. 115–18.

60. Tugwell, *Democratic Roosevelt*, pp. 326–27; Rexford G. Tugwell, "Roosevelt and Frankfurter: An Essay Review," *Political Science Quarterly* 85 (March 1970): 99–114; Frankfurter to Arthur Schlesinger, June 18, 1963, in *Roosevelt and Frankfurter*, p. 25; Frankfurter to Geoffrey Parsons, April 17, 1933, in Rosen, *Hoover, Roosevelt*, p. 328. Murphy also claims that Frankfurter and Moley developed a good working relationship in the early days of the New Deal. In contrast, Parrish, Dawson, and Hirsch all tend to see Frankfurter and the Brains Trust as representing fundamentally different approaches to reform. Murphy, *Brandeis/Frankfurter Connection*, pp. 106–11; Parrish, *Frankfurter*, p. 205; Nelson Lloyd Dawson, *Louis D. Brandeis, Felix Frankfurter, and the New Deal* (Hamden, 1980), pp. 33–39; H. N. Hirsch, *The Enigma of Felix Frankfurter* (New York, 1981), pp. 102–05.

61. Hirsch, *Frankfurter*, p. 104; Daniels to Franklin Roosevelt, October 1, 1934; January 7 and 15, 1935; March 4, 1938, JD MS; Daniels to Homer Cummings, February

12, 1937, JD MS. On Daniels, see also Hawley, *New Deal*, p. 290; E. David Cronon, "A Southern Progressive Looks at the New Deal," *Journal of Southern History* 24 (May 1958): 151–76.

62. Daniels to Roosevelt, January 7, 1935; Frankfurter, Memo for Roosevelt, December 28, 1935, in *Roosevelt and Frankfurter*, p. 297.

63. Hawley, *New Deal*, p. 421; Stimson, Diary, September 17, 1940, HS MS; Richberg to Franklin Roosevelt, April 23, 1938, DR MS/LC. After 1935, Richberg consistently called for a revision of the anti-trust laws to make possible some of the cooperative practices which he claimed were used successfully in the NRA. Richberg, "A Suggestion for Revision of the Anti-Trust Laws," *University of Pennsylvania Law Review* 85 (November 1936): 1–14; Richberg, "Future Federal Regulation of Business," *Vital Speeches* 3 (February 1, 1937): 238–41; Richberg, "Government and Business: The Strength of a Responsible Democracy," *Vital Speeches* 4 (February 15, 1938): 280–82; Richberg, *Hero*, pp. 299–301.

64. Louis D. Brandeis, *Other People's Money*, edited with an introduction and notes by Richard Abrams (New York, 1967 ed.); Frankfurter to Walter Lippmann, March 11, 1933, in *Roosevelt and Frankfurter*, p. 117; Daniels, Diary, May 28, 1933, JD MS.

65. For background on the Securities Act of 1933 and on subsequent New Deal legislation affecting the financial markets, see Ralph E. de Bedts, *The New Deal's SEC* (New York, 1964); and Michael E. Parrish, *Securities Regulation and the New Deal* (New Haven, 1970).

66. Frankfurter to Franklin Roosevelt, February 22, 1934, in *Roosevelt and Frankfurter*, p. 195.

67. In addition to the sources cited in footnote 65, see also Schlesinger, *Coming of the New Deal*, pp. 456–67.

68. Cronon, "Southern Progressive," p. 161; Dawson, *Brandeis, Frankfurter*, pp. 119–22. Baruch opposed the Holding Company Act's death sentence. Baruch, Testimony, in U.S. Congress, Senate, Special Committee to Investigate Unemployment and Relief, 75th Cong., 3d sess., *Hearings*, February 28 and March 1, 1938.

The banking laws passed in 1933 and 1935 separated commercial and investment banking functions, as Frankfurter had previously advocated, created the Federal Deposit Insurance Corporation, and strengthened the Federal Reserve Board. The nature and impact of the Brandeisian approach to regulation, however, is well illustrated by the securities legislation examined in the text. In discussing the banking reforms of the 1930s, Ellis Hawley concludes that by the time of the New Deal, the power of investment bankers had, in fact, already waned, largely because of the growing strength and financial independence of the great corporations which had evolved during the 1920s. Hawley, *New Deal*, pp. 304–24.

69. Schlesinger, *Coming of the New Deal*, p. 444; Stimson to Franklin Roosevelt, October 31, 1933, copy in FF MS; Stimson to Frankfurter, December 5, 1933 and January 26, 1934, FF MS.

Frankfurter ended the correspondence on the subject as follows: "A story that I love dearly is Carlyle's account of his friendship with John Sterling. You may remember Carlyle's telling of one of his talks with Sterling, when they talked way into the morning, canvassing differences between them which they had threshed out again and again. Carlyle concludes that early in the morning 'we parted, agreeing in all things except opinion.' That, in a way, is not a bad summary of the relation between us for now more than twenty-five years. Ever since our break over T.R., back in 1912, we have differed about things political, but these differences have never touched a relationship that I prize so very, very dearly. Certainly whatever 'personal feeling' I may have shown in my earlier letter—and I can assure you that I was not conscious of any such feeling—

was not at all directed towards you. How could it have been!'' Frankfurter to Stimson, February 20, 1934, FF MS.

70. Frankfurter, ''The Federal Securities Act,'' *Fortune* 8 (August 1933): 5–24; Vincent P. Carosso, *Investment Banking in America: A History* (Cambridge, 1970), p. 352. See also Bedts, *SEC* and Parrish, *Securities Regulation*, for similar assessments of the significance of the securities legislation.

71. Frankfurter, ''Federal Securities Act,'' pp. 5–24.

72. Hawley, *New Deal*, p. 311.

73. Bedts, *SEC*, pp. 199–200; Frankfurter, ''Review of *Curse of Bigness*,'' *Atlantic Monthly* 155 (May 1935): 14–16; Frankfurter to Franklin Roosevelt, May 23, 1933, in *Roosevelt and Frankfurter*, p. 220.

74. Frankfurter, ''The Young Men Go to Washington,'' originally in *Fortune* 13 (January 1936), reprinted in *Law and Politics: Occasional Papers of Felix Frankfurter, 1913–1938*, ed. by Archibald MacLeish and E. F. Prichard, Jr., (Gloucester, 1971), p. 242; Frankfurter, ''What Standard of College Education Is Defensible?'' radio address, May 22, 1933, FF MS; Daniels to Franklin Roosevelt, March 29, 1938, JD MS.

75. Frankfurter to Arthur Perry, September 13, 1933, in Baker, *Frankfurter*, p. 160.

76. Bedts, Parrish, and Carosso all agree that the financial community came to value the regulatory system created by the New Deal.

77. For the statistic on the level of private investment, see Herbert Stein, *The Fiscal Revolution in America* (Chicago, 1969), p. 89.

78. On the political climate created by Huey Long's Share-Our-Wealth campaign, see Schlesinger, *Politics of Upheaval*, pp. 62–68, 325–26. Frankfurter to Franklin Roosevelt, May 16, 1935, in *Roosevelt and Frankfurter*, p. 271. The previous year, Daniels wrote to FDR to advise him to consult with Brandeis before drawing up the next tax bill. Daniels to Franklin Roosevelt, September 26, 1934, JD MS.

79. Hawley, *New Deal*, pp. 344–59; Dawson, *Brandeis, Frankfurter*, pp. 114–19; Murphy, *Brandeis/Frankfurter Connection*, pp. 159–65.

80. Frankfurter, Draft of the 1936 Democratic platform, in *Roosevelt and Frankfurter*, p. 352; Frankfurter, Memo for FDR on tax policy, October 31, 1937, in *Roosevelt and Frankfurter*, p. 430.

81. Brandeis is quoted in Hawley, *New Deal*, p. 344; Frankfurter, Draft of tax message, 1937, in *Roosevelt and Frankfurter*, p. 437; Daniels to Franklin Roosevelt, March 5, 1936, JD MS. On Daniels' support for tax reform, see also Cronon, ''Southern Progressive,'' pp. 167–68.

82. Frankfurter, Draft of tax message, 1937, p. 435.

83. Frankfurter, Draft of tax message, 1937, p. 436; Frankfurter, ''Some Observations Regarding Taxes,'' memo sent to Franklin Roosevelt, October 8, 1939, in *Roosevelt and Frankfurter*, p. 502.

84. Schwarz, *Speculator*, p. 314.

85. Baruch to Daniels, March 16, 1936, JD MS; Baruch, Senate testimony, March 1, 1938.

86. Baruch to Sen. Joseph Robinson, June 28, 1935, BB MS; Baruch to Daniels, March 16, 1936.

87. Stimson to John Lee, March 1, 1934, HS MS.

88. Ibid.

89. Richberg, ''Essentials for Sustained Recovery,'' *Proceedings of the Academy of Political Science* 18 (May 1938): 38.

90. James T. Patterson, *Congressional Conservatism and the New Deal: The Growth of the Conservative Coalition in Congress, 1933–1939* (Lexington, 1967), p. 69. On the provisions and impact of the tax legislation of the Thirties, see Sidney Rattner, *Taxation and Democracy in America* (New York, 1980 ed.), pp. 465–90; Randolph E. Paul, *Tax-*

*ation for Prosperity* (Indianapolis, 1947), pp. 40–61; Hawley, *New Deal,* pp. 344–59; *Historical Statistics,* p. 713. Schwarz notes that "conservatives dubbed the 1938 tax bill 'the Baruch bill' " because of his influence over the Senate deliberations on the act. Schwarz, *Speculator,* p. 323.

91. For a discussion of the strength of Congressional opposition to FDR's tax reform proposals, see Patterson, *Congressional Conservatism.*

92. Frankfurter to Walter Lippmann, April 7, 1932, FF MS; Robin Barlow, Harvey E. Brazer, and James N. Morgan, *Economic Behavior of the Affluent* (Washington, 1966), pp. 2–7.

93. See Gabriel Kolko, *Wealth and Power in America: An Analysis of Social Class and Income Distribution* (New York, 1962), pp. 30–45, for a discussion of the problem of individual tax avoidance. I have already briefly discussed the issue of corporate tax avoidance in Chapter 5.

94. Stein, *Fiscal Revolution,* p. 4.

95. For a clear statement of the development of Keynes' theory, see Robert Lekachman, *The Age of Keynes* (New York, 1975 ed.).

96. Stein, *Fiscal Revolution,* pp. 130, 148.

97. Stein, *Fiscal Revolution,* pp. 6–38.

98. Stein, *Fiscal Revolution,* pp. 27, 46.

99. Frankfurter to Franklin Roosevelt, July 6, 1933; November 23, 1933; and May 7, 1934, all in *Roosevelt and Frankfurter,* pp. 147, 167–73, 213; J. M. Keynes, "An Open Letter to President Roosevelt," in *Roosevelt and Frankfurter,* p. 180. See also Murphy, *Brandeis/Frankfurter Connection,* pp. 126–29.

100. Murphy, *Brandeis/Frankfurter Connection,* pp. 165–78; Frankfurter to Roosevelt, May 30, 1935, p. 275; Daniels to Franklin Roosevelt, January 18, 1935, JD MS; Baruch, *Public Years,* p. 256; Baruch to Franklin Roosevelt, April 30, 1936, BB MS.

Brandeis and Frankfurter argued that unemployment insurance ought to be based on the Wisconsin approach which taxed industries differentially according to their past records as employers, though they also favored leaving the various states a considerable amount of discretion in the administration of such a program. Other New Dealers backed a unified national system which would not have attempted to treat firms on an individual basis. On Frankfurter's views, see also Frankfurter "A Distinctively American Contribution," *American Labor Legislation Review* 23 (December 1933): 169. Richberg, interestingly, recommended back in 1931 that individual industries ought to begin absorbing the expense of creating old-age pensions for their employees, since such expenses ought properly to be considered an "industrial cost," rather than as a responsibility of government. This was clearly an example of Richberg's corporatist leanings. Richberg, "Report on Old Age Pensions to RLEA," July, 1931, DR MS/CHS.

101. Stein, *Fiscal Revolution,* p. 56.

102. Broadus Mitchell, *Depression Decade: From New Era through New Deal* (New York, 1947), p. 446; *Historical Statistics,* p. 73; Paul A. Baran and Paul M. Sweezy, *Monopoly Capital: An Essay on the American Economic and Social Order* (New York, 1968 ed.), p. 242; Hawley, *New Deal,* pp. 386–87; Leuchtenburg, *FDR and the New Deal,* pp. 243–44.

103. Stein, *Fiscal Revolution,* pp. 91–130; Lekachman, *Keynes,* pp. 124–25, 137–43; Baruch, Senate testimony, March 1, 1938; Baruch, *Public Years,* p. 125.

104. Stein, *Fiscal Revolution,* pp. 105–07. For a discussion of the ease with which FDR's spending bill went through Congress, see Patterson, *Congressional Conservatism,* pp. 233–42.

105. John Maynard Keynes, *The General Theory of Employment, Interest, and Money* (New York, 1964 ed.), p. 129.

106. *Historical Statistics,* p. 711; Carey E. Brown, "Fiscal Policies in the Thirties: A

Reappraisal," *American Economic History Review* 46 (December 1956): 863–66; Le-kachman, *Keynes,* pp. 124–25, 138–43.

107. *Historical Statistics,* pp. 73, 139; Baran, *Monopoly Capital,* p. 242; Gilbert Burck and Charles E. Silberman, "Why the Depression Lasted So Long," *Fortune* 51 (March 1955): 84–88+.

108. Stein, *Fiscal Revolution,* pp. 117–18.

109. Stein, *Fiscal Revolution,* pp. 83–90; Schwarz, *Speculator,* p. 315.

110. On the shift from direct to work relief and the restrictions placed on WPA projects, see Frances Fox Piven and Richard A. Cloward, *Regulating the Poor: The Functions of Public Welfare* (New York, 1972 ed.), pp. 94–98.

111. Keynes, "Open Letter," p. 180; *Historical Statistics,* p. 711.

112. Lekachman, *Keynes,* p. 285. See also Stein, *Fiscal Revolution,* pp. 89–90.

113. See especially the final chapters in Richard Hofstadter, *The Age of Reform: From Bryan to F.D.R.* (New York, 1955); and Leuchtenburg, *FDR and the New Deal.* See also Otis L. Graham, Jr., *An Encore for Reform: The Old Progressives and the New Deal* (New York, 1967).

114. *Historical Statistics,* pp. 710–11.

115. Graham, *Encore for Reform,* p. 193; Arthur S. Link and William B. Catton, *American Epoch: A History of the United States Since 1900* Vol. I: *An Era of Economic Change, Reform, and World Wars 1900–1945* (New York, 1980 ed.), pp. 389, 413. Schlesinger sees the New Deal as a struggle between those who were heirs of Theodore Roosevelt's New Nationalism and those who identified with Woodrow Wilson's New Freedom. In Schlesinger's account, the dominance of first the New Nationalism and then the New Freedom defined the transition from the First to the Second New Deal. Patterson concludes from his study of conservative Congressional opposition to the New Deal that the "welfare state" which emerged in the 1930s was fundamentally different from the "Wilsonian" regulatory state of the Progressive era, and that this difference accounts for the opposition of many Southern Democrats who had earlier supported Wilsonian progressivism. A recent study of the old Republican progressive bloc still surviving in the Senate during the New Deal demonstrates the difficulty of neatly labeling most former progressives as either pro- or anti-New Deal. Ronald Feinman has found virtually unanimous support among progressive Senate Republicans for such key elements of the Second New Deal as Social Security, the Wagner Act, and tax reform, but most of the individuals he has studied ultimately turned against FDR because of the court packing controversy and foreign policy differences. Schlesinger *Politics of Upheaval,* pp. 214, 393; Patterson, *Congressional Conservatism,* p. 133; Ronald L. Feinman, *Twilight of Progressivism: The Western Republican Senators and the New Deal* (Baltimore, 1981), pp. 93–94, 203–05. I believe it is important not to overemphasize the supposed differences between the New Nationalism and New Freedom legacies, since, as I have argued earlier, the two approaches were essentially compatible.

116. See, for instance, Carl N. Degler, *Out of Our Past: The Forces That Shaped Modern America* (New York, 1970 ed.), pp. 379–413.

117. *Historical Statistics,* pp. 166–67; Jeffrey G. Williamson and Peter H. Lindert, *American Inequality: A Macroeconomic History* (New York, 1980), p. 54; Douglass C. North, *Growth and Welfare in the American Past* (Englewood Cliffs, 1966), pp. 178–79.

118. Ornati estimates that 46 percent of American households in 1935–36 lived below a "minimum adequacy" standard of living. Lebergott notes that by government standards of the 1970s, 56 percent of American families lived below the poverty line in 1935–36. I have been unable to find precise statistics for 1939, though, by 1941, Ornati calculates tht the number of Americans living in poverty fell to 32 percent of the population. By 1941, however, the country was already beginning to experience the stimu-

lative effects of war production. Oscar Ornati, *Poverty Amid Affluence* (New York, 1966), pp. 148, 158; Stanley Lebergott, *The American Economy: Income, Wealth, and Want* (Princeton, 1976), p. 3; *Historical Statistics,* p. 95.

119. *Historical Statistics,* p. 573.

120. Graham, *Planned Society,* pp. 67–68

## IX. Liberalism's Ambiguous Legacy

1. For two sharply critical views of Frankfurter's career on the Supreme Court, see H. N. Hirsch, *The Enigma of Felix Frankfurter* (New York, 1981); and Joseph P. Lash, Biographical Essay, in *From the Diaries of Felix Frankfurter,* ed. by Lash (New York, 1975). For a thorough examination of Frankfurter's extrajudicial activities while on the bench, see Bruce Allen Murphy, *The Brandeis/Frankfurter Connection: The Secret Political Activities of Two Supreme Court Justices* (New York, 1982).

2. Vadney argues that Richberg himself remained ideologically consistent throughout his career, but that the times changed and left him behind. Thomas E. Vadney, *The Wayward Liberal: A Political Biography of Donald Richberg* (Lexington, 1970). For Richberg's later views, see Richberg, *Government and Business Tomorrow: A Public Relations Program* (New York, 1943); Richberg, *Labor Union Monopoly: A Clear and Present Danger* (Chicago, 1957); Richberg and Albert Britt, *Only the Brave Are Free: A Condensed Review of the Growth of Self-Government in America* (Caldwell, 1958).

3. Grant McConnell observes that businessmen, workers, and farmers in America continue to exhibit a "conspicuous" degree of "agreement" in their "loud and persistent appeal for liberty. It is very easy to discount this avowed devotion as propaganda and the use of an overworked cliché. To dismiss it thus, however, is to do injustice to the sincerity of those who voiced it and to ignore much of its significance. Several points should be noted here. First, liberty is seen by business, labor and agriculture in very simple terms—as absence of compulsion. Second, compulsion is seen as coming almost exclusively from the state. Third, liberty is seen as an attribute not merely of the individual, but more especially of certain kinds of private association." *Private Power and American Democracy* (New York, 1970 ed.), p. 89.

For a brief but broad survey of the continuities in the American political economy during the first half of the twentieth century, see Arthur M. Johnson, "Continuity and Change in Government-Business Relations," in *Change and Continuity in Twentieth-Century America,* ed. by John Braeman, Robert Bremner, Everett Walters (Columbus, 1964).

4. Edward C. Budd, ed., *Inequality and Poverty* (New York, 1967), p. xxii; Jeffrey G. Williamson and Peter H. Lindert, *American Inequality: A Macroeconomic History* (New York, 1980), pp. 53–57; James T. Patterson, *America's Struggle Against Poverty, 1900–1980* (Cambridge, 1981), p. 158.

5. U.S. Department of Commerce, Bureau of the Census, *1976 U.S. Fact Book: The American Almanac (The Statistical Abstract of the United States)* (New York, 1976), pp. 502–03.

6. See Theodore J. Lowi, *The End of Liberalism: The Second Republic of the United States* (New York, 1979 ed.) for an excellent analysis of modern-day liberalism.

7. Lowi, *End of Liberalism;* McConnell, *Private Power,* p. 29. See also Otis L. Graham, Jr., *Toward a Planned Society: From Roosevelt to Nixon* (New York, 1976).

8. See especially McConnell, *Private Power* for a critique of the liberal assumption that decentralized private associations are more likely to be democratic in spirit and practice than large constituency based public institutions.

9. Lowi uses the term "incrementalism" in his critique of the basic assumptions of interest group liberalism. See especially, *End of Liberalism,* pp. 38, 211, 236.

10. John Braeman, "The New Deal and the 'Broker State:' A Review of the Recent Scholarly Literature," *Business History Review* 46 (Winter 1972): 428–29.

# Bibliography

## Manuscripts

Bernard M. Baruch Papers, Princeton University Library.
Josephus Daniels Papers, Library of Congress.
Felix Frankfurter Papers, Library of Congress.
Donald R. Richberg Papers, Chicago Historical Society.
Donald R. Richberg Papers, Library of Congress.
Henry L. Stimson Papers, Yale University Library.

## Public Documents

U.S. Congress, House, Committee on Naval Affairs. *Hearings on Estimates Submitted by the Secretary of the Navy,* 64th Cong., 1st sess., 1916.
U.S. Congress, Senate, Committee on Finance. *Hearings on Investigation of Economic Problems,* 72nd Cong., 2nd sess., 1933.
U.S. Congress, Senate, Committee on Public Lands. *Hearings on Leasing of Oil Lands,* 64th Cong., 1st sess., 1916.
U.S. Congress, Senate, Special Committee to Investigate Unemployment and Relief. *Hearings,* 75th Cong., 3rd sess., 1938.
U.S. Department of Commerce, Bureau of the Census. *Historical Statistics of the United States: Colonial Times to 1957,* 1960.
U.S. Department of Commerce, Bureau of the Census. *1976 U.S. Fact Book: The American Almanac (The Statistical Abstract of the United States).* New York: Grosset and Dunlap, 1976.
U.S. National Resources Planning Board. *The Structure of the American Economy,* Part II: *Toward Full Use of Resources: A Symposium by Gardiner C. Means, D.E. Montgomery, J.M. Clark, Alvin H. Hansen, Mordecai Ezekiel,* 1940.

## Newspapers

Raleigh *News & Observer.* 1894–1948.

## Books and Articles

Adelman, M.A. "The Measurement of Industrial Concentration," *Review of Economics and Statistics* 33 (November 1951): 269–296.

Aldcroft, Derek H. *From Versailles to Wall Street 1919–1929*. London: Allen Lane, 1977.

Altschuler, Glenn C. *Race, Ethnicity, and Class in American Social Thought, 1865–1919*. Arlington Heights, Illinois: Harlan Davidson, 1982.

Arnold, Peri Ethan. "Herbert Hoover & the Continuity of American Public Policy," *Public Policy* 20 (Fall 1972): 525–544.

Baker, Liva. *Felix Frankfurter*. New York: Coward-McCann, 1969.

Baltzell, E. Digby. *The Protestant Establishment: Aristocracy & Caste in America*. New York: Vintage, 1966, or. ed. 1964.

Baran, Paul A., and Sweezy, Paul M. *Monopoly Capital: An Essay on the American Economic and Social Order*. New York: Monthly Review Press, 1968, or. ed. 1966.

Barlow, Robin; Brazer, Harvey E.; and Morgan, James N. *Economic Behavior of the Affluent*. Washington: Brookings Institution, 1966.

Barton, Bruce. "Bernard M. Baruch Discusses the Future of American Business," *American Magazine* 107 (June 1929): 26+.

Baruch, Bernard M. *American Industry in the War: A Report of the War Industries Board (March 1921)*, ed. by Richard H. Hippelheuser. New York: Prentice-Hall, 1941.

——. *Baruch: My Own Story*. New York: Henry Holt, 1957.

——. Baruch: The Public Years. New York: Holt, Rinehart and Winston, 1960.

——. "The Consequences of the War to Industry," *Current History* 29 (November 1928): 189–197.

——. "Educating Ourselves for Peace and Freedom: Today, Thinking Has Become a Neglected Art," *Vital Speeches* 19 (June 1, 1953): 510–12.

——. "Output as Inflation Cure," *United States News* 20 (April 5, 1946): 73–75.

——. "Regulating One's Behavior: False Gospel of Security by Deficit Spending," *Vital Speeches* 16 (June 15, 1950): 523–25.

——. "Self-Discipline, The Key to Peace," *Vital Speeches* 17 (June 1, 1951): 487–89.

——. "This I Believe," *Reader's Digest* 64 (April 1954): 69.

——. "The Wilsonian Legacy For Us," *New York Times Magazine* (December 23, 1956): 12+.

Bell Daniel. *The End of Ideology: On the Exhaustion of Political Ideas in the Fifties*. New York: Collier, 1962, or. ed. 1960.

Bellush, Bernard. *The Failure of the NRA*. New York: W.W. Norton, 1975.

Berle, Adolph A., Jr., and Means, Gardiner C. *The Modern Corporation and Private Property*. New York: Macmillan, 1932.

Bernstein, Irving. *A History of the American Worker, 1933–1941: Turbulent Years*. Boston: Houghton Mifflin, 1970.

———. *The Lean Years: A History of the American Worker, 1920–1933.* Baltimore: Penguin, 1966, or. ed. 1960.

———. *The New Deal Collective Bargaining Policy.* Berkeley: University of California Press, 1950.

Best, Gary Dean. *The Politics of American Individualism: Herbert Hoover in Transition, 1918–1922.* Westport, Connecticut: Greenwood, 1975.

Bickel, Alexander. "Applied Politics and the Science of Law: Writings of the Harvard Period," in *Felix Frankfurter: A Tribute,* ed. by Wallace Mendelson. New York: Reynal, 1964.

Blair, John M. *Economic Concentration: Structure, Behavior and Public Policy.* New York: Harcourt Brace, 1972.

Boorstin, Daniel. *The Genius of American Politics.* Chicago: University of Chicago Press, 1958, or. ed. 1953.

Braeman, John. "The New Deal and the 'Broker State:' A Review of the Recent Scholarly Literature," *Business History Review* 46 (Winter 1972): 409–29.

Brandeis, Louis D. *Other People's Money: And How the Bankers Use it,* ed. with an introduction and notes by Richard Abrams. New York: Harper & Row, 1967, or. ed. 1913.

Brown, Carey E. "Fiscal Policy in the Thirties: A Reappraisal," *American Economic History Review* 46 (December 1956): 857–79.

Brody, David. *Steelworkers in America: The Nonunion Era.* New York: Harper & Row, 1960.

Budd, Edward C., ed. *Inequality and Poverty.* New York: W.W. Norton, 1967.

Buenker, John D. *Urban Liberalism and Progressive Reform.* New York: Scribner's, 1973.

Burck, Gilbert, and Silberman, Charles E. "What Caused the Great Depression," *Fortune* 51 (February 1955): 94–99+.

———. "Why the Depression Lasted So Long," *Fortune* 51 (March 1955): 84–88+.

Burner, David. *Herbert Hoover: A Public Life.* New York: Alfred A. Knopf, 1979.

Burns, Arthur Robert. *The Decline of Competition: A Study of the Evolution of American Industry.* New York: McGraw-Hill, 1936.

Carosso, Vincent P. *Investment Banking in America: A History.* Cambridge, Massachusetts: Harvard University Press, 1970.

Chalmers, David M. *Neither Socialism nor Monopoly: Theodore Roosevelt and the Decision to Regulate the Railroads.* Philadelphia: Lippincott, 1976.

Chambers, Clarke A. *Seedtime of Reform: American Social Service and Social Action, 1918–1933.* Ann Arbor, Michigan: University of Michigan Press, 1967, or. ed. 1963.

Chambers, John Whiteclay II. *The Tyranny of Change: America in the Progressive Era, 1900–1917.* New York: St. Martin's, 1980.

Chandler, Alfred D., Jr. *The Visible Hand: The Managerial Revolution in American Business.* Cambridge, Massachusetts: Belknap, 1977.

Chandler, Lester V. *America's Greatest Depression, 1929–1941.* New York: Harper & Row, 1970.

Clark, Lawrence E. *Central Banking Under the Federal Reserve System: With Special Consideration of the Federal Reserve Bank of New York.* New York: Macmillan, 1935.

Clarkson, Grosvenor B. *Industrial America in the World War: The Strategy Behind the Line, 1917–1918.* Boston: Houghton Mifflin, 1923.

Cochran, Thomas C. *The American Business System: A Historical Perspective, 1900–1955.* New York: Harper & Row, 1962, or. ed. 1957.

——, and Miller, William. *The Age of Enterprise: A Social History of Industrial America.* New York: Harper & Row, 1961, or. ed. 1942.

Coit, Margaret L. *Mr. Baruch.* Boston: Houghton Mifflin, 1957.

Comanor, William S., and Smiley, Robert H. "Monopoly and the Distribution of Wealth," *Quarterly Journal of Economics* 89 (May 1975): 177–194.

Crawford, Finla G. "Constitutional Developments, 1867–1915," in *History of the State of New York: Modern Party Battles,* ed. by Alexander C. Flick. New York: Columbia University Press, 1935.

Cronon, E. David. *Josephus Daniels in Mexico.* Madison, Wisconsin: University of Wisconsin Press, 1960.

——. "A Southern Progressive Looks at the New Deal," *Journal of Southern History* 24 (May 1958): 151–176.

Cuff, Robert D. "Bernard Baruch: Symbol and Myth in Industrial Mobilization," *Business History Review* 43 (Summer 1969): 115–133.

——. "The Cooperative Impulse and War: The Origins of the Council of National Defense and Advisory Commission," in *Building the Organizational Society: Essays on Associational Activities in Modern America,* ed. by Jerry Israel. New York: Free Press, 1972.

——. "Herbert Hoover, the Ideology of Voluntarism and War Organization During the Great War," *Journal of American History* 64 (September 1977): 358–372.

——. *The War Industries Board: Business-Government Relations During World War I.* Baltimore: The Johns Hopkins University Press, 1973.

——. "Woodrow Wilson and Business-Government Relations During World War I," *Review of Politics* 31 (July 1969): 385–407.

——, and Urofsky, Melvin I. "The Steel Industry and Price-Fixing During World War I," *Business History Review* 45 (Autumn 1970): 291–306.

Current, Richard N. *Secretary Stimson: A Study in Statecraft.* New Brunswick, New Jersey: Rutgers University Press, 1954.

Dahl, Robert A. *Pluralist Democracy in the United States: Conflict and Consent.* Chicago: Rand McNally, 1967.

Daniels, Jonathan. *End of Innocence.* Philadelphia: J.B. Lippincott, 1954.

Daniels, Josephus. "Above all—Patriotism! A Seven-Point Remedy for Our Hectic After-War Fever," *Forum* 63 (March 1920): 298–306.

——. "According to Plan: A Review of Woodrow Wilson's First Year in the White House," *Harper's Weekly* 58 (March 7, 1914): 8–9.

——. "Building the World's Most Powerful Warships," *Saturday Evening Post* 193 (March 26, 1921): 21+.

——. *The Cabinet Diaries of Josephus Daniels, 1913–1921,* ed. by E. David Cronon. Lincoln, Nebraska: University of Nebraska Press, 1963.

——. *Editor in Politics.* Chapel Hill, North Carolina: University of North Carolina Press, 1941.

——. *The Navy and the Nation: War-Time Addresses by Josephus Daniels.* New York: George H. Doran, 1919.

——. *Our Navy at War.* New York: George H. Doran, 1922.

——. *Shirt-Sleeve Diplomat.* Chapel Hill, North Carolina: University of North Carolina Press, 1947.

——. *Tar Heel Editor.* Chapel Hill, North Carolina: University of North Carolina Press, 1939.

——. *The Wilson Era: Years of Peace, 1910–1917.* Chapel Hill, North Carolina: University of North Carolina Press, 1944.

——. *The Wilson Era: Years of War and After, 1917–1923.* Chapel Hill, North Carolina: University of North Carolina Press, 1946.

Dawson, Nelson Lloyd. *Louis Brandeis, Felix Frankfurter, and the New Deal.* Hamden, Connecticut: Archon, 1980.

De Bedts, Ralph E. *The New Deal's SEC: The Formative Years.* New York: Columbia University Press, 1964.

Degler, Carl N. *Out of Our Past: The Forces That Shaped Modern America.* New York: Harper & Row, 1970, or. ed. 1959.

Derber Milton, and Young, Edwin, eds. *Labor and the New Deal.* Madison, Wisconsin: University of Wisconsin Press, 1961.

Dowd, Douglas F. *The Twisted Dream: Capitalist Development in the United States Since 1776.* Cambridge, Massachusetts: Winthrop, 1974.

Edwards, Richard; Reich, Michael; and Weisskopf, Thomas E. *The Capitalist System: A Radical Analysis of American Society.* Edgewood Cliffs, New Jersey: Prentice-Hall, 1978, or. ed. 1972.

Fabricant, Solomon. *The Trend of Government Activity in the United States Since 1900.* New York: National Bureau of Economic Research, 1952.

Fainsod, Merle, and Gordon, Lincoln. *Government and the American Economy.* New York: W. W. Norton, 1948, or. ed. 1941.

Faulkner, Harold Underwood. *American Economic History.* New York: Harper & Bros., 1949, or. ed. 1924.

——. *The Decline of Laissez Faire, 1897–1917.* New York: Harper & Row, 1968, or. ed. 1951.

Fausold, Martin L., and Mazuzan, George T. *The Hoover Presidency: A Reappraisal.* Albany, New York: State University of New York Press, 1974.

Feinman, Ronald L. *Twilight of Progressivism: The Western Republican Senators and the New Deal.* Baltimore: The Johns Hopkins University Press, 1981.

Ferrell, Robert H. *American Diplomacy in the Great Depression: Hoover-Stimson Foreign Policy, 1929–1933.* New York: W.W. Norton, 1970, or. ed. 1957.

Field, Carter. *Bernard Baruch: Park Bench Statesman.* New York: Whittlesey House, 1944.

Fine, Sidney. *The Automobile Under the Blue Eagle: Labor, Management, and* the Automobile Manufacturing Code. Ann Arbor, Michigan: University of Michigan Press, 1963.

——. Laissez Faire and the General-Welfare State: A Study of Conflict in American Thought, 1865–1901. Ann Arbor, Michigan: University of Michigan Press, 1964, or. ed. 1956.

Fite, Gilbert C. George N. Peek and the Fight for Farm Parity. Norman, Oklahoma: University of Oklahoma Press, 1954.

Forcey, Charles. The Crossroads of Liberalism: Croly, Weyl, Lippmann and the Progressive Era, 1900–1925. New York: Oxford University Press, 1967, or. ed. 1961.

Frankfurter, Felix. Address to Harvard Law Society of Illinois, April 28, 1955. Privately bound pamphlet.

——, and Landis, James M. The Business of the Supreme Court: A Study in the Federal Judicial System. New York: Macmillan, 1927.

——, and Hart, Henry M., Jr. "The Business of the Supreme Court at October Term, 1934," Harvard Law Review 49 (November 1935): 68–107.

——. "Child Labor and the Court," New Republic 31 (July 26, 1922): 248–250.

——. The Commerce Clause Under Marshall, Taney and Waite. Chapel Hill, North Carolina: University of North Carolina Press, 1937.

——. "The Conservation of the New Federal Standards," Survey 41 (December 7, 1918): 291–293.

——, and Pound, Roscoe, eds. Criminal Justice in Cleveland. Cleveland: Cleveland Foundation, 1922.

——. "A Distinctively American Contribution," American Labor Legislation Review 23 (December 1933): 169.

——. "The Federal Securities Act," Fortune 8 (August 1933): 5–24.

——. Felix Frankfurter on the Supreme Court: Extrajudicial Essays on the Court and the Constitution, ed. by Philip B. Kurland. Cambridge, Massachusetts: Harvard University Press, 1970.

——. Felix Frankfurter Reminisces (recorded in talks with Dr. Harlan B. Phillips). New York: Reynal, 1960.

——. "Industrial Relations: Some Noteworthy Recent Developments," Bulletin of the Taylor Society 4 (December 1919): 12–16.

——, and Greene, Nathan. The Labor Injunction. New York: Macmillan, 1930.

——. Law and Politics: Occasional Papers of Felix Frankfurter, 1913–1938, ed. by Archibald Macleish and E.F. Prichard, Jr. Gloucester, Massachusetts: Peter Smith, 1971, or. ed. 1939.

——. "Letter: A Difference in Figures," Independent 113 (November 1, 1924): 352.

——. "The Manager, the Workman, and the Social Scientist," Bulletin of the Taylor Society 3 (December 1917).

——, ed. Mr. Justice Brandeis. New Haven, Connecticut: Yale University Press, 1932.

——. Mr. Justice Holmes and the Supreme Court. Cambridge, Massachusetts: Harvard University Press, 1938.

——. *Of Law and Life & Other Things That Matter: Papers and Addresses of Felix Frankfurter, 1956–1963,* ed. by Philip B. Kurland. New York: Atheneum, 1965.

——. *Of Law and Men: Papers and Addresses of Felix Frankfurter, 1939–1956,* ed. by Philip Elman. New York: Harcourt, Brace, 1956.

——. "The Palestine Situation Restated," *Foreign Affairs* 9 (April 1931): 409–434.

——. *The Public & Its Government.* New Haven, Connecticut: Yale University Press, 1930.

——. "Public Opinion and Democratic Government," *Reference Shelf* 20 (1947): 145–149.

——. "The Question of a Minimum Wage Law for American Industry," *Congressional Digest* 15 (November 1936): 271–273.

——. "Rationalization in Industry and the Labor Problem," *Proceedings of the Academy of Political Science* 13 (June 1928): 171–177.

——. "Reply to Protest from Clothing Manufactures' Association," *New Republic 25 (January 12, 1921): 202.*

——. "Review of *Curse of Bigness* by Louis D. Brandeis," *Atlantic Monthly* 155 (May 1935): 14–16.

——. "Review of *Encyclopedia of the Social Sciences* v. 1," *Harvard Law Review* 43 (May 1930): 1168–1171.

——. "Review of *Interstate Transmission of Electric Power* by H.L. Elsbree," *Harvard Law Review* 45 (February 1932): 762–764.

——. "Review of *Trade Association Activities and the Law* by F. D. Jones," *Columbia Law Review* 23 (June 1923): 601–602.

——. "Robert Grosvenor Valentine, '96," *Harvard Alumni Bulletin* (December 14, 1916).

——. "Social Unrest," *Current Affairs* 10 (January 5, 1920): 5+.

——. "Summation of the Conference," *American Bar Association Journal* 24 (April 1938): 282–286.

——. "Surveys of Criminal Justice," in *Proceedings of the National Conference of Social Work.* Chicago: University of Chicago Press, 1930.

——. "The Utilities Bureau," *Annals of the American Academy of Political and Social Science* 57 (January 1915): 293–294.

——. "The Worth of Our Past: Civilization Our Business," *Vital Speeches* 7 (July 15, 1941): 601–603.

Fraser, Hugh Russell. "One Man Beats 150," *Outlook* 147 (October 5, 1927): 149–152.

Frederickson, George M. *The Inner Civil War: Northern Intellectuals and the Crisis of the Union.* New York: Harper & Row, 1968, or. ed. 1965.

Freedman, Max, ed. *Roosevelt and Frankfurter: Their Correspondence, 1928–1945.* Boston: Atlantic-Little, Brown, 1967.

Friedman, Milton, and Schwartz, Anna Jacobson. *The Great Contraction 1929–1933.* Princeton, New Jersey: Princeton University Press, 1965.

Galambos, Louis. *Competition & Cooperation: The Emergence of a National Trade Association.* Baltimore: The Johns Hopkins University Press, 1966.

Galbraith, John Kenneth. *The Great Crash, 1929*. Boston: Houghton Mifflin, 1961, or. ed. 1954.

Gilbert, James. *Designing the Industrial State: The Intellectual Pursuit of Collectivism in America, 1880–1940*. Chicago: Quadrangle, 1972.

Girvetz, Harry K. *The Evolution of Liberalism*. New York: Collier, 1963.

Goldman, Eric F. *Rendezvous with Destiny: A History of Modern American Reform*. New York: Vintage, 1977, or. ed. 1952.

Goldschmid, Harvey J.; Mann, H. Michael; and Weston, J. Fred, eds. *Industrial Concentration: The New Learning*. Boston: Little Brown, 1974.

Gordon, Robert Aaron. *Business Fluctuations*. New York: Harper & Bros., 1961, or. ed. 1952.

Gosnell, Harold F. *Boss Platt and his New York Machine: A Study of the Political Leadership of Thomas C. Platt, Theodore Roosevelt, and Others*. Chicago: University of Chicago Press, 1924.

Gould, Lewis L. *Reform and Regulation: American Politics, 1900–1916*. New York: Wiley, 1978.

Graham, Otis L., Jr. *An Encore for Reform: The Old Progressives and the New Deal*. New York: Oxford University Press, 1967.

——. *Toward A Planned Society: From Roosevelt to Nixon*. New York: Oxford University Press, 1976.

Haber, Samuel. *Efficiency and Uplift: Scientific Management in the Progressive Era, 1890–1920*. Chicago: University of Chicago Press, 1964.

Hansen, Alvin Harvey. *Full Recovery or Stagnation*. New York: W. W. Norton, 1938.

Hartz, Louis. *The Founding of New Societies: Studies in the History of the United States, Latin America, South Africa, Canada, and Australia*. New York: Harcourt, Brace & World, 1964.

——. *The Liberal Tradition in America: An Interpretation of American Political Thought Since the Revolution*. New York: Harcourt, Brace & World, 1955.

Hawley, Ellis W. *The Great War and the Search for a Modern Order: A History of the American People and Their Institutions, 1917–1933*. New York: St. Martin's, 1979.

——, ed. *Herbert Hoover as Secretary of Commerce: Studies in New Era Thought and Practice*. Iowa City: University of Iowa Press, 1981.

——. "Herbert Hoover, the Commerce Secretariat, and the Vision of an 'Associative State,' 1921–1928," *Journal of American History* 61 (June 1974): 116–140.

——. *The New Deal and the Problem of Monopoly: A Study in Economic Ambivalence*. Princeton, New Jersey: Princeton University Press, 1966.

Heilbroner, Robert L. *The Economic Transformation of America*. New York: Harcourt, Brace, Jovanovich, 1977.

Hicks, John D. *Republican Ascendancy, 1921–1933*. New York: Harper & Row, 1963, or. ed. 1960.

Higham, John. "The Cult of 'American Consensus': Homogenizing American History," *Commentary* 27 (February 1959): 93–100.

Himmelberg, Robert F. "Business Anti-Trust Policy and the Industrial Board of the Department of Commerce, 1919," *Business History Review* 42 (Spring 1968): 1–23.

——. *The Origins of the National Recovery Administration: Business, Government, and the Trade Association Issue, 1921–1933.* New York: Fordham University Press, 1976.

——. "The War Industries Board and the Antitrust Question in November, 1918," *Journal of American History* 52 (June 1965): 59–74.

Hirsch, H. N. *The Enigma of Felix Frankfurter.* New York: Basic, 1981.

Hofstadter, Richard. *The Age of Reform: From Bryan to F.D.R.* New York: Vintage, 1955.

——. *The American Political Tradition: And the Men Who Made It.* New York: Vintage, 1948.

——. *The Progressive Historians: Turner, Beard, Parrington.* New York: Alfred A. Knopf, 1968.

Holt, Charles F. "Who Benefited from the Prosperity of the Twenties," *Explorations in Economic History* 14 (1977): 277–289.

Hoogenboom, Ari and Olive. *A History of the ICC: From Panacea to Palliative.* New York: W. W. Norton, 1976.

Hudson, Winthrop S. *American Protestantism.* Chicago: University of Chicago Press, 1961.

Huthmacher, J. Joseph. *Senator Robert F. Wagner and the Rise of Urban Liberalism.* New York: Atheneum, 1971, or. ed. 1968.

——, and Susman, Warren I., eds. *Herbert Hoover and the Crisis of American Capitalism.* Cambridge, Massachusetts: Schenkman, 1973.

Ickes, Harold L. *The Autobiography of a Curmudgeon.* Chicago: Quadrangle, 1969, or. ed. 1943.

——. *The Secret Diary of Harold L. Ickes: The First Thousand Days, 1933–1936.* New York: Simon and Schuster, 1954.

Jenkins, Innis L. "Josephus Daniels and the Navy, 1913–1916: A Study in Military Administration." Ph.D. dissertation, University of Maryland, 1960.

Jessup, Philip C. *Elihu Root,* Vol. II: *1905–1937.* New York: Dodd, Mead, 1938.

Johnson, Arthur M. "Continuity and Change in Government-Business Relations," in *Change and Continuity in Twentieth-Century America,* ed. by John Braeman, Robert Bremner, and Everett Walters. Columbus, Ohio: Ohio State University Press, 1964.

Johnson, Hugh. *The Blue Eagle from Egg to Earth.* Garden City, New York: Doubleday, Doran, 1935.

Johnson, Thomas. "Postwar Optimism and the Rural Financial Crisis of the 1920's," *Explorations in Economic History* 11 (Winter 1973/74): 173–192.

Keller, Morton. *The Life Insurance Enterprise, 1895–1910: A Study in the Limits of Corporate Power.* Cambridge, Massachusetts: Belknap, 1963.

Keller, Robert. "Factor Income Distribution in the United States During the 1920's: A Reexamination of Fact and Theory," *Journal of Economic History* 33 (March 1973): 252–273.

Keynes, John Maynard. *The General Theory of Employment, Interest, and Money.* New York: Harbinger, 1964, or. ed. 1936.

Knappen, Theodore M. "Looking at the Farmers' Side: An Interview with Bernard M. Baruch," *World's Work* 43 (March 1922): 474–480.

Koistinen, Paul A. C. "The 'Industrial-Military Complex' in Historical Perspective: World War I," *Business History Review* 41 (Winter 1967): 378–403.

Kolko, Gabriel. *Railroads and Regulation, 1877–1916.* New York: W.W. Norton, 1970, or. ed. 1965.

——. *The Triumph of Conservatism: A Reinterpretation of American History, 1900–1916.* Chicago: Quadrangle, 1967, or. ed. 1963.

——. *Wealth and Power in America: An Analysis of Social Class and Income Distribution.* New York: Praeger, 1962.

Kuznets, Simon. *National Income: A Summary of Findings.* New York: National Bureau of Economic Research, 1946.

Lampman, Robert J. *The Share of Top Wealth-Holders in National Wealth, 1922–1956.* Princeton, New Jersey: Princeton University Press, 1962.

Larner, Robert J. *Management Control and the Large Corporation.* New York: Dunellen, 1970.

Lasch, Christopher. "Donald Richberg and the Idea of a National Interest." M.A. thesis, Columbia University, 1955.

Lash, Joseph P. *From the Diaries of Felix Frankfurter: With a Biographical Essay and Notes by Joseph P. Lash.* New York: W.W. Norton, 1975.

Lebergott, Stanley. *The American Economy: Income, Wealth, and Want.* Princeton, New Jersey: Princeton University Press, 1976.

Lee, Susan Previant, and Passell, Peter. *A New Economic View of American History.* New York: W.W. Norton, 1979.

Lefler, Hugh Talmage, and Newsome, Albert Ray. *North Carolina: The History of a Southern State.* Chapel Hill, North Carolina: University of North Carolina Press, 1973 ed.

Lekachman, Robert. *The Age of Keynes.* New York: McGraw-Hill, 1975, or. ed. 1966.

Leuchtenburg, William E. *Franklin D. Roosevelt and the New Deal, 1932–1940.* New York: Harper & Row, 1963.

——. "The New Deal and the Analogue of War," in *Change and Continuity in Twentieth-Century America,* ed. by John Braeman, Robert Bremner, and Everett Walters. Columbus, Ohio: Ohio State University Press, 1964.

——. *The Perils of Prosperity, 1914–1932.* Chicago: University of Chicago Press, 1958.

Link, Arthur S. "What Happened to the Progressive Movement in the 1920's?" *American Historical Review* 64 (July 1959): 833–851.

——. *Wilson: The New Freedom.* Princeton, New Jersey: Princeton University Press, 1956.

——. *Wilson: The Road to the White House.* Princeton, New Jersey: Princeton University Press, 1947.

——. *Woodrow Wilson and the Progressive Era, 1910–1917.* New York: Harper & Row, 1963, or. ed. 1954.

——, and Catton, William B. *American Epoch: A History of the United States*

*Since 1900:* Vol. I: *An Era of Economic Change, Reform, and World Wars 1900–1945.* New York: Alfred A. Knopf, 1980, or. ed. 1955.

Lipset, Seymour Martin. *Political Man: The Social Bases of Politics.* Garden City, New York: Anchor, 1963, or. ed. 1960.

——, and Bendix, Reinhard. *Social Mobility in Industrial Society.* Berkeley, California: University of California Press, 1964, or. ed. 1959.

Lombardi, John. *Labor's Voice in the Cabinet: A History of the Department of Labor from Its Origins to 1921.* New York: Columbia University Press, 1942.

Lowi, Theodore J. *The End of Liberalism: The Second Republic of the United States.* New York: W. W. Norton, 1979, or. ed. 1969.

McConnell, Grant. *The Decline of Agrarian Democracy.* New York: Atheneum, 1969, or. ed. 1953.

——. *Private Power and American Democracy.* New York: Vintage, 1970, or. ed. 1966.

Marmor, Theodore R., ed. *Poverty Policy: A Compendium of Cash Transfer Proposals.* Chicago: Aldine, 1971.

Martin, Albro. *Enterprise Denied: Origins of the Decline of American Railroads, 1897–1917.* New York: Columbia University Press, 1971.

Mason, Alpheus Thomas. *Brandeis: A Free Man's Life.* New York: Viking, 1946.

May, Henry F. *The End of American Innocence: A Study of the First Years of Our Own Time, 1912–1917.* Chicago: Quadrangle, 1964, or. ed. 1959.

——. *Protestant Churches and Industrial America.* New York: Harper & Row, 1967, or. ed. 1949.

Means, Gardiner C. *The Corporate Revolution in America: Economic Reality vs. Economic Theory.* New York: Crowell-Collier, 1962.

Merwin, C. L. "American Studies in the Distribution of Wealth and Income by Size," in *Studies in Income and Wealth,* Vol. III. New York: National Bureau of Economic Research, 1939.

Mitchell, Broadus. *Depression Decade: From New Era Through New Deal, 1929–1941.* New York: Rinehart, 1947.

Morgan, Edmund S. "The Puritan Ethic and the Coming of the American Revolution," *William and Mary Quarterly* 24 (January 1967): 3–43.

Morison, Elting E. *Turmoil and Tradition: A Study of the Life and Times of Henry L. Stimson.* New York: Atheneum, 1964, or. ed. 1960.

Morison, Samuel Eliot; Commager, Henry Steele; and Leuchtenburg, William E. *The Growth of the American Republic,* Vol. II. New York: Oxford University Press, 1969, or. ed. 1930.

Morrison, Joseph L. *Josephus Daniels Says, 1894–1913.* Chapel Hill, North Carolina: University of North Carolina Press, 1962.

——. *Josephus Daniels: The Small-d Democrat.* Chapel Hill, North Carolina: University of North Carolina Press, 1966.

Morton, Marian J. *The Terrors of Ideological Politics: Liberal Historians in a Conservative Mood.* Cleveland: Press of Case Western Reserve University, 1972.

Mowry, George E. *The Era of Theodore Roosevelt and the Birth of Modern America, 1900–1912.* New York: Harper & Row, 1962, or. ed. 1958.

Murphy, Bruce Allen. *The Brandeis/Frankfurter Connection: The Secret Political Activities of Two Supreme Court Justices.* New York: Oxford University Press, 1982.

Murray, Robert K. *The Politics of Normalcy: Government Theory and Practice in the Harding-Coolidge Era.* New York: W.W. Norton, 1973.

Nash, Gerald D. "Experiments in Industrial Mobilization: WIB & NRA," *Mid-America* 45 (July 1963): 157–174.

National Popular Government League. *To the American People: Report Upon the Illegal Practices of the United States Department of Justice.* Washington, D.C.: National Popular Government League, 1920.

Noble, David F. *America by Design: Science, Technology, and the Rise of Corporate Capitalism.* New York: Alfred A. Knopf, 1977.

Noggle, Burl. *Into the Twenties: The United States from Armistice to Normalcy.* Urbana: University of Illinois Press, 1974.

——. *Teapot Dome: Oil and Politics in the 1920's.* Baton Rouge: Louisiana State University Press, 1962.

North, Douglass C. *Growth and Welfare in the American Past: A New Economic History.* Englewood Cliffs, New Jersey: Prentice-Hall, 1966.

Olson, James Stuart. *Herbert Hoover and the Reconstruction Finance Corporation, 1931–1933.* Ames: Iowa State University Press, 1977.

Ornati, Oscar. *Poverty Amid Affluence: A Report on a Research Project Carried Out at the New School for Social Research.* New York: Twentieth Century Fund, 1966.

Parrish, Michael E. *Felix Frankfurter and His Times: The Reform Years.* New York: Free Press, 1982.

——. *Securities Regulation and the New Deal.* New Haven, Connecticut: Yale University Press, 1970.

Patterson, James T. *America's Struggle Against Poverty 1900–1980.* Cambridge, Massachusetts: Harvard University Press, 1981.

——. *Congressional Conservatism and the New Deal: The Growth of the Conservative Coalition in Congress, 1933–1939.* Lexington: University of Kentucky Press, 1967.

Paul, Randolph E. *Taxation for Prosperity.* Indianapolis: Bobbs-Merrill, 1947.

Perkins, Frances. *The Roosevelt I Knew.* New York: Harper & Row, 1964, or. ed. 1946.

Peterson, Merrill D. *The Jeffersonian Image in the American Mind.* New York: Oxford University Press, 1962, or. ed. 1960.

Peterson, Shorey. "Corporate Control and Capitalism," *Quarterly Journal of Economics* 79 (February 1965): 1–24.

Piven, Frances Fox, and Cloward, Richard A. *Regulating the Poor: The Functions of Public Welfare.* New York: Vintage, 1972, or. ed. 1971.

Pound, Roscoe. "The Law School, 1817–1929," in *The Development of Harvard University: Since the Inauguration of President Eliot, 1869–1929,* ed.

by Samuel Eliot Morison. Cambridge, Massachusetts: Harvard University Press, 1930.

Radosh, Ronald. "The Corporate Ideology of American Labor Leaders from Gompers to Hillman," in *For a New America: Essays in History and Politics from 'Studies on the Left,' 1959–1967*, ed. by James Weinstein and David W. Eakins. New York: Vintage, 1970.

——, and Rothbard, Murray N. eds. *A New History of Leviathan: Essays on the Rise of the American Corporate State.* New York: E.P. Dutton, 1972.

Rattner, Sidney. *Taxation and Democracy in America.* New York: Octagon, 1980, or. ed. 1942.

Rauch, Basil. *The History of the New Deal 1933–1938.* New York: Capricorn, 1963, or. ed. 1944.

Richberg, Donald R. "The Black-Connery Bill," *Vital Speeches* 3 (July 15, 1937): 585–587.

——. "Constitutional Aspects of the New Deal," *Annals of the Academy of Political and Social Science* 178 (March 1935): 25–32.

——. "Cooperating with Competitors," *Academy of Political Science: Proceedings* 11 (April 1925): 501–508.

——. "Democratization of Industry," *New Republic* 11 (May 12, 1917): 49–51.

——. "Developing Ethics and Resistant Law," *Yale Law Journal* 32 (December 1922): 109–122.

——. "Essentials for Sustained Recovery," *Proceedings of the Academy of Political Science* 18 (May 1938): 35–42.

——. " 'Five Brothers' or 'Trust Triplets'?: A Vital Issue Between Democrats and Progressives," *Outlook* 106 (March 21, 1914): 638–641.

——. "Future Federal Regulation of Business," *Vital Speeches* 3 (February 1, 1937): 238–241.

——. "The Future of Power and the Public," *Annals of the Academy of Political and Social Science* 159 (January 1932): 148–155.

——. *G. Hovah Explains.* Washington, D.C.: National Home Library Foundation, 1940.

——. "Government and Business: The Strength of a Responsible Democracy," *Vital Speeches* 4 (February 15, 1938): 280–282.

——. *Government and Business Tomorrow. A Public Relations Program.* New York: Harper & Bros., 1943.

——. "The High Cost of Low Thinking," *New Republic* 32 (October 18, 1922): 193–195.

——. *In the Dark.* Chicago: Forbes, 1912.

——. "Industrial Civilization," *American Federationist* 39 (March 1932): 265–274.

——. *Labor Union Monopoly: A Clear and Present Danger.* Chicago: Henry Regnery, 1957.

——. "Legislative Reference Bureaus for Political Parties," *Proceedings of the American Political Science Association at Its Tenth Annual Meeting, Sup-*

*plement to the American Political Science Review* 8 (February 1914): 222–233.

———. *A Man of Purpose: A Novel.* New York: Thomas Y. Crowell, 1922.

———. "Mutualism," *Academy of Political Science Proceedings* 13 (June 1928): 185–194.

———. *My Hero: The Indiscreet Memoirs of an Eventful but Unheroic Life.* New York: G.P. Putnam's Sons, 1954.

———. "N. R .A.," *Congressional Digest* 14 (January 1935): 14–15.

———. "The National Emergency Council," *Vital Speeches* 1 (October 22, 1934): 54–60.

———, and Britt, Albert. *Only the Brave Are Free: A Condensed Review of the Growth of Self-Government in America.* Caldwell, Idaho: Caxton, 1958.

———. "A Permanent Basis for Rate Regulation," *Yale Law Journal* 31 (January 1922): 263–282.

———. "Planning and Controlling Business Activities," *Vital Speeches* 1 (December 17, 1934): 168–172.

———. *The Rainbow.* Garden City, New York: Doubleday, Doran, 1936.

———. "The Same Door Wherein I Went," *University of Chicago Magazine* 4 (June 1912): 268–271.

———. "Security—Without a Dictator," *New York Times Magazine* (January 28, 1940): 1–2+.

———. "Seeking the Law in Vain," *Survey* 49 (December 1, 1922): 289–292+.

———. *The Shadow Men.* Chicago: Forbes, 1911.

———. "A Suggestion for Revision of the Antitrust Laws," *University of Pennsylvania Law Review* 85 (November 1936): 1–14.

———. *Tents of the Mighty.* Chicago: Willett, Clark & Colby, 1930.

———. "A University Consciousness," *University of Chicago Magazine* 2 (March 1910): 156–161.

Robertson, Ross M. *History of the American Economy.* New York: Harcourt, Brace & World, 1964, or. ed. 1955.

Rogin, Michael Paul. *The Intellectuals and McCarthy: The Radical Specter.* Cambridge, Massachusetts: M.I.T. Press, 1969, or. ed. 1967.

———. "Voluntarism: The Political Functions of an Antipolitical Doctrine," *Industrial and Labor Relations Review* 15 (July 1962): 521–535.

Romasco, Albert U. *The Poverty of Abundance: Hoover, the Nation, the Depression.* New York: Oxford University Press, 1968, or. ed. 1965.

Roosevelt, Franklin D. *Nothing to Fear: The Selected Addresses of Franklin D. Roosevelt, 1932–1945,* ed. by Ben D. Zevin. New York: Popular Library, 1961, or. ed. 1946.

Rosen, Elliot A. *Hoover, Roosevelt, and the Brains Trust: From Depression to New Deal.* New York: Columbia University Press, 1977.

Rudy, S. Willis. *The College of the City of New York: A History.* New York: City College Press, 1949.

Schlesinger, Arthur M., Jr. *The Age of Roosevelt,* Vol. I: *The Crisis of the Old Order, 1919–1933.* Boston: Houghton Mifflin, 1957.

——. *The Age of Roosevelt*, Vol. II: *The Coming of the New Deal, 1933–1935*. Boston: Houghton Mifflin, 1958.

——. *The Age of Roosevelt*, Vol. III: *The Politics of Upheaval, 1935–1936*. Boston: Houghton Mifflin, 1960.

Schwarz, Jordan A. *The Interregnum of Despair: Hoover, Congress, and the Depression*. Urbana, Illinois: University of Illinois Press, 1970.

——. *The Speculator: Bernard M. Baruch in Washington, 1917–1965*. Chapel Hill, North Carolina: University of North Carolina Press, 1981.

Soule, George. *Prosperity Decade: From War to Depression, 1917–1929*. New York: Harper & Row, 1968, or. ed. 1947.

Stein, Herbert. *The Fiscal Revolution in America*. Chicago: University of Chicago Press, 1969.

Stein, Leon. *The Triangle Fire*. Philadelphia: Lippincott, 1962.

Sternsher, Bernard. *Consensus, Conflict, and American Historians*. Bloomington, Indiana: University of Indiana Press, 1975.

Stimson, Henry L. *American Policy in Nicaragua*. New York: Charles Scribner's Sons, 1927.

——. "Bases of American Foreign Policy During the Past Four Years," *Foreign Affairs* 11 (April 1933): 383–396.

——. "The Basis for National Military Training," *Scribner's Magazine* 61 (April 1917): 408–412.

——. "Defend Our Seas with Our Navy: Freedom Cannot Be Saved Without Sacrifice," *Vital Speeches* 7 (May 15, 1941): 450–453.

——. *Democracy and Nationalism in Europe*. Princeton, New Jersey: Princeton University Press, 1934.

——. "The Effects of Popular Ownership on Public Opinion," *Academy of Political Science: Proceedings* 11 (April 1925): 488–490.

——. *The Far Eastern Crisis: Recollections and Observations*. New York: Harper & Bros., 1936.

——. "First-Hand Impressions of Philippine Problem," *Saturday Evening Post* 199 (March 19, 1927): 6–7+.

——. "Future Philippine Policy Under the Jones Act," *Foreign Affairs* 5 (April 1927): 459–471.

——. "Inaugural Address of Henry L. Stimson, Governor-General of the Philippines," *Far Eastern Review* 24 (May 1928): 212–213.

——. "A National Budget System—II," *World's Work* 38 (September 1919): 528–536.

——. "The Needs of Our Army," *Harper's Weekly* 56 (August 31, 1912): 12.

——. "No Time for National Complacency," *World's Work* 41 (April 1921): 545–547.

——, and Bundy, McGeorge. *On Active Service in Peace and War*. New York: Harper & Bros., 1948.

——. "Responsible State Government: A Republican Constitution Program," *Independent* 79 (July 6, 1914): 14–16.

——. "The Secret Center of Our Government: A Remedy for Inefficient Legislation," *Harper's Weekly* 57 (June 21, 1913): 15+.

———. "Why I Shall Vote for Mr. Hughes," *New Republic* 8 (October 28, 1916): 317–319.

Stocking, George W., and Watkins, Myron W. *Monopoly and Free Enterprise.* New York: Twentieth Century Fund, 1951.

Storr, Richard J. *Harper's University: The Beginnings.* Chicago: University of Chicago Press, 1966.

Temin, Peter. *Did Monetary Forces Cause the Great Depression?* New York: W.W. Norton, 1976.

Thelen, David P. *The New Citizenship: Origins of Progressivism in Wisconsin, 1885–1900.* Columbia, Missouri: University of Missouri Press, 1972.

———. *Robert La Follette and the Insurgent Spirit.* Boston: Little, Brown, 1976.

Thernstrom, Stephan. *The Other Bostonians: Poverty and Progress in the American Metropolis, 1880–1970.* Cambridge, Massachusetts: Harvard University Press, 1973.

Thorne, Christopher. *The Limits of Foreign Policy: The West, the League and the Far Eastern Crisis of 1931–1933.* New York: Capricorn, 1973, or. ed. 1972.

Tugwell, Rexford G. *The Brains Trust.* New York: Viking, 1969, or. ed. 1968.

———. *The Democratic Roosevelt: A Biography of Franklin D. Roosevelt.* Baltimore: Penguin, 1969, or. ed. 1957.

———. "Roosevelt and Frankfurter: An Essay Review," *Political Science Quarterly* 85 (March 1970): 99–114.

Urofsky, Melvin I. *Big Steel and the Wilson Administration: A Study in Business-Government Relations.* Columbus, Ohio: Ohio State University Press, 1969.

———. "Josephus Daniels and the Armor Trust," *North Carolina Historical Review* 45 (July 1968): 237–263.

Vadney, Thomas E. *The Wayward Liberal: A Political Biography of Donald Richberg.* Lexington, Kentucky: University of Kentucky Press, 1970.

Wagner, Susan. *The Federal Trade Commission.* New York: Praeger, 1971.

Warren, Harris Gaylord. *Herbert Hoover and the Great Depression.* New York: W.W. Norton, 1967, or. ed. 1959.

Weber, Max. *The Protestant Ethic and the Spirit of Capitalism,* trans. by Talcott Parsons. New York: Charles Scribner's Sons, 1958, or. ed. 1904–1905.

Weinstein, James. *The Corporate Ideal in the Liberal State, 1900–1918.* Boston: Beacon, 1969, or. ed. 1968.

White, Morton. *Social Thought in America: The Revolt Against Formalism.* Boston: Beacon, 1957, or. ed. 1949.

White, W. L. *Bernard Baruch: Portrait of a Citizen.* New York: Harcourt, Brace, 1950.

Wiebe, Robert H. *Businessmen and Reform: A Study of the Progressive Movement.* Chicago: Quadrangle, 1968, or. ed. 1962.

———. *The Search for Order, 1877–1920.* New York: Hill & Wang, 1967.

Williamson, Jeffrey G. "American Prices and Urban Inequality Since 1820," *Journal of Economic History* 36 (June 1976): 303–333.

———, and Lindert, Peter H. *American Inequality: A Macroeconomic History*. New York: Academic, 1980.

Wilson, Joan Hoff. *Herbert Hoover: Forgotten Progressive*. Boston: Little, Brown, 1975.

Wirth, Louis. "The Social Sciences," in *American Scholarship in the Twentieth Century*, ed. by Merle Curti. Cambridge, Massachusetts: Harvard University Press, 1953.

Wise, Gene. *American Historical Explanations: A Strategy for Grounded Inquiry*. Minneapolis: University of Minnesota Press, 1980, or. ed. 1973.

Woodward, C. Vann. *Origins of the New South, 1877–1913*. Baton Rouge, Louisiana: Louisiana State University Press, 1966, or. ed. 1951.

———. *Tom Watson: Agrarian Rebel*. New York: Oxford University Press, 1963, or. ed. 1938.

Woolf, S. J. "The President's No. 1 Man," *Literary Digest* 118 (December 1, 1934): 5–6.

# Index